THE FIRST ASIANS IN THE AMERICAS

The First Asians in the Americas

A Transpacific History

DIEGO JAVIER LUIS

HARVARD UNIVERSITY PRESS

Cambridge, Massachusetts, and London, England   2024

Publication of this book has been supported through the generous provisions
of the Maurice and Lula Bradley Smith Memorial Fund.

First printing

Library of Congress Cataloging-in-Publication Data

Names: Luis, Diego Javier, 1992– author.
Title: The first Asians in the Americas : a transpacific history / Diego Javier Luis.
Description: Cambridge, Massachusetts : Harvard University Press, 2024. |
    Includes bibliographical references and index.
Identifiers: LCCN 2023009534 | ISBN 9780674271784 (cloth)
Subjects: LCSH: Asians—Latin America—History. | Asians—Migrations—Latin America—
    History. | Slavery—Latin America—History. | Racism against Asians—Latin America—
    History. | Asians—Race identity—Latin America—History. | Mexico—History—Spanish
    colony, 1540–1810. | Asia—Emigration and immigration—History. | Latin America—
    Emigration and immigration—History.
Classification: LCC F1419.A84 L85 2023 | DDC 973/.0495—dc23/eng/20230515
LC record available at https://lccn.loc.gov/2023009534

For my parents, William Luis and Linda Lee Tracey

Contents

A Note on Terminology

The terms *asiático / a* and *Asia* (for *Asian* and *Asia*) do not consistently appear in Spanish colonial sources. In colonial Mexico, one phrase commonly used to refer to the lands across the Pacific was *la china*. Since people of Asian provenance became known as *chinos* upon arrival, *Asian* and *Asia* are the most accurate translations for "chino / a" and "la china" in Mexico. Thus, this book uses *Asian* and *Asia* in their contemporary meanings as shorthand for the great diversity of peoples in this history and the locales from the Indian Ocean World to East Asia, respectively.

Filipino is a similarly complicated term, since nothing resembling the contemporary Filipino national identity existed in the early modern period. In fact, during the late colonial period, *Filipino* often referred to Spaniards born in the Philippines and not to the land's Indigenous inhabitants.[1] Most often, Spanish sources characterized Philippine peoples as *indios* (Indigenous vassals) or *moros* (enslavable Muslim enemies). In some cases, colonial-era authors differentiated among specific ethnic groups like Tagalogs, Kapampangans, Visayans, Ilocanos, and so forth. When it is possible to identify the ethnicity of an individual or community, I use labels that privilege specificity. When this is not possible or when I refer to a group consisting of multiple ethnicities autochthonous to the Philippines, I use "Philippine" with a corresponding noun.

The goal is to avoid, as much as possible, reproducing the colonial rhetoric of "indio / a" (*indiyo* in Tagalog) unless the reference is to its specific employment in primary sources and / or Spanish colonial systems of categorization. This word is derogatory not only in contemporary Tagalog but also in many areas throughout Latin America.[2] I have also placed the names of other *castas* (castes) of New Spain—including "chino / a"—in quotes to cite the language of colonial sources. In a similar vein, I refer to enslaved or formerly enslaved peoples by either first name or first and last names and not solely by their last names (e.g., "Catarina" in lieu of "San Juan"), which were often markers of possession.[3] These are imperfect approaches to irresolvable issues of colonial nomenclature and power that, for the sake of intelligibility, are nonetheless essential to the narration of this history.

Timeline

Mid–late 1400s	Tupac Inca meets Pacific Islanders at Tumbez and launches an expedition into the Pacific.
1492	Christopher Columbus believes he has reached Asia after crossing the Atlantic and landing in the Caribbean.
1522	The *Victoria* returns with eighteen survivors to Sanlúcar de Barrameda, completing the first known circumnavigation.
1548	In his will, the first bishop of Mexico, Juan de Zumárraga, frees an enslaved Indian man of Calicut named Juan Núñez, the first Asian man known to have lived in the Americas.
1565	The Afro-Portuguese Lope Martín pilots the first ship to complete the *tornaviaje* (return voyage) from the Philippines to the Americas, inaugurating the era of the Manila galleons. Miguel López de Legazpi burns Cebu and establishes the first Spanish colony in Asia on top of its ruins.
1565–1815	Spanish ships known as the Manila galleons regularly sail across the Pacific in both directions, connecting the Philippines and Mexico.
1571	The Rahjanate of Maynila is destroyed, and the Spanish Intramuros rises over the ashes.
1580–1640	The Union of the Two Crowns of Spain and Portugal leads to an era of intercolonial mobility and slave trading.
1585	Juan González de Mendoza publishes in Rome a best-selling account of China titled *Historia de las cosas mas notables, ritos y costumbres del gran reyno dela China*. In the following years, hundreds of Catholic missionaries flock to Asia.
1587	Pedro de Unamuno's expedition lands at Morro Bay, California, with eight Philippine Natives of Luzon.

1588–1589	The Tondo Conspiracy, led by don Agustín de Legazpi and don Martín Panga, is brutally repressed, isolating elites on Luzon from direct connection and kinship with Muslim Southeast Asia.
1590	Treasury officials in charge of the Caja de Acapulco (cashbox of Acapulco) attempt the first consistent recordings of Manila galleon traffic and labor in Mexico.
1593	En route to the Spice Islands, "Sangley" (Chinese) rowers mutiny and kill the Spanish governor of the Philippines, Gómez Pérez Dasmariñas.
1596	Nine Chinese captains and eighteen merchants in Manila present a formal complaint of unfair treatment to the bishop of Nueva Segovia, Miguel de Benavides.
1597	The former governor of the Philippines, Luis Pérez Dasmariñas, pens an elaborate proposal to deport all unconverted "Sangleyes" from Manila.
1602	Sebastián Vizcaíno recruits Asian crew members from Acapulco for an expedition up the coast of California that reaches present-day Oregon.
1603	Several thousand "Sangley" rebels attack Manila, and an army including Spanish, Japanese, and Philippine troops burns the Parian (Chinese quarter) and massacres many thousand "Sangleyes"—militants and innocent bystanders alike.
1604	Bernardo de Balbuena's epic, *Grandeza mexicana,* celebrates the flow of Asian goods from across the Pacific to Mexico City.
1606–1663	With the assistance of thousands of Philippine Natives from Luzon, the Spaniards occupy Ternate, one of the famed Spice Islands.
c. 1610–1688	Catarina de San Juan (born Mirra) of South Asian origin is traded across the Pacific as a slave, earns her freedom, and becomes an exemplar of ascetic Catholic devotion in Puebla, Mexico.
1614	A Japanese embassy under the command of Hasekura Rokuemon Tsunenaga lands in Acapulco en route to Rome.
1615	Multiethnic labor gangs break ground on the Fort of San Diego in Acapulco. All Asians become "chinos" in the port's treasury records as of this date, ending the fluidity of terms that had proliferated since 1590.
1639	A second major uprising cripples Manila and ends in yet another wholesale massacre of "Sangleyes" on Luzon.
1644	The Ming dynasty falls to northern invaders, and Qing rule commences.

1645	All "mestizos," "mulatos," "negros," "chinos," and *"zambaigos"* (mixed Afro-Indigenous people) are banned from carrying arms after an outbreak of violence in Veracruz.
1671	Fernando de Haro y Monterroso submits an influential petition to the colonial court in Guadalajara to free enslaved "chinos" within its jurisdiction.
1672	Queen Regent Mariana of Austria confirms Fernando de Haro y Monterroso's petition and expands it to include all "chinos" in Mexico. However, corruption in Mexico City slows the progress of emancipation.
1700	The last Hapsburg emperor, Carlos II, dies without an heir in Madrid, and the Bourbons inherit the Spanish Crown.
1751	The largest Manila galleon ever, *La Santísima Trinidad y Nuestra Señora del Buen Fin,* makes its maiden voyage with 407 crew members.
1762–1764	The British seize Manila during the Seven Years' War. Spanish economic reforms in the aftermath of the conflict severely undermine the Manila galleon route.
1806	The first shipment of Chinese conscripted laborers arrives in Trinidad, inaugurating a new wave of Asian labor migration to the Americas— primarily the Caribbean.
1810	Miguel Hidalgo's speech, the Grito de Dolores (Cry of Dolores), announces the call to arms against the New Spanish colonial government and begins the Wars of Mexican Independence.
1813	The rebel army under José María Morelos besieges and burns Acapulco.
1815	The Spanish Crown declares a formal end to the Manila galleons, and the last of these ships, the *Magallanes,* sails back to Cavite with little profit.
1821	Agustín de Iturbide proclaims the independence of Mexico. In the next year he becomes emperor of this new nation.
1822	The Mexican rejection of reparations to the Spanish Philippines for commercial losses signals a long-term break between the eastern and western nodes of the old Manila galleon route.
1838–1917	Half a million conscripted and indentured South Asians arrive at the plantations of the British Caribbean.
1847–1874	125,000 Chinese land in Cuba to labor under the stipulations of their contracts, yet most are reduced to a life of de facto bondage.

1848	Through the Treaty of Guadalupe Hidalgo, Mexico cedes an enormous territory to the United States. Soon after, the first Chinese laborers and gold prospectors arrive in the newly occupied California territories, particularly San Francisco.
1849–1874	100,000 Chinese are contracted to work in Peru under conditions similar to the brutal ones of their compatriots in Cuba.
1855	Forty-five Chinese workers arrive in Puntarenas, Costa Rica.
1864	The first Chinese railroad workers land in Mexico.
1898	The United States intervenes in the Cuban and Philippine Wars of Independence against Spanish rule and occupies Cuba, Puerto Rico, the Philippines, and the Mariana Islands in the aftermath.
1911	303 Chinese and 5 Japanese residents of Torreón are massacred during the Mexican Revolution.
1915	William Schurz inaugurates the historiography on the Manila galleons after drafting and defending his dissertation under the tutelage of Herbert Eugene Bolton at the University of California at Berkeley.

THE FIRST ASIANS IN THE AMERICAS

INTRODUCTION

AT 4:04 A.M. ON JANUARY 5, 1688, Catarina de San Juan breathed her last in Puebla de los Ángeles, Mexico.[1] Her ascetic life of perpetual suffering had reached its holy and inevitable end. A few devotees carried the corporeal relic that was her body from her dilapidated home (containing only one small room) to the house of Hipolyto del Castillo y Altra "to have in death a more decent place" for the customary postmortem washing and shrouding.[2] In the blue light before sunrise, the Jesuit fathers rang the bells of the College of the Holy Spirit to announce her passing. They prepared a palm leaf and a crown of flowers to honor Catarina as a virgin.[3]

Word spread quickly, and by 5:00 a.m., the city had swelled with "innumerable people" from miles around hoping to catch a glimpse of the sacred corpse.[4] Nobles and the poor alike hurried to the home of Castillo y Altra, so that it looked like "a church on Maundy Thursday, where the public of the entire city enters and exits and performs the stations [of the cross]."[5] However, this orderly procession did not last for long. As eager spectators converged on the home, their patience waned, and they rushed the door. The doorframe groaned and split, and the pious mob crowded around the body, eager to kiss Catarina's hands and feet, touch her rosaries, take flowers from her shroud, and even cut off her fingers and pieces of flesh to keep as holy relics.[6]

In this state, Catarina's body remained on display until the next afternoon, when a religious procession arrived to inter her in the main chapel of the Jesuit college. According to one of her confessors and hagiographers, Alonso Ramos, "The large crowd that gathered and attended the burial is inexplicable . . . even on the rooftops, balconies, and windows of the houses that correspond to the doors of the temple of our College of the Holy Spirit, there appeared a multitude of men and women."[7] As the pallbearers approached the college, they needed to extract Catarina's body from the coffin, which had to be rotated to fit inside the narrow doorway. When the crowd spotted her holy figure, they stormed in "to rob her of the few decorations that had remained on the deceased."[8] They grasped the last shreds of her tunic, hair, and flesh and the final flowers from her shroud, and they even made off with her shoes.

Within the chapel, the undeterred Jesuits buried Catarina by a presbytery in a vault that also held stillborn infants—similarly valued for their purity. Two keys sealed the vault. In a speech given shortly after her interment, the Jesuit Francisco de Aguilera proclaimed that "all that the world adores as most precious, it makes holy, without claiming it, nor searching for it, [it found] a poor little *china*, slave, foreigner, who made us fill our tongues with her praises, our hearts with jubilation, and even our eyes with tears."[9]

But for all the acceptance she eventually found among Puebla's denizens, Catarina continued to be a "a poor little *china*" (the colonial Mexican term used to refer to any Asian person) and a "slave, foreigner." This was so although she had lived almost seventy years in Puebla, most of them as a free woman. Those who knew Catarina speculated that she might have been born on the Arabian Peninsula or lived in her youth as a princess of the Mughal royal family in India. The Jesuit Joseph del Castillo Graxeda's conjecture was the least ambitious and, therefore, perhaps the most persuasive: "Catharina was native to the Mughal Kingdom. The place where she was born is unknown, and even she did not know it for being such a young age when she was taken from it."[10] As a child, Catarina had been a victim of a Portuguese slave raid in South Asia. She was eventually sold in Spanish Manila. Then, at the nearby port of Cavite, she was made to board a Spanish galleon destined for Mexico. The journey across the world's largest ocean on an early modern ship, even one advanced for its time, lasted many months under horrid conditions. In 1621, Catarina disembarked at the port of Acapulco in chains and was sent overland to Puebla. There, she eventually gained her freedom and, through her piety, became a renowned symbol of holy virtue and global Catholic hegemony.[11]

Despite her celebrity, Catarina—the person behind the reputation—remained an unknown and unknowable entity, a "Thesaurus absconditus" (hidden treasure) in the words of the Jesuit Antonio Plancarte.[12] For the funerary procession, Plancarte painted a dark, sealed box of Asian design and penned a poem to accompany it:

> Here from *china,* you see
> my color; inside the gold
> I save as greater treasure,
> that hidden here you will find.
> Although the more turns you give
> the key, it will not open, none will understand it;
> since the cipher only God
> knows, for you
> [only] in his time will he reveal it.[13]

According to Plancarte, the inner quality of Catarina's soul lay beyond the human grasp. What those attending her funeral perceived, instead, was her exotic difference—her body "here from *china*" (meaning Asia) now laid out before them. Catarina remained inextricably tied to the thousands of hands seeking to defile and consume her, desiring to turn the key that would expose her interior, yearning for the total submission she withheld in life and reserved for the Holy Trinity alone. As silent as stone, Catarina had become her foreignness.

Today, Catarina de San Juan is erroneously known by another name, the China Poblana (the "china" of Puebla). In his 1897 book *Historia de la Puebla de los Angeles,* the Mexican historian Antonio Carrión conflated the China Poblana, a popular nineteenth-century form of dress that was a symbol of Mexican femininity, with the distant memory of an Asian woman who had once lived in Puebla.[14] He wrote that the women of Puebla had known Catarina de San Juan as "la *China,* which they called her affectionately," and thus, Catarina had become the China Poblana.[15] The allure of the *castor* (patterned skirt), white slip, white blouse, and shawl of the China Poblana melded with Carrión's resurrection of an Asian-infused Baroque past. From this orientalist conflation of the two "chinas," Catarina de San Juan shape-shifted into folklore.[16]

The coordinated efforts to suppress Catarina de San Juan's story shortly after her death enabled Carrión's invention and others like it.[17] From 1689 to 1692, Alonso Ramos published an ambitious hagiography of Catarina in three enormous volumes that commemorated his confessant as a religious icon and made a daring case for her beatification (figure I.1). Because it celebrated Catarina's celestial visions and ethereal visitations with the Holy Trinity, however, Ramos's hagiography aroused inquisitorial suspicion. Throughout the post-Tridentine (1563–) Catholic world, the worship of persons who had not been formally beatified or sanctified was strictly prohibited.[18] In the end, Ramos's dream of crafting a holy figure to elevate Puebla as a sacred site of the Catholic world was not to be realized. He had overplayed his case by prematurely declaring that Catarina had performed miracles and other acts of God: only the Sacred Congregation of Rites and the pope could make this determination. Even one of the theologians who supported Ramos's first volume warned that Catarina's "visions, revelations, and prophecies" could make a reader "seasick."[19] In 1692 the Spanish Inquisition banned Ramos's magnum opus for "containing revelations, visions, and apparitions [that are] unfit, implausible, full of contradictions and comparisons [that are] inappropriate, indecent, reckless, and that *sapient blasphemiam* (that reveal or that nearly are blasphemies)."[20]

Ramos's hefty three-volume work was the longest text ever published in colonial Mexico, and hardly anyone would read it.[21] The New Spanish Inquisition confirmed the Spanish ban on printing and distribution in 1696 and dismantled the public altar in the little room where Catarina had lived.[22] Inquisitors then confiscated most of the remaining publications about her and burned them.[23] From the outstretched hands that had despoiled her body to the suppression of her devotion, Catarina had become a myth within a decade of her passing. In the words of Kate Risse, she was "too spectacular, too unorthodox, too popular."[24] She was also, I would add, too foreign.

Yet although Catarina de San Juan was distorted by her erstwhile hagiographers and modern eulogizers, she remains one of the very few Asians in the early modern Americas whose name has endured. In this sense, she is exceptional. Although thousands of Asian people traveled to and through the colonial world during this period, Catarina's life was recorded with a level of detail afforded to few others of her time. Her commemoration is

I.1 Portrait of Catarina de San Juan

This portrait appeared in the first volume of Alonso Ramos's hagiography of Catarina de San Juan (1689) and is the only historical image that survives of an Asian individual who lived in New Spain. By 1691, an inquisitorial edict outlawed the circulation of this and other portraits of Catarina, which had already become images of popular devotion thought to have healing power. The caption reads, "The virgin Catarina de San Juan of the Great Mughals died at the age of eighty-two on January 5 of 1688 in Puebla de los Angeles of New Spain. She was buried in the College of the Holy Spirit of the Company of Jesus (La v[irgen] Catharina de S[an] Ioan del g[ra]n Mogor murio de edad de 82 años a 5 de enero de 1688 en la Puebla de los Angels de Nueva España. Enterrose en el Colegio del Espíritu Santo de la comp[añí]a de Iesvs)."

Alonso Ramos, *Primera parte de los prodigios de la omnipotencia y milagros de la gracia, en la vida de la venerable sierva de Dios Catharina de San Ioan* (Puebla, Mexico: Imprenta Plantiniana de Diego Fernandez de Leon, 1689), Sig. 3 / 18733, 1:1. Reproduction courtesy of Biblioteca Nacional de España.

even more remarkable given that her identity as a formerly enslaved Asian woman made her an unlikely candidate for remembrance.

While she had achieved a rare degree of fame by the end of her life, in many ways Catarina's story is also more broadly emblematic of other Asian peoples in the early Americas, about whom only fragments survive. Catarina was one of many people who boarded a Spanish galleon in the Philippines—either voluntarily or in captivity—and crossed the tempestuous Pacific to reach a strange land beyond the horizon. Once they arrived in New Spain, the haggard survivors of this journey faced a new challenge: the violent colonial realities of the Spanish Americas. Collectively, these free and enslaved Asians represented a new kind of migrant in global history, and their experiences shifted endlessly along a continuum between the two poles of coming and going, bondage and freedom, assimilation and foreignness, and recognition and repudiation.

How many of their histories have been lost to human memory or to infinite entombment as a decaying shred of discarded paper in the archives of a dead, Baroque empire? The experiences of Asian peoples in colonial Mexico and the Spanish Americas are neither folklore nor myth: they are history. The traces of their lives that can be recovered from the oblivion of time and the fickleness of human memory populate this book and constitute a history of unlikely survivals, perseverance against prejudice, and spectacular convergences of distant peoples.

The First Asians in the Americas is the first book to examine the mobility of both free and enslaved Asians to and through the Americas during the 250 years that Spanish ships sailed the Pacific Ocean between the Philippine port of Cavite and Acapulco, Mexico. The book's scope is necessarily global, and its approach attends to the grain of lived experience. At the heart of this story are the desires both to understand what Asians made of their new lives in new lands and to uncover how regimes of difference making impacted the search for just treatment in a deeply race-conscious colonial world. Regardless of their origin, the vast majority of Asians who disembarked in Acapulco became known as "chinos," like Catarina. This invented term slotted Asian peoples into New Spain's *casta* (caste) system, alongside more familiar casta designations that variously defined Afro-Mexican and Indigenous peoples as "indios," "mulatos," and "negros." Formally, becoming "chino / a" conditioned Asian peoples' status within the New Spanish social order. It restricted their ability to work in certain trades and made them legally vulnerable to enslavement and the Inquisition.[25] Informally, in the ears of Spaniards, the word "chino / a" alone often conjured up the expectation of servitude, criminality, and un-Catholic behavior. Even Catarina's popularity could not overcome her nature as a "*china*, slave, foreigner" in the eyes of her admirers.

Facing these perils, "chinos" recalibrated their social relationships and blended into existing Indigenous and Afro-Mexican communities as they sought to secure their freedom, acquire sustenance, and live with dignity. From the bustle of Manila to the rural rhythms of the Costa Grande, and from the height of Spanish imperial power to the early struggles for independence in Mexico, this book tracks the little-known forms of Asian mobility that defined the deep entanglement of the Pacific world with the colonial lifeblood of the Spanish Americas. From archival shadows, it produces names, networks, and communities. And from the locked sepulcher of Catarina de San Juan, it offers not a new cipher as in Plancarte's vision, but a multitude of epigraphs, attesting to the lives of other people—just as extraordinary and just as worthy of our attention, analysis, and empathy as Catarina—hundreds of years after they passed from earthly memory.

Through this history, it is my aim to offer three interventions: the first geographic, the second temporal, and the third methodological. First, I join a growing cohort of scholars invested in restoring the importance of the Pacific to the history of colonial Latin America, a field traditionally focused on the Atlantic.[26] Rooted in the passage of Spanish galleons sailing between the Philippines and Mexico, the history of transpacific Asian mobility presents a strong case for adopting a Pacific orientation in the study of Latin America. Second, I make a chronological intervention in the long history of Asian migration to the Western Hemisphere. While the story of Asian migration conventionally begins in the nineteenth century, this book builds on a recent turn in the scholarship to the importance of the early modern period. The story that I tell unfolds between the late sixteenth and early nineteenth centuries. To the history of Asians in the Americas, it offers a new inception, one in which mobility was free and forced.

Third, this book focuses methodologically on the racialization of mobile, non-Spanish communities in Hispanic colonies. Through the use of the word "chino / a"—and the numerous sociolegal repercussions of that designation—the colonial bureaucracy effectively collapsed the diverse ethnolinguistic groups that made the Pacific passage into a single, racialized collective. We have not yet completed the picture of how this legal form of difference making developed, or of how it impacted the day-to-day lives of Asians in the Hispanic World. Similarly, we have yet to uncover the full range of Asian responses to racialization. Many Asian peoples sought to differentiate themselves from "chino / a" stereotypes to achieve social mobility, while others engaged in multiethnic collaborations with Indigenous and Afro-Mexican communities to mitigate the conditions of bondage. This book tracks the evolution of both colonial praxes of difference making and Asian peoples' adaptations in the face of this adversity to reconstruct the human experience of long-distance mobility across the world's largest ocean during the early modern period.

The Spanish Pacific

By the late sixteenth century, the Spanish Crown had created the world's first transpacific empire. The vessels that connected the Asian and American ports of this domain between 1565 and 1815 are widely known today as Manila galleons, though the name is somewhat misleading for several reasons. First, the port of Cavite, near Manila—not Manila itself—was the ships' most frequent point of embarkation and disembarkation in Asia. Second, Spanish records from the period refer to the ships not as *galeones de Manila* (Manila galleons) but as *naos de china* (Asia ships). Third, the ships often varied greatly in size from small galliots to full-sized galleons, and during the last half century of the trade route, they consisted solely of mid-sized frigates. In total, this transpacific line comprised roughly 332 departures from Mexico to the Philippines and 379 from the Philippines to Mexico.[27] The most consistent periods of transpacific navigation occurred from the late sixteenth to the mid-seventeenth centuries, while significant disruptions transpired during the 1650s, 1670s, 1680s, 1740s, and 1760s. Of course, even during decades of relative stability, many ships never reached their destinations. Captaining a galleon on the formidable Pacific crossing certainly required a degree of hubris.

During the years of their operation, the Manila galleons constituted a critical lifeline from Spanish-held regions in the Americas to those in Asia. This enormous zone fell under the governance of Mexico City, the seat of the Viceroyalty of New Spain. In the eyes of one governor of the Philippines, Manila "is a fort or outpost of New Spain," more a colonial Mexican territory than a Spanish one.[28] At the orders of New Spanish viceroys, Spaniards in the Philippines conducted diplomatic missions with nearby kingdoms, assigned missionaries to convert wary Indigenous populations, and launched violent incursions into neighboring regions with limited success. By the same token, New Spain "was as much an American entity as an Asian one."[29]

Over the past fifteen years, scholars in the new field of Spanish Pacific studies have argued that colonialism in the Americas cannot be fully understood without attending to the global nature of the sprawling Spanish empire.[30] While this scholarship has begun to demonstrate the importance of the Pacific to the Hispanic World, the entanglements of Spanish imperial ambition, the fragility of colonial societies in Pacific littorals, and the experiences of free and enslaved Asian subjects remain imperfectly understood. The task at hand, then, is to delineate the human experience of the Spanish Pacific from the perspective of its most marginalized subjects.

It is now widely recognized that reaching Asia was the principal aim of early Iberian overseas voyages, beginning with Portuguese navigators who sought a route to India in the fifteenth century. The Genoese Christopher Columbus was no exception, though he sought to emulate Marco Polo by sailing across the Atlantic instead of traveling east from Europe. In 1493, he returned to Barcelona, claiming to have found a new route to Asia. Thereafter, generations of millenarian missionaries, imaginative officials, and covetous merchants continued the dream of reaching distant Asian kingdoms by sailing westward into the setting sun. As the American continents slowly gained recognition as distinct landmasses, they became an inconvenient obstruction separating the Iberian Peninsula from the silks and cloves of China and the Spice Islands.

The Pacific would similarly prove to be a significant barrier in the quest to reach Asia. Spaniards reluctantly acknowledged the ocean's colossal size during the sixteenth and seventeenth centuries, and consequently, most aspiring colonialists eventually reoriented their ambitions toward the Americas, their Indigenous populations, their natural resources, and the profitability of the transatlantic slave trade. Understandably, the Atlantic World has dominated oceanic historiographies of the Americas for these reasons. The Atlantic framework has produced a rich scholarly discourse on the multidirectional movement of people and ideas, the blending of borderlands between empires, and—more recently—the lives of African,

Indigenous, and mixed peoples facing captivity or pursuing a tenuous freedom.[31] Yet this framework struggles to accommodate the full global connectedness of the early modern world.[32]

An earlier generation of historians fostered a more expansive view of empire, though they were not without their limitations. The US seizure of the Philippines in 1898 ignited Anglophone academic interest in its new and distant territorial possessions. Perhaps the most prolific scholars of this wave of Pacific-facing research were Emma Helen Blair and James Alexander Robertson. From 1903 to 1909, they published a staggering fifty-five volumes of translated documents, manuscripts, and books pertaining to the Spanish period in the Philippines.[33] Robertson was a librarian at the National Library of the Philippines in Manila from 1910 to 1915. On his return to the States, he helped create the *Hispanic American Historical Review,* and he served as the journal's editor in chief from its founding in 1918 until his death in 1939.[34] Also in 1939, William Schurz published a groundbreaking monograph on the Manila galleons that drew attention to the Pacific as a generative force in early modern history, as well as the historical connections between the Americas and the Philippines.[35] This subject became more popular among historians in the latter half of the twentieth century, when world-system theorists began connecting the flows of silver from the Americas across both the Atlantic and the Pacific to the formation of a global economy and the rise of capitalism.[36]

While the Pacific turn has its origins in historicizing long-distance economic circulation, it has recently come to encompass the movements of people, cultural exchanges, literary imaginaries, and institutional adaptations to transpacific trade.[37] According to Christina Lee and Ricardo Padrón, Spanish Pacific studies conceives of a space that "is not precisely physical and certainly not natural" but that nonetheless "helped produce a social, cultural, and political space whose frontiers were ragged and whose borders were malleable."[38] While limited in its reach, the Spanish Pacific created a new zone of global encounter and exchange that linked Asia and the Americas materially, demographically, and culturally. The transformative implications of these contacts for the early Americas have often been understated, but Déborah Oropeza makes a case for examining transpacific movement most explicitly: "if the Asian population that integrated into New Spanish society is not considered, then our vision of New Spain is incomplete."[39] This book is likewise grounded in the understanding that transpacific mobility is foundational to the history of the Spanish Americas.

The importance of the Pacific Ocean to the Hispanic World is perhaps nowhere more visible than in the 1601 map of the royal chronicler Antonio de Herrera y Tordesillas, "Descripcion de las Yndias ocidentales" (Description of the West Indies; figure I.2).

Herrera y Tordesillas's maps were the official cartographic representations of the Spanish empire at the beginning of the seventeenth century.[40] As Padrón points out, the "Descripcion" reinforced the long-standing claim

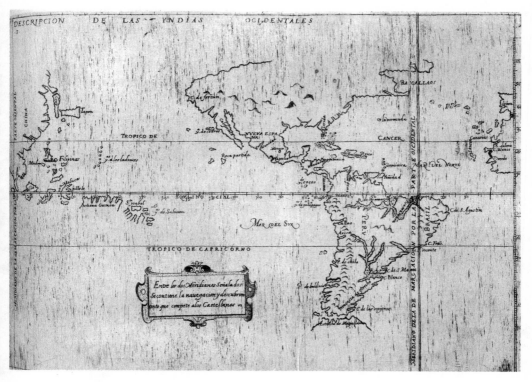

I.2 Description of the West Indies

The cartouche reads, "The two marked meridians contain the navigation and discovery of all that pertains to the Castilians" (Entre los dos Meridianos señalados se contiene la nauegacion y descubrimiento que compete a los Castellanos).

Antonio de Herrera y Tordesillas, "Descripcion de las Yndias ocidentales," in *Historia general de los hechos de los castellanos en las islas i Tierra Firme del Mar Oceano* (Madrid: En la Emprenta Real, 1601), 4:1–2. Reproduction courtesy of the John Carter Brown Library.

that all lands and waters between the two meridians designated by the Treaties of Tordesillas (1494) and Zaragoza (1529) belonged to the Spanish Crown.[41] This enormous territorial assertion encompassed fully half of the globe and all the peoples residing therein. To represent this domain visually, the map put New Spain in the center, featured the Pacific prominently (although compressing its true size to extend the Zaragoza meridian on the left side of the map), and even marginalized the Iberian Peninsula (placing it in the upper right) to accommodate the colonial domain.[42] In the words of Padrón, the map "make[s] central what was peripheral to everyone else."[43]

For Herrera y Tordesillas, the ships that made a Spanish presence possible in these far-flung possessions had allowed Spain to surpass the glory of the ancients.[44] In exemplifying this claim, he cited four key trade routes, the newest being the transpacific galleon line that connected Asia to the Americas. The addition of this route extended his conception of the "West Indies" from the Western Hemisphere all the way to Southeast and East Asia, since all Hispanic colonies were "western with respect to Castile."[45] In this new imperial imaginary, New Spain became the crossroad of the Atlantic and Pacific, a nexus of grandeur, wealth, and new embarkations to ever more distant lands. In Herrera y Tordesillas's conception, the nature of Spain's early modern empire was unequivocally global.

Yet his projection reveals disturbingly little about the on-the-ground realities of this colonial world. In truth, Spanish presence was minimal outside of a handful of urban settlements. Spain's outlandish claim to the entirety of the Pacific was actualized almost solely through the passage of a couple of ships sailing in either direction each year.[46] Strictly speaking, the Spanish presence in the Pacific during most of the colonial period existed within a narrow navigational corridor, a transpacific space "as shallow as the amount of seawater displaced by the weight of Iberian sailing vessels."[47] In the words of Lee and Padrón, "Spanish Pacific studies begins by recognizing that Spain's presence in the Pacific was always slim, tenuous, and contested."[48]

Despite the extremely limited scope of the Spanish encounter with the Pacific, it sufficed to facilitate "an unprecedented global *mestizaje* [intermingling and intermixture]" in the movement of thousands of free and enslaved Asians to the Americas for the first time.[49] During their 250 years of operation, the Manila galleons confronted the most challenging seafaring conditions of their era to ferry merchandise and people between Cavite in the Philippines and Acapulco in Mexico. The survivors of this arduous journey were forever marked by it.

The people disembarking in Mexico's torrid Pacific port had come from Gujarat to the southwest, Nagasaki to the northeast, and everywhere in between. Most sailors and free migrants were born on Luzon in the Philippines, while captives had often been ensnared throughout the Philippines or, like Catarina de San Juan, by Portuguese enslaving operations in the Indian Ocean World.[50] Smaller concentrations came from elsewhere in Southeast Asia, Japan, or China.

Though most remained in central Mexico after they disembarked in Acapulco, many dispersed further afield on long journeys to Central America, Peru, and even across the Atlantic to Spain. The pioneering scholarship of Edward Slack, Melba Falck Reyes, Héctor Palacios, Oropeza, Tatiana Seijas, and Rubén Carrillo Martín has established the study of these early Asians in Mexico as a distinct field of inquiry.[51] Focusing primarily on the late sixteenth and seventeenth centuries, these authors have examined a wide range of questions pertaining to the scale of Asian transpacific movement, Asian integration within New Spanish society, Asian experiences under regimes of bondage, and the ways in which colonial institutions and officials adapted to the entry of this new population.

Despite these important advances, there is much left to uncover about the history of the earliest Asians who migrated or were displaced to the Spanish Americas. Fundamental questions remain unanswered: What propelled Asian mobility across the Pacific? How did the "chino / a" label emerge? How did Asians respond to incipient colonial forms of race making? Moreover, the full range of early modern Asian movement to and through the Americas has yet to be articulated. It extended far beyond Mexico, the geographic focal point for the current historiography. In addition, this movement continued into the eighteenth and early nineteenth centuries, which are regarded as periods when Asians largely disappeared from the archival record in colonial Mexico. How might these elongated trajectories reshape the emerging historical canon on Asians in colonial Mexico?

In answering these and other questions, this book takes an expansive archival approach to locate the extant shards of information on Asian subjects of Spanish empire. It draws on documents from archives and libraries across Spain, Mexico, the United States, and the Philippines. Often, the relevant fragments are few and far between: an examination of thousands of pages of accounting records at the Archivo General de Indias in Seville, for example, turned up sparse notations on Asian galleon crews and port laborers in Cavite and Acapulco. These transactional memoranda—along with parish, matrimonial, criminal, licensing, manumission, inquisition, ordinance, and land-claim records—represent the canonical genres of social history for the colonial period. Where possible, as in the case of Catarina de San Juan, I paired these fragments with printed narratives, manuscript accounts, official correspondence, and private letters. As historians of transatlantic enslavement have long remarked, such a broad range is ultimately required to write the history of fundamentally marginalized colonial populations.[52]

In every instance, I endeavor to restore the human element to expansive yet vacuous imperial imaginaries, like that of Herrera y Tordesillas. In so doing, I rely heavily on the methodologies of global microhistory, which use the stories of highly mobile individuals to arrive at new metanarratives that challenge the Eurocentrism of traditional global histories.[53] In John-Paul Ghobrial's formulation, global microhistory turns our attention to the border crossers, the links between movement and identity, and the space between belonging and unbelonging.[54] The fragmentary nature of the Spanish Pacific archive lends itself to this approach, whereby minuscule details of individual lives—in the words of Matt Matsuda—"take on full meaning only when linked to other stories and places."[55] People embodied the Pacific connection to the Spanish Americas, and the varied ways in which they lived their lives defined the human realities of global empire in the early modern era.

Asians in the Americas

Traditionally, the historiography of Asian diasporic movement to the Americas has focused on the United States from the nineteenth to the twenty-first centuries. These temporal and geographic biases are especially present in the field of Asian American studies, which has often overlooked hemispheric histories of Asians based in Latin America—to say nothing of those histories rooted in the early modern period. Early social histories of colonial Mexico did little to ameliorate this problem. They often sidelined the experiences of "chinos" due to the assumption that these people were demographically insignificant compared with Indigenous, mixed, and Afro-Mexican populations. And while the flourishing literature on early modern Asians in Latin America has done much to situate their experiences within the Spanish empire, this scholarship remains disconnected from studies focused on Asian diasporas more broadly. In fact, early modern Asian movement to and through the Americas is rarely described as diasporic.

Although inconsistent record keeping means that we will never know the precise number of Asians who crossed the Pacific and reached the early Americas, we now know that this movement was not insignificant in its scope. Estimates of the scale of the transpacific slave trade and of free Asian migration vary widely, however. On the lowest end, Oropeza has calculated that 7,375–20,000 free or enslaved Asian peoples arrived in the Spanish Americas during the colonial period. On the high end, Slack has conjectured that a minimum of 40,000–60,000 and a maximum of 100,000 Asians arrived during the same period.[56] Slack's range is often dismissed as improbable, especially because the basis for his measurement is unclear. Yet while it may overestimate the number of Asians disembarking from the galleons in Mexico, I believe Slack's range comes closest to a realistic count of Asians who boarded a galleon for the Americas (including those who died en route) and their descendants who were born there during the early modern period.[57]

I arrive at this conclusion in the following manner. Seijas has estimated that 8,100 enslaved Asians were shipped to Mexico from the late sixteenth to the late seventeenth centuries. This estimate, which seems probable, is based on a calculation that the galleons sailing to Mexico during this period each held sixty enslaved Asians on average.[58] Her total also falls within Oropeza's proposed range for Asian captives who arrived in Acapulco: from 3,776 (a minimum of 32 captives per ship on approximately 118 vessels) to 10,000 (if the same ships were filled to capacity).[59]

Of course, these calculations do not account for the free Asians who continued to cross the Pacific until the end of the galleon line in 1815. According to anecdotes of desertions by Asian sailors, central Mexican notarial documents, and parish records from the midcolonial period, the number of free Asian migrants undoubtedly exceeded the number of enslaved Asians, especially since the transpacific slave trade in Asian captives had largely ended by the final decades of the seventeenth century. For the combined number of free and enslaved Asians entering Mexico before 1815, Carrillo Martín and Oropeza agree on an upper estimate of 20,000.

At the same time, I believe that an accurate account of the early modern Asian mobility to and through the Americas requires us to consider a few additional factors. Of chief importance are the thousands of itinerant Asian sailors (often at least a hundred per year) who disembarked in Acapulco or elsewhere along the coast and then sailed back to the Philippines at the end of the trade season. Also significant are the thousands of Asians who perished during the Pacific crossing due to storms, the bitter cold, exposure, shipwreck, violent punishment, contagion, and malnourishment. Furthermore, an untold number of Asians and their descendants were born in the Americas over half a dozen or more generations, and many of them are untraceable in colonial documents because they were of mixed heritage. Finally, several ships sailed directly to Peru during the sixteenth century and to San Blas, Mexico, in the eighteenth and nineteenth centuries, and including their crews yields a larger total. According to this view, Slack's numbers might not be unreasonable if reframed as estimates for the total number of Asians who boarded galleons for the Americas and their descendants who were born there.

Such large estimates also prompt a new question: did these populations constitute early modern Asian diasporas to the Americas? Though *diaspora* can be used informally to refer to any dispersion or migration, the term has at least three formal characteristics: dispersal to two or more sites, a homeland consciousness, and the maintenance of a sociocultural identity distinct from that of the receiving community.[60] Invoking the diaspora studies framework allows us to shift our perspective from the top-down model of the Herrera y Tordesillas map to the bottom-up model of the life of Catarina de San Juan.[61]

However, the question presents a fundamental problem. If a migratory community must exhibit a documentable connection to a homeland (real or imagined) and, often, a desire to return to be considered diasporic, then it is nearly impossible to verify whether most marginalized populations of the early modern period qualify as diasporic. Colonial archives hold only traces of evidence that meets these requirements because their records rarely foreground non-European voices and never do so in an unmediated manner.[62] For enslaved people, the problem deepens.[63] Captives could almost never record a desire to return to their life before captivity, and most appear in the archive solely as names in notarial records, property in wills, or criminals in court cases.

Despite these limitations, there are some examples of diasporic activity among the first Asians in the Americas. The clearest cases often correspond to specific trades and geographies in which larger ethnolinguistic concentrations could be found, especially within the jurisdictions of today's Mexican states of Guerrero, Michoacán, Colima, and Jalisco. For example, when Domingo de Villalobos, a Kapampangan Philippine trader of Michoacán, fell sick, he stayed in the home of another Kapampangan man named Alonso Gutiérrez, his friend and business associate. As a gesture of thanks, Villalobos gave a petticoat from the Philippine region of Pampanga to Gutiérrez's Indigenous wife, doña Mariana. It was an object of both material and sentimental value to both Villalobos and Gutiérrez from a homeland neither would see again. Before he succumbed to disease in 1618, Villalobos willed his possessions to his mother, Monica Binangan, who still lived in the Philippines, and he made Gutiérrez his executor.[64] Based on the importance of his friendship with a fellow Kapampangan man in Mexico and the enduring connection to his home and mother, Villalobos's experience was diasporic.

Outside of a few cases of intra-ethnic solidarity like this, the broader question of communal identity is more difficult to answer. Although social historians of Mexico for a long time assumed that the "chinos" of Mexico were either only Chinese (an erroneous translation of "chino" in the colonial Mexican context) or Indigenous people of the Philippines (a misleading assumption), we now know that people categorized as "chino / a" were very diverse in terms of ethnicity, language, and social condition.[65] This variation means that there was little intrinsic to this population that made it a coherent community.[66] Instead, both the extreme difficulties of the Pacific crossing and colonial racial classification schemes generated new commonalities and social intersections where none or few had existed previously. Many people met in the commercial entrepôt of Manila and remembered the names of the ships that had borne them across the Pacific, as well as the people they had known on board.

After their arrival in Acapulco, most Asian subjects received the designation "chino / a." Though Spaniards on the Iberian Peninsula and in the Philippines clearly and consistently used the word to mean Chinese from China, in Mexico the label could apply to anyone perceived as originating from the lands across the Pacific—that is, coastal Asia. This linguistic invention was a uniquely Mexican orientalism that subsumed a population of enormous diversity into a new social identification system with adverse legal implications. It was the first time in the history of the Americas that Asian peoples were categorically racialized as belonging to a single group. Like the all-encompassing "indio / a" label that applied to Indigenous subjects of the crown from the Americas to Asia, becoming "chino / a"—the process that I term *chino-genesis*—similarly "speaks to the lack of Spanish interest in distinguishing the ethnic diversity of subject peoples."[67] There was no "affectionate" use of the term, despite Carrión's claim that benevolent *poblanos* (people from Puebla) welcomed Catarina de San Juan as a "china."

While the "chino / a" label formally racialized diverse ethnolinguistic Asian communities as an undifferentiated monolith, Asian people also learned to deploy the category at times to their own benefit. For example, a man named Juan Alonso appeared before the royal court in Mexico City in 1591 and argued successfully that restrictions against "indios" riding horseback should not apply to him, since he was a "chino."[68] In other cases, "chinos" found new commonalities through their mutual displacement and frequently formed intimate bonds with other "chinos," even those belonging to different ethnolinguistic groups.[69] They also founded confraternities that offered mutual assistance and selected each other as godparents for their children.[70] In specific circumstances, then, being "chino / a" served as a "strategic essentialism," an expedient form of identity making in which established stereotypes are manipulated for the sake of both situational gain and broad solidarity among multiple groups.[71] "Chino / a" was a fluid category, one that indicated both foreignness and new articulations of identity and subjecthood.

Yet as Dana Murillo has observed, "social change or acculturation does not equal cultural annihilation."[72] The extant documentation suggests that the first Asians in the Americas often retained a distinct sense of their identities, even as they received baptism, married across ethnolinguistic lines, emphasized their assimilation to Hispanic mores, conversed in Spanish and Nahuatl, and acculturated into existing communities of other castas. Thus a more flexible definition of *diaspora* is needed—one that is attentive to the limitations of colonial archives, the survival strategies of marginalized subjects, and the contingencies of early modern empire.

As scholars of diaspora studies have long noted, no "ideal type" of diaspora has ever existed.[73] In studying the great exodus of Chinese out of their
homeland after World War II, Dominic Yang argues that the multifaceted
nature of overseas movement—including the impossibility of return—
need not preclude the existence of "diasporic" characteristics related to
community formation, social integration, and memories of a homeland.[74]
Yang's intervention is also relevant to the early modern context and its at-
tendant archival limitations. Communal cohesion occurred both within
and in opposition to the formal requirements of diaspora.

David Ruderman's reflection on the early modern period is particularly
useful here. He defines the era "on the basis of intense communication
and exposure to other groups and communities," so that "the historian
might be better able to speak about a common cultural experience while
recognizing the perpetuation of distinct regional and local identities."[75]
This book incorporates both global synthesis and localism into the framework of mobility, which it treats as a broad construction that encompasses
both assimilation and cultural continuity, voluntary and involuntary movement, permanent settlement and transience, and geographic dispersion
and change over time. In tracking Asian mobility, rather than movement
bound by social condition or geography, this book establishes a new
chronology for Asian diasporic history. It situates the first Asians in the
Americas as the earliest iteration of the more recent and better-known
Asian migrations to the Western Hemisphere that began in the nineteenth
century and that still define the commencement of Asian diasporic history.

Colonial Race Thinking

Spaniards understood Asians in the Hispanic World through comparative
ethnography, based on Asians' degree of perceived similarity to or difference from preexisting archetypes. This disposition toward categorization
and stereotyping indicates that Asian subjects, like other marginalized
peoples, lived in a deeply race-conscious colonial world. Understanding
how these ethnographic discourses operated and how non-Spaniards negotiated and responded to them is essential in reconstructing Asian experiences in the imperial domain. And yet, this approach remains contested
in colonial Latin American historiography. In the words of Stuart Schwartz,
"There may be no topic in early Latin American history that has generated

more interest and debate than the issue of race and racial identity."[76] While many researchers working in adjacent fields (such as Atlantic World history) have found great use for methodologies of racial formation, the efficacy of race as a category in colonial Latin America continues to generate debate and disagreement.[77]

Many of those who consider race anachronistic to the early modern period in Latin America have argued that early modern humoral theory and the fluidity of castas, for example, defy the rigidity of modern racialization. Rebecca Earle best articulates this argument. In an effective study on how food and climate affected perceptions of the body, she maintains that the early modern reception of Galenic philosophy in Spain enabled flexible thinking about inherent natures. Modern ideas of race, she argues, are therefore inappropriate because "Spaniards in the new world constructed lasting social hierarchies that served the interests of colonial rule without resorting to the idea that the bodies of the colonisers and the colonised were incommensurately different."[78]

Similarly, María Eugenia Chaves concludes that early modern Spaniards marked difference in the colonial world by deploying a discourse that went beyond the frame of race making: "It seems to me that applying a conceptual criterion such as that of 'race,' for the sake of a coherent explanation . . . reduces the heterogeneity and dispersion of the colonial enunciative regimes to an order which is fundamentally foreign to them."[79] For Chaves, as for Earle, the term *race* treats as rigid what were actually fluid modes of perceiving and categorizing difference in the Hispanic World.

These apparent incompatibilities between early modern and modern conceptions of difference have been enormously influential in the field and, at the very least, have motivated historians to use extreme caution in discussing the applicability of *race* to colonial Latin America. For example, Robert Schwaller has declared that he will not use *race* to refer to early colonial Mexico "except in order to draw specific parallels with later concepts and beliefs"—although at the same time he notes that early modern Spaniards encoded stereotypes in language that "served to naturalize difference and entrench prejudice in racial ways."[80] His seeming ambivalence about the word reflects these broader tensions in the field.

What these claims about the inapplicability of race to early modern history have in common is an interpretation of race as a modern, biological determinant concerned primarily with hereditary descent and phenotypical traits. Francisco Bethencourt has described this Enlightenment-era philosophical position as the "theory of race," a codified, scientific system that relied on natural divides in humanity to justify discriminatory action.[81] Reacting to definitions of this kind, Earle reasons that "the early modern Hispanic world provides little evidence for the existence of racial thinking."[82] This tendency to use Enlightenment and post-Enlightenment racial ideologies as foils to dismiss early modern operations of race is especially widespread in the field of colonial Latin American history.

However, as any ethnic studies scholar can affirm, modern conceptions of race are rarely immutable and fixed.[83] David Nirenberg expresses this position very clearly: "We premodernists often rely on the questionable axiom that modern racial theories depend upon evolutionary biology and genetics, in order to leap to the demonstrably false conclusion that there exists a truly biological modern racism against which earlier forms of discrimination can be measured and judged innocent."[84] Destabilizing these basic assumptions about racial thought and its historical applications allows us to arrive at more nuanced and elastic understandings of race making in the early modern world.

Geraldine Heng's theorization of premodern racial thought is the natural step forward from Nirenberg's contention. Heng has constructed a powerful methodological tool for understanding how race functions in different times and places. She has argued that race demarcates "human beings through differences . . . that are selectively essentialized as absolute and fundamental, in order to distribute positions and powers differentially to human groups." In this formulation, race need not be rooted in biological or even physical markers: it can also refer to culture and religion, as well as intersect with class, gender, and sexuality. She continues, "Race-making thus operates as specific historical occasions in which strategic essentialisms are posited and assigned through a variety of practices and pressures, so as to construct a hierarchy of peoples for differential treatment." These hierarchies may be fluid, contingent, and contested, but their existence is key. She concludes, "My understanding, thus, is that race is a structural relationship for the articulation and management of human differences, rather than a substantive content."[85] According to these criteria, perceptions of difference in colonial Latin America—and, indeed, in the early modern world—qualify as "race thinking" or "racial formation" in countless forms.[86]

Following Heng's framework, I argue that the racialization of diverse Asian ethnolinguistic groups into undifferentiated "chinos" in the Spanish Americas was dependent on the Spanish perception of Asian difference from the model Hispanic and Catholic subject. As in Heng's definition, these differences were "fundamental," although some individuals found inventive ways to contest their legal implications in colonial courts. Furthermore, as colonial subjects, Asians were arranged in hierarchies of power managed by colonial institutions and influential Spaniards who selectively favored some phenotypical, social, linguistic, religious, sexual, and gendered traits over others. These hierarchies produced "differential treatment" and profoundly shaped the lived experiences of free and enslaved Asians in colonial societies.

In the Hispanic World, race thinking colloquially and institutionally positioned wealthy, white Spanish Catholic male lives above all others. Individuals with these markers had never been and never would be legally vulnerable to colonial regimes of bondage in the Americas.[87] There could never be a so-called just war or a colonial war of extermination against them.[88] Requirements of *probanzas de limpieza de sangre* (proofs of blood purity [needed for travel, advancement to nobility, and proving innocence before the Inquisition]) did not threaten them, since they were of documentable, old Christian stock (and even considered themselves the descendants of the Biblical Tubal, the grandson of Noah). They did not suffer from any of the exclusionary economic or social restrictions that were fundamental to the ordering of colonial society. According to Antonio Feros, "[The idea of Spain] existed primarily and fundamentally not in the laws or institutions or state but in its people—the descendants of the original inhabitants of Hispania."[89] These notions of a Spain and a Spanish people were themselves racial imaginaries.

The existence of a privileged class of wealthy, white Spanish Catholics clearly indicates that race thinking structured and ordered the fundamental operations of colonial society, even if the process of determining who could be defined as belonging to that class was sometimes imprecise and variable. Indeed, there is a growing cohort of scholars of colonial Latin America who agree and study the relations of power between colonial groups through the analytical framework of race. Jorge Cañizares-Esguerra argues that the sometimes nebulous distinctions among Spaniards, Indigenous peoples, and Black people began to rigidify in the late sixteenth century when American-born Spaniards postulated "clear-cut racial distinctions and [began] to construct separate bodies for Indians and Creoles."[90] Any deviation from the Hispanic standard marked an individual or community as other and vulnerable to adverse perceptions and laws, often driven by fear of un-Hispanic activity, conspiracy, violence, and even rebellion. Miguel Valerio describes this discourse of fear and its repercussions (including confinement, brutal labor regimes, torture, and executions) as constituting a veritable "anti-Black culture" in colonial Mexico during the early seventeenth century.[91] Ann Twinam summarizes this point well: "Spanish America . . . was universalist and racist in its assignation of blackness as an inferior category justifying discrimination. It was constructionist in that it recognized variable statuses between white and black and brown and Spanish and African and Native and permitted movement among categories."[92] Fluidity, then, does not discount the operations of race.

Movement between racialized categories required assimilation, which consisted of undergoing holy baptism, adopting a Spanish name, celebrating Catholic holidays, entering a monogamous and heterosexual Catholic marriage, following Catholic cultural and sexual prohibitions, wearing Spanish clothes, becoming ladino / a (Spanish-speaking), and instructing one's children in the tenets of the Catholic faith. Integration necessitated a public excision of most non-Hispanic and non-Catholic cultural signs, which often entailed a renunciation of a pre-Hispanic and pre-Christian past and heritage. Rather than challenging the applicability of race, this incorporationist model of governance illuminated and accentuated the traits that could mark colonized populations as other.

However, this growing scholarship on race in the Spanish empire has yet to incorporate the Pacific or "chinos" into its analytical frame. Juan de Medina, an Augustinian missionary writing in Manila in 1630, provides one of the clearest examples of the racial implications of incorporationist imperial thinking:

> and if these very bad-tempered people [Zambales and Chinese] were settled and tied down with laws and civilization, they would come in time to lose their natural arrogance and gain different customs; because if animals incapable of reason are domesticated with treatment and lose their strength, men capable of reason will do much better. We have an example in the Blacks [*negros*], that being a people

that seem the scum of the earth, so untamed [bozales] when they are
brought, that even though they seem greater beasts than they really
are, in the end, in dealing with civilized people, they come to learn
the comportment of men; because how much better did the Indigenous peoples [indios] of these islands [the Philippines] do in whom
much ingenuity has been discovered for all that has been taught
them?[93]

According to Medina, if Spaniards could domesticate animals, then they
could assimilate Black people, and if they could Hispanicize Black people,
then the Indigenous Zambales of the Philippines and the Chinese could
be brought into the fold as well. Through his comparison of racial others
to animals, Medina delivered an optimistic assessment of the colonial mission. These peoples could change their inherent natures through contacts
and dealings with "civilized people"—that is, Spaniards. Racial discourse,
therefore, developed not in isolation but relationally.[94]

Similarly, the scholarship on the "chinos" of New Spain has yet to seriously consider the implications of early modern racialization for the lives
of Asian subjects. While this important body of work has unpacked the
rhetoric that justified Asian enslavement and studied the categorical exclusions of casta society, it has not considered these developments in the
context of race or engaged with the idea that race making was itself a historical process that drove overseas movement and determined the lived
experience of transpacific mobility. To examine the first Asians in the Americas through the lens of race thinking is to study, for the first time, how
the confluences of ethnographic discourse, colonial inclusion (or lack
thereof), Spanish fears of multiethnic coalitions, the threat of enslavement, and the liminality of social advancement came to structure social
and economic possibilities for Asian peoples. The processes by which
Asians became visible, stereotyped, and subordinated in Spanish colonial
societies exemplify how forms of racialization both emerged and came to
justify systemic discriminatory action. From the tactics of ethnic extermination used in Manila to the wholesale bans on "chino" weapon bearing
in Mexico, the ramifications of these discourses cannot be understated.
Difference was often inscribed spatially as well. Whether confined to an
urban ghetto or a textile mill (obraje), Asians experienced the genealogies
of spatial control and segregation meant to encourage conversion and

orderly behavior in the colonies.[95] As "chinos" within the casta system, Asians had become yet another homogenized mass of potentially rebellious others in need of oversight and control. Many "chinos" sought to contest this negative characterization by creating new nodes of collaboration across ethnic lines or by asking the colonial administration for specific privileges based on merit and service.

As Kris Manjapra reminds us, "Racialization is as much about the fact of survival and vital reclamations among the colonized as it is about the social violence inflicted by colonizers."[96] Like other colonial subjects, Asians consistently negotiated their second-class statuses for individual and, occasionally, mutual benefit. Challenging the colonial order took many forms and could range from attempts at social advancement to outright resistance to enslavement. These tensions—sometimes coherent, sometimes contradictory—are at the heart of this history. Uncovering them elucidates the many structural and individual challenges that Asians faced in the Hispanic World and how they sought to resolve them.

The Structure of This Book

By the time the Hapsburgian Cross of Burgundy first appeared off Philippine shores in 1521, Asian places and peoples had already enraptured European imaginations for hundreds of years.[97] The lures of spice and silk led Iberians to take up the cross and the sword to invade those distant lands for commercial gain. To access those gateways to wealth and opulence, Spaniards invaded the Philippine Islands. The islands possessed few resources that inspired mercantile interest, but they represented a crucial crossroad that linked Spanish American metropoles to Asian markets. As Spaniards accumulated years of experience in the Philippines and neighboring regions, officials and missionaries struggled to decipher the enormous social and cultural complexities of the peoples they encountered. They tried to resolve their confrontation with unfathomable difference by imposing their own standards and expectations of civilized, Hispanic behavior on Indigenous and foreign populations.[98] Yet these incorporationist ideals failed in the Philippines, where the minimal Spanish population—even in the heart of Manila—deployed exclusionary and often violent tactics as a means to manage non-Spanish populations resisting assimilation.

Chapter 1 opens with the climax of these tensions in Manila—the Chinese uprising of 1603, the suppression of which was among the most violent episodes of its era. Thousands of Chinese residents in Manila, militants and bystanders alike, fell to the blades of the colonial coalition army composed of Spanish, Japanese, Tagalog, and Kapampangan warriors. These massacres decisively recalibrated the possibilities of colonial collaboration, regimes of labor and bondage, and the frequency of Spanish flight from the city in ways that increased the already growing numbers of free and enslaved Asians sailing to the Americas. The year 1603 was a watershed moment of racially motivated violence that substantively influenced the emergence of one of the most important patterns of long-distance migration and displacement in the early modern world. Beginning with this flash point, the book proceeds geographically, tracing the Pacific, Western Hemispheric, and Atlantic trajectories of Asian subjects like roots sprouting from a blood-soaked seed.

As Asian sailors, *criados* (servants), enslaved people, and free travelers boarded the Manila galleons for Mexico, they faced a grueling journey: the Pacific passage. Chapter 2 examines the repercussions of this jarring dislocation. Asians, irrespective of ethnicity, most often occupied the lowest rung of the shipboard hierarchy as *grumetes* (cabin boys). Under horrific conditions, they performed menial tasks that were essential for the survival of everyone on board. Shipboard labor structures, along with the omnipresence of maritime religious rituals, forced Asians of all ethnicities into close proximity and mutual dependency. It was on board the galleons, I argue, that the process of gathering disparate ethnic groups under a single socioracial category began. When the voyage's survivors arrived in Acapulco, most of them were legally classified as "chino / a," again regardless of their ethnolinguistic identity. As "chinos," they entered the *sistema de castas* (caste system), becoming vulnerable to enslavement, the Inquisition, a wide range of socioeconomic restrictions, and negative stereotypes that framed them as disloyal and criminal.

As they trudged from the Pacific coast to the highlands of central Mexico, the newly christened "chinos" (sometimes called "indios chinos") often tried to distance themselves from the legal penalties associated with these labels. Chapters 3 and 4 examine the strategies whereby both free and enslaved "chinos" negotiated the repercussions of their legal statuses. Chapter 3 argues that free "chinos" in central Mexico tried to circumvent negative social perceptions and racialized laws by submitting petitions for exceptional treatment. Through petitions for licenses to trade and possess weapons, free "chinos" presented the Real Audiencia (Royal Court) of Mexico City with evidence of Hispanic and Catholic assimilation. If awarded, the licenses opened new possibilities for social mobility. However, they did little to curtail acts of discrimination by local magistrates and petty officials who consistently disregarded and negated privileges conferred to individual "chinos."

While privileged "chinos" struggled for recognition through formal channels, the enslaved had to find alternative means of negotiating and contesting the conditions of their bondage. Though the field of Afro-Asian studies in Latin America has yet to consider the early modern period, Chapter 4 contends that the history of enslavement in colonial Mexico marks the beginning of Afro-Asian convergence in the Western Hemisphere. During this period, "chinos" responded to the brutalities of enslavement specifically by collaborating with other enslaved populations. In conjunction with Indigenous and Afro-Mexican communities, enslaved Asians ran away, blasphemed to protest unjust treatment, and formed hybrid spiritualities that went far beyond the precepts of Catholic dogma. They were neither passive nor voiceless subjects.

Although most of the first Asians in the Americas remained in central Mexico, some individuals traveled much farther through the empire: reaching the present-day borders of Oregon to the north and the Andes to the south, and even going across the Atlantic to the Iberian Peninsula. Chapter 5 follows their trajectories, which were hemispheric and global in ways many other early modern mobilities were not. As distance from New Spain increased, so too did the instability of central Mexican labels, legal precedents, and stereotypes. In South America and on the Iberian Peninsula, the categorization of Asians as "chinos" was less consistent, and Asian peoples found themselves better able to use other categories for social and legal expediency. In Lima, for example, many Asians were counted among the city's Indigenous population in a tribute register from 1613–1614. Similarly, in Seville, Asians frequently appealed as Indigenous subjects for charity that would allow them to return to Asia by crossing first the Atlantic and then the Pacific. In these distant locales, Asian populations were also generally much smaller than in Mexico—which presented unique challenges for these subjects, who sometimes lamented their social and cultural isolation. Given these local distinctions, we cannot look to Mexico alone to build a complete picture of Asian experience in the Spanish Americas or in Spain.

Over time, the demographic composition of Asian populations in the Americas changed significantly. The greatest shift occurred after 1672, when Queen Regent Mariana of Austria signed an emancipation order into law that freed all "chinos." In Chapter 6, the book takes a temporal turn to the aftermath of emancipation. A prevailing thesis in the historiography suggests that Asians disappeared from Mexico in the eighteenth century, given that the "chinos" of the so-called casta paintings produced in this period are Afro-Indigenous and not Asian. However, I argue that Asian people not only remained visible in Mexico until the end of the colonial period but also adapted to shifts in coastal economic development and new trade routes that eventually undermined the primacy of the Manila galleons. Despite lower rates of migration, Asians continued coming to and going from Acapulco and other Pacific ports until the Mexican Wars of Independence (1810–1821). The last Asian participation in the galleon trade coincided with the early stirrings of Asian labor conscription in 1806 and the modern indenture of East and South Asians in the Western Hemisphere. The interimperial competition that brought about the end of the Manila galleons simultaneously enabled the emergence of these modern migratory trajectories.

From the sixteenth to the nineteenth centuries, the Asians arriving in the Americas defined a new chronology that predates the canonical histories of Asians in the Western Hemisphere more broadly. The Pacific World and Asian mobility were fundamental to daily life in colonial Mexico and beyond. These spheres were intricately connected politically, economically, and socially. People made this global colonial world cohere, and through the ways they chose to live their lives, they created new realities, imaginaries, and identities. These stories are immediately relevant to the founding of an Asian America, and incorporating them into its study requires a significant recalibration of Asian American origins and their connections to Latin American history.

I THE FRAGILE CONVIVENCIA
OF COLONIAL MANILA

ON NOVEMBER 14, 1603, four thousand victorious Tagalog and Kapampangan warriors paraded through Spanish Manila. They marched over the
ashes of the once bustling Parian (the Chinese quarter), waving captured
banners before grateful Spanish onlookers.[1] This coalition and their Spanish
captains had just returned from a month-long pursuit of rebels from the
Pasig River to Batangas that ended in the near obliteration of the "Sangleyes,"
their Chinese neighbors.[2]

Six weeks earlier, thousands of "Sangley" rebels had attacked Manila's
city walls with two siege towers in an attempt to scale the formidable ramparts of Intramuros, the inner city. Only the timely intervention of the
engineer Rodrigo de Figueroa had prevented the rebels from overrunning
the defenses: he successfully installed a naval cannon capable of firing
22-kilogram shot on the ramparts and used it to destroy the siege towers.
This desperate action cost Figueroa his life.[3] Nearly half of the soldiers of
the Spanish garrison had also fallen in the city's defense, including many
of its most experienced veterans, a former governor, and the sitting governor's nephew.[4]

The provident arrival of Indigenous reinforcements prevented the colony's complete downfall, and now these troops trod over the rubble of the
district that had represented the greatest existential threat to Spanish colonial rule in the Philippines. The "savage retribution" of the Spaniards—
as even the imperial apologist William Schurz termed it—was a violent
expression of decades of racializing discourse and discrimination targeting
Chinese residents.[5] Although hawkish Spaniards also considered the colony

untenable without Chinese laborers and merchants, negative stereotypes that focused on fundamental cultural differences became entrenched over time. "Sangleyes" came to occupy a liminal space within the colonial imaginary as both necessary neighbors and unassimilable enemies of Hispanic Catholic society. These new essentialisms were defining features of early modern racial formation as it developed in the Hispanic World.

As stereotypes of Chinese "undifferentiated differentness" under colonial rule ossified over time, Spaniards learned to deploy these discourses to justify violent action.[6] By the start of 1603, Spanish officials—including some previously sympathetic to "Sangleyes"—had executed those accused of sodomy, impressed poor "Sangleyes" as galley slaves in numerous expeditions, and penned petitions to deport the unconverted. Tensions reached a height in October when a couple thousand "Sangley" peasants raised arms against the colony and rallied more people to their cause.

According to the report of an anonymous soldier, the Spaniards had debated three extreme actions as the rebels closed in: preemptively murdering everyone in the Parian, setting fire to it, or sacking it to obtain its riches, allegedly worth 80,000 pesos. As time was short, the decision was made to incinerate Manila's most populous neighborhood. The soldier concluded that "divine justice had shown that sins, like the ones committed [in the Parian], were deserving of such punishment."[7] Thus, the "Sangleyes" (even those not involved in the uprising) could only be absolved of their sins in flame. What had begun as an armed conflict between warring parties had devolved into ethnic extermination enacted through the wanton murder of thousands of "Sangley" noncombatants.

The greatest heroes of the mid-November parade were two Indigenous nobles, don Ventura de Mendoza and don Guillermo Dimarocot, who had fought at the head of the Tagalog and Kapampangan contingents, respectively. Dimarocot (the name means "he whose feet are spared of mud") came from the town of Guagua on the northern edge of Manila Bay and had a record of colonial service dating back to 1585.[8] In 1593, he had been promoted to captain fifty Kapampangan soldiers fighting against the headhunting Zambales, their pre-Hispanic adversaries. During that campaign, he had suffered no fewer than seven head wounds. His commanding officers described him as a "sharp and reliable person."[9] At his side marched his son, don Diego Dimarocot, whom he had appointed as his lieutenant. After the parade, Hernando de los Ríos Coronel, an advocate of colonial policy reform, wrote that the Natives of Laguna de Bay and Pampanga "fought very well and with much loyalty and willingness against the Sangleyes." Coronel went on to name don Guillermo and don Ventura as especially worthy of reward and noted that they and their people should no longer be mistreated or whipped.[10]

The unprecedented opportunities afforded to loyal collaborators after the 1603 campaign were only one of the developments that would impact the dispersion not just of Philippine Natives but of all Asians who willingly or unwillingly traveled on the galleons from Cavite in the Philippines to Acapulco. After the war, Tagalog and Kapampangan veterans with extensive records of military service began appearing with greater frequency in archival records on the other side of the Pacific. Don Guillermo's son, don Diego, would board a galleon headed for Mexico in 1621 to then cross the Atlantic to petition the Spanish Crown for royal favor. The 1603 uprising was a turning point in Spanish transpacific history.

In recent years, scholars have understood Asian mobility from the Philippines to central Mexico as an extension of regional slave markets and as a by-product of galleon trade and the labor necessary to maintain it.[11] These factors were indeed central to the overall contours of the eastward movement across the Pacific, grounding a new and important metanarrative about the exploitative and violent nature of early Asian movement. Yet because this existing narrative elides the local politics of colonial Manila, it ultimately provides an incomplete picture of transpacific Asian mobility and why that mobility occurred as it did. The fallout from the "Sangley" rebellion accentuated Spaniards' dependency on other populations, and it crucially informed the demographic and social compositions of galleon travelers.

Schurz remains one of the few scholars to notice that discrimination against the Chinese in the Philippines shaped the development of Manila galleon history.[12] Although Schurz referred principally to the impact of discrimination on the circulation of material goods, geopolitics, and economic prosperity, prejudice was also fundamental to the history of the people that the galleons ferried to the Americas. As Schurz noted almost a century ago, "no [other] ship ever played the part in a city's life which the galleon did in that of Manila."[13] The reverse was true as well: what transpired in the city deeply impacted the human contours of galleon travel. The development of racialized categorical thinking and the violence it spawned in Manila framed and generated the movement of thousands of Asians east across the Pacific.

The relationship between the violence of 1603 and Asian mobility to the Americas has gone unnoticed. Spanish race making in the Philippines produced conflict along ethnic and religious confessional lines that structured and shaped both spatial and social mobility. The phenomenon of transpacific movement precedes 1603, of course. However, not coincidentally the years after the uprising witnessed an increase in the number of slaves arriving in Manila, the eastward movement of Spanish officials and their retinues in search of safer posts, and new forms of social mobility through collaboration. These local processes, directly catalyzed by the violence of 1603, in turn affected transpacific movement by both limiting and enabling numerous avenues for long-distance connection to the Americas. In other words, Manila's social politics and the evolving processes of racial formation, rooted in the lived experiences of the city's multiethnic population, defined the transpacific movement of Asians (both free and enslaved) during the early seventeenth century.

Manila at the Beginning of the Seventeenth Century

As Seville's population neared 100,000, the residents of Manila—the remote colony wrested from Rajah Sulayman only in 1571—came to account for half of the population of its Spanish counterpart.[14] The Jesuit Francisco Colín did not exaggerate his claim that Manila had one of the highest populations in the Spanish Indies.[15] However, it was the Chinese, not the Spaniards, who allowed Manila to hold this distinction. During the late sixteenth century, Chinese captains and merchants turned their attention to Spanish silver, and by 1600, thirty to forty Chinese ships were arriving in Manila Bay every year.[16] In comparison, during the middle of the sixteenth century, just over 100 vessels of all sizes left Seville every year for the Americas.[17]

The Chinese were fundamental to both the survival of the frontier colony and the transpacific trade that made the prospect of colonialism in Asia attractive. Through Chinese merchants, a plethora of luxury products entered the Hispanic World and filled the holds of ships destined for Mexico. This merchandise included refined and unrefined silks, porcelain from Jingdezhen (景德镇), lacquerware, foodstuffs, and more.[18]

Estimates of the Chinese population in Manila from the late 1590s to 1603 reach 20,000–30,000 at their peak, compared to a mere 1,000–2,000 Spaniards. For this reason, Guillermo Ruiz-Stovel writes, "Manila may have been a Spanish possession, but for all practical purposes it was a Chinese town, inhabited not only by Chinese merchants but also by a skilled contingent of [Chinese] workers and artisans who kept the colony afloat."[19] Nearly all of the Chinese were men, and many of them had families in Fujian (福建).[20]

This considerable population growth owed much to earlier Chinese-Philippine contacts. By the early fifteenth century, over 150 years before Spanish settlement, numerous Philippine polities had already established diplomatic communications with Ming China. By the mid-sixteenth century, one or two ships from Fujian arrived in the Philippines every year to trade, and a fledgling population of forty Chinese families resided in the Rahjanate of Maynila prior to its seizure by the Spanish. Visayans were so familiar with Chinese trade vessels and merchants that when Esteban Rodríguez, a Spanish navigator, attempted to persuade the townspeople of a small polity that he and his sailors were Chinese and therefore to be respected, the Visayans did not hesitate to state that they knew the Spaniards were not, in fact, Chinese, but thieves.[21]

Spanish silver mined from Potosí, Zacatecas, and elsewhere enhanced the economic attraction of Manila and subsequently drew considerable attention from southern Japanese traders, Fujianese ship captains traversing Southeast Asia, and Portuguese merchants based in Macau, Nagasaki, Melaka, Goa, Kochi, and Makassar.[22] These overlapping trade circuits rapidly diversified Manila's demographics, creating fluid cultural frontiers and connecting the early modern world in new ways. Within the multiethnic alleys of Manila's markets, pidgin languages—based on Spanish, Hokkien Chinese, and Tagalog—abounded.[23] According to one curious observer, "Every nation [*nación*] has formed a jargon through which they are understood . . . the Chinese, to say 'alcalde' [magistrate], 'español' and 'indio', say this: *alicaya, cancia, juania.*"[24] The city's economic viability would rely on the tolerance of numerous non-Hispanic and non-Catholic populations, a dynamic that did not exist to such an extreme anywhere else in the Hispanic World.

For an empire that had defined itself by its imagined ability to integrate and assimilate diverse Indigenous populations in the Americas, the inability to project power and cultural influence in Manila created a unique crisis of *convivencia* (the state of living together). Although convivencia typically has medieval Iberian connotations, Antonio García-Abásolo, Ryan Crewe, and José Antonio Cervera have observed that the concept was on the minds of secular and ecclesiastical administrators in colonial Manila.[25] Initially, convivencia referred to premodern Iberian multiconfessional communities (Catholic, Muslim, and Jewish) living side by side. As David Nirenberg argues, such an arrangement did not indicate a society of utopian harmony. On the contrary, physical, symbolic, and discursive violence was fundamental to these faiths' ability to coexist: "*Convivencia* was predicated upon violence. . . . Violence drew its meaning from coexistence, not in opposition to it."[26] By the sixteenth century, the convivencia in Spain had effectively ended with the forced expulsion of Jews and Muslims and the implementation of an inquisition that terrorized recent Jewish and Muslim converts to Catholicism (known as *conversos* and *moriscos,* respectively).

As large numbers of Chinese merchants and laborers began settling in Manila, the Spanish royal court continued to debate what was referred to as the morisco question. Nirenberg concludes that, although Catholics and moriscos were mutually dependent economically, "such recognition [of economic utility] did not preclude violence."[27] Proposals for dealing with Spain's morisco population oscillated between begrudging toleration and outright expulsion.[28] In the Philippines, Spaniards developed an acute economic dependence on their Chinese neighbors, and consequently the polemics of the morisco debate soon appeared in reference to "Sangleyes." Indeed, well-established anti-Muslim and anti-Jewish discourses conditioned Spanish intolerance of unconverted or insincerely converted populations in the colonies. Not only did the presence of "Sangleyes" threaten the pillars of Spanish colonial identity, but it also destabilized and undermined conversion efforts among the spiritually vulnerable neophytes, the Indigenous population of the colony.

For Spaniards, the necessity of safeguarding Philippine Catholicism was all the more critical because the people living on the northern outskirts of Manila, across the Pasig River from the rest of the city, prominently maintained Muslim customs into the late 1580s. Spaniards in the Philippines viewed their conflicts with local Muslim populations as a continuation of the Reconquista (711–1492) that had shaped Spanish Catholic identity in opposition to the monolith of Mediterranean Islam.[29] More than a decade after the Spanish seizure of Manila in 1571 and the ousted Rajah Sulayman's failed insurrection in 1574, Spanish officials began to realize that they had been shockingly ineffective at converting Tagalog elites north of the Pasig River, in the districts of Tondo and Quiapo. For example, from 1581 to 1582 the Augustinian missionary Diego de Mújica imprisoned a *datu* (elite) from Tondo named don Luis Amanicalao. The missionary accused Amanicalao of having sex with the sister of his deceased wife (which Spaniards considered incest) and then arranging a Muslim wedding with her. The criminalization of pre-Hispanic sexual customs had become a fundamental mode of cultural control and anti-Muslim policy in and around Manila.[30]

In June 1582, Amanicalao—with Calao, his son from his first marriage—joined a group of forty datus from towns near Manila to testify against the consistent persecution of Spanish *alcaldes mayores* (magistrates and provincial heads).[31] The most outraged of the datus were don Martín Panga and his cousin, don Agustín de Legazpi, the former governor of Tondo who was married to the Sultan of Brunei's daughter. In 1585, Legazpi had given his mother a Muslim burial and had been imprisoned for doing so.[32] While behind bars, Legazpi and numerous other datus (including Amanicalao and his son) recognized the realities of their waning power under Spanish rule and pledged to support each other financially and, eventually, militarily against the Spaniards.

Central to their grievances were differences between pre-Hispanic and Spanish customs of enslavement. For datus on Luzon, owning enslaved people was a primary form of building long-term wealth and prestige.[33] Spanish colonial rule and norms of enslavement conspired to divide datus from this customary source of hierarchical legitimacy. The brutality of tribute exploitation through the forced sale of goods at set prices (*vandala*) and rotational forced labor drafts (*polo*) depopulated Luzon and hampered the ability of elites to acquire and retain slaves. The polo was a loose version of its predecessor in Mexico, the *repartimiento*. Levies varied from season to season and were mustered and dissolved as needed for short-term assignments. Labor often consisted of construction projects, servicing ships at port, and cutting timber for galleon construction. Polo work regimes tended to be extremely arduous, and pay was virtually nonexistent.[34]

After 1581, Spanish administrators at least nominally sought to prevent the direct enslavement of Philippine Natives formally designated as protected "indios."[35] While legal measures like the New Laws of 1542 often failed to keep Indigenous people from captivity, the vassal status of "indios" within the Spanish empire opened the possibility of contesting the legitimacy of one's enslavement in colonial courts. Under the Spanish system, the enslaved of Philippine elites could now prosecute their enslavers on the ground that they were illegally kept in bondage. The judge and writer Antonio de Morga commented in 1609 that these pleas for freedom were the most frequently litigated cases in Spanish courts.[36]

After the Union of the Two Crowns of Spain and Portugal in 1580, Spaniards in Manila gained access to enslaved labor through Portuguese traders operating throughout the Indian Ocean World and East Asia. Thus, not only were Indigenous elites losing access to traditional routes of enslavement, but there were now more enslaved peoples entering the Philippines from elsewhere than ever before. Across the Pacific, Spanish officials in Mexico considered the possibilities of tapping into the enslaved labor market in the Philippines as early as 1572.[37] In 1584, the attorney general of "miners and owner of mines in Ixmilquilpan" (due north of Mexico City) requested 3,000–4,000 Africans and "if possible to also send Chinese, Japanese, and Javanese people from the Philippines" to support dwindling Indigenous labor pools.[38] Locked out of the nascent transpacific slave trade, Philippine elites came to view the growing gap between Spanish and Indigenous access to captives as a glaring sign of inequality.

After being released from confinement, don Agustín de Legazpi and don Martín Panga sought alliances with the other datus of central Luzon but had limited success. Their most ambitious plan called for coalitions with Japanese pirates and the Sultanate of Brunei through their shared kinship networks. Not only had Brunei resisted Spanish incursion in the early 1580s, but it was also the central gateway to Muslim Southeast Asia from the Philippines.[39] Unfortunately for the conspirators, an Indigenous man named don Antonio Surabao leaked the plot to his Spanish patron, who rushed to Manila with news of an imminent uprising. Governor Santiago de Vera immediately rounded up and interrogated all high-level conspirators, which resulted in twenty-four guilty verdicts. It is entirely unclear whether these denunciations were based on direct evidence or, in at least some cases, they functioned as excuses to punish nobles linked to Islam.

Don Agustín de Legazpi and don Martín Panga were decapitated, and their heads were displayed in iron cages. Spaniards confiscated their estates and salted their fields so that nothing would grow there. Don Luis Amanicalao and Calao were exiled for three and four years, respectively, and were soon deported on a ship bound for Acapulco with a handful of their co-conspirators.[40] They were among four exiled elites who survived the passage to Acapulco.[41]

The violence of Vera's retribution indicates the surprise, anguish, and fear so common in Spanish accounts of having found Muslims, their ancient enemies, on the far side of the world. Although the suppression of Legazpi and Panga's conspiracy in 1588–1589 definitively severed Luzon elites from outward expressions of their pre-Hispanic Muslim heritage, Spanish fears of spiritual backsliding remained. Thus, Spaniards believed that their survival relied on their ability to incentivize others to ally themselves with the colony and convert to Christianity, limit the means by which non-Spanish people could find solidarity, and preserve the status quo of convivencia.

The arrival of Chinese merchants and laborers in large numbers only exacerbated Spanish anxieties. The prospect of multiethnic coalitions, coupled with the ideological strain of hosting a rapidly growing male Chinese population in Manila, introduced a new rhetoric of fear that doomed the project of colonial convivencia. During the late sixteenth century, Manila experienced a tremendous growth in trade with the Southern Min (閩南), a seafaring people originating primarily from Fujian. A major province of foreign commerce since the Yuan dynasty (1271–1368), Fujian had a low agricultural output relative to its population, which encouraged many residents to turn to the sea and seek their fortune abroad.[42] Although illicit trade occurred throughout the sixteenth century, Spanish settlement in the Philippines coincided with the Ming dynasty's formal opening of the port of Yuegang (月港) to overseas trade in 1567.[43] This maritime allowance also intersected with the promulgation of the Single Whip Reform (一條鞭法) in 1580, which meant that taxes in China were now collected in the form of silver instead of rice. This increased demand for silver aligned Chinese trade interests with those of Spanish suppliers of silver in the Philippines.[44] Traveling 15–20 days from coastal Fujian, ship captains typically arrived in Manila after the Lunar New Year and stayed for several months, leaving numerous passengers and sailors behind before departing (figure 1.1).[45]

1.1 Hydrographic and Chorographic Map of the Philippine Islands

The Jesuit Pedro Murillo Velarde's "Carta hydrographica y chorographica de las Yslas Filipinas" is the iconic colonial-era projection of the Philippines. Designed with the contributions of two Philippine artists, Nicolás de la Cruz Bagay and Francisco Suárez, the map features a Chinese ship (*champan de china*) off the "Yloco" (Iloco) coast to the northwest of Luzon. To the east, Manila galleons sail in either direction near the Embocadero (the eastern entrance to the Philippines). The map's left side contains six panels featuring the diverse array of ethnic groups residing in the islands, while the right side has inset maps of cities and illustrations of modes of crop cultivation and hunting.

Pedro Murillo Velarde, "Carta hydrographica y chorographica de las Yslas Filipinas" (Manila, 1734). World Digital Library.

In a letter to King Felipe II in 1590, Domingo de Salazar, the Dominican bishop of Manila, wrote that these new arrivals, the "Sangleyes," had turned an inhospitable swamp into a well-ordered and productive district (the Parian). According to him, the energetic trade that occurred there was unparalleled in the world. The abundant goods and marvelous wonders of China and elsewhere could be bought for prices so low "that it is shameful to say it."[46] Salazar admired the district's doctors, pharmacists, specialists in mechanical arts, restaurants (where all could eat well and cheaply), silversmiths, and goldsmiths. In the comparative imaginary so common to early modern observers, Salazar viewed Chinese artistry, bookbinding, and farming in the Philippines as superior to the equivalents in Europe and Mexico.

Salazar's wide-eyed awe mirrored Hernando Cortés's admiration of the legendary market of Tlatelolco that is a defining feature of his second *carta de relación* (report) to King Carlos V.[47] Salazar articulated a colonial discourse that deployed the language of orientalistic *maravilla* (wonder) to encourage missionary activity in Asia and bring the riches and territories of those distant polities into the universal Catholic kingdom. Millenarian writers believed these conjunctures to be the destiny of the world. The best-known example of this discourse was Juan González de Mendoza's *Historia de las cosas mas notables, ritos y costumbres, del gran reyno dela China* (History of the most notable things, rites and customs, of the grand kingdom of China), published in Rome in 1585—just five years before Salazar penned his letter to King Felipe II.[48] Mendoza's unequivocal praise of Chinese people and civilization spread widely throughout Europe (his book had forty-five editions and was published in seven languages in just fifteen years), stoking the imaginations of several generations of European readers.[49] According to Mendoza, the Chinese had the advantage over Europeans in everything except Christianity. He wrote that Saint Thomas had visited China long before and that the signs of his journey remained in certain elements of Chinese religiosity. In other words, Chinese people would be receptive to the reintroduction of Christianity, and if they were converted, their kingdom would become Christendom's greatest prize.[50]

Efforts at Catholicization both in the Philippines and on the Chinese mainland met with very limited success, however. The overwhelming majority of Chinese settling in Manila never received baptism. Nonetheless, several hundred Chinese decided to conform to Hispanic expectations and managed to leverage their new status as converts to achieve a considerable degree of social mobility. Chinese Christians were permitted to live outside of the Parian, could marry Indigenous women, and had fewer tribute obligations than their unconverted peers. Christian weddings between Chinese men and local women were highly encouraged, as the prevailing view was that these women would attach new converts to good Catholic and Hispanic customs.[51] The push toward Catholic unions was also intended to curb Chinese bigamy, or the incidents in which men with families in Fujian would take a concubine, lover, or additional wife in the Philippines. A child of a Chinese-Indigenous licensed marriage was known as a "mestizo / a" or "mestizo / a de sangley," and these mixed descendants quickly acquired reputations as loyal and dependable subjects of the Spanish Crown through the moderating influence of their Philippine mothers. The ambiguity of "mestizos" in the Philippines as both Spanish-Indigenous and Chinese-Indigenous reinforces the argument that, in the prevailing Spanish view, Hispanic and Chinese lineages were equally capable of producing a mixed population of service to the colony.

Some converts, like Juan Sami, taught Hokkien and Mandarin Chinese to dedicated Dominican missionaries like Juan Cobo, and still others crafted devotional art, built churches, and even prepared the ninety-seven illustrated pages of the ambitious "Boxer Codex" manuscript (figure 1.2).[52] Undoubtedly, the most economically successful and socially influential Chinese Christian of the early cohort was a man named Eng Kang, who was baptized as Juan Bautista de Vera.

Morga wrote that Kang was a "Christian Sangley known in the land . . . rich and well favored by the Spaniards, feared and respected by the Sangleyes . . . and he had many godchildren, and dependents, and he was very Hispanicized and spirited."[53] Kang owned twelve *trapiches* (sugar mills), one *ingenio* (sugar refinery), and half of the salt flats of Nabotas, to the north of Manila. Collectively, he and the other Chinese Christian landowners managed sugar and agricultural operations with over 100 enslaved laborers and thousands of Chinese field hands. Kang also participated directly in transpacific trade with Mexico. Although it is unlikely that he crossed the Pacific, the name Juan Baptista de Vera appears in the log of people who entered Acapulco in 1592. In that year, Asian sailors and nine passengers registered an unusually large quantity of merchandise at the Mexican port.[54] De Vera was likely a dependent or godson of Kang who served as his intermediary in transpacific trading. By 1594, Kang was employing a

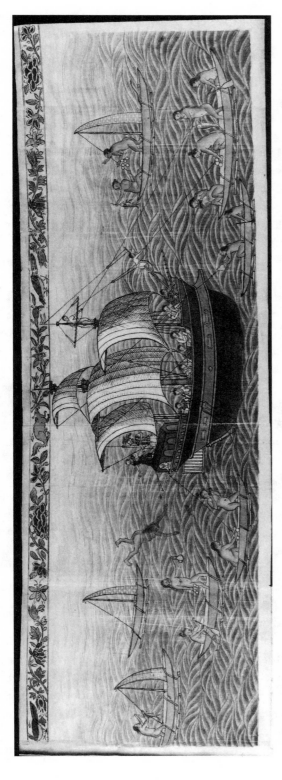

1.2 Manila Galleon Trading with Chamorros

This opening illustration of the Boxer Codex from around 1590 depicts a galleon in the Mariana Islands trading with Chamorros. This ship is likely the *Santiago*, which carried Gómez Pérez Dasmariñas and Luis Pérez Dasmariñas to Manila to take up their posts. One or more talented Chinese artists in Manila drew this and other elaborate scenes featured in the Boxer Codex.

"Sino-Spanish Codex (a.k.a. Boxer Codex)," circa 1590. Reproduction courtesy of the Lilly Library.

Spaniard, Luis Hernández, as his middleman in Acapulco. During one trading season, Kang sent twenty-six boxes of clothes to Spain, collectively worth 25,000 pesos—a significant portion of the total value of goods loaded on the galleon. He subsequently earned a cask of riches so heavy that not even four men could lift it.[55]

Still, the optimism that Salazar communicated and that people like Kang inspired proved to be more exceptional than typical in Manila. As early as the 1580s, Spaniards began stereotyping "Sangelyes" as "materialistic, self-interested, and unreliable due to their inherent lack of morality."[56] One of the first ordinances targeting "Sangley" cultural customs expressly invoked the dangers of their influence on the spiritually vulnerable Indigenous population. In 1592, Cristobal de Salvatierra, an ecclesiastical judge, recommended that Chinese Lunar New Year plays be banned because "superstitions and idolatries are mixed . . . all of which is of great scandal to the New Christians."[57] Any "Sangley" violating the order would be fined twenty pesos (likely the equivalent of several months' wages), forfeit their costumes, receive two hundred lashes, perform forced labor for a year, and be exiled forever. In 1594, King Felipe II issued a royal proclamation reinforcing the intention of the new rule: he ordered that unconverted "Sangleyes" be kept physically separate from the New Christians (figure 1.3). In the same year, an inquisitor of the Holy Office in Mexico City received six letters from the Philippines, some of which strongly condemned the public practice of Chinese rites, ceremonies, and idolatries.[58]

The crescendo of Spanish fear increased when two ragged Spaniards arrived in Manila in 1593 with the shocking news that the governor, Gómez Pérez Dasmariñas, had been murdered on his flagship during a mutiny of "Sangley" rowers. Against the wishes of his advisers, the governor had impressed 250 Chinese men for an expedition to retake the Spice Islands and organized the men into five companies under Chinese Christian captains.[59] After a week at sea, the governor's flagship encountered strong currents and contrary winds that the impressed rowers were unable to overcome. The Spanish crew harassed and beat them, despite the governor's previous promise of good treatment. When verbal and physical abuse failed, the governor told the Chinese that if they did not row harder, he would chain them and cut their hair. Haircutting had been a highly controversial requirement of Chinese conversion to Catholicism that symbolized the passage from orientalistic femininity to Hispanicized masculinity. As Christina Lee notes, hair was fundamentally important in Confucian discourse extending

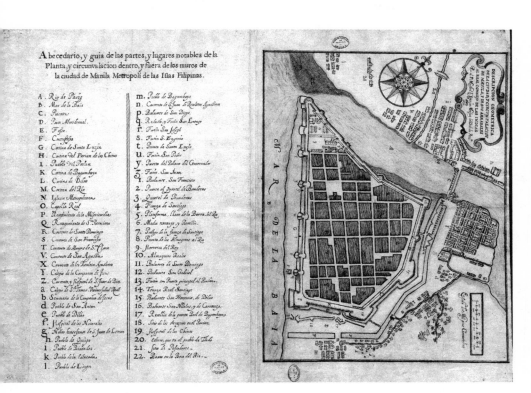

A becedario, y guia de las partes, y lugares notables de la
Planta, y circunvalacion dentro, y fuera de los muros de
la ciudad de Manila Metropoli de las Islas Filipinas.

1.3 Geometric Description of Manila

Manila's spatial organization exemplifies the Spanish obsession with urban segregation to limit moral corruption. The walled city is the Spanish quarter (Intramuros), which is isolated and protected. Just east of Intramuros ("I") is the Chinese Parian. South of the Parian ("e") is the Japanese quarter of Dilao. The Hospital de los Chinos (Chinese Hospital) is separated by the Pasig River from the Parian, and the Hospital de los Naturales (Hospital of the Natives) is west of Dilao.

"Descripción geométrica de la ciudad y circunvalación de Manila y de sus arrabales al Consejo de las Indias," 1671, AGI, MP-Filipinas, 10. Reproduction courtesy of the Archivo General de Indias.

back to the Han period's *Xiaojing* (孝經, *Classic of Filial Piety*) and *Liji* (禮記, *Book of Rites*).[60] Hair conveyed notions of personhood, civility, and honoring the bodily inheritance one received from parents and more remote ancestors. Its removal symbolized severing "familial and social ties" with the motherland.[61]

Rather than face this disgrace, the Chinese rowers decided, as one, to seize the ship the next night. The *Ming Shilu* (明實錄, Ming dynasty annals) commemorate this moment by including a speech. According to the annals, Pan Hewu, the leader of the mutineers, said: "Let us revolt and die in that way. Should we submit to being flogged to death or suffer any other such ignominious death? Should we not rather die in battle? Let us stab this chieftain to death and save our lives. If we are victorious, let us hoist the sails and return to our country. If we should succumb and be fettered, it will be time enough to die."[62]

The two Spanish survivors, Francisco Montilla and Juan de Cuellar, recounted how the "Sangleyes"—both the unconverted and their Christian captains—had armed themselves with *katanas* (Japanese swords) during the night. They dressed in white shirts and carried candles to distinguish themselves from their enemies during the fighting. Then, each rower pretended to sleep next to a Spaniard, waiting for the whistle that signaled the ambush. The Spanish and Philippine crew members had stayed up late gambling and, due to the heat, slept naked in the corridors and on the rowers' seats. When the whistle pierced the night, the Chinese mutineers slit the Spaniards' throats. Belowdecks, the commotion woke Dasmariñas. The Chinese called for him to stop the fighting, but they were waiting for him to lift the hatch to his cabin. As Dasmariñas pulled himself up, a katana split his head, and pikes impaled his body "with more than barbarian ferocity," according to one chronicler.[63]

After seizing control of the ship, the mutineers steered it north to make the crossing to China. In the imaginative narration of Bartolomé Leonardo de Argensola, the mutineers began summoning spirits to guide them through a period of contrary and calm winds.[64] The mutineers' inexperience at sea and an ambush in the Ilocos allegedly heightened their reliance on supernatural means to escape the Philippines. These phantasmagoric details appear only in Argensola's retelling and are clearly deployed to demonize the Chinese. The appearance of folk practices presents a firm dichotomy between Catholic dogma and Chinese paganism, or between holy faith and abominable ritual.

At wit's end, one mutineer who was possessed by a spirit purportedly tied a Philippine captive to the foremast. For the sake of conjuring favorable wind, the mutineer then pulled out a dagger and opened the victim's chest. As the bound man struggled, the mutineer reached his hand into the cavity, removed a handful of organs, put it in his mouth, and threw the rest down. This sacrifice filled the Spanish witnesses with "horror and hate," and for Argensola's audience it surely recalled the tales of Mexica sacrifice and cannibalistic rituals that had served to legitimize the Cortés invasion of Tenoch-titlan.[65] Having completed the grisly ceremony, the Chinese crew, at the behest of the possessed man, abandoned the rest of their prisoners in a skiff and continued on toward China, only to be blown off course again.[66]

The death of Dasmariñas at the hands of a mutinous Chinese crew and the subsequent horrors of the journey marked a turning point in Sino-Spanish relations in the Philippines. Rather than merely suspecting that the Chinese community contained rebellious and corrupting elements, Spaniards began to assume that such characteristics were inherent. Das-mariñas's death intensified exclusionary discourse against the Chinese and culminated in several high-level petitions for wholesale expulsion. These petitions typically argued that despite the integral role of the Chinese and their Parian to the colonial economy, they were ultimately too disruptive to the status quo to remain. The coexistence of Spanish, Indigenous, and Chinese people became intolerable to many administrators, and relations only became increasingly strained as the "Sangley" population swelled.

The son of the slain governor, Luis Pérez Dasmariñas, soon assumed the governorship, and in 1595 he unsuccessfully attempted to impose se-vere restrictions on the "Sangleyes." For example, the restrictions stated that the Parian could neither be extended to within 100 paces of the city wall nor contain more than 100 shops for artisans. All "Sangley" denizens would also need special permission to remain in the city, on pain of de-portation.[67] In the wake of his father's death, the younger Dasmariñas perceived all "Sangleyes" of the Parian as military threats to the colony.

After his tenure as governor, Dasmariñas penned the most ambitious pe-tition of his career. In a letter to King Felipe II in 1597, he proposed that all unconverted "Sangleyes" be deported from Manila immediately.[68] Defini-tive expulsion relied on the notion of inherent racial characteristics that distinguished "Sangleyes" from Spaniards and Philippine neophytes. As Dasmariñas put it, "experience" had hardened Spanish perceptions of Chinese people and customs. He described all "Sangleyes" as "extremely greedy and thieving and traitorous *in their being.*"[69] They corrupted Philip-pine Natives, turning them away from Catholicism through "an abomi-nable and nefarious sin" (meaning sodomy); funneled wealth away from Spaniards; successfully competed against Christians for jobs; and could murder Spaniards in their homes if they wanted.[70] For Dasmariñas, the very nature of "Sangleyes" was incompatible with Hispanic society.

As evidence, Dasmariñas listed a slew of ship mutinies and accusations of cultural malignity. Though he did not directly reference the death of his father, he described the 1593 mutiny as being "so costly, woeful, and harmful and that it impeded so much good and service both of God and of His Majesty."[71] He also mentioned other Chinese mutinies: on a ship en route to Cagayan, on a Portuguese ship headed to Melaka, and on a vessel sailing to Mindanao. The fact that the Chinese continued to rebel—despite supposedly receiving good treatment—was indisputable evidence that they could not be persuaded to abandon their inherent vices. Dasmariñas summed up "Sangleyes" as "a people so ruinous, insolent, depraved, and shameless."[72]

He ended this extraordinary letter with an eight-point plan that culminated in expulsion and highly restricted contact thereafter. The first step required the governor to list all the trades that non-Christian Chinese worked in that could be done by Christian replacements. Chinese who could not be replaced and were neither hagglers nor gamblers could stay, at least until a converted Christian could replace them. However, "all the rest of the infidel Sangleyes of these islands are to be gathered up, embarked on ships, and sent to their lands with much care, rigor, and punctuality."[73] Dasmariñas also recommended that only necessary sailors and merchants should be allowed to disembark and that they would all have to leave again in the same year to prevent unwanted immigration. Licenses to travel into the countryside beyond two *leguas* (leagues) from Manila would be denied.[74] No non-Christian "Sangley" would be able to seek refuge in a convent or Intramuros, nor would they be given licenses to make rice wine. Citizens caught helping the "Sangleyes" break any of these rules would be punished severely.[75]

Dasmariñas was not the only Spaniard to respond radically to the 1593 mutiny. Daily discrimination against "Sangleyes" became the norm by the late 1590s. Guided by fear, Spanish administrators responded to the "Sangley" presence with economic abuse, spatial containment, religious restrictions, and political disenfranchisement. In 1596, hundreds of "Sangley" merchants and ship captains took the unprecedented step of lodging a formal, written complaint in Chinese. Led by the nine most powerful captains and eighteen merchants, they submitted their letter to the Dominican bishop of Nueva Segovia, Miguel de Benavides. His colleague, Diego Aduarte, prepared a translation of the letter (figure 1.4).

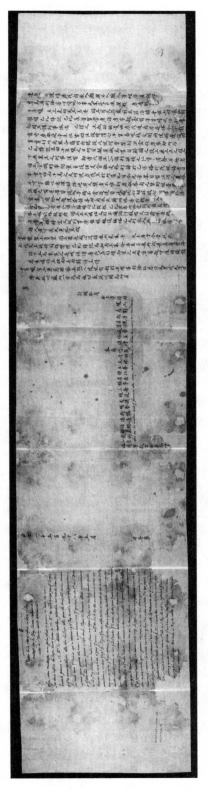

1.4 A Chinese Petition by Merchants and Captains

The Chinese petition is in beautiful calligraphy from a well-trained hand. Written right to left, the signatures appear in the center. Diego Aduarte's Spanish translation is on the left side. This document is the earliest extant Chinese-language petition in the Philippines.

"Carta del obispo de Nueva Segovia Miguel de Benavides sobre quejas de los chinos," 1598, AGI, Filipinas, 76, N.41. Reproduction courtesy of the Archivo General de Indias.

Although Aduarte's translation is largely faithful, the Chinese text offers a more detailed report of daily abuses.[76] The letter attested to rampant mistreatment in the Parian. The merchants and captains reported that
Spanish administrators and functionaries "are all greedy and corrupt," de-
manding bribes, stealing Chinese wares, and having the protection of
judges. "Sangley" travel permits to trade elsewhere in the islands had
been categorically denied and disregarded as well. The merchants and
captains ended the letter as follows: "What a miserable life, and we
sign in despair! . . . With tears in our eyes, we are grateful to submit this
petition."[77]

The convivencia that kept the colony afloat and enabled the riches of
Asia to flow to the Americas—thus maintaining the very legitimacy of the
colony—was balanced on a razor's edge. Framed as the central threat to
moral order, the "Sangleyes" were transformed into a monolith of impu-
rity and subversion. The hardening of racialized stereotypes and their indiscriminate projection predisposed the populace to perform mass violence
against their neighbors. Murdering "Sangleyes" could now be construed
as an act of protection not only of Spanish Intramuros, but also of the easily
corrupted Philippine New Christians. The discriminatory ideology of
the past decade directly enabled the mass violence that erased the Parian
in 1603.

Saving Manila: The 1603 Massacre

On May 23, 1603, three Chinese officials from the mainland arrived in Manila with a formidable entourage, triggering "a period of increased racial
and ethnic tension in a city that was already marked by considerable un-
ease."[78] Led by an ambitious eunuch named Gao Cai (高寀), the officials
inquired about rumors of a mountain of gold in what they called Keit (the
port of Cavite), which they had heard from a carpenter named Zhang Yi.[79]
During their stay, they assumed jurisdictional authority over the "Sangleyes" of the Parian and imposed punishment for various offenses. One
Chinese Christian translator named Gabriel Yaocon was accosted and
beaten in the Parian for working with the Spaniards and forced to kowtow
before the entourage. The brother-in-law of a Chinese Christian bailiff
named Aychuan was tortured with needles in his knuckles. According
to one Spanish witness of these and other punishments, "all are afraid to
see that a barbarian made justice in the land of our lord."[80] Fundamen-

tally, these acts represented the unbalancing of the status quo and a sway toward a colony governed by Chinese legal customs rather than Spanish institutions.

After discovering that no gold mountain existed in Cavite, the officials asked Zhang Yi why he had spread these rumors. Benavides, then arch-bishop of Manila, translated the carpenter's chilling response for Gov-ernor Pedro de Acuña: "If you want that this be gold, it will be, but if you do not want it to be, it will not. What I say is cut the heads of the indios of this land, and you will find the neck filled with hoop skirts and necklaces of gold. This is the gold I speak of."[81] Although the officials departed shortly thereafter at the governor's insistence, Zhang Yi's answer spooked Spanish authorities, who feared an imminent invasion by the Chinese.[82] If the mainland Chinese sought to seize Manila, the Spaniards reasoned, then surely the 30,000 "Sangleyes" of the Parian would rise as a fifth column to join them.

In the uncertain aftermath, Benavides rescinded his former support of the "Sangleyes." He delivered several inflammatory public sermons that warned of an impending uprising and penned a thorough letter to King Felipe III, urging him to approve the immediate expulsion of the "Sangl-eyes."[83] He entreated the king to recall his ancestors, Fernando and Isabel, who solved problems of moral degradation through forceful deportation: "In one blow they threw out all the Moors and Jews of Spain, and they took that for their coat of arms. Do not think, your majesty, that these people [Sangleyes] are only in Manila or next to Manila but through all the land . . . and spreading this devilry [sodomy] and other vices through it all."[84] With Benavides's encouragement, Acuña began hurried preparations to safeguard the city.

The governor stockpiled rice from Pampanga; demolished houses in the Parian next to the walls; instructed "Sangley" laborers to dig a moat around Intramuros; ordered Spanish merchants to purchase all available metal and weapons from "Sangley" blacksmiths; mandated that Parian officials com-pile registries of individuals with notations about their weapon owner-ship and trustworthiness; and began secretly arming units of Japanese, Tagalog, and Kapampangan warriors.[85] The Franciscan Juan de Garro-villas remembered the tension of the summer of 1603 as if "we were all with knives at our throats."[86]

Aduarte wrote that several impetuous Spanish officials had already drafted plans to exterminate the "Sangleyes" to avoid fighting against both external and internal enemies at the same time. He noted that "after this, the people of less capacity looked at [the Sangleyes] already like enemies, and they treated them very badly, whereupon they went about restless and afraid."[87] After Acuña began mobilizing Japanese and Philippine warriors, they too began harassing the "Sangleyes" and calling them dogs and traitors.[88]

When a cohort of two thousand disgruntled "Sangley" laborers finally raised arms on October 3, none other than Eng Kang raced to warn Acuña and pressed him to find a bloodless resolution to the crisis.[89] Rather than receiving the governor's gratitude, Kang was imprisoned and conveniently accused of inciting the revolt. The most powerful man in Manila, the consistently loyal Kang, had become the victim of a sweeping racial discourse that painted all "Sangleyes" as enemies. Kang had been a man who was "rich and well favored by the Spaniards," but now he had become a subversive agent who "feigned loyalty" and acted "as a faithful thief."[90]

Acuña had Kang summarily executed on October 11. Kang swore to the end that he was innocent of treason. He said that "for the rut he was in, he did not owe his death and that he had always been a loyal vassal of his majesty and that God knew what he had in his chest and carried in his heart."[91] After the hanging, the Spanish executioners quartered his body, displayed his head in a cage, and destroyed his home.

During the rebels' initial attacks, Luis Pérez Dasmariñas defended the Tondo church with a contingent of the colony's most experienced soldiers. Emboldened by an early victory but against Acuña's directives, Dasmariñas ordered the first Spanish pursuit of the rebel forces. When his captains hesitated to disobey Acuña by marching their tired troops into bad terrain, Dasmariñas allegedly retorted, "What chicken has sung to your ear?" and demanded "that they should keep going, for twenty-five soldiers are enough for all of China."[92] With this Cortés-like pretension, he and his company of 130 crack pikemen and harquebusiers trekked north after the retreating "Sangleyes" into marshland with high grasses on a path so narrow that no more than two men could walk side by side. They marched directly into an ambush. The "Sangleyes" "came onto [Dasmariñas] so intently that they crushed him and broke his legs. And on his knees, he fought a long time, until they beat him senseless, without a strong helmet to defend him."[93]

After this triumph, the "Sangleyes" advanced on the walls with their siege towers and the decapitated heads of the defeated Spaniards (figure 1.5). Only Figueroa with his cannon and a contingent of five hundred Japanese

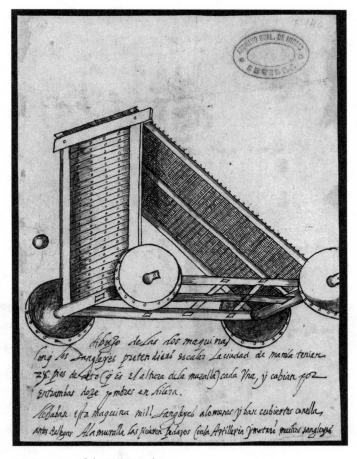

1.5 Drawing of the Two Machines

Modeled after the loquat cart (杷车) of the eleventh-century *Complete Essentials for the Military Classics,* soldiers in two of these towers attacked Intramuros during the 1603 uprising. The cannonball to the left presumably depicts the shot that destroyed the towers. The caption reads, "Drawing of the two machines. Those with which the Sangleyes intended to scale the city [walls] of Manila were 28 feet high (which is the height of the wall) each, and they fit 12 men in a row between them. At least a thousand Sangleyes took this machine and protected themselves with it until arriving. The artillery tore them to pieces and killed many Sangleyes." *Wujing qishu zhijie* (武經七書直解), in *Zhongguo bingshu jicheng* (中国兵书集成), vol. 10 (Beijing: Jiefangjun Chubanshe [解放军 出版社], 1988).

"Dibujo de las dos máquinas con que los sangleyes pretendieron escalar la ciudad de Manila," 1606, AGI, MP-Ingenios, 237. Reproduction courtesy of the Archivo General de Indias.

soldiers under Spanish command succeeded in repulsing the attackers. The
counterattack ended in the complete destruction of the Parian and the
murder of thousands of noncombatants. The deaths were on a scale comparable only to the most horrific episodes of colonial violence, like the hei-
nous siege of Tenochtitlan in 1521. Spaniards deployed mass slaughter as
an essential technique to achieve their ambitions of eliminating those
deemed unassimilable challengers of colonial intent and rule.

Facing imminent destruction, many wealthy "Sangley" merchants chose
death on their own terms by hanging themselves. Even Argensola, who
elsewhere described "Sangleyes" as "monsters," reflected that "although
it would be less meticulous to kill them all, or to try, it did not seem just
to punish people whose offense was uncertain."[94] Both he and Juan de
Bustamante placed the blame for the slaughter on the Japanese, Tagalog,
and Kapampangan "butchers" and thus absolved Spaniards of the responsibility for the indiscriminate killings (figure 1.6).[95]

1.6 The Massacres of 1603

Displayed in the Bahay Tsinoy Museum in Intramuros, Manila, this contemporary rendition in miniatures depicts the brutal, chaotic killing in the Parian in 1603 that claimed many
civilian lives.

Photo courtesy of the author.

Acuña's reinforcements (four thousand Tagalog and Kapampangan auxiliaries) chased the surviving "Sangleyes" into the countryside.[96] The steadfast Dimarocots displayed exceptional initiative on numerous occasions during the pursuit. For example, during the attack on the "Sangley" fort at San Francisco del Monte, don Guillermo "always [went] to the most dangerous and risky positions."[97] He later advanced at the head of seventy men with harquebus, lance, and pavis (large shield) toward the "Sangley" fort at San Pablo. He cut off the fort's food supply and killed any who left in search of provisions.[98] Harassing the "Sangleyes" toward Batangas, don Guillermo and Martín de Herrera, a Spanish captain, cornered the "Sangley" rearguard by the Tiao River, and in desperation, many "Sangleyes" jumped into the water and drowned.[99] The chase continued, and the Dimarocots gave no quarter. Don Guillermo and Herrera surrounded one of the last groups of "Sangley" troops on a hill near Batangas. Don Guillermo posted his twenty-seven Kapampangan harquebusiers by a river to keep the "Sangleyes" from collecting drinking water. While looking for an attack route, he stumbled upon a patrol of forty rebels. Although the skirmishers shattered don Guillermo's shield with rocks and fireworks, the Kapampangan harquebusiers routed their foes.[100] This encounter formed part of a larger, six-hour battle at Batangas against the last "Sangley" column, which was trapped between Philippine warriors and the sea. Don Ventura fought at the head of two hundred Tagalogs and reported no survivors.

Once the bloody campaign had subsided and the Tagalog and Kapampangan reinforcements had returned victorious from Batangas, Spanish treasury officials auctioned off what remained of Kang's impressive estate. The extensive inventory included a horse, a silver sword, and five enslaved servants who had survived the uprising.[101] Some of these goods were later shipped across the Pacific to New Spain.[102] The other three hundred Chinese Christians who returned to the city with a pardon also suffered major losses. Property worth more than seventy thousand pesos had been looted, and only a tiny portion was restored to survivors, despite sweeping promises of restitution.[103] Starting on November 7, 1603, Spanish administrators called on survivors to provide testimony about the holdings of dead "Sangleyes" so that they could repossess their lands at very cheap prices. After a protracted series of litigations, all the salt flats of Nabotas and most sugar plantations formerly owned by prominent Chinese Christians and their descendants fell into Spanish hands. Assets acquired over decades were wiped out over the course of several years. Much of this property would later be sold or donated to the University of Santo Tomas after its founding in 1611.[104]

Adaptive Slave-Trading Practices

Both the execution of Kang and the appropriation of land and wealth after the uprising removed the emerging class of affluent, ambitious, and landed Chinese Christians from direct participation in transpacific trade and travel. Over the next decade, Chinese Christians had few opportunities to reclaim their once privileged status as the colony's most prosperous and mobile demographic group. One Chinese Christian of this cohort, Miguel Lonte, died in prison at eighty years of age: he had been convicted of committing adultery and fraud and defaulting on his debts.[105] Chinese Christians' reacquisition of their assets, Spanish trust, enslaved labor, and land would come slowly. After 1603, the "Sangleyes"—once Manila's largest and most prosperous non-Spanish demographic group—were generally excluded from transpacific migration. The magnitude of this immobility becomes apparent only after consulting sources on the other side of the Pacific, which rarely document the presence of ethnic Chinese in the Americas. This de facto exclusion supports Kerilyn Schewel's argument that "mobility and immobility are often two sides of the same coin, mutually constitutive and reinforcing."[106] Large numbers of Chinese would not arrive in the Americas until the period of indenture during the nineteenth century. The special allowances that had once permitted the passage of two Chinese monks to study Catholicism in Mexico in 1585 became forgotten vestiges of an earlier era.[107] The few documented cases of "Sangleyes" in Mexico after 1603 indicate that they had crossed the Pacific through humbler means, including outright enslavement.

With nearly the entire population of thirty thousand "Sangleyes" either massacred or otherwise driven from the city in 1603, the colonial economy ground to a halt. There were suddenly very few farmers, artisans, dock-hands, or poor wage laborers of any variety. All goods, even basic foodstuffs, became scarce. The royal cashbox of Manila ran a deficit of seventy-six thousand pesos in the immediate aftermath of the war.[108] Spaniards, including those who had just participated in the massacres, waited anxiously for trade ships from China to appear, since their absence would have been, in Acuña's words, an "irreparable damage."[109] Although the ships did slowly return during the next several years, the demand for trade, financial subsidies from Mexico (called the *situado*), and additional labor became increasingly urgent.[110]

Despite the relatively low cost of purchasing enslaved people in Manila, "Sangleyes" had become the cheapest and highest-skilled workforce in and around the city by the beginning of the seventeenth century. For example, a "Sangley" field hand could be compelled to work for the paltry sum of one peso per month.[111] The availability and affordability of "Sangley" labor was especially important due to the precipitous demographic decline of Philippine Natives on Luzon during the same period. Linda Newson estimates that disease, war, and brutal colonial labor regimes had reduced the population just north of Manila by 16 percent from 1570 to 1598, despite high rates of internal migration to the area. The Indigenous tribute-paying subjects of Manila declined at least another 25 percent by 1630.[112] Demographic losses on Luzon and in the Visayas reached 36 percent during the same period.[113]

Spaniards responded to the eradication of poor "Sangley" wage laborers in 1603 by strengthening regimes of bondage in Manila. Juan de Artiz's 1605 report on the survivors of the 1603 uprising reflects this new reality.[114] The 597 "Sangley" rebels who had been captured during the fighting had been sentenced to labor: 262 rowed in Spanish galleys, 10 served on a ship sailing from Cavite to Mexico, and 26 worked in smithies. Benavides described them as enslaved.[115] The remaining 299 could not be accounted for, since they had run away, died in captivity, or been granted their freedom.[116] Although "Sangleyes" from overseas soon returned to Manila (457 residence permits were issued in 1604), the captives of 1603, together with newly imported enslaved men and women from Macau and Guangzhou, totaled a larger population of enslaved "Sangleyes" than had ever before resided in the city.[117]

Even the *Santiaguillo*, the vessel tasked in 1604 with reporting news of the uprising in Macau, returned with a sweltering hold containing fifty-four enslaved individuals.[118] It is particularly telling that this ship, sent to repair relations with the mainland, had the double purpose of returning with dozens of captives—so desperate were Manila's denizens for new labor. The enslaved became part of a rapidly increasing captive population already swelling with the enslaved of the Imjin War (1592–1598) and other regional conflicts. Spaniards welcomed these captives from abroad, many of whom were girls, for their perceived utility in domestic settings and for the sex trafficking that characterized much of the slave trade in Japanese, Korean, and Chinese girls and women in East Asia.[119] Spaniards frequently abused enslaved children from the Philippines as well.[120]

After 1603, the Manila slave market would become as frenzied and diverse as that of any in the major entrepôts of the Indian Ocean World. This surge in demand coincided with the Iberian Union (1580–1640) and the Portuguese *asiento* (monopoly) on slave trading to the Hispanic World in 1595, which facilitated unprecedented access to Portuguese channels of enslavement throughout Asia and Africa.

As captives changed hands, the fluid local nuances of peonage and bondage common to coastal Asian polities were "erased by European slave traders."[121] Ohmura Yuko, a horrified Japanese observer, wrote of the enslaved: "Their hands and feet are chained, and they are driven into the bottom of the ships. This is far beyond the punishment in Hell."[122] Formal prohibitions on European slave trading and sex trafficking in Japan began with Toyotomi Hideyoshi's 1587 restriction on "'trade in persons' (*hito no baibai*)."[123] This measure, along with a subsequent ban by the Tokugawa shogunate in 1616, ultimately failed to outlaw enslavement until all Portuguese were expelled from Japan in 1639.[124]

During the Iberian Union, Portuguese enslavers frequently sailed to Manila to exchange captives for silver. They often used the silver to buy Indian textiles, which were traded in turn for the highly coveted cloves and nutmegs of the Spice Islands.[125] Departing from bases in Macau, Melaka, and Makassar, these trade missions both directly and indirectly linked slave trading in Manila to more distant sites of enslavement like Nagasaki, the Bay of Bengal, the Coromandel Coast, Malabar, Goa, Gujarat, and the Zambezi Delta, among numerous other locales. Through Portuguese shipping lanes, the famed Catarina de San Juan (born Mirra) of the "Mughal Kingdom" arrived in Manila.[126] She had been enslaved as a child of eight or nine while playing on a beach with her little brother and other children. In Kochi she received baptism, and her later confessor, Alonso Ramos, considered her survival there amid rampant sexual abuse (and "all of the furies of hell") to be the work of divine "providence."[127]

Summaries of cases heard in the Inquisition's Goa Tribunal corroborate this wide range of displacements in their notations of Bengali, Malabari, Sinhalese, Gujarati, Javanese, Chinese, Japanese, Burmese, and East and Southern African slaves.[128] During the early seventeenth century, each Portuguese household in Goa may have had up to ten slaves, putting the colony's enslaved population as high as eight thousand.[129] Despite the diversity of ethnic groups enslaved in Goa, the shared experience of displacement created new connections among people in bondage. For example, two Japanese captives named Tomás and Marta had been born in Goa, and they both ended up in Lima during the early seventeenth century, where they married each other after enduring a geographic dislocation of over thirty thousand kilometers.[130]

The expansion and recession of kingdoms in South Asia often drove slave production in the Indian Ocean World. In particular, the Mughal Emperor Akbar I's conquests in 1556–1605 and the collapsing Vijayanagara empire of Southern India fueled cycles of famine and debt that the Portuguese consistently exploited to acquire slaves (primarily in Gujarat, Malabar, and Goa).[131] One merchant later baptized as Antón had done nothing more than fall asleep on a Portuguese vessel docked at Kochi. When he awoke, he had become a slave on a ship at sea, and he was sold in Melaka.[132] Portuguese mercenaries also raided the region around the Bay of Bengal for captives, assisted by the Taungoo Kingdom (in modern-day Burma) and the Arakanese further west.[133] A man named Mateo de la Torre had been ensnared somewhere on the Bengali coast at the age of seven. He had been watching a bag of rice on a beach for his family when Portuguese enslavers captured him.[134]

Wars in Southeast Asia steadily added more enslaved people to Portuguese ships as well. Siamese-Cambodian conflicts netted captives for the Iberian market, particularly during the mid- and late 1590s.[135] Portuguese expansion into Ambon, Melaka, and the Spice Islands also created new slave-trading ventures. By the early seventeenth century, Portuguese slave trading had shifted from the northern coasts of Java and Sumatra to these regions.[136] António Manuel Hespanha estimates the ratio of enslaver to enslaved in Melaka during the 1620s and 1630s as being between 1:25 and 1:10.[137] Away from the Malaysian coast, eighty Portuguese enslavers owned as many as three thousand slaves in 1609.[138]

Traders added a couple hundred East Africans from the Zambezi Delta and the Horn of Africa to the Indian Ocean slave market every year. Labeled "negros" or *cafres* (from the Arabic *kāfir*, meaning nonbeliever), enslaved East Africans became highly coveted in Iberian ports from Goa to Acapulco.[139] Not only was owning them a symbol of wealth and prestige, but they had also developed considerable reputations for being skilled mariners and soldiers in the Indian Ocean World.[140] From these exchanges, large-scale enslaved African populations were formed in the Spanish Pacific, perhaps most prominently in Manila toward the middle of the seventeenth century.[141]

All of these captives entered Spanish enslavement through justifications of capture during a *guerra justa* (just war), affiliation with a Muslim state or Islam, and *rescate* (ransom) of captives. This final category (frequently employed in the Mediterranean World, the Canary Islands, and the Caribbean) proved decisive: in this case, any person enslaved in lands claimed by the Portuguese throughout Asia could be accepted as a slave without question in Manila, regardless of the legitimacy of that person's enslavement, if they had been captured in Spanish territory.[142] This practice became a common method of keeping Indigenous peoples in bondage despite the protections of the New Laws of 1542.[143] Although influential writers like Juan de Solórzano Pereira criticized the legitimacy of Asian enslavement at the hands of the Portuguese, his *Política Indiana* (1648) did little to sway enslavers in Manila during this period.[144]

Numerous examples of these diverse networks of enslavement appear in inventories of slave ownership in Manila after the uprising of 1603. For example, Governor Acuña's will in 1606 listed twelve captives: Antonio ("negro," sixteen years old), Tomas (a Korean, no age given), Breynte (a Korean, no age given), Lucia (Javanese, ten years old), Menera (Chinese, eight years old), Luissa (Chinese, six years old), Luissa (Chinese, ten years old), Luissa Mechacha (Chinese, ten years old), Lucia (Cambodian, eleven or twelve years old), Madelena (Chinese, eleven years old), Pedro (Bengalese, twenty-four years old), and Antonio ("negro" of Mozambique, twenty-four years old).[145] Perhaps not coincidentally, the number of enslaved Chinese girls was disproportionately high in the inventory of the governor who oversaw the destruction of the "Sangleyes" in 1603.

Similarly, the Spanish enslaver Joan Baptista de Manila owned fifteen enslaved people in 1611: ten from Java, one "mulata" who had been born in Manila, three from China, and one from Ternate. The thirteen from Java or China had likely been acquired through Portuguese channels.[146] Finally, in 1643 Francisco Díaz de Montoya's estate of enslaved men and women included Francisco (Chinese, thirty years old), Francisco (Malabar, twenty-two), Agustin (Chinese, thirty), Joseph ("mulato," thirty), Francisca (Visayan, "old"), Tomasa Colunbi ("old"), Ysauel (Jolo, thirty), Antona (Bengala, fifty), Ynes ("criolla," forty and "sick"), Lorenza ("casta baeilan," twenty), Andrea Caraga (eight), and Beatriz (Java, forty).[147] Apart from Francisca of the Visayas and Ysauel of Jolo, all of these men and women or their parents had likely been enslaved and sold by the Portuguese.

The zenith of this new slave trade occurred from roughly 1620 to the end of the Iberian Union, during a period of relative economic recovery between the 1603 uprising and another major Chinese revolt in 1639.[148] After the separation of the crowns of Spain and Portugal in 1640, a subsequent ban on interimperial trade in 1644 severely limited (though it did not exclude) Spanish enslavers from Portuguese networks.[149] Growing Dutch naval supremacy and Mughal opposition to Portuguese enslavement further impeded the continuity of these networks.

After arriving in Manila, captives entered enslaved communities in the Philippines that were already swelling with numerous *moro* (Muslim) captives. In 1621, Miguel García Serrano, the archbishop of the Philippines, estimated that 1,970 slaves lived within the city walls, with many more in the surrounding lands.[150] These numbers continued to rise over the next couple of decades due to accelerated Portuguese slave trading in Manila and conflicts internal to the Philippines. For example, Governor Sebastián Hurtado de Corcuera's wars against Mindanao (1637) and Jolo (1638) netted forty-three captives, mostly women and children, for the public market, in addition to the more than a hundred that the soldiers had already claimed for themselves.[151] Corcuera sent several of these girls to New Spain with his niece in 1642.[152]

Despite formal bans, a clandestine slave trade in non-Muslim Filipinos also thrived under the Spanish colonial administration. For example, in the middle of the seventeenth century, six-year-old Domingo de la Cruz was snatched from his parents' home in the jurisdiction of Tutuli near Cebu by a Captain Antonio Rodriguez. Domingo would not know his own origin and, thus, the illegality of his enslavement, until he overheard the details during his sale from Captain Don Pedro de Urbina to Juan Sánchez Bañales in Salagua, Mexico.[153] Children were especially vulnerable to this form of trafficking, and sometimes those as young as four were enslaved. Moreover, enslavers often preferred trading in children because they had to pay only half of the usual import duty for them in Acapulco.[154] Stories like Domingo de la Cruz's contextualize Ben Vinson III's findings that when Asians in Mexico in 1605–1700 were asked for their parents' names, twenty out of twenty-two people said they did not know those names.[155] Catarina de San Juan similarly could not recall her father's name, nor could she remember the name of her homeland "for being so young when she was taken from it."[156]

The expanding slave market in Manila extended to Acapulco via private license and contraband. Crucially, that expansion coincided with rising labor demands in central Mexico, spurred by a diminishing Indigenous population. In 1597, only enslaved people intended for personal service to elites were permitted to cross the Pacific, albeit in limited numbers. The growth of the transpacific slave trade in subsequent years, particularly after the 1603 uprising, produced more lenient oversight. In 1620, the Spanish Crown reluctantly allowed lowly passengers and sailors—many of whom were acting as proxies for merchants in Manila—to transport one enslaved person each, though sailors regularly embarked with more than one captive.[157] This change meant that a galleon could now legally carry as many of the enslaved as it could hold. Though the total volume may appear relatively small next to transatlantic crossings of the same period, Manila galleon holds were crammed with valuable Asian wares, meaning that the enslaved generally filled the decks to capacity.[158]

These slave traders stood to make several times their investments if they had a successful sale in Mexico.[159] The main hindrances to transpacific enslavers were the high import duties charged when they arrived in Acapulco, which reached fifty pesos per enslaved person by 1626.[160] In some cases, this sum exceeded a fifth of the enslaved person's assessed value. Despite these hurdles, galleons regularly registered numerous contingents of enslaved people for sale in Acapulco. For example, the *San Ambrosio* logged forty-five slaves when it reached that port in 1639 (table 1.1). Diego Perez, a scribe on the ship's crew, and Joseph de Vides, a passenger, each registered seven captives.[161]

Table 1.1 List of Enslaved People per Crew Member or Passenger on the *San Ambrosio* in 1639

Crew member or passenger's name in the order of their appearance in Acapulco	Crew member or passenger's position	Number of enslaved people (45 in all) on arrival in Acapulco	Additional details about the enslaved
Diego Perez	Scribe	7	
Juan Camacho	Sailor	1	Antonio Malabar
Juan Domingo	Pilot	1	Juan of Malabar land
Antonio Pinto	Sailor	1	Benito
Francisco Suarez	Artilleryman	1	Antonio "cafre"
Nicolas Mezia	Artilleryman	1	Sold to Antonio Morgaxo
Juan Dominguez	Pilot	3 (Dominguez received 1 from a Lieutenant Francisco de Lescomo in Manila)	
Juan Esteban Picana	Sailor	2 (Picana sponsored the transpacific journey of 1 for Lucas García, sailor)	
Joseph de Vides	Passenger (captain)	7	
Gaspar de Sossa	Sailor	1	
Diego Nunez	Sailor	1	
Manuel Lopez	Sailor	1	
Domingo Gonzalez de la Tereza	Sailor	1	
Francisco de Aguirre	Sailor	1	
Manuel Hernandez de Cavite	Sailor	1	
Simon Cordero	Quartermaster	1	
Grauiel Perezon	Sailor	1	
Pedro Gallardo	Sailor	1	
Francisco Delizalde	Sailor	1	
Juan de Silva	Constable	2	
Miguel Costentino	Caulker	1	
Pedro de Oliua	Sailor	1	
Tomas Delgado	Pilot assistant	2	
Vicente de Oria	Unknown	5 (Oria sponsored the transpacific journey of 1 for Lucas García and 1 for Nicolas de Rriuas, sailor)	

Source: "Caja de Acapulco," 1637, Archivo General de Indias, Contaduría, 905A, fols. 363r–399r.

Notes: This table demonstrates the broad participation in transpacific slave trading that the system of private licenses entailed. Treasury officials assessed each enslaved person at a value of three hundred pesos and charged enslavers fifty pesos in import duty per each enslaved person. Déborah Oropeza has published a similar table for the *San Ambrosio* but arrived at different numbers (*La migración asiática en el virreinato de la Nueva España: Un proceso de globalización [1565–1700]* [Mexico City: El Colegio de México, 2020], 141). This discrepancy emerges from the archival record: Spanish treasury officials in Acapulco tabulated the enslaved cargo of the *San Ambrosio* three times, and each record has slight variations from the others. The table here uses data from all three tabulations.

Even at the end of the Union of the Two Crowns in 1640, the galleons carried significant numbers of enslaved people. The *Nuestra Señora de la Concepción*, which docked in Acapulco in 1640, officially reported carrying sixty-two of them.[162] Even as late as 1645, the *Nuestra Señora de la Encarnación* held thirty-seven enslaved people, and the *San Luis Rey de Francia* reported another twenty-five in 1646.[163]

Inconsistent record keeping in Acapulco, due to bribery and carelessness, meant that official restrictions on transpacific slave trading were regularly exceeded and rarely documented.[164] For example, a thorough inspector named Pedro de Quiroga y Moya found to his surprise that the *San Juan Bautista* and *Nuestra Señora de la Concepción* carried a total of 186 enslaved people when they landed in Acapulco in 1637, a number far beyond the official figures for previous years.[165] A further example of this contraband trafficking appears in an uncommon treasury record for the *Espíritu Santo*, which landed in Acapulco in 1618 with fifty-three unregistered enslaved people. Treasurers charged the enslavers 32 percent of the assessed value of their contraband and then promptly repossessed all unregistered slaves for a meager twenty-three pesos, two *tomines,* and eight *granos* each.[166] These officials would have made a small fortune from the resale of these confiscated slaves.

Although scholars generally agree that transpacific enslavement was never intended to replace the transatlantic slave trade, an unsigned and undated proposal from the seventeenth century suggested just that.[167] If the proposal had been adopted, the Chamorros of the Mariana Islands would have taken the place of enslaved Africans from Guinea and Cape Verde in New Spanish mines.[168] However, no such large-scale enslavement from the Marianas to Mexico occurred, as Sevillian slave traders managed to protect their monopoly on captives shipped across the Atlantic and suppress their transpacific competitors.[169] In fact, the transpacific slave trade contracted severely before the end of the seventeenth century. In 1672, Queen Regent Mariana of Austria (urged on by Fernando de Haro y Monterroso, a fiery attorney in Guadalajara) announced the emancipation of all enslaved Indigenous peoples, including "chinos," in the colonies. As Chapter 6 reveals, the process of establishing those freedoms on the ground was a difficult one at best. Nevertheless, by the end of the century, the transpacific slave trade would be reduced to the trafficking of East African captives and a handful of clandestinely enslaved Asians.

New Opportunities in a Broken City

New and adaptive patterns in slave trading were but one repercussion of the utter destruction of Manila's former social order in 1603. For some people, new opportunities arose in this fragmented landscape of colonial power, fear, and labor demand. On the recommendations of Coronel and several Spanish captains, don Ventura de Mendoza and don Guillermo Dimarocot received promotion to the illustrious rank of *maestre de campo* (chief of staff) for their service during the 1603 insurrection.[170] Almost immediately after the campaign, Governor Acuña began planning to retake Ternate, one of the Spice Islands, from the Dutch and to displace its Muslim ruler. In 1606, Acuña launched the invasion that would keep Ternate under Spanish control until 1663. Having earlier depended on Tagalog and Kapampangan reinforcements to defend Intramuros against the "Sangleyes," he mobilized many of these veterans for war in the Spice Islands, including the Dimarocots.

The uprising and this war represented a turning point. After 1603, Indigenous peoples of Luzon would form the backbone of Spanish military operations throughout Southeast Asia, opening new channels of mobility for daring nobles and common soldiers steeped in long-standing martial traditions. José Eugenio Borao Mateo estimates that as many as 30,000–40,000 Philippine soldiers served with Spanish forces from 1575 to 1640 and that they outnumbered their Spanish counterparts by an average of 5:1 in overseas expeditions.[171] Over the course of a campaign in the Spice Islands or *La Isla Hermosa* (Taiwan), for example, an experienced Kapampangan soldier could expect to make a considerable sum (at least a thousand pesos, minus expenses) and earn a promotion.[172] In fact, so many Kapampangan soldiers served in colonial wars that by 1630, the Augustinian Juan de Medina expressed considerable surprise that Pampanga had any men left at all.[173]

Matthew Furlong has argued that one central motivation for these collaborations was the steadily increasing isolation of Philippine elites from pre-Hispanic modes of wealth accumulation, as we have already seen in the case of enslavement.[174] Spanish control of the China trade had gradually edged out Philippine translators, merchants, and middlemen whose connections to Fujianese traders had predated the Spanish arrival in Luzon. In addition, the colonial-era influx of inexpensive goods from

China flooded Philippine artisan markets and outperformed local products. In contrast, soldiering for the crown promised a reasonable salary,
as well as informal rewards like access to war booty and state-sanctioned
slave raiding.[175]

Indigenous social mobility in Manila, then, became entangled with several distinct forms of collaboration. Soldiering was a far better choice than
the brutal and thankless polo, which often consisted of port-related labor.
Such assignments frequently included long treks into the mountains to cut
wood for galleon construction and repair. Other conscripted polo laborers
worked as carpenters, blacksmiths, caulkers, porters, ship loaders, and low-
ranking sailors.

Near-constant war during the early seventeenth century, particularly
with the Dutch, placed increasing pressure on the Indigenous communities that supplied laborers to maintain high levels of agricultural production at their own expense while their populations plummeted.[176] Internal
and external pressures forced more and more Philippine Natives into debt-
based relationships with Spanish officials. The Spaniards habitually impressed debtors and members of forced labor pools to work as galley rowers
and impressed mariners to work on the galleons. Though it was extraor-
dinarily high-risk labor, many people preferred impressment because it
often supplied a quicker route to economic independence than working
on a labor gang in the Philippines.[177] Even an experienced carpenter in
Cavite could expect to make only one real in three days, amounting to only
a dozen or so pesos per year.[178] Although this appallingly low sum was regularly supplemented with rations of rice, such an income could hardly
support life on its own.[179]

In comparison, the typical Asian grumete on a transpacific galleon made,
on average, forty-eight pesos per year.[180] This wage was very low but still
several times higher than what their port-based counterparts in Cavite
made. Moreover, even the poorest dockhands in Acapulco made five pesos
per month plus rations.[181] This was only slightly below the standard payment of eighteen granos per day for unskilled labor in Mexico during the
early seventeenth century, a rate that had doubled in the decades following
the Spanish seizure of Manila.[182] Someone with experience and skill could
earn more than double these amounts in Acapulco. Thus, with the promise
of significantly higher wages, there was a clear and obvious economic in-
centive to making the Pacific crossing.[183] Asian sailors enabled the trans-

pacific voyages that defined the early modern Asian connection to the Americas. Retired Philippine soldiers seeking to resettle in the Americas also typically embarked as sailors to pay their passage to Mexico. Only the wealthiest, like don Diego Dimarocot, could board as passengers. After arriving in Acapulco, sailors often abandoned their posts for a new life in that new land.

There were many reasons beyond financial incentives that a free Asian might travel east from Manila. Spanish settlements in Asia were under constant attack during the seventeenth century. Manila's inhabitants continually watched the seas for invasions by Japanese pirates, Chinese corsairs and warlords, British privateers, Dutch fleets, and others, and there was the possibility of another devastating "Sangley" uprising as the Chinese slowly returned.[184] Throughout the seventeenth century, war parties from Maguindanao, Jolo, the Sulu Archipelago, and elsewhere conducted stunningly effective raids in Spanish territory that often netted hundreds of captives and left hundreds more dead.[185] In fact, the raids were so successful that over time they resulted in considerable demographic declines and lower population densities in the affected areas.[186]

If this were not enough, Portuguese refugees fleeing the Dutch arrived in Manila every year from outposts in South and Southeast Asia with tales of the latest conquest by the Vereenigde Oost Indische Compagnie (Dutch East India Company). Spanish Manila's survival hung by a thread.[187] In comparison, Mexico was a land of abundance, the center of viceregal power, and relatively isolated from external geopolitical threats, apart from the occasional piratical raid. Thus, many Asians who traveled willingly to Mexico were refugees.

Spanish officials in the Philippines habitually sought reassignment as well. Beginning with Francisco Tello (1603), five governors in a row had died prematurely (including Acuña from poison in 1606). In 1638, Governor Guillermo de Bañuelos y Carrillo wrote that without "great support, I could not stay in [Manila]."[188] When the bitter Governor Sabiniano Manrique de Lara left the Philippines in 1669, he proclaimed, "I shit on all of Manila."[189] With a few exceptions, administrators and missionaries typically departed after a few years of service. Morga petitioned for a post in the Americas no fewer than four times before he was reassigned to Mexico City's city council in 1604.[190] He likely crossed the Pacific with the six enslaved Asians that later served his household in the viceregal capital.[191]

That Morga returned to Mexico in the company of Asian servants and slaves was not uncommon. The writer don Fernando Valenzuela arrived at Mexico City in 1690 after fifteen years in the Philippines. Valenzuela died during a horse-riding accident in January 1692, and a report on his will gives a strong indication of his transpacific entourage from two years prior. He left 39 reales to "a chino who served him and of whom it seems he had great confidence; to another chino [he left] 19 reales . . . for the affection he had for him and for having raised him. To the other chinos (since his family consisted of only them, and they were many), he left [his inheritance to them] to the recommendation of his executor. He gave liberty to his slaves, which it seems there were eight."[192] Even a single Spaniard could transport a large household of Asians across the Pacific.

Spaniards also departed the Philippines with their enslaved retinues simply because trade opportunities in Manila had begun to decline toward the middle of the seventeenth century. With Japan's formal expulsion of the Portuguese in 1639, a second major "Sangley" uprising in Manila that same year, the fall of the Ming to northern invaders in 1644, and shortages of American silver in the Philippines, the opportunities that had originally attracted Spanish investors and millenarian missionaries to Manila had become severely limited.[193] Spanish corruption, indecision, and fear provoked more uprisings, wars, and massacres throughout the seventeenth century. With the China trade threatened, the steady recession of Iberian control in the Spice Islands, the Spanish defeat in Taiwan, the dissolution of key Portuguese strongholds in the Indian Ocean, and the diversion of trading power to Dutch-controlled ports like Batavia and Melaka, Spanish optimism about the Philippines was replaced by the fear that it had become a "Pacific purgatory."[194] During the tumultuous summer of 1603, many of Manila's wealthiest residents fled the city aboard the *San Antonio* with their valuables and captives, only to succumb to the sea.

The violent destruction of the myth of colonial multiethnic stability had shattered the dream of a Catholic Asian utopia. Manila was a city constantly torn between economic and geopolitical prerogatives, and between its own viability and cultural coherence. The reinforced walls of Intramuros and its cannons perched above the gates did little to comfort the timorous Spanish population. The Spanish propensity for flight from the Philippines coincided with the abovementioned loosening of restrictions on transpacific slave trading in New Spain, which facilitated the entry of higher numbers of Asians into Mexico. In the end, Acapulco would receive thousands of Asians, free or enslaved. A few were wealthy, many had arrived in chains, some were war veterans, some had been deported, and some were refugees.

Before arriving in the Americas, however, they would have to endure the Pacific passage. This harrowing journey across the world's largest ocean scarred any voyager brave enough to confront it and lucky enough to survive it. The dangers of the route and the physical, social, and religious conditions that defined life on the galleons foreshadowed the difficulties Asians would later face in the Americas.

2 THE PACIFIC PASSAGE

LIKE THE ATLANTIC, the Pacific was a space of vulnerability, racialization, and transformation. Those who survived "the mother of all oceans" arrived ragged and feverish in Acapulco, some in bondage and some free.[1] The scheduled eastward route spanned over 15,500 kilometers and lasted six months on average (figure 2.1). In the words of William Schurz, "No other regular navigation has been so trying and dangerous as this, for in its two hundred and fifty years the sea claimed dozens of ships and thousands of men and many millions in treasure."[2] However, the perils of the crossing varied significantly among travelers. On the galleons, wealthy passengers had the privilege of using lading space and cabins below deck. Although the cabins were only five square feet and were stifling, having one of them would have been luxurious compared to sleeping on a soggy, flea-infested cloth beneath the stars or stuffed into the fore- or aftercastle.[3] Most Asians crossing the Pacific experienced the worst of these conditions and accounted for the majority of lives lost at sea.

The value of the cargo consistently surpassed that of human life, and this reality magnified the galleons' deadly squalor. Captains heavily invested in the transpacific trade normalized the preferential accommodation of Chinese silks, Japanese furniture, Philippine textiles, and so on over people. Topside, the enslaved, most crew members, and poor passengers endured ferocious storms, the arctic chill, and exposure to the sun. While most colonial records on Asians in the Americas make little or no mention of how or when an individual arrived, all transpacific survivors endured the Odyssean challenges of the Pacific passage. The common suffering of this grueling journey between the ports of Cavite, in the Philippines, and Acapulco,

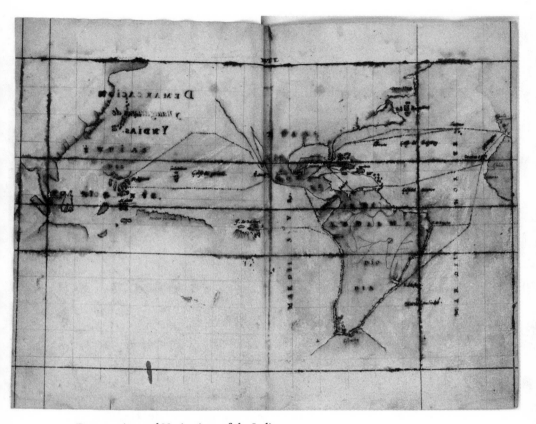

2.1 Demarcation and Navigations of the Indies

This map by the royal cosmographer Juan López de Velasco depicts the galleon routes between the Philippines and New Spain. The voyage west is a horizontal line, and the passage east rises, crosses the Pacific, and finally drops down by California to central Mexico. Velasco compressed the Pacific to enhance the visual connectedness of the Spanish Pacific empire and to extend the meridian of the Treaty of Zaragoza (1529) and thus claim as much territory as possible for Spain instead of Portugal. See Ricardo Padrón, "A Sea of Denial: The Early Modern Spanish Invention of the Pacific Rim," *Hispanic Review* 77, no. 1 (2009): 14–16.

Juan López de Velasco, "Demarcacion y nauegaciones de Yndias," circa 1575. Reproduction courtesy of the John Carter Brown Library.

in Mexico, defined the lived experience of transpacific mobility. Moreover, the conditions of the journey began to create Asian social and communal relations that differed from those in the Spanish Philippines.

The first half of this chapter posits that Asians underwent a sociocultural reorganization amid the horrors of the transpacific route. On board the galleons, maritime hierarchy was structured around laboring status. Although the Asians who boarded these ships had often experienced institutions that divided them based on perceived ethnic identification or geographic provenance, they were now thrust into seafaring roles irrespective of origin. The two salient categories were the enslaved (who were both a source of labor and a transpacific commodity) and the sailors designated primarily as infantilized grumetes. Like ethnicity, religious life on the ships played an important role in reconstituting familiar categories and, consequently, reshaping communities of Asians on board. In the Philippines, Spanish Catholic conversion efforts had been organized by ecclesiastical jurisdictions, as members of missionary orders were assigned to administer particular ethnic groups, provinces, and islands. On the galleons, Asians experienced Catholic religious instruction collectively for the first time, regardless of their ethnicity or place of origin.

Therefore, the Pacific crossing and its many dangers initiated a transition between two distinct forms of Spanish race thinking and contributed to a flattening of social and spiritual organization. These processes later hardened in Acapulco and culminated in a clear racialization: the production of the "chinos" of Mexico. The second half of this chapter traces this transformation in Acapulco and unfolds its widespread implications. The "chino / a" label must have bewildered Asians arriving from the Philippines, where "chinos" were literally Chinese. During the early seventeenth century, however, "chino / a" became a consistent referent to any Asian (including but not limited to the Chinese) in treasury records from Acapulco. This new nomenclature marks the first time in either the Hispanic World or the Americas that a single label was used to refer to all Asians regardless of ethnicity, language, or religious background. The invention of this category and its stunning demographic breadth is one of the clearest examples of race making in Latin America during the long seventeenth century and is comparable only to the extensive scope of the "indio / a" marker.[4] As "chinos," survivors of the Pacific passage became part of the New Spanish casta system, joining an array of castas already enshrined in New Spanish discourse and law, such as "negro / a," "mulato / a," and "mestizo / a." This discursive transition had important secular and ecclesiastical juridical ramifications that limited social, spatial, and legal mobility in Mexico. Becoming "chino / a" drove some individuals to form multiethnic Asian social and kinship bonds, and it thrust others into relationships with existing Indigenous, Afro-Mexican, and mixed populations.

Like other casta labels, "chino / a" denoted a socially constructed grouping, one that replaced the wide array of ethnolinguistic identifications more common to racialized discourses of allegiance and assimilation in the Philippines.[5] Inventing "chino / a" was an orientalist process of extreme erasure that subsumed dozens of ethnolinguistic identities under a single word. The conditions of the Pacific passage—specifically, its entrenched labor hierarchies and religious rituals—became central to the essentialism that climaxed in this new form of racialized identification.

New Spanish forms of race making should thus be seen as a response to the new ways in which long-distance empires in the early modern period connected the world. The consolidation of new racializing language across the long seventeenth century was driven by intensifying waves of Asian movement (both free and forced) to the Americas in the context of post-1603 Manila. Central Mexico was at the heart of these demographic transformations. It became a society of people from all over the world who acquired and invented new identities and cultural communities. The region was the core of the Spanish Pacific empire and the Spanish Atlantic empire. The interactions, convergences, and conflicts among groups in its tremendously diverse population determined the contours of lived experience in this dynamic "contact zone."[6] At the same time, this population felt the local impact of changing conditions across the empire, which included increasing regulation of galleon routes and shipboard culture, the emergence of a global imaginary from the viceregal core, and the heightening importance of casta categorization in law.

The capaciousness of the invented term "chino / a"—which could encompass both Blackness ("*chino negro*") and Whiteness ("*chino blanco*"), freedom and slavery, rebelliousness and colonial service, and every gradation between—makes Acapulco one of the most revealing contexts for the study of racialization in the early modern world. In its vagueness, "chino / a" certainly had similarities to other terms of its time, like "negro / a" and "indio / a." Yet at the same time, "chino / a" was exceptional in its range of reference: it grouped together people whose skin colors and social conditions would have otherwise seemed mutually exclusive to Spanish observers. Chino-genesis was the defining experience of Asian arrival in Acapulco because to become "chino / a" was to acquire a new kind of colonial subjectivity. The term explained how Asians were perceived in the social order, their legal status within that order, their relative social mobility, and their vulnerability to enslavement and the Inquisition. Despite their diversity, "chinos" entered a world where their categorization and, therefore, juridical foreignness indicated both heightened exposure to legal dangers and structural constraints to social, spatial, and economic advancement.

Preparation in Cavite

Whether Asian subjects at sea had been enslaved or hired as low-ranking grumetes, their social statuses determined how they experienced the Pacific crossing. The horrors of the route, both environmental and man-made, initiated an important transition between the forms of ethnolinguistic racialization prominent in the Philippines and the use of castas in Mexico. The passage created a point of commonality among Asian travelers, as shipboard laboring life blurred the distinctions between ethnolinguistic communities and reorganized them around new maritime realities.

Adversity defined this transition. In the words of Pablo Pérez-Mallaína, "it is not difficult to agree that whoever traveled on a ship in the Carrera de Indias entered into a type of hell."[7] Yet the hell of the Manila galleons began long before the ships left harbor. At Cavite, the port that never slept, thousands of laborers converged to build and service the galleons.[8] Spanish officials ordered *cabezas de barangay* (Indigenous leaders) to muster hundreds of hands from their communities for the forced labor drafts called polos.[9] The place-based nature of these drafts meant that labor gangs were often divided by their members' geographic origin and ethnicity. For example, in 1609 Juan María Sanguitan organized 120 Indigenous people of Cagayan to cut wood and haul it to the port.[10] This assignment is typical, as logging and woodworking were the most common tasks. Laborers trekked deep into the mountains for timber and towed it overland or brought it down rivers to reach Cavite.[11] Shifts could last sixteen hours "without breaks for eating or resting."[12] The workers' compensation amounted to a small ration of rice or a paltry sum averaging 9–12 pesos per year, though they often went years without pay.[13]

Polo labor extraction and the accessibility of building materials relatively near the port meant that ship production and repair in the Philippines was many times cheaper than in Mexico.[14] By Captain Sebastián de Pineda's count, Luzon produced six main varieties of wood used in galleon construction: *María, arquijo, laguan, banaba, María de monte,* and *dongón.*[15] Harvesting laguan (also called *lanang*) and dongón (also known as *molave*) on Luzon had significant advantages. Lanang trees were quite tall, resistant to worms, and so strong that they could repel bullets and even cannonballs.[16] Though molave was similarly renowned for its toughness, its prime disadvantage was that it rotted quickly, and decks made of it needed to be torn out and replaced every two years.[17]

Spanish officials paid influential "Sangleyes," often Christians, to mobilize Chinese caulkers, ironworkers, carpenters, porters, and others to accompany the polo gangs. This practice began before 1603 and continued once more "Sangleyes" arrived in subsequent years. Each assigned group often numbered over a hundred men. Treasury officials also rented captives from enslavers for port labor. Most of the enslaved worked as caulkers and were described as "negro," which likely suggested an East African origin.[18] In other words, labor organization at the port of Cavite was largely structured around the mobilizing efforts of intermediaries linked to particular geographies and social statuses. This custom meant that labor gangs tended to share perceived ethnic identifications.

The daily realities of shipboard labor hierarchies represented a significant departure from this practice. The social condition of grumetes and enslaved people was far more important than ethnolinguistic identity in determining how they experienced the crossing. One of the most important ramifications of this transition was that Asians of diverse origin needed to communicate and collaborate with each other to survive. One artilleryman's report on a journey in the *Santo Cristo de Burgos* in 1692 supplies a rare and provocative observation of this process. He wrote that the navigator's incompetence caused "the natives [*naturales*]," meaning the Philippine sailors, to confer among themselves, since they knew the route out of the Philippine Islands better than their Spanish peers did.[19]

Although once thought to be exclusively from the Philippines, some Asian crew members originated from South Asia or Japan, and Southeast Asians and Chinese were represented as well—but in smaller numbers. Philippine Natives usually made up at least 50 percent of a ship's crew. Those who originated from coastal communities on Luzon were especially prized for their navigational and seafaring proficiencies. Most of these people came from towns like Parañaque, Dongalo, Malate, Kawit, San

Roque, and Las Piñas.[20] Together with Tatiana Seijas's estimate that each galleon carried an average of sixty enslaved Asians, these figures indicate that the number of Asians traveling east across the Pacific exceeded that of their Spanish counterparts in nearly every year.[21]

Once a galleon was built or repaired, sailors and dockhands began the enormous task of loading it—using pulley systems and brawn—with diverse merchandise from Asian markets, provisions for the voyage, large water jugs for drinking and ballast, and travelers' trunks.[22] Spanish vessels worthy of the Pacific crossing ranged from small *pataches* ("tender, a small, shallow boat") with crews of 20–30 to full-sized galleons capable of carrying 400 people.[23] Larger ships had better chances of weathering the trials of the open ocean.[24] Anywhere between one and six ships made the crossing in a single year, though it was rare for more than two galleons (called the *capitana* [first in command] and the *almiranta* [second in command]) to do so in a year. Ship size generally increased over time until the mid-eighteenth century.

Everyone on board knew that the west-to-east crossing was nothing short of a Herculean effort. The galleons navigated for one or two months through the Visayas to the Embocadero, at which point they turned north, sent toward Japan by the southwest monsoon called Habagat and by the Kuroshio current.[25] At latitudes varying between 31 and 37 degrees, they entered the North Pacific. Andrés Reséndez calls this zone "one of the most forbidding regions on Earth" and "the most active tropical cyclone region in the world."[26] There, ships struggled against fickle winds, dark skies, the cold, and persistent storms until they finally hit the Californian coast and headed south past the port of Navidad, finally reaching Acapulco in central Mexico (figure 2.2).[27] The route's brutal conditions sank no fewer than forty galleons during their 250-year history.[28]

The Passage

The journey lasted roughly six months on average, with no opportunities to dock and resupply between the Philippines and Mexico. The rocky Californian coast made it impossible to stop for water or provisions north of Navidad under most circumstances. Indeed, the route was so treacherous that in 1613 the crown estimated that it had lost a staggering eight million

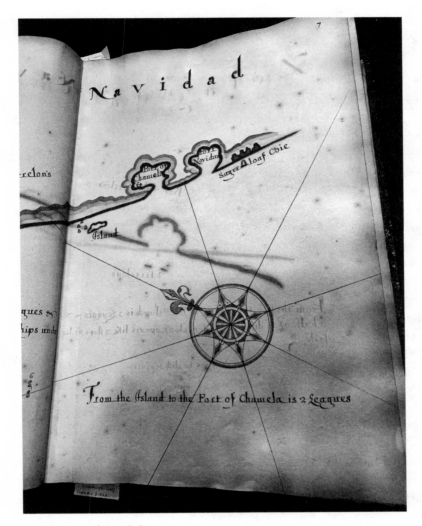

2.2 The Port of Navidad

The Manila galleons regularly stopped at Navidad on their way south to central Mexico. From Navidad, it took about another week to arrive at Acapulco. Stops in Navidad offered illicit and profitable opportunities to disembark and sell enslaved people. The Hacke atlas also depicts other sites of possible unregistered visits, such as Metenchill, the plantations of Maxenteluca and Ponteque, Pilots Sallina, Chametla, Zelagua, Chasapi, Marbata, Tesupan, and Signatelejo. Note that the names are Anglicized pronunciations of Spanish and Indigenous place names. The atlas was based on sailing charts captured on a Spanish ship in 1669.

William Hacke, "An accurate description of all the harbours riuers ports islands ricks and dangers between the mouth of California & the Straights of Lemaire in the South Sea of America as allso of Pepys's Island in the north sea near to the Magellan Straghts," circa 1698, John Carter Brown Library. Photo courtesy of the author.

pesos in ships and goods to the tumultuous Pacific over the previous eleven years.[29]

Asian crew members and enslaved people invariably experienced the worst conditions aboard these ships. To begin with, they almost always spent their time aboard working as the lowest-ranking grumetes and *pajes* (apprentices), and thus they were at the disciplinary mercy of the *contra-maestre* (boatswain).[30] Only a handful of Spanish grumetes (usually three to five people) worked alongside them. Although later banned from beating sailors, boatswains on the Manila galleons had full license to imprison lower-ranking people with "stocks or shackles and other tortures" for disciplinary violations.[31] In extreme cases, insubordinate crew members "could be thrown overboard for even minor infractions like falling asleep twice during their watch."[32] Contramaestres habitually considered their Asian crew members to be expendable. Asian grumetes regularly re-ceived half the pay of Spanish grumetes (48–60 pesos versus 100 pesos per year) and half as much rice.[33] The lowliest made as little as 1–2 pesos per month.[34] During times of scarcity at sea when rations were cut, theirs were reduced first.[35]

According to Diego García de Palacio in 1587, the ideal number of gru-metes was two for every three *marineros* (full sailors), and the ideal ratio of apprentices to marineros was 1:10. In practice, however, Manila galleons often carried more grumetes than marineros, while the reverse was true for the smaller patches. At least half of the shipboard grumetes needed to know how to hoist the topsail, the fore-topmast sail, the mizzen sail, and the spritsail. They had to row if necessary, know how to tie basic knots, understand all seafaring vocabulary (even if they could not understand much else in Spanish), operate the bilge pumps, and launch skiffs. Mari-neros had to know how to handle and use all sails, complex knots, the an-chor, and the helm; discern cardinal directions and the positions of the sun and moon; and navigate the ship during the night.[36] These were high-risk and high-labor jobs. During storms, grumetes spent days in their ship's dark, damp hull fighting leaks and operating the bilge pump.[37] During the journey, enslaved people were often expected to perform grumete labor.

Beginning in the early seventeenth century, Asian grumetes were as-signed an experienced disciplinary *guardianejo* (guardian) from their own ranks to mediate between them and higher-ranking officials. The guardi-anejos typically made considerably more than the grumetes, earning an average of 150 pesos per year—which exceeded the pay of most Spanish grumetes (100 pesos per year) but did not reach the amounts paid to the marineros.[38] During this period, even after many years of service, skilled Asian sailors rarely achieved the rank of marinero.[39] The only other route of advancement was as a carpenter. Most of whom were from Cagayan, and so many ship carpenters came from there that Pineda believed that "Cagayan" translated to carpenter "in their language."[40] These were the only cases in which galleon labor structures preserved a consistent ethnic grouping of Asian people. Large ships typically carried 2–4 Cagayan carpenters on their payrolls. Their earnings varied widely: the median was 150 pesos per year, but don Diego Cagayan received the exceptional amount of 300 pesos in 1610 on the *San Juan Baptista*—a sum equal to that paid to Spanish carpenters.[41]

As hard to bear as the route was for even high-ranking naval officers and wealthy passengers, those with fewer means—Asian crew members and enslaved people—suffered a near-unimaginable journey.[42] In 1607, Hernando de los Ríos Coronel submitted a lengthy petition to the king, arguing that various reforms were needed in the Philippines. His petition began an important discussion on regulating and improving overall sailing conditions, with particular attention to those of the Asian grumetes. Coronel wrote that ships were so overloaded, usually with Asian merchandise, that they were not properly stocked with food. As a result, the provisions they did carry had to be stored on deck and were swept away in the first storm. Wealthy passengers and high-ranking crew members brought their own supplies, so losing the official provisions would not have been an irreparable catastrophe for them. Asian crew members often had to supply their own food as well, and their significantly fewer resources meant that they were the first to be forced to subsist solely on rice. Over long periods of time, this vitamin-deficient diet invariably resulted in scurvy and beriberi. The absence of live chickens (a common cure for shipboard ailments) by the end of the journey meant that the malnourished crews, "especially the Indigenous cabin boys [grumetes]," had no way to return to health.[43] Living in squalid, overcrowded cabins and on deck, crew members had to deal with all manner of vermin in their *bizcocho* (hardtack), broth, clothing, and trunks.[44] The Jesuit Francisco Colín commented that illness from corrupted food supplies was "an ordinary thing on this route."[45] During storms, crew members' belongings, stored on the deck, were "to be offloaded before those below deck."[46]

By the end of the journey, even the wealthiest passengers felt the effects
of sickness, lack of hygiene, and poor provisions. An Italian slave trader,
Francesco Carletti, described a method of consuming hardtack to avoid
feeling hunger or thirst:

> And it was ordered that, so that we should not drink, the cooking be
> stopped, that we should eat nothing but biscuits dipped in water and
> in oil, on which a little sugar was sprinkled, a thing very helpful in
> mitigating thirst. But I discovered that by eating in the morning a sop
> dipped in wine and then drinking water on top of it, I could keep my-
> self a whole day without feeling hunger or thirst. Others took a lot
> of sugar and put it into both salt and sweet water, thus making a drink
> that was neither very good nor very healthful.[47]

Carletti's method was merely one of many adaptations designed to keep
a ship functioning while its crew members and passengers slowly starved.
By the end of the seventeenth century, royal proclamations advised galleon
officials to merely "distract and entertain with nice words" sailors asking
about rations.[48]

The missionary Pedro Cubero Sebastián wrote that the last month of
the passage was the deadliest: "all of those who come [are] touched by
scurvy, or the illness of Loanda [beriberi], which are the most pestiferous
ailments that this voyage gives, and later [comes] dysentery. Rare is he who
escapes [them]."[49] He recorded that three or four people died every day as
the ship neared Acapulco, and although he did not state it directly, we can
assume that Asian grumetes died at disproportionate rates on the ship.
Only 192 of the original 400 people on his voyage survived. Other ships
also registered high mortality rates. The *Altamira* arrived in Acapulco in
1606 with eighty fewer people than had been on board when the ship left
Manila. An astounding 150 out of 200 crew members on one ship perished
in 1616 due to a lack of provisions, and a 1620 crossing resulted in ninety-
nine deaths and many survivors being sick.[50] Perhaps the most haunting
example is that of the derelict *Nuestra Señora de la Victoria,* which floated
past the Mexican coast in March 1657. It landed far to the south, at the port
of Amapal (in modern-day Honduras). Only a handful of those who originally boarded the ship survived.[51]

Thomas Gage, an English Dominican missionary and traveler, never crossed the Pacific, but his description of how Spanish crews disposed of bodies at sea is the closest approximation we have of how Manila galleon crews did the same:

> [The dead man] had weighty stones hung to his feet, two more to his shoulders, and one to his brest; and then the superstitious *Romish Dirige* and *Requiem* being sung for his Soul, his Corpse being held out to Sea on the ship side, with Ropes ready to let him fall, all the Ship crying out three times, *buen Viaci* [sic] (that is good Voiage) to his [Soul] chiefly, and also to his Corpse ready to Travel to the deep to feed the Whales: at the first cry all the Ordnance were shot off, the Ropes on a suddain loosed, and *John de la Cueva* with the weight of heavy Stones plunged deep into the Sea, whom no mortal eyes ever more beheld.[52]

On the Manila galleons, like all other long-distance nautical travel at the time, death was omnipresent.

The high latitude of the Pacific passage presented additional problems. Coronel noted that storms and other delays often kept galleons from ascending high enough to cross until September or October, which resulted in their exposure to more storms and frigid, arctic weather, "and having left warm land, many people die. Their gums cannot tolerate it, and their teeth fall out."[53] Lamp oil would freeze into "pieces like lard."[54] The Dominican Diego Aduarte recorded that "these winds were so cold that those who died were frozen, without any other infirmity than the cold, by which the waves met the rigging many times, and soaked those who did not have a coat (which was almost everyone), with which the cold increased greatly, and having left such a hot temple like that of this land [Philippines], and entering so suddenly in another so cold, [the cold] could not but cause many illnesses, and like this, many died in this voyage, and among them the general, the first mate, and a rich merchant."[55] Like the dearth of food, the cold affected Asian crew members disproportionately. Colín wrote that "neither those born nor raised in [the Philippines] can identify by sight the color of snow, nor the appearance of ice."[56] Coronel noted that Asian sailors, levied from both inland and coastal tropical regions, did not have coats to protect them against the winter chill or the cold sea, and even if given access to coats, they could not have afforded to buy them. In response to Coronel's petition, a cluster of *cédulas* (royal decrees) recommended harsh punishment for the mistreatment of Asian grumetes attempting to acquire rations and cold-weather clothing.[57] Unfortunately, enforcing these royal decrees relied upon the whims of individuals who typically did not share these concerns.

In addition, the Pacific passage became even more difficult during the second half of the seventeenth century due to the Maunder Minimum, a slowing in the rate of sunspots generally lowering temperatures world-wide between 1645 and 1715. Colder weather exacerbated harsh conditions at high latitudes, produced more storms, and according to Arturo Giráldez, ultimately lengthened voyages by as much as 40 percent from 1640 to 1670.[58]

Enslaved Asians and East Africans experienced still more appalling shipboard treatment than other groups did. For them, the Pacific passage would have been only the most extreme displacement in a lengthy series that often began with Portuguese slave trading in the Indian Ocean World (see Chapter 1). Their lives were inconsequential to Spanish officials. For example, Diego Fajardo Chacón, a governor of the Philippines, downplayed losses at sea by assuming that the dead were merely enslaved people who had been stowed away to save their owners from having to pay duties in Acapulco.[59] As early as 1607, Governor Juan de Silva wrote that stowaways were common despite measures to stop the practice.[60] By the end of the seventeenth century, official ordinances authorized the execution of anyone found hiding on a ship.[61]

The stowaways were overwhelmingly enslaved women, whom traffickers hid belowdecks because of restrictions on importing them and to avoid paying duties. At Coronel's insistence, King Felipe III ordered in 1608 that no enslaved women be permitted to embark on the galleons to avoid offending God, a direct reference to the sexual assault, rape, concubinage, and sex trafficking that typified daily life on these ships.[62] In 1620, however, Coronel testified that the abuses had not ended: he wrote that one Spaniard had taken fifteen enslaved women aboard a ship and impregnated them.[63] Officials in Mexico were similarly culpable for what transpired on the galleons. For example, during the same period, the viceroy of New Spain sent a letter to the governor of the Philippines, ordering him to locate and ship to Acapulco "a few good-looking female slaves."[64] Similarly, Captain Miguel de Sosa and his wife, doña Margarita de Chaves, charged a Portuguese merchant with bringing a "chinita" from Manila to them in Puebla.[65]

Men of the sea had also acquired notorious reputations as lustful deviants and predators, isolated as they were from opportunities to participate in legitimate Catholic relationships for many months or years at a time.[66] The enslaved Catarina de San Juan had been disguised as a boy on the galleons to avoid registry and, undoubtedly, to protect her from the unending sexual torment she had suffered in captivity.[67] Her misery was such that she would later pray for Jesus to change her appearance from "beautiful" (and "white") to "ugly" (and "brown-colored china").[68] She was not the only girl or woman to have to change her appearance for her safety and for the benefit of her enslaver to avoid royal restrictions. Still, scattered examples exist of enslavers registering enslaved women in Acapulco despite the prohibitions on doing so, like the captains of the *Nuestra Señora de la Concepción* in 1643 and the *San Luis Rey de Francia* in 1646.[69] Only wealthy merchants and officials would have been able to reliably smuggle enslaved women into Mexico. For this reason, Seijas estimates a 3:1 ratio of males to females among enslaved Asians on the galleons.[70] Comparably, Déborah Oropeza calculates that 23 percent of enslaved "chinos" in Mexico City were women, and Pablo Sierra Silva estimates a 4.25:1.00 ratio of "chinos" to "chinas" based on the sales of enslaved people in Puebla.[71]

Cultures at Sea: Instituting Hispanicization on the Galleons

To shipboard officials, the manner of transpacific survival was nearly as important as the fact of it. The anxieties over the sincerity of conversion that dominated early modern ecclesiastical discourse in the Philippines seeped into the regulation of life at sea. Given the difficulties of the voyage, Spanish officials recognized that travelers on the galleons would need the guidance of Catholic dogma and the promise of salvation to persist against great odds.[72] However, during desperate moments at sea religious disillusionment and blasphemous outcries frequently threatened the spiritual discipline of the galleons, recalling the tenuousness of the Catholic mission in the Philippines. Consequently, religion became foundational to the racialized collapsing of social and cultural difference that characterized the

Pacific passage. The importance of Christianity on the Manila galleons cannot be overstated.[73]

Shipboard religiosity derived its urgency from the Philippine context. In the islands, as in the Americas, the papal bulls of 1522 known as the *Omnímoda* had given the mendicant orders broad jurisdiction to autonomously administer sacraments and perform other parish functions.[74] Consequently, missionaries and friars became the vanguard of the Catholic faith in the colonies. However, missionaries in the Philippines confronted severe setbacks at every turn as they sought to Catholicize spiritually plural populations. Often, the missionaries attributed resistance to conversion to ethnic shortcomings.[75] Nonetheless, the act of conversion held the promise of transcending the racialized prejudices of many Spaniards against pre-Catholic people. In 1604, the Jesuit Pedro Chirino declared that conversion was responsible for transforming the Indigenous "Negrillos" (Aeta and Ati Austronesian peoples) from "wild beasts" to "peaceable and tame" beings.[76] For the Dominican missionary Diego Aduarte in 1640, Catholic marriage between a Japanese woman and a Chinese man "seems to have negated both of their origin [*nación*] because neither in her was found the deceitfulness and choleric spirit of the Japanese, nor in him the covetousness and the nonsense of the Chinese."[77] Through willing submission to Catholic ritual, the couple surpassed their racialized limitations.

Additionally, each missionary order administered to populations by "geo-ethnic distribution" in the Philippines.[78] For example, the Augustinians and Franciscans had the largest jurisdictions on Luzon (often separated by linguistic group), and Governor Santiago de Vera gave the Dominicans authority over the Chinese Parian in 1589.[79] Therefore, the various peoples designated as the grumetes and the enslaved of the galleons had largely been sermonized separately by ecclesiastical jurisdictions in the Philippines. On the ships, missionaries provided spiritual instruction with little to no regard for the jurisdictions over which they fought bitterly in the islands: ethnicity and geography no longer determined these contacts. Thus, the galleons reorganized and, to some extent, homogenized Asian encounters with the Catholic faith.

In so doing, galleon life furthered the universalist aspirations of Catholic discourse and practice. Hence, the ships functioned as mobile exercises in Hispanicization. One funerary poem written in honor of Catarina de

San Juan suffices to demonstrate this point. The Jesuit Antonio Plancarte wrote:

> I am an Asia ship [*nao de China*]
> that a china disembarked,
> Acapulco is not much a ship
> to encompass this china.
> Catarina is my name,
> my course without wind current:
> The Holy Spirit the wind
> San Ignacio the captain
> their navigators will put me
> on the land of salvation.[80]

Accompanying this poem was the image of a ship unloading passengers in Acapulco.[81] Catarina de San Juan stood at its side in a small boat, with San Ignacio on the mainmast bearing a banner with the words "Salva facta est" ("It [the boat] was saved").[82] The galleons represented holy salvation. The poem's conflation of Catarina with the ship through the first person in the first five lines indicates that the miraculous extended not only to transpacific survival but also to the conversion of people from distant lands across the Pacific.

Asians aboard the galleons were typically either Christian neophytes or enslaved people with ambiguous confessional identities. Most of them had been baptized, used a Spanish name, recognized Catholic rhetoric and ritual, understood the basic structures of colonial social organization, and had circulated through multiethnic colonial settings like Intramuros. Before boarding, all of them were required to "confess and take communion, fulfilling the Christian's obligation."[83] For these reasons, the consistency of Catholic ritual and the importance of religious figures on the ships reinforced certain expectations of behavior and custom.

From start to finish, Catholic ritual played a prominent role in the day-to-day life of galleon travel. On both sides of the Pacific, departure and arrival were met with fervent prayers and joyous church bells.[84] In the Philippines, Our Lady of the Good Voyage and Peace protected the galleons from harm. Beginning in the middle of the seventeenth century, this Marian devotional image crossed the Pacific no fewer than eight times. It accompanied the *San Luis* in 1641, 1643, and 1645, and it departed one final time from the Philippines in 1746 aboard the *Nuestra Señora de Pilar*.[85] When the image came aboard, "a procession of friars carried the statue of the line's virgin-patroness along the walls and delivered it . . . accompanied by a salvo of gunfire," in a ritual that sent the galleon on its way.[86] In 1672, Andrés de Ledesma wrote that "mariners and seafarers come [to her shrine in Antipolo] to request the happy outcome of their voyage."[87]

The ship's sails and bonnets carried the letters AMGP, an acronym for the *"Ave Maria, gratia plena"* of the Hail Mary, which allowed sailors to quickly arrange the sails, based on their knowledge of the letters' correct order in the prayer.[88] Grumetes kept time on the ship "by turning sand clocks every half hour while reciting religious invocations, which were answered in chorus. They also chanted the 'Good Day' each day, and before evening, they recited other prayers and the main tenets of the Christian faith, the *Credo*."[89] Through this daily repetition, everyone on board soon memorized these prayers and recognized them as marking the passage of time.[90]

Missionaries, friars, clerics, and vicars also occupied prominent roles on the galleons. Manila officials gave the following instructions to the crew of the *Santo Cristo de Burgos* in 1693: "On the days that the weather allows, mass and the *Salve* will be said in the afternoons with all of the reverence of life and devotion possible, since doing so like this, one will achieve a very safe voyage and happy outcomes."[91] Ordinances issued during the eighteenth century would later standardize these practices: "It will be of [the ship's] care that the established prayers are done with total reverence, in the customary places and times, in a loud voice. And on Sundays and other holidays, time willing, and in agreement with the ship captain, it will be possible to explain the Doctrine and prayers to the grumetes and other people aboard, like the crew and garrison, and that all can sequentially join these acts of devotion and religion; and those who miss it, without legitimate cause, or in malice, will be punished."[92] In this way, missionaries raised morale and steadfastly celebrated the religious calendar, inspiring weary travelers with their humility and determination to persevere through suffering. For example, Cubero Sebastián's galleon had ascended to 34 degrees when on October 22, 1678, 866 leagues from the Philippines, they hit a horrific storm that lasted eighty grueling hours.

The waves striking the galleon were said to have thundered like artillery fire. During such a storm, no one could sleep or eat, and the labor required to keep the ship afloat would have been tremendous. Everyone, even the pilot, came to Cubero Sebastián for confession. The pilot spoke with him privately so as "to not upset those on the ship. Señor Padre, I have navigated many oceans, but in my life, having seen such a storm, I come undone."[93] When the clouds finally parted, everyone on board sang *Te Deum Laudamus.*[94]

During one storm in the 1609 crossing, friars whipped themselves on deck until they drew blood to satiate God with their public devotion. When another storm struck, sailors held the Jesuit Pedro de Montes atop the aftercastle so that he could confess as many people as possible from the safest location on deck.[95] Exemplary behavior of this sort encouraged some crews to keep rotting bodies on board so that they could be given a Christian burial in Acapulco.[96]

Throughout the voyage, sailors and passengers alike paid careful attention to the *señas* (signs) that marked different stages in the journey. According to Cubero Sebastián, the first sign was spotting San Lazaro, which marked the exit from the Philippines. Upon sighting it, "[all] say loudly, as if about to fall and die: in your hands, Señor, we commend ourselves; our miserable boat has to be in your care [to arrive safely so] that one risks navigating this very vast Archipelago, and all in one voice say, like this we hope for [your care]. And giving the sail to the winds, they begin to sail . . . not another thing is seen . . . until arriving to recognize the signs that seem that divine providence brought them there, so that the galleon is not lost."[97] Survival against such odds was so miraculous and seemed, at times, so unlikely that spotting the signs could only be an act of deliverance. The second, third, and fourth signs were *porras, balsas,* and *lobillos.* Rubén Carrillo Martín classifies the porras as "giant sargasso, *Marcrocystis prifera,* an algae local to the Pacific-American littoral."[98] A balsa was simply a large clump of porras, and lobillos were animals that floated and played on top of them.[99] Lest anyone doubt the existence of the lobillos, Cubero Sebastián wrote, "and by my own eyes I saw them."[100] He described them as "fish in the style of bodices."[101] These were probably what Antonio de Morga termed *perrillos* (small dogs) and what Carrillo Martín identifies as "marine seals and lions and elephants."[102]

According to Cubero Sebastián, seeing these signs generated more happiness than arriving at port. That same day, the crew relieved the pain and frustration of the passage by conducting a theatrical trial:

> The sailors, dressed ridiculously, have a Trial, and they bring imprisoned all of the most important people on the galleon, beginning with the General, and for each one they have an investigation of what happened. And taking charge, they make a condemnation, according to each, which is a day of much merrymaking for all: to the General they pile on that he did not want to give leave that they open the hatch to get water, which had made them perish from thirst. To the Sergeant Major (who was also the Doctor) that he had spilled much human blood because he had bled more than two hundred people. To the Pilot who had always gone about fighting with the sun.[103] To me [the friar], who, sitting in a chair always went about reprimanding and that I was the Lazarillo of death because those who I went down to visit between the bridges under the hatch the next day were thrown overboard. And later, they condemned us and sentenced us: one was to give chocolate, another hardtack, another sweets, another other different things.[104]

This description resembles the early modern carnivalesque tradition that inverted hierarchy and power to expunge woes and placate the masses. It also highlights the fact that Cubero Sebastián, a missionary, was considered among the most important people on the ship, known for "reprimanding" others (probably in matters of faith) and for preceding death as the giver of last rites and final confession. The connection to Lazarillo is also significant, because books of dogma and pleasure (like *Orlando Furioso, Amadis de Gaula,* and *La Araucana*) were often read aloud on board, inviting passengers and sailors to imagine worlds and delights beyond the confines of the ship or their social condition.[105] For example, when the *Nuestra Señora de la Asunción* landed in Acapulco in 1590, sailors and passengers registered numerous "books of pastime and devotion," specifically including "books of chivalry and papal history and hourly prayers."[106]

Of course, as Catholicism played an important role in maintaining stability, crew members often expressed their frustrations through sinful behavior. In 1636, the governor of the Philippines complained of Spanish and

Kapampangan sailors having problems with discipline in Cavite.[107] This commentary was consistent with stereotypes of sailors as the "fex maris (dregs of the sea)."[108] The crown officially banned card gambling (a notorious occasion for blasphemous outcries) on the galleons in 1679 on threat of severe punishment because officers tended to rig the games against passengers.[109] Any curse against "the holy name of God in vain [or] of his holy mother [or] offending the divine majesty" was expressly forbidden."[110] Like other decrees, though, these had limited impact.

In 1608, Antonio de Olivera, a pilot, denounced the boatswain on his ship, Martín Costa, to the Inquisition upon arrival in Acapulco. Witnesses reported a collection of potentially damning statements. Costa had remarked that "God did much against the said ship." On another occasion when the vicar was offering prayers, Costa said, "Father, give your Hail Mary over there. If I go to hell, everyone has more work." As Guillermo de Guerrera prayed for the souls in purgatory, Costa gave him a bell and said, "commend also those who are in hell."[111]

Costa's objections emerge directly from the difficulty of the passage and follow known patterns of blasphemy under extreme physical and psychological duress.[112] His comments were also scathingly sarcastic. He interpreted the strain of the voyage as a sign that God had turned against the people on board and reasoned that the only consequence of his dying and going to hell was that everyone on the ship would have more work to do. The denunciation does not record any punishment, perhaps suggesting that such offenses were so common or minor that the inquisitor decided not to follow up on the denunciations with a full trial. After all, *reniego a dios* (I renounce God) was a common profanity.[113]

The cultural life on the galleons mediated between the spiritual tension of life at sea and the proscriptions of Catholic society. The cramped space of the ship itself functioned as an aspirational vehicle of assimilation for non-Spanish passengers, sailors, and enslaved people (figure 2.3). When they landed, those well enough to walk proceeded to mass at the parish church immediately after completing administrative formalities.[114] By this point, many Asians could recite Catholic prayers and speak some Spanish, even if they could not do either before going on board. Still others questioned Catholic ritual and blended it with other beliefs, and they would continue to do so after arriving in New Spain (see Chapter 4). Even the life of Catarina de San Juan, the religious icon, demonstrated these lingering tensions born of the Pacific passage. Francisco de Aguilera described Catarina's ecclesiastical

2.3 The Rebuilt *San Salvador*

The narrow deck of the rebuilt *San Salvador* shows the limited living space
that thrust the galleon's multiethnic crew, passengers, and enslaved people
into close contact. The *San Salvador* was the first European ship to visit the
bay that is now San Diego and would have been somewhat smaller than a
full-sized galleon crossing the Pacific during the seventeenth century.

Photo courtesy of the author.

knowledge after landing in Acapulco as "neither very much of the day, nor of the night," meaning that it was neither strong nor weak.[115] Numerous writers also called her *bozal* (wild or unacculturated) in her speech, and that word was similarly used to describe and denigrate recently arrived Africans. In a funerary poem, Plancarte wrote, "Neither does the confessor divine / what she says."[116] In his hagiography, Joseph del Castillo Graxeda recorded her speech in broken Spanish and provided a "translation" with the understanding that her awkward language represented communication from God. Therefore, galleon travel endowed many Asian subjects, like Catarina, with a hybrid subjectivity that both was and was not Hispanic or Catholic.

More broadly, the experience of the Pacific passage created new bonds among travelers. Asians long remembered the names of their ships, their year of arrival, and the people they crossed the ocean with.[117] For example, in 1611 an enslaved Asian man named Antonio Geronimo produced Juan Barco and Domingo de Ortega, both enslaved Asians, as witnesses to testify that he was single and legally available to marry. Both Juan and Domingo claimed to have known Antonio for eight years, including four in Manila, and to have sailed together on the same galleon.[118] Perhaps these dynamics explain why Oropeza found that "chinos" later married each other at high rates in Mexico City, even though they often did not come from the same ethnic group. Despite the wide availability of partners from other groups, "chinas" selected "chinos" for marriage more than any other casta, and "chinos" married "chinas" at rates that were exceeded only by their unions with women of Indigenous heritage ("indias" and "mestizas")—a function, in part, of the far greater number of Asian men than Asian women on the galleons.[119] Carrillo Martín determined that in cases where both parents of a baptismal candidate were identified as "chinos," the selection of "chino / a" godparents was more likely.[120] The crossing had therefore become a defining feature in the social memory and acculturation of the first Asians in the Americas and formed a new, critical node of diasporic commonality for the "chinos" of New Spain.[121]

Landing in Acapulco

The first sign of arrival at Acapulco on a Manila galleon coming from the north was a mountain twenty-five kilometers back from the sea called La Brea (pitch). The ship then passed through a channel between the shore and the island of La Roqueta near El Grifo (today's Punta Grifo) that "although it seems narrow, . . . is good with a depth from 15 to 20 Castilian yards." After the galleon cleared the channel, the Fort of San Diego (which overlooked the bay) came into view on the headland, and finally the crew members could see some 250 houses tucked into a corner of the bay (figures 2.4 and 2.5). Two densely forested mountains with "small white spots that look like grazing sheep" flanked the town.[122] Crew members roped the galleons to thick trees on the beach, unloaded the cargo onto small skiffs operated by the enslaved people of Acapulco and Asian rowers, and

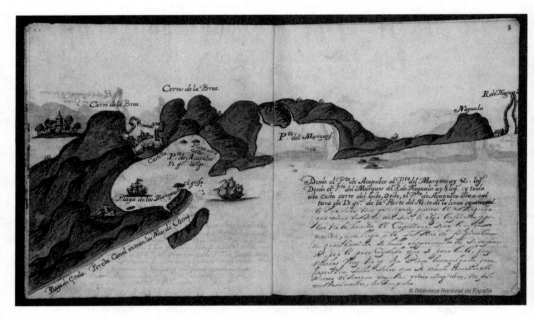

2.4 The Port of Acapulco

Beyond providing an exceptional depiction of Acapulco and its surroundings, this map's text is significant for describing the popular opinion of Acapulco as a port town. A portion of the text reads: "It is one of the most important ports of the South Sea, that of Acapulco. It is somewhat unhealthy, and as such, the castellan does not reside in it, except when the ship from the Philippines arrives. It causes great shame that its defense is found to be unprepared, for the little care that is placed in it. So, oftentimes there is not a mounted [artillery] piece to salute [the ships], which should be remedied."

"Mapas de las costas de América en el mar del Sur, desde la última población de españoles en ellas, que es la ciudad de Compostela, en adelante," circa 1600s. Reproduction courtesy of the Biblioteca Nacional de España.

2.5 The Port of Acapulco in the Kingdom of the New Spain in the South Sea

Adrian Boot's spectacular rendition of Acapulco features a galleon passing through the channel and another in the bay with a prominent Cross of Burgundy on display. Several smaller boats await by the shore to haul merchandise into the town. On the headland to the left of the town is the Fort of San Diego. In the foreground, a figure that presumably is Boot himself gazes out across the Pacific. The image is unusually attentive to labor, perhaps a sign of Boot's participation in the fort's construction. Also in the foreground, one man cuts wood to the right, while a porter just to the right of the figure on horseback walks down the mountain to the port. For more information on this image, see Dana Leibsohn and Meha Priyadarshini, "Transpacific: Beyond Silk and Silver," *Colonial Latin American Review* 25, no. 1 (2016): 1–15.

Adrian Boot, *Puerto de Acapulco en el Reino de la Nueva España en el Mar del Sur*, 1628. Reproduction courtesy of the Benson Latin American Collection, University of Texas at Austin.

proceeded immediately to mass. Those too sick to attend were rushed to the Hospital Real (Royal Hospital) for rest and nourishment. Its rooms for treatment were divided by the patients' category: one room for Spaniards and the other for "indios, negros and mulatos and chinos."[123] Convalescing sailors and enslaved people were fed a diet of bread and fish or meat, supplemented by a few products procured from apothecaries in Mexico City during the off-season.[124]

However, the number of sailors requiring treatment often meant that the hospital's supplies were inadequate. In 1595, a report testified that there were so many sick mariners that no medicine remained to treat the town's poor.[125] In 1616, Bartolome de Nasera, a priest who administered the hospital's finances, complained that he had found "the said hospital building in such a state that if it was not covered before the rainy season, it was not possible to occupy nor live [in it]."[126] These sodden conditions were what grumetes disembarking on the verge of death faced.

As much as galleon crews nearing the journey's end yearned for land, arriving at Acapulco began a new and perhaps equally disheartening conflict, this time with corrupt officials. In town, galleon survivors would have been immediately recognizable, due to their ragged clothing, haggard complexions, distinctive red *bonetes* (caps), and blue sea capes.[127] According to one report, "[the sailors] fear arriving at the ports for the executors of the royal duties more than the storms of the sea, and it is a great pain that after seven months and more of travel, arriving at port where you think to find refreshment and rest from so much work, they find that all, from the youngest to the oldest, seem conspired against them."[128] The *almojarifazgos* (import duties) amounted to 10 percent on all goods and accompanied a 6 percent *alcabala* (sales tax).[129] Other duties were sometimes added to supplement the cost of building and repairing Acapulco's Fort of San Diego.[130] And invented charges regularly compounded these high rates.[131]

Little more than an arid, insalubrious fishing village for most of the year, Acapulco came alive solely for transpacific trade with the Philippines and trans-American trade with Peru. Everyone who could profit did so, through either legal or illicit means. Price inflation was so rampant that in 1616 the cost of a chicken rose to a full peso from six reales. Chickens were the principal means of nursing dying sailors back to health at the Hospital Real.[132]

It was well known that sailors, including grumetes, engaged in transpacific trade to the extent that they could fill their trunks with merchandise to peddle at the port, an economic activity well established by transatlantic sailors selling coveted Spanish clothing in the Americas.[133] In 1608, a cédula limited marineros to a single trunk and noted that sailors had previously filled up to three trunks each, for which there was no room aboard.[134] After a ship arrived in Acapulco, the fort's castellan would conduct an inspection of shipboard goods and impound sailors' trunks unless bribed not to do so.[135] This was a rampant abuse of authority, but there was virtually no oversight to prevent it. If a trunk was held for three days, it would be forfeit. Furthermore, sailors could only leave the port legally with a special permit from the castellan.[136] The castellan also had the authority to punish sailors for any crimes committed at sea. Once in prison, sailors could procure food only at exorbitant prices that they typically could not afford, because many had lost their earnings in illegal gambling dens that the castellan had organized.[137]

Dead sailors also presented unique opportunities for the castellan and parish priest. Last wills and testaments made at sea were often declared null and void, and officials routinely pocketed dead sailors' goods and their back pay—which sometimes amounted to 400–500 pesos (closer to 30–60 pesos for grumetes). Families back in the Philippines never got the money for which their relatives had perished, leaving them in "extreme need."[138] A cédula from 1670 concluded that "the persecution of the ports arrives even to the dead."[139] Gemelli Careri, an Italian traveler, noted that the castellan stood to make 20,000 pesos in a year and the parish priest 14,000 pesos, although the castellan's official annual salary amounted to only 180 pesos.[140]

These woes intensified the daily difficulties of life at the port. The Dominican Domingo Fernández Navarrete was not alone in believing incorrectly that "Acapulco" in Nahuatl translated to the "mouth of Hell" in Spanish.[141] Cubero Sebastián lamented that the land was dry, and the only fresh water came from "a little, very weak spring, that barely puts out a trickle of water, which they name the Chorrillo [little stream]. To fill a pitcher of water, it takes two hours."[142] After commenting on the small plaza, he ironically concluded, "this is what the celebrated port of Acapulco has."[143] Careri was more incisive: "Regarding the city of Acapulco, it seems to me that it should be given the name of humble hamlet of fishers (so low and contemptible are its houses, made of wood, mud and straw) [rather] than the deceitful [name] of the main emporium of the South Sea and way station to Asia."[144] Carletti, who wrote almost a hundred years earlier, had a similar impression and noted that Acapulco "abounds with gnats and scorpions and other animals and bugs, all very poisonous. If they bite you, you will die. And if by some accident you eat or drink them in wine or water, they will drive you insane."[145] Although land must have provided some measure of rest for weary crew members, true respite was in short supply in Acapulco. For free and enslaved Asian subjects stepping onto American soil for the first time, the conditions of the port dramatically belied the Viceroyalty of New Spain's global reputation and foretold the difficulties they would face in the future.

Spanish officials in the Philippines and on the Iberian Peninsula concerned themselves with the treatment of transpacific sailors because life in Acapulco and the hardships of the passage resulted in frequent desertions and severe manpower shortages.[146] One official wrote in 1633, "[Sailors from the Philippines] get completely discouraged from returning."[147] Francisco de Acuña, a Philippine sailor from Parañaque who made no fewer than twenty-seven transpacific round trips, was an extreme exception to these trends.[148] For example, in 1606 Lieutenant (alférez) Alonso de Medina paid fifty-five pesos and four tomines to commission bounty hunters to capture four Asian grumetes "who had fled with their advance pay [socorro], named Alonso Baean, Pedro Loc, Simon Manapa, and Don Juan."[149] These hunters frequently tracked grumetes as far as to Mexico City and dragged them back to Acapulco.

The best-known example of desertion is that of the Espíritu Santo's surviving Asian grumetes: seventy out of seventy-five of them fled upon arrival from Acapulco to Colima in 1618. They had found employment as producers of fermented and distilled tuba (coconut wines).[150] These beverages were and still are popular in the Philippines, and grumetes like those of the Espíritu Santo transplanted the cultivation of coconuts and production of the wines to Mexico's Pacific coast beginning in the Manila galleons' earliest years. As in the Philippines (particularly the Visayas), "chinos" in Mexico cut stairs into palm trees to access their coconuts, which they used to make clothing and medicine as well as wines.[151] In 1619, Pineda expressed considerable concern that Colima's Indigenous population "enjoys [coconut wine] more than the wine that comes from Spain."[152] In fact, they craved it so much that they would travel to Acapulco when the galleons arrived and recruit Asian sailors to produce it. Pineda believed that the beverage's notoriety in the region would result in significant monetary losses for Spanish merchants and ultimately reduce the volume of Castilian wine arriving in Mexico. Pineda could imagine only one solution: that "they load up [all the Natives of the Philippine Islands] and return them . . . and that they burn the palm plantations . . . and cut down the palm trees."[153]

Pineda's proposal of violent deportation, so reminiscent of the calls to send "Sangleyes" back to China, was never accepted.

On the contrary, the Acapulco-to-Colima pipeline developed so rapidly that by 1619, the town of San Joseph Tecolapa in Colima boasted a population of fifty married "chinos" with their own alcalde.[154] In fact, "chinos" were so active as wage laborers, bonded debtors, and enslaved workers on the tuba plantations in that town (and in other towns like Tecpan, Acoyac, Atoyaque, and Caxitlan) that coconut wine overtook cacao monoculture in Colima during the seventeenth century.[155] Indigenous and Afro-Mexican laborers quickly learned how to "climb the palm trees like chinos" as well.[156] Five "indios chinos," named Miguel Pano, Sebastián de la Cruz, Juan de Triana, Francisco Ramos, and Nicolás Mananquel, were operating their own tuba plantations by 1644.[157]

At the behest of the Manila city council, the crown responded to the perennial problems of desertion to places like Colima with economic incentives. To limit the corruption of the castellan, it repeatedly ordered that sailors' trunks not be sequestered or opened.[158] For marineros, it offered them the rights to transport up to a thousand pesos and to sell small trade goods at the port.[159] In 1639, the viceroy of New Spain even declared that marineros would be exempted from duties on trade goods worth up to four hundred pesos, and that grumetes would be exempted for duties on goods worth up to two hundred pesos—a significant allowance.[160] Ultimately, even these generous measures would not prove to be sufficient compensation to overcome the difficulties of the voyage, discrimination at port, and delays in receiving pay. Sailors sometimes had to wait up to fifteen years and complete the return journey to receive their promised wages.[161] In 1676, Diego de Villatoro summarized that "[the sailors] experience the same prejudices" recorded in cédulas from the 1620s.[162] Consistently high rates of mortality and desertion exacerbated labor shortages over time and resulted in a swelling Asian population in Mexico during the long seventeenth century.

The Production of "Chinos"

The world that came into view on the port side of the galleons as they dropped south past scattered chapels, humble ports, distant mountains, and the occasional plantation underwent significant changes during the sixteenth century. In 1521, Tenochtitlan—one of the world's largest cities, a metropolitan wonder built on a lake—fell to an army of Indigenous and Spanish troops. The extraordinary violence of the city's fall became the subject of numerous elegies, recited for generations in memory of a fading past.[163] Hernando Cortés's expedition in 1519–1521, which began the invasion of central Mexico, coincided with Ferdinand Magellan's storied circumnavigation of the globe. Magellan's five ships sailed west from the Iberian Peninsula in 1519, and several years later, one of them (the *Victoria*) limped up the West African coast to Sanlúcar de Barrameda in 1522. It carried eighteen survivors, who were all that remained of the first European voyage to cross the world's largest ocean.

Subsequent transpacific expeditions departed from the American coast and represented a direct continuation of the wars of Cortés and his captains against the Indigenous polities of central Mexico. Indeed, "all the captains who set off to explore regions of Mesoamerica in 1521 . . . were instructed to look for a way to sail from the Caribbean to the Pacific (or South Sea)."[164] Cortés was responsible for organizing and outfitting no fewer than five Pacific expeditions, and a sixth was in preparation when he departed from Mexico for the last time in 1541.[165] Burgeoning missionary fervor, the desire to conduct long-distance trade with Asia, and zealous advocacy for continued conquest ensured that what became the Viceroyalty of New Spain remained deeply invested in its Pacific connections.[166]

The first successful west-to-east crossing from the Philippines to Mexico occurred in 1565, after more than five unsuccessful attempts across four decades.[167] An Augustinian missionary named Andrés de Urdaneta typically receives the sole credit for this navigational achievement: he and his ailing crew aboard the galleon *San Pedro* arrived at Acapulco on October 8, 1565, four months after departing from the Philippines. In truth, an unlikely patache christened the *San Lucas* had managed to reach the port of Navidad on August 9 of the same year after three months and twenty days with no more than twenty men aboard. The ship's pilot, the Afro-Portuguese Lope Martín, had therefore achieved a success equal to Urdaneta's two months earlier, marking the beginning of the transpacific route that transformed global connectivity in the early modern age.[168]

Meanwhile, Mexico had been transformed in the decades following the fall of Tenochtitlan. During the second half of the sixteenth century, the infamous colonial mines, plantations, and textile mills continued to decimate Indigenous populations struggling to recover from decades of disease, enslavement, and war.[169] Supplementing these diminishing labor pools, thousands of enslaved Africans arrived every year through the ports of Veracruz and Campeche. As Mexico's multiethnic populations rapidly diversified and formed mixed populations, they were categorized in ways that were rapidly codified within colonial law, and over time these laws constituted the sistema de castas.

Robert Schwaller argues that the sistema emerged from a transposed framework originally developed in the Iberian Peninsula, which categorized people based on perceptions of difference and inherited traits.[170] Over time, peninsular ideas of religious purity and nobility created new "social divisions" in the Americas that legally differentiated Spaniards from Indigenous laboring and tribute-bearing subjects.[171] When castas entered colonial discourse, they did so as groups that needed to be controlled, regulated, and castigated. As early as 1533, colonial ordinances characterized "mestizos," predominantly the mixed offspring of Spanish men and Indigenous women, as mobile vagabonds in need of surveillance and guidance.[172] Comparably, in the words of Pablo Sierra Silva, "the earliest legislation on Puebla's African-descent population [1536] defined black men as criminal slaves subject to corporal punishment."[173] Colonial fears born from ideas of inherent difference, discourses of *buen gobierno* (good governance), and local concerns and precedents hardened over time into legal praxis and stereotypes about casta ascriptions.

Each casta collapsed ethnolinguistic identities into metaconstructs that initially meant more in the world of discourse and law than in lived reality. For example, "indio / a" designated an Indigenous, vassal status within the Hispanic World but failed to differentiate among hundreds of discrete communities that had little in common otherwise. Most individuals initially categorized as such recognized the label for what it was: a sociolegal classification and not quite an identity.

Only over time did the castas become meaningful signifiers in the communities to which they were applied. In the case of colonial Zacatecas, Dana Murillo argues that survival in the mines required Indigenous peoples "to create new communities without the organizing structures of the *tlaxilacalli* (the altepetl's neighborhood subunits), juridical autonomy, and a hereditary civil leadership."[174] Thus, spatial proximity, labor, and religiosity had reorganized colonial identities away from strictly ethnolinguistic categories.[175] Similarly, Miguel Valerio demonstrates that "mulatos" in Mexico

City in 1568 found cause for unity around Juan Bautista's petition for a "mulato" hospital. Although the petition failed due to categorical exclusions and prejudices, "a common goal brought the mulatos together and a process of community-building through petitioning ensued."[176] These prescient studies show that as Spanish administrators invented sociolegal categories, new ideas that synthesized disparate communities based on colonial exclusions formed among non-Spanish people.

For Asian subjects, becoming a member of the colonial Mexican sistema de castas as a "chino / a" represented the culmination of a racialized flattening process begun during the transpacific galleon crossing. This was the first time that a single word in the Americas referred to all peoples perceived as Asian and represented a uniquely colonial Mexican orientalism. While the circumstances of the passage—including labor arrangements, physical conditions, and spiritual practices—initiated this process, chinogenesis created a new legal designation for recently disembarked Asians that essentialized an incredible breadth of ethnolinguistic and religious identities into a new people. As "chinos," many Asians in colonial Mexico found new commonalities born of their shared displacement or journey across the Pacific to the Americas.

Curiously, there is no definitive explanation in colonial documents for why Asians became known as "chinos" in Acapulco. Throughout the colonial period, when Asian grumetes received their advances in Manila and Cavite, they were almost always paid as "indios grumetes," with occasional additions to specify their provenance. When they received their pay in Acapulco, they became "chinos." The royal treasury used separate identificatory markers to reference the same individuals when they were in different locations. They had been protected "indio" vassals in the Philippines, but they were vulnerable "chinos" in Mexico.

The transition to "chino / a" was uneven, at least initially. The earliest surviving treasury record volumes from Acapulco, which covered 1590–1592, primarily refer to non-Spanish galleon crews as "indio chino" and sometimes use other identifiers like "lascar" and "pampanga."[177] The "indio chino" label maintained the "indio" designation that predominated in the Philippines, and the addition of "chino" essentially distinguished between the "indios" of Asia and those of the Americas. In the context of Acapulco, the "indios chinos" performed specific, port-related labor, while "indios" of the surrounding areas most often appeared in repartimiento rosters and as local artisans. As more Asians became visible in these treasury records in the late 1590s, "indio / a chino / a" became roughly synonymous with "chino / a."

The exchangeability of terms in Acapulco persisted until 1615, when "chino / a" became the dominant referent. This transition was likely driven by an uptick in the numbers of free and enslaved Asians arriving in Acapulco, consistent with the post-1603 realities of Spanish Manila. It also coincided with the entry of six hundred Indigenous men from Igualapa, Zacatula, Tixtla, and elsewhere, who were assigned through the repartimiento to build Acapulco's Fort of San Diego from November 1615 to April 1617.[178] Thus, the decisive move to label Asians as "chinos" may have been born of the pragmatic need to juridically differentiate Asians at the port from repartimiento laborers.

Sometimes (particularly in settings conferring privilege), *nación* (nation, people, or origin) accompanied the "chino / a" category to differentiate an individual of a specific origin from the "chino / a" mass. Through these descriptive appendages (either ascribed or claimed), historians can track the Asian provenance of individual "chinos." Outside of Acapulco, free Asians often sought to retain the "indio / a" and "indio / a chino / a" labels to reinforce the fact that they could not be enslaved and to confirm their protected status as tribute-paying Indigenous vassal subjects (see Chapter 3).[179]

"Chino / a" itself was an anomaly. Literally it meant Chinese outside of the Americas, and in the Philippines, it was used interchangeably with "Sangley."[180] Thus, as a casta in central Mexico, it should be treated as an entirely separate word. Over time, New Spanish officials became increasingly conscious of the constructed nature of the term. An extraordinary report from 1672 by Martín de Solís Miranda in Mexico City clarifies this process. He wrote that "chino" was a "name used abusively and not with accuracy since [those that] are called and termed this [are] the indios of the Philippine Islands, which are very distant from the Great China [*la gran china*] whose inhabitants are those who should accurately be called chinos and not Filipinos [*filipinenses,* Philippians], who observe different rites and different dogmas."[181] In 1675, Fernando de Haro y Monterroso expanded Miranda's definition of "chino" to all "indios born in the Philippine Islands, who are Japanese, Tartars, Malukan, Sangleyes, Mindanaos, Bengalas, Makassars, Malays, and of other nations . . . next to and close to the great island of Great China which provided the word that is [used in] New Spain and even all of Europe."[182] Geographic anomalies aside, his and Miranda's definitions of "chino" are careful and unique reflections on the word's inaccurate and artificial nature. In puzzling over Catarina de San Juan's ethnicity as a "china," Alonso Ramos repeated the consensus in 1689 that "chinos" were "those who come to these parts from the Orient by way of the Philippine Islands."[183]

Furthermore, the commentaries of these men are consistent with early modern Spanish onomastic traditions. In his *Libro de grandezas y cosas memorables de España* (Book of the great and memorable things of Spain; 1549), Pedro de Medina clarified the metonymical structure of Spanish naming customs. He wrote that the term "moro" (Moor or Muslim) came originally from "mauro," the Spanish word for people from Mauritania in Northwest Africa. Since "mauros" had been Muslims for centuries, all Muslims eventually became known as "moros," regardless of their provenance.[184] This account mirrors Geraldine Heng's observation that "from the late eleventh and the twelfth century onward *Saracens* streamlined a panorama of diverse peoples and populations into a single demographic entity defined by their adherence to the Islamic religion."[185]

Comparably, Samar—the first island in the Philippines to be spotted on the journey west across the Pacific—had originally been called "la Isla Filipina," but eventually, this name "was extended to the entire archipelago."[186] Colín noted that the Philippines had often been called "Islas de los Luzones" and "Las Manilas" after the island and city in the Philippines that Spaniards knew best. He traced this practice to the naming of "las Canarias" (the Canary Islands) after the one island of Gran Canaria.[187]

In New Spain, the best-known Asian polity was unquestionably the Kingdom of China—due, in part, to the crates of Chinese goods arriving every year on the galleons. La China quickly became a cartographic and textual stand-in for all of Asia, complementing the equally common referents of Indias Occidentales (West Indies) and Indias del Poniente (Indies of the Setting Sun).[188] However, Domingo Fernández Navarrete was aware that even China was a foreign construction. In 1676, he wrote that "China" came from the fusion of two words: "Chìn" or "Zing," a common Chinese greeting (perhaps from 幸會), and "Nan" (south, 南).[189] He considered this usage (and others like it) to be an ignorant linguistic imposition by interlopers when the Chinese themselves most commonly referred to their country as "Chung Kue; that is, the Kingdom in the middle" (中國).[190]

Navarrete's awareness was uncommon among Spaniards. Following the tradition of "mauro," "Gran Canaria," and "La isla Filipina," the use of La China as a signifier for all of Asia led to the people who came from those regions becoming known simply as "chinos." Like other casta ascriptions, "chino / a" was a vaguely ocular category, since it was used as a descriptor both in runaway slave notices posted publicly in chapels and cathedrals and in Inquisition records to sequester and physically describe the denounced (see Chapter 4). Still, few could agree on what "chinos" looked like. To exemplify the confusion, in 1665 an unnamed enslaved blasphemer was denounced to the Inquisition for criticizing the Catholic God, the Holy Spirit, and the saints. The inquisitors called witnesses, but they could not agree on how to identify the man. He was variously called a "chino" and a "chino or mulato," and one witness said that "he seemed blacker than mulato."[191] Clearly, "chino / a" was a visual identifier associated with the appearance of non-European descent, but beyond that, details were hazy and situationally contingent. One of the best descriptions from the period comes from Domingo de la Cruz's litigation for freedom in 1678. Originally from Cebu in the Philippines, he argued that the king had freed all "chinos" following rulings in 1659 and 1672, and he should be free "because of how my face looks . . . and [my] features are those of a chino, not mulato, nor any other type [*genero*] of slaves."[192] Therefore, the "chino" category could sometimes conjure up an array of physical signs in the discursive imaginary both associated with and distinct from Blackness.

For Catarina de San Juan and her hagiographers, "china" (like categories of Blackness) equated to ugliness. Catarina miraculously changed her appearance to look more "china" to repel men seeking to abuse her. Ramos provided a great amount of detail about this racial transformation: "in short order, her flesh dried and consumed itself bit by bit, and her facial features molted. Her hair grayed, and the color of her face became more Asian [*se achinó*], such that she looked more old than young, more ugly than beautiful, more brown-colored china than white and Mughal blond, more like a hazel india of the darkest of the Occident than a white and beautiful Oriental of the confines of Arabia Felix."[193] The darkness of the "china" severely contrasted with the implicit beauty of imagined Arabian whiteness. Catarina's virginity and survival depended on her ability to transform herself into a darker, older, and therefore (in the eyes of her hagiographers) less attractive woman.

As these descriptions indicate, over time "chinos" obtained common physical stereotypes despite their numerous differences. Gradually, the urge to impose sameness upon the "chino / a" category merged with the very different drive of "chinos" to find commonalities based on shared social settings. In some respects, these new relationships were not dissimilar from those forged by people within other castas. What differentiated "chinos" was precisely their transpacific context. They had endured a horrific Pacific passage that had collapsed an enormous diversity of physical, social, and cultural signs into a single category in Acapulco. An enslaved woman from the Bay of Bengal, a Kapampangan warrior, and Japanese converts from Nagasaki had all become "chinos." The tremendous essentialism of the "chino / a" label after arrival in the Americas reinforced and expanded the sea-born need to overcome enormous differences to found new communities. Therefore, in more ways than one, the "chinos" who disembarked in Acapulco were not the "indios" who had boarded in Cavite.

Acapulco, the Gateway to Mexico

During the trading season, the population of the port of Acapulco swelled with merchants, missionaries, soldiers, mule trains, the enslaved, sailors, and hangers-on. As the primary destination of the galleons, Mexico's Pacific coast consistently had the largest number of "chinos" in the Americas during the long seventeenth century. Each ship unloaded its contingent of sailors, travelers, and enslaved people in Acapulco, adding to the communities of "chinos" that had stayed on in the off-season. In 1615, the capitana called *Santiago* unloaded sixty "chinos" grumetes and two Cagayan carpenters. The almiranta christened the *San Andrés* carried a contingent of thirty-nine "chinos" grumetes, one "of the Japanese caste," two Cagayan carpenters, and one "chino" guardianejo. The smaller *fragata* (frigate) *Santa Margarita* had nine "chinos" grumetes.[194] These numbers of surviving grumetes were not unusual. In that year, twelve "chinos" had stayed on during the off-season to work in the royal warehouses (receiving 60 pesos per year) or as carpenters (150–200 pesos per year) or blacksmiths (60 pesos per year).[195] Although these twelve accounted only for those who remained on the royal treasury's payroll, their number was smaller than usual. A more typical year was 1600, which better exemplifies the wide range of professions that "chinos" practiced in Acapulco.

In that year, a "chino" named Juan Baptista made 150 pesos per year as the sacristan of the church. A longtime resident of the port named Diego Nunez, described variously as a "lascar" and a "chino," operated one of the *chinchorros* (rowboats) in the bay. He made sixty pesos during the six-month period from November 1, 1599, to the end of April 1600. The chinchorro's crew included five "indios chinos" grumetes, who each made fifty pesos per year. There were eight Asian carpenters in the port, and one of them— Juan Vanegas—was also a *bombero* (fireman). Two of these carpenters, Francisco Cagayan and Juan Cagayan, cut wood in the mountains to build artillery mounts. They labored alongside eight other "chinos" and fourteen "indios."[196] Most "chinos" who remained in Acapulco during the off-season resided in the "neighborhood [*barrio*] that they call of the chinos."[197]

Multiethnic labor gangs that were organized around a trade or an assignment in Acapulco were common. For example, eighty "negros, mulatos, and chinos, free and enslaved by citizens of the said port" repaired the capitana *San Luis,* which had arrived in 1631 without its mainmast. This labor gang hiked into the mountains to cut a new mast and hauled it to the beach, being paid at the significant rate of one peso per person per day. Payment to the enslaved people was awarded to the enslavers.[198] As another example, twenty free or enslaved "negros," "mulatos," and "chinos" worked from September 2 to September 20, 1632, to open trails into the mountains and to cut wood to mount artillery at the Fort of San Diego.[199] Dozens of free or enslaved "chinos" labored in smithies, as carpenters or porters, in quarries, and elsewhere to construct and repair the defenses that protected the bay from enemy incursion. The Spanish demand for labor was so high that one Philippine trader named Marcos Garcia ("chino") traveled overland to Acapulco when the galleons arrived in 1608 and was illegally conscripted into "personal services," meaning a forced obligation to labor for an individual.[200]

Unquestionably, Acapulco relied on "chinos" for a wide range of port-related functions. Most "chinos" had acquired these skills in Cavite and continued practicing their trades aboard the galleons. Some, like a man named Pedro Elen, rose to prominence. He had been the guardianejo aboard the *San Andrés* in 1615, and for the next thirty-one years he served as the drummer of the garrison stationed at the Fort of San Diego.[201] He made 171 pesos per year, and by 1620 he had bought an enslaved "mulata" named Madalena.[202] Even those who made significant earnings, though, had to face substantial restrictions. For example, Diego Nunez, a "chino lascar," worked as a carpenter during the construction of the Fort of San Diego in 1616 and made a maximum of four reales per day, an amount that "he was rated for being chino."[203] As a comparison, even the lowest-paid Spanish carpenters laboring alongside him made one peso per day (double Nunez's rate).[204]

While it is difficult to determine the total numbers of free and enslaved "chinos" in Acapulco in any given year during the seventeenth century, it is safe to say that Asians made up a significant percentage of the population. In 1622, the city had an estimated 70 Spanish residents, and by 1643, the number of Indigenous tribute-payers in the area had declined to 185. By the middle of the seventeenth century, Acapulco had become a predominantly Afro-Mexican town.[205] These demographic realities indicate that as soon as Asians entered colonial society in central Mexico, most found themselves laboring and socializing with Afro-Mexicans at the port; in taverns owned by Black women; and in numerous labor gangs assigned to cut wood, break rocks, and repair ships and buildings. As "chinos" began to articulate new forms of community and identity in Acapulco, distinct from those in the Philippines, they did so within this multiethnic social world organized around Mexico's societies of castas. Matthew Furlong considers this process an adaptation of "traditions of pre-colonial insular Southeast Asian practice which emphasized collateral alliance, tracing of bilateral lineages, exogamous networks, and cross-ethnic social networks."[206]

One of the clearest examples of these relations comes from a bigamy case involving a "chino" tried by the Inquisition in 1669. Gregorio de Benavides (the owner of the hacienda of Apusagualcos in Acapulco) denounced Baltazar Melchor (his "chino" servant) for having married twice. The second wife was an enslaved woman (owned by Benavides) named Bernarda de los Reyes. Though Melchor had been an "indio" in the Philippines (and therefore not subject to the Inquisition), in New Spain he could be prosecuted because he had become a "chino."

In 1619, Pineda had reported a "great offense": that since married grumetes "are not known [as married in Mexico], they marry again."[207] Melchor exemplified the trend: he had married only two months after disembarking in Mexico. A diverse slew of witnesses testified that they had either heard or knew that Melchor had been married to a woman named

Fulana Sinio in Lolo (in Cagayan, the Philippines). The first witness was a "mulata" widow named Isabel de Aracas (also known as Isabel Guerra), who had heard about Melchor's marriage to Sinio from a recently disembarked "chino" named Francisco. The second witness, Francisca de Pineda (a free Black woman), gathered that Benavides had discovered the scandalous situation from a "chino" named Juan, who had written him a letter about it. The third witness, a "mulata" named Geronima Arias, declared that her son, Luis Hortiz, had read Juan's letter aloud, and everyone who heard it had laughed at Juan's awkward writing style and language. The fourth witness, a "chino" (also from Lolo) named Domingo de la Peña, had traveled with Melchor across the Pacific to Acapulco and knew that Melchor had been married. However, this witness had left Cagayan six years before and did not know if Fulana Sinio was still alive. The fifth witness, Phelipe Cortes (a "chino" from Maribeles in the Philippines and a *vecino* [citizen] of Acapulco), had discussed the matter with Peña and don Andres (a "chino" grumete), and the latter had confirmed Melchor's previous marriage.[208]

This case wonderfully exhibits how networks of information functioned through the maintenance of transpacific social relations, the closeness of members in the diverse community of "chinos" in Acapulco, and the development of multiethnic social and kinship relations. Residents of the port, like the Afro-Mexican witnesses, also had access to the latest news and gossip on the galleons and even found comedic relief in the linguistic differences between themselves and recently arrived "chinos." In the end, the inquisitors could not determine with certainty if Fulana Sinio was still alive, so they ordered that she be located. The case ended with this order, and we can assume that the time required for transpacific crossings and the necessity of traversing Luzon either discouraged or outright prevented the order from being carried out. Although he had caused a scandal and possibly angered his new bride, Melchor received no punishment.

From the second-class brutalities of the transpacific journey to chinogenesis in Acapulco, the Pacific passage marked Asian subjects' transition to a new space of race thinking in the Hispanic World. After disembarking, Asians suddenly became members of an undifferentiated mass within an existing web of social relations of power.[209] It is true that Asians were not always reminded of their juridical "chino / a" status in many of their daily encounters. But in legal settings that decided their access to privilege, their casta mattered deeply—especially as colonial administrators developed new ordinances and ossified stereotypes intended to control non-Spanish, poor, and enslaved populations.

With the salt stench of the Pacific trailing them inland, the survivors of the galleon odyssey trekked into a strange environment filled with incipient dangers and, for a few people, tenuous opportunities. Inland from the Pacific coast, Asian subjects generated even more curiosity—and suspicion— among their new neighbors. Throughout central Mexico, Asians began seeking new ways to distinguish themselves from popular stereotypes, with the goal of integrating into marketplaces, parishes, and neighborhoods filled with Spanish, Indigenous, Afro-Mexican, and mixed residents.

3 Merchants and Gunslingers

THE TREK INLAND from the hot lowlands of Acapulco to the viceregal capital would have been a brutal introduction to life in Mexico beyond the transpacific port. As "chinos" confronted the punishing terrain in their effort to reach the central highlands, they became visible subjects of the Viceroyalty of New Spain's cosmopolitan core. With the eyes of the colonial elite on them, they became characterized as yet another subset of Mexico's unruly urban poor. Combating this conception, numerous "chinos" sought to differentiate themselves to achieve some measure of social mobility against the grain. The path inland, therefore, represented a transition away from a coastal zone slowly adapting to transpacific contact toward an area in which the presence of non-Spanish people conjured up the specter of subversion, rebellion, and non-Hispanic customs.

The route from Acapulco to Mexico City covered 280 miles and was widely known as the *camino de china* (Asia Road; figure 3.1). Couriers on horseback regularly covered this ground in three days, but fully packed mule trains traveled at a top speed of twelve miles per day (even less in the mountains).[1] For most people, the journey lasted many weeks. The globe-trotting Spanish missionary Pedro Cubero Sebastián wrote that the Asia Road was one "of the most rugged that I have walked in my life because there is nothing but ravines, mountains, crags, and precipices, the deepest that there are in the world, and I can assure that it is only this until arriving at [Tixtla]. It is one of the most rugged paths of all that I have walked."[2] In fact, the route was so onerous that the Jesuit Pedro de Montes (already weak from the Pacific crossing) died along it in 1610, halfway to Mexico

3.1 A Map of Mexico or New Spain, from the Latest Authorities

This map of Mexico from the late colonial period provides an excellent view of the towns along the Pacific coast with notable Asian populations: Acapulco, Petatlán, Colima, and so on. It also usefully represents the distance from Acapulco to Mexico City. The winding paths through the mountains greatly elongated the journey, which would have been far shorter had it been possible to travel in a straight line.

John Lodge, *A Map of Mexico or New Spain, from the Latest Authorities* (London: J. Bew Pater Noster Row, 1782). Reproduction courtesy of the John Carter Brown Library.

City.[3] After berating previous authors for exaggerating the hardships of the road from Veracruz to Mexico City, Domingo Fernández Navarrete described the Asia Road as follows: "yes, it is bad and arduous, mountains up to the clouds, as rugged as can be said, mighty rivers. . . . I assume there are no bridges, mosquitos, yes, and many, and biting things [*Caribes*], as many as can be said. Some nights, one sleeps under the stars."[4]

In the mountains, the climate quickly turned wet. After five days, the Italian Giovanni Francesco Gemelli Careri complained of the cold.[5] When he reached San Agustín de las Cuevas, the last stop before Mexico City, it snowed.[6] Traveling in lumbering mule trains, free and enslaved "chinos" ascending to higher altitudes confronted the Papagayo River, "one of the most feared in all of New Spain for having drowned so many men."[7] The Balsas River was another deadly obstacle. When the rivers were high, travelers sat on their saddles on a raft of gourds bound together, while Indigenous and enslaved porters swam alongside to guide the rafts across. After witnessing this ordeal, Navarrete commented, "seeing that ridiculous assemblage causes disgust."[8] According to the Italian Francesco Carletti, "even the viceroy passes by there with the same difficulty and danger when he goes from Mexico [City] to embark at that port of Acapulco."[9]

Along the way, the mule trains passed various customs inspection posts, the trapiche of Bazatlán, the corn-growing valley of Chilpancingo, the inland trade crossroad of Huejotzingo, and Huichilaque (a summit town near Cuernavaca), known for its *pulque* (alcohol made from maguey cactus). The caravans typically stopped at inns with names like *Peregrino* (Pilgrim) and *Los dos caminos* (The Two Paths) in Indigenous towns, which were required to provide travelers with accommodations and provisions.[10] According to Careri, mule trains moving between settlements relied on hunting birds in the mountains (such as parrots, turtledoves, and chachalacas) for sustenance and searched for flat ground on which to camp.[11] During the wet season, travelers like Navarrete constantly battled swarms of mosquitos, venomous snakes in the trees, and even pumas.[12]

The contrast between the grueling trek through the mountains and the arrival in Mexico City, the sprawling viceregal core, cannot be overstated. Having overcome the deadliest sea and land journeys of their time, "chinos" finally arrived in the largest metropolis in the Americas (figure 3.2). Here, they participated in the social interactions, economic exchanges, and religious rituals that constituted colonial public life and discourse. In so doing, they caught the attention of local diarists and observers who were already marveling at the stunning array of newly available Asian merchandise in the plazas.

Shortly after the arrival of the first Manila galleons in the 1560s, the capital's denizens became increasingly aware of how transpacific connections transformed colonial society and culture. For them, the maritime link to Asia was visible primarily through the arrival of trade goods. As early as 1574, Mexico City's cosmopolitan elite had begun praising the quantity, quality, and variety of Chinese products available in the city.[13] Bernardo de Balbuena crafted timeless stanzas in his *Grandeza mexicana* (1604) on how the city contained more trade and treasure "than the north cools or even the sun warms."[14] He provided a spectacular list of commodities available in the city's markets, roughly half of which came from Asia—including

3.2 View of the Plaza Mayor of Mexico City

Cristóbal de Villalpando's iconic view of the Baroque capital was an aspirational vision of a cosmopolitan world centered on trade, spectacle, and opulence. The walled market in the foreground was the Parian, named after the famed Chinese quarter of Manila. It was not complete in 1695, when the painting was created, but its construction was a microcosm of the city's grandeur and marvels. It is particularly significant that Mexico City appears here as a thriving metropolis, since the painting omits any evidence of the uprising in 1692 that had destroyed much of the plaza. "Chinos" were thought to have been among the ringleaders of the riot. For more information on the Villalpando and the uprising, respectively, see Stephanie Merrim, *The Spectacular City, Mexico, and Colonial Hispanic Literary Culture* (Austin: University of Texas Press, 2010), 245; "Sumaria contra Antonio de Arano y otros: Motín de México," AGI, 1692, Patronato, 226, N.1, R.6; R. Douglas Cope, *The Limits of Racial Domination: Plebeian Society in Colonial Mexico City, 1660–1720* (Madison: University of Wisconsin Press, 1994), 139.

Cristóbal de Villalpando, *Vista de la plaza mayor de la Ciudad de México,* 1695.

"from Ternate / Fine cloves, and cinnamon from Tidore. / From Cambray textile, from Quinsay captives [*rescate*] . . . of the great China, colored silks."[15] For Balbuena, the commercial realm morphed into a cabinet of curiosities, a sublime metaphor for "cultural capital," viceregal pride, and divine favor.[16]

However, the maravilla at the core of Balbuena's praise of Asian products rarely extended to the influx of people who accompanied them. "Chinos" entering the capital evoked a range of conflicting responses from its European residents. Local observations ranged from occasional hopefulness about the benefits of transpacific connection to denigrations that centered on the social dangers of casta mobility. Thomas Gage and Careri represent the two ends of this continuum. Of Mexico City, Gage noted that "above all the goldsmiths' shops and works are to be admired. The Indians, and the people of China [Asia] that have been made Christians and every year come thither, have perfected the Spaniards in that trade."[17] In contrast, Careri described a violent event during the Easter festivities of 1697. Three days before Easter, he recalled a procession of confraternities and, in particular, the presence of the brothers of San Francisco, "which is called the procession of the chinos, for being of indios of the Philippines." The celebration quickly turned violent: "arriving at the royal palace, a conflict started up between the chinos and the brothers of the Santísima Trinidad over who would go first, such that they fought with maces and the crosses on their backs in such a way that many were left wounded."[18]

Careri's description of disruptive "chinos" was far more representative of opinion in the capital than Gage's praise. The fastidious diaries of Gregorio Martín de Guijo and Antonio de Robles (written in 1648–1664 and 1665–1703, respectively) registered the presence of "chinos" primarily through the criminal acts attributed to them and the ensuing punishments. Robles's notation for Monday, June 2, 1681, exemplified the trend: "They hanged two men, a chino and a mulato."[19] "Chinos" also frequently appeared alongside "negros," "mulatos," and "mestizos" in ordinances issued by the Real Audiencia. Motivated by fears of public disturbance and violent acts, the ordinances sometimes prevented members of these castas from moving freely throughout central Mexico, joining Spanish guilds, and practicing various trades.

Broadly speaking, the non-Spanish, non-Indigenous masses represented vagabondage, unassimilated behavior, and rebelliousness—stereotypes that time only reinforced. Catarina de San Juan's introduction to central Mexican society illustrates many of these tropes. Priests and residents of Puebla often regarded her as a "trickster" for the seeming contrast between her "china" identity and her piety.[20] Captain Miguel de Sosa tested her "loyalty" by leaving a few reales on the ground to see if she would steal or return them.[21] She threw them in the trash.

From the humiliating disarming of don Balthazar de San Francisco in 1612 to the imprisonment of a man named Lorenzo for cutting hair during a religious festival in 1650, the treatment of the "chinos" of central Mexico exemplifies the limits of colonial social mobility. The Spanish assumption that "chinos" were inherently devious made their participation in even mundane tasks and trades risky endeavors. Nevertheless, several scholars have characterized the free "chinos" of Mexico as exceptional subjects, whose treatment allegedly demonstrates the openness and lenience of colonial society. Edward Slack delivered one such defense, writing that "a willing acceptance or tolerance of Asian people and products [in New Spain] . . . stands in stark contrast to the historical experiences of European nations during the same time frame."[22] Similarly, in studying the family of the very wealthy Japanese majordomo of the Guadalajara cathedral, Melba Falck Reyes and Héctor Palacios note that the family's success "reveals, on the one hand, a flexible society that knew to recognize the genius entrepreneur [the Japanese Juan de Páez] without import given to his racial origin, and on the other hand, a capacity to ascend to the top of that society."[23] Finally, though with more nuance, Rainer Buschmann, Edward Slack, and James Tueller write the following about the Chinese-Philippine Antonio Tuason's social advancement: "In [contrast to the Philippines, in] Nueva España someone with Tuason's résumé—in spite of his racial status—would have been incorporated into the ranks of the local political elite."[24] Taken together, these interpretations project the image of an equitably integrated colonial society populated by exceptional and free Asian subjects. Examples of enslaved "chinos" remain conspicuously absent from these arguments.

This scholarship has, even if unintentionally, framed early modern "chinos" as the earliest example of the trope of the exceptional Asian immigrant, known in its most recent formulation as the model minority myth. In the twentieth century, this trope crystallized around the encouragement of obedience, the idealization of meritocracy, and the application of a good / bad immigrant framework to the achievement (or not) of social mobility.[25] "Compliant subjectivity and hard work," in the words of Yoonmee Chang, became the key traits of model minority behavior.[26]

Applying the rhetoric of the exceptional migrant to global diasporic populations (including the early modern Asians who are the subject of this book) ultimately contributes to this assimilative racial project. Like contemporary model minority discourse, the scholarship on "chino / a" success in New Spanish society implies that other casta groups failed because they were less industrious and ideologically conforming, and it normalizes the expectation of productivity in Asian communities.[27] Such romanticized accounts of New Spanish cultural pluralism and Asian assimilation in the Americas form an apologistic image of colonial society. The exceptional cases cited in these texts that are meant to exemplify the egalitarianism of New Spain in fact, in the words of Stanley and Barbara Stein, preserve "the essence of social stratification."[28] They actually signal that the majority of "chinos" and people in other castas could not reach the upper echelons of colonial society. Without Spanish kinship ties or lineage, most "chinos" struggled.

Moreover, as the Steins suggest, arguments for New Spanish cultural pluralism also misread the exceptions. "Chinos" who achieved significant social mobility did so only with great difficulty and much good fortune. For example, three Asians attained the notable distinction of enrolling in the Royal University of Mexico (operational from 1553 to 1865).[29] They were the Japanese "indio" Manuel de Santa Fe (who earned a bachelor of philosophy degree in 1674), the Kapampangan Nicolás de la Peña (who enrolled in 1691 as a student of rhetoric), and the Philippine Native Ignacio de Oruega Manesay (who enrolled as a student in 1695). To study at this institution, all three confronted statute 226 of its constitution, which banned "chinos morenos" and members of other castas. These students were permitted to enroll only because they had light skin and argued successfully that they had no discernible Muslim background and were not descended from slaves.[30]

To practice their trades and feed their families without abuse, socially mobile Asians similarly navigated Baroque bureaucracies and interpersonal prejudices. Examining the complexities of these troubled attempts to climb the social ladder reveals the quotidian manifestations of colonial racial discourse. Furthermore, Asians' confrontations with colonial law occurred when the region's non-Spanish populations had begun to create a new status quo by articulating new "ideas of protection, liberty, possession, guilt, autonomy, voice, common good, rebellion, and reconciliation" during the early seventeenth century.[31] These contestations emerged from the ascendance of the first truly "colonial" generation in central Mexico: a generation whose members were born into a world in which no one had experienced the region's pre-Hispanic past.[32] Rather than raise arms, this generation often pursued social and economic advancement through litigation.

As new constituents of this multiethnic cohort, free "chinos" entered courtrooms to contest exclusionary laws. To do so, they first had to differentiate themselves from discriminatory stereotypes about unacculturated non-Spaniards in colonial Mexican discourse and law. To prove that they had assimilated Hispanic culture and to acquire social prestige linked to confessional and mercantile communities, many joined confraternities, became godparents, entered Catholic marriages, and established multiethnic credit networks.[33] One of the most important ways in which Asians could mitigate the disadvantages of their "chino / a" categorization and improve their social status was integration into Indigenous communities.[34] By reclaiming the "indio / a" status they had lost in Acapulco, "chinos" could benefit once more from the "royal paternalism" that at least nominally sought to protect Indigenous peoples from the violent intentions of many mid-ranking colonial officials.[35] Even after the "chino / a" label became dominant in Acapulco, many Asians continued to describe themselves as "indios chinos" elsewhere in Mexico for precisely this reason.[36]

Some Asians succeeded in formalizing their transition to "indio / a" by paying tribute to *encomenderos* (holders of *encomiendas* [grants of Indigenous tribute and labor]) and other colonial officials via tribute collectors.[37] The amounts that Indigenous people paid depended on an individual's *cabecera* (political and economic unit), *sujeto* (place), and status in a variety of social hierarchies.[38] Paying these tributes was an assertion of colonial personhood and freedom, since most Indigenous peoples were formally protected from indefinite bondage (though this was never a guarantee).[39] However, some Asians evaded the tribute obligations and legal restrictions of "indio / a" categorization when it was juridically expedient, principally when they were attempting to join the local elite. Otherwise, free "chinos" paid tribute taxes equal to those paid by free Afro-Mexican communities. For example, in Acapulco in 1640 the tributes of "free chinos, mulatos, and negros" (averaging 1 or 2 pesos per person per year) funded repairs to the Fort of San Diego.[40] Similarly, "chinos" were ordered to pay their tributes alongside "negros" and "free mulatos" in and around Toluca in 1676.[41] Therefore, what Norah Gharala has so aptly called the colonial "tax on blackness" occasionally applied to Asians.[42]

However, the genres of licenses and license petitions most clearly exemplify the legal efforts of "chinos" to counter the effects of discriminatory stereotypes. To carry weapons, sell various products, and practice specific trades, "chinos" in Mexico City and other densely populated settlements in central Mexico had to apply for licenses. To "chinos" coming from Acapulco and the Pacific coast, where licensing was uncommon, these requirements must have initially seemed unusual. During the seventeenth century, it was not uncommon to find "chinos" in Acapulco serving in the garrison at the Fort of San Diego (fifty did so in 1672), as shore sentinels along the Pacific coast, or as traders, all without licenses.[43] For example, the 1618 will of Domingo de Villalobos, a Kapampangan merchant and citizen of Michoacán, inventories a sword, dagger, harquebus, pistol, and katana. No record exists that legally permitted him to possess these weapons or sell goods.[44] The fact that there were "chinos" who were armed and traveled (sometimes both at once) should not be surprising. As we saw in Chapter 1, Tagalog and Kapampangan peoples had already distinguished themselves as steadfast allies of Spanish troops in Southeast Asia, especially after 1603, and many sought to maintain this reputation in the Americas. Elites often retained or invented "don" titles after the Pacific crossing and quickly joined the ranks of the upwardly socially mobile.

By contrast, Spanish officials made it clear that "chinos" in the viceregal core could not enjoy the flexibility of life in Acapulco or the countryside, where institutional oversight tended to be minimal or nonexistent. In Mexico City and other heavily populated urban areas, "chinos" found themselves distrusted and suspected of criminal intent. To combat these perceptions, "chinos" approached Spanish authorities with written claims of loyal, Hispanic behavior to acquire "social legitimacy" through special privileges.[45] According to R. Douglas Cope, petitions of this variety answered "unspoken accusations of laziness, immorality, and unreliability."[46]

Yet social advancement for "chinos" remained uneven and contested at best. Robert Schwaller has argued that weapon licenses allowed individuals "to undercut and transcend . . . the negative views of prevailing society."[47] In other words, licenses designated exceptions to racializing laws against castas, thereby functioning as tacit declarations of allegiance by the colonial administration to non-Spanish individuals. But although licenses awarded special privileges in name, in practice they typically failed to enable what they authorized. Local magistrates and officials habitually impeded "chinos'" ability to make use of licenses. Of the thirty-three "chino" licenses and license petitions between 1591 and 1666 that I have examined, only two do not explicitly complain about such cases of illegal impediment. In this sense, petitions for licenses had much in common with contemporaneous Indigenous petitions seeking *amparo* (protection) against abusive officials.[48] The constant abuse documented in license and amparo petitions indicates that the licenses did little to curb inequity and intolerance over time. In fact, they made no pretense of doing so. In the words of Brian Owensby, such protections merely sought "to secure an environment within which accommodations could be reached that would promote social peace," and therein lay their failure to enact the protection they prescribed.[49]

This chapter centers on two key types of licenses and petitions: one for bearing weapons and the other for merchants and traders to demonstrate how "chinos" sought to circumvent the repercussions of restrictive legal regimens and discrimination. Securing a license for bearing weapons signified the acquisition of social capital and prestige, while a trading license portended economic growth. However, anecdotes about impediment and abuse surrounding both kinds of licenses reveal the daily frictions that hampered the pursuit of these legally sanctioned paths to advancement. Furthermore, the petitions and licenses exhibit a set of increasingly complex rhetorical and textual strategies, in which "chinos" articulated new forms of identity to confront and surmount deeply rooted perceptions of otherness. Cases of licensing ultimately demonstrate that transpacific migrants were far from being exceptional subjects and experienced the same sort of daily struggles as non-Spaniards facing similar exclusions in Mexico.

The Armed "Chino"

On Santo Domingo's feast day, August 4, in 1645, two militia battalions of free Afro-Mexican men wielding swords and shields took to the streets of Veracruz, vowing to kill all "white faces."[50] In their fury, they left five dead and two seriously wounded, prompting the colonial administration to pass an *ordenanza* (ordinance or bylaw) fourteen days later banning all "negros," "mestizos," "mulatos," "chinos," and "zambaigos" (mixed Afro-Indigenous people) from carrying arms. The ordinance also nullified licenses that had already been approved. Habitually in fear of subversive activity and multiethnic coalitions, administrators tended to lump multiple casta groups together, regardless of their members' alleged involvement in any action. Anyone violating the order would be publicly whipped, receiving two hundred lashes; have an ear cut off; and be sent to labor in one of New Spain's notorious textile mills for the "time necessary." If more than three individuals categorized as "negro," "mestizo," "mulato," "chino," or "zambaigo" were caught out together at night, they would all receive two hundred lashes, have an ear cut off, and be sentenced to labor in a textile mill for three years. If more than four were found walking about together during daylight hours, all would receive two hundred lashes, have both ears cut, and be sent to labor for six months in a textile mill.[51] Allegations against a few individuals resulted in the enactment of legislation that affected multiple groups.

Weapon bans like this order echoed past, unevenly implemented measures to limit non-Spanish people's access to arms that stretched back to 1537.[52] Despite the harsh terms of the ordinances, exceptions had been made before and would be made again in the form of approvals for and reissuing of weapon licenses. Schwaller characterizes this process as an example of the paradox of Spanish colonial law, which simultaneously restrained and exempted people—creating uneven loci of power based on Iberian notions of privilege and honor.[53]

But why might a "chino"—or, for that matter, a member of any other casta—with weapons have been considered a threat? Exemplifying Homi Bhabha's concept of "colonial mimicry," the weapon-toting "chino" had become a transgressive symbol, blurring distinctions between the assimilated and unassimilated or the Hispanicized and un-Hispanicized.[54] The weapons—typically swords and daggers, and sometimes harquebuses—

located agency and power in subjects whose motives and allegiance were open to suspicion.[55] "Chino" knowledge of how to use the weapons further destabilized the line between colonizer and colonized, for the early modern science of swordplay had become a metaphor used to justify violent action in wars of colonial conquest.[56] Nonetheless, the license to bear arms was a weapon of the colonial bureaucracy used to designate privilege and allegiance. It was a form of recouping and reclaiming the power that weapons gave to non-Spaniards. In this sense, both the license and the discriminatory legislation to which it responded were entangled in the same process of consolidating colonial hegemony.

To receive a license, a person had to submit either a written or oral petition to the viceroy, who called in witnesses as needed before making a decision. An *escribano* (scribe) then made a written notation of the case, adding or omitting details as they saw fit. Approved licenses and the scribe's record would then be transcribed into volumes of license briefs. It is these volumes that historians have access to today, along with a few loose-leaf petitions. The license petition often included requests to waive tribute obligations or *alcabalas* (sales taxes imposed on members of free, non-Indigenous castas), signaling the text's work as a document of upward mobility.[57] Courts awarded most of these licenses to heads of households who demonstrated financial need, had good reputations, hailed from certain regions, and had proved their allegiance or pacification. Schwaller demonstrates that Afro-Mexican petitioners strategically appealed to these Iberian expectations of honor and masculinity.[58]

Indeed, Black men in the Americas had petitioned for merit based on military service since at least the 1530s and some (such as guards in Mexico City during the Gil Ávila-Martín Cortés conspiracy of 1566) had been successful.[59] Ann Twinam identifies the 1578 petition of Sebastian de Toral, a Black man from Portugal living in the Yucatan, as among these first cases in which "the traditional reciprocity that existed between the king and his white vassals might also extend to the castas."[60] Merit, proof of loyalty, and Hispanicization allowed Toral to argue successfully that he should be exempt from paying tribute. Twinam concludes that this move "was a first step in blurring ethnic identity over the generations."[61]

However, even the awarding of a license or exemption from tribute or taxes is better described as a process than as a decisive event. *Justicias* (local magistrates and judges) regularly prevented "chinos" and members of other castas (and even dark-skinned Spaniards) from acquiring or possessing weapons.[62] They requested to see licenses for proof of lawful carrying, but they often disregarded or destroyed these licenses, forcing frustrated subjects back to Mexico City (the viceregal capital) to request reissuance. Justicias constantly revised or overturned the actions of high-ranking court officials and exercised their power to impede, enforce, and deny within their jurisdictions. Kathryn Burns argues that Spanish officials' unlawful removal of weapons based on physical appearance was an early modern form of racial profiling.[63] Although the probability of justicia interference certainly increased for "chinos" after the 1645 ordinance, problems existed from the earliest petitions, since weapon bans were already in effect when the first Asians landed in colonial Mexico.[64]

Juan Alonso, an "indio chino," was the first Asian to receive licenses in New Spain: first to ride horseback in 1591 and then to lead a larger pack of mules and carry a sword and a dagger in 1597. Riding a horse with bit and saddle (as opposed to riding bareback) was not only a utilitarian allowance but also a sign of acculturation. Between 1591 and 1597, however, justicias prevented Alonso from using a pack of twenty mules for farm work. Citing an ordinance that prohibited "indios" from owning more than six mules, they interrupted his labor and punished him by ordering him to pay as tribute the corn he had grown in ten *brazas* (Castilian yards) for each mule.[65] Alonso contested this ordinance by arguing that as a "chino," he was exempt from orders pertaining to "indios" and from the meddlesome justicias that enforced them.

Ten days later, Alonso appeared before the court again, testifying that his rights to ride horseback with bit and saddle, as well as to wear a sword, had been ignored again. Once more, justicias cited an earlier ordinance that banned "indios" from both riding horseback and carrying swords. Ignoring Alonso's designation as an "indio chino" or a "chino," the justicias merely observed that a man they recognized as an "indio" had violated colonial ordinances. However, the court ruled that since Alonso was not *natural* (native) to the region with this restriction, "the said order should not apply."[66] As an "indio chino," therefore, he was not held to the same rules as "indios" from New Spain.

At this early date, the viceregal court clearly had not yet established a fixed standard for categorizing people who came from across the Pacific and issuing rulings based on those categories. Alonso's rhetorical strategies exemplify the casuistic or individualistic nature of Spanish colonial law, since administrators adapted historical precedents in their jurisdictions rather than applying "unswerving" law codes.[67] Alonso managed to use both sides of his "indio chino" identification to play the court against the justicias. From 1599 to 1612, six "chinos" copied Alonso's strategy to be allowed to ride horseback.[68]

The petition of Melchior de los Reyes, a Kapampangan man, reveals another salient rhetorical strategy. De los Reyes approached the court in 1610 to decry justicia impediment, not unlike Alonso. The timing of the complaint coincided with a wave of Spanish paranoia about Black rebellion and maroon communities (like the one founded by the famed Gaspar Yanga) which intensified fears of other non-Spanish populations.[69] De los Reyes sought a license to carry a sword and a dagger and considered himself an "amigo" in dealing with Spaniards. This word established him as the opposite of a maroon and referenced the decades-long history that Kapampangan warriors had in Spanish colonial armies. Kapampangans had fought with distinction most recently alongside the Dimarocots against the "Sangleyes" in 1603 and in Pedro de Acuña's campaign to retake Ternate in 1606. In distinguishing himself from those non-Spanish populations whom the Spanish feared would rebel, De los Reyes successfully leveraged his own and his people's transpacific history of collaboration to win special privilege in Mexico.[70]

The Spanish fear of rebellion affected other Asian petitioners as well. In 1612, don Balthazar de San Francisco requested a reissuance of his license to bear arms after Juan Carlos, an alcalde mayor, had disregarded his previous license, unceremoniously disarmed him, and fined him eight pesos. San Francisco was an "indio chino" from Manila, and the "don" in his name suggested noble heritage. The timing of his petition was crucial, as 1612 marked a feverish pitch (a "colonial psychosis") of anti-Black sentiment in Mexico City and its environs.[71] In the days before Easter, rumors had spread throughout the city of an imminent Black uprising that sought to overthrow colonial rule and brutalize Spanish women. "Was it not [started by] some mischievous Spanish youth?" wondered don Domingo de San Antón Muñón Chimalpahin Quauhtlehuanitzin, an Indigenous intellectual and chronicler.[72] As Miguel Valerio demonstrates, these rumors manifested the existential Spanish fear of Afro-Mexican festive culture, maroons in the countryside, and a Black protest in 1611 against the wrongful death of an enslaved woman at the hands of her enslaver.[73]

Several days before Easter, town criers had read new bans on the carrying of weapons and wearing of Spanish clothes by Black and mixed men. No more than two "chinos" were now permitted to be in the personal retinues of Spanish elites. By May 2, twenty-eight men and seven women, allegedly conspirators in the planned uprising, had been hanged.[74] San Francisco's disgrace at the hands of the alcalde mayor occurred amid these heightened fears of casta conspiracy. Like De los Reyes, he had been driven to the courts by the impediments of local officials, and he sought redress from stereotypes against people who looked like him and shared his casta.[75]

In the years immediately following 1645, the increasingly elaborate nature of the petitions implies that over time such redress became more difficult to procure and exercise. In 1653, Francisco de Lima penned two petitions for licenses to carry a sword, a dagger, and a harquebus. In both petitions, he categorized himself as a "free chino from Bengala" (he was one of the few free individuals from the Bay of Bengal in the Americas) and a vecino of Querétaro.[76] He operated a mule train that sold food and other goods to miners in Escanela in exchange for silver. Such mercantile businesses in mining towns tended to be very lucrative throughout the colonial period.[77] Like most other petitioners, Lima defined his occupation as the source of the income he needed to pay tributes to the king and support his family (in his case, a wife and children). Traveling to Escanela, Mexico City, and Querétaro, he had to pass through land contested by the "Chichimeca," a general term applied to nomadic or rebellious peoples in the northern reaches of the viceroyalty who resisted Spanish incursions.[78] Itinerant "mestizos" before him had often used the threat of Chichimeca violence to procure licenses for weapons.[79] During the early and middle parts of the seventeenth century, Chichimeca bandits often ambushed poorly armed muleteers.[80] According to Dana Murillo, in New Galicia Indigenous peoples' "familiarity with the terrain and their sharpened martial skills often left the colonizers on the defensive."[81] Lima insisted that his petition was to carry arms not for mere decoration because the Chichimeca and highwaymen robbed merchants every day along the roads he traveled and he needed weapons to train them to respect travelers. He claimed that the only way to let "indios" know he carried weapons (and keep them from ambushing him) was to fire a harquebus periodically through the night.

These two petitions illuminate a web of relations and perceptions that reveal the in-between status of socially mobile "chinos." Lima claimed to need weapons to protect himself against the Chichimeca. Whether or not this was true, it was believable that the Chichimeca were an enemy of both "chinos" and Hispanic society and that the Chichimeca saw "chinos" as their enemy. Lima positioned his own interests alongside those of the Spaniards who received his petition. Like Alonso, he distanced himself from the category of "indio" by highlighting the distinction between himself and Chichimeca bandits. He relied on the fact that the Spanish feared the Chichimeca more than they feared him, even referring to a new ordinance that allowed people to get a license to carry weapons to defend themselves on the road.[82]

Although no direct evidence remains to show whether Lima received a license, we do know that his mule trains were so successful that in 1661 he could afford to pay seven hundred pesos for a trapiche in Xilitla, to the northeast of Querétaro. Operating a trapiche required significant resources, not least of which were enslaved people, oxen, horses, and mules to turn the machinery, as well as mule trains for transporting goods across long distances.[83] The timing of his purchase coincided with a broader turn in the New Spanish economy away from mining, which had begun to falter, and toward agricultural production. Like other early entrepreneurs, Lima made what he thought would be a more stable investment. Over time, he also managed to acquire an *estancia de ganado mayor* (a square league of land to raise horned cattle) and three *caballerías* (about 100 acres of agricultural land each).[84] He may have found temporary success, but by 1693, his land was described as "depopulated," and only one free "mulato," Antonio Enriques, was left to look after the abandoned warehouses. Juan de Lima, Francisco's son and heir, failed to prevent a nearby convent from repossessing the land after his father died.[85]

After 1645, other "chinos," like Juan Tello de Guzmán, presented themselves as pacified subjects to convince Spanish authorities to allow them to carry a sword and a dagger. Like Francisco de Lima, Guzmán was a traveling merchant, and he presented a petition in 1651 on grounds similar to those used by Lima. To practice the trade that allowed Guzmán to pay tributes and sustain his family, he claimed to need to carry a sword and a dagger. He also noted "decoration of his person" as an additional reason for carrying weapons, which signifies a departure from a rigidly pragmatic petition like Lima's.[86] The viceroy approved Guzmán's petition on the grounds that he was "a calm and peaceful man and that he lives honorably."[87] This "free chino," a citizen of Mexico City, posed no threat to the colonial order and could therefore carry weapons to advance his station.

Dedicated and loyal militarism was an effective rhetorical positioning as well. A Kapampangan man named Marcos de Villanueva arrived in Mexico in 1646, where he married a Spanish woman and was quickly licensed to carry a harquebus. After his license had been annulled in response to the 1645 disturbance in Veracruz, he petitioned to have it reissued. The document he submitted recounted his long and decorated list of service on Luzon at the head of eighty infantrymen during the "Sangley" uprising of 1639, on Ternate, on Mindanao, and against the Dutch. He even summoned don Sebastián de Corcuera, a former governor of the Philippines, to testify on his behalf and confirm his military record. Villanueva received a new license in 1654 with an acknowledgment that "chinos" from the province of Pampanga had special privileges for their services to the crown.[88] For individuals seeking privilege in Mexico after 1645, claiming Hispanicization and past participation in wars of colonial power projection in Asia remained significant strategies.

Two Japanese petitions for a license to carry weapons survive, one written before 1645 and the other written after. In their attempts to avoid being classified as "chino," the petitioners described themselves as "of the Japanese nación." Just as Villanueva had invoked the Kapampangans' military reputation, these petitioners relied on Spanish ethnographic awareness of the Japanese as a distinct people. During the late sixteenth and early seventeenth centuries, several Japanese embassies traveled through Mexico en route to Spain and Rome to meet with European sovereigns and to visit the religious center of the Catholic world. They generated widespread interest in Mexico, as the presence there of foreign representatives of sovereign states was exceedingly rare. Chimalpahin wrote that the Japanese ambassadors "seem bold, not gentle and meek people, going about like eagles," and that "their hair is rather long at the neck; they put together something like a *piochtli,* which they tie in twisted, intertwined fashion, reaching the middle of the head with close shaving."[89] His reference to pi-ochtli likened Japanese hairstyles to those of Indigenous Nahua boys of central Mexico.

Chimalpahin believed that the arrival of embassies in 1610 (led by Tanaka Shōsuke) and 1613 (led by Hasekura Rokuemon Tsunenaga) deserved to be a matter of public record. Both of the Japanese petitions, from 1644 and 1666, took advantage of this heightened awareness of Japanese people and allowed the petitioners to achieve greater success at distinguishing them-selves from the "chino / a" monolith than was the case with members of other ethnolinguistic groups considered to be "chino / a." Nevertheless, each of the Japanese petitioners still had to prove that they were excep-tional individuals who did not embody negative casta stereotypes.

In 1644, Juan de Cárdenas petitioned the court on behalf of himself and his son to carry harquebuses and swords in the port of Huatulco and its environs. Huatulco was deeply integrated into Pacific coastal trading, and ships coming from Guatemala, Nicaragua, and Peru sometimes favored it over Acapulco because it had a direct road to Veracruz.[90] Cárdenas had been a vecino of Huatulco for over thirty years, and one can infer that his twenty-five-year-old son had been born there. Cárdenas likely settled in New Spain after participating in either the 1610 or the 1613 embassy.[91] He and his son had helped fight off "enemies" who were known to attack the port periodically, likely referring to the many Dutch attacks that ultimately destroyed the port during the seventeenth century.[92] Huatulco had been a popular target of coastal raiding since Sir Francis Drake's sack of the town in 1579.[93] Therefore, to continue defending themselves and the port, both father and son needed a license to carry arms. While they had wielded weapons under dire circumstances without hindrance (as was common along the Pacific coast), having a license formalized a favorable relation-ship with the Real Audiencia that likely increased the Cárdenas family's so-cial standing in Huatulco.

The Japanese petition of 1666 is among the latest extant cases of Asian weapon licensing. The three surviving sons of Juan de la Barranca (Diego, Juan, and Bernabé) used their father's legacy to petition for licenses to carry arms and confirm their tribute exemptions. The sons also acted on behalf of their sisters (María, Josepha, Ysabel, Ana, and Bonifacie), and they had the means to hire a Spaniard, Luis de Deseña Matienzo, to represent them and submit their petition. Juan de la Barranca had traveled across the

Pacific as an ambassador (likely with Hasekura) from Japan to Europe before settling in Veracruz. He would have been one of the very few free Asians living along the Gulf Coast during this period.[94] There, he married Ana Díaz (who may have been Spanish, since there is no record of her casta) and served in a company of Spanish soldiers, which was exceedingly rare for Asian subjects in Mexico. According to Barranca's descendants, "he was a person of quality."[95] Given the father's meritorious record and the children's status as vecinos of Veracruz, the family had long been exempted from paying tribute to the colonial administration. As in the Cárdenas case, Barranca's deeds as a military ally of the colony and distinguished place in Veracruz society advanced the position of his children. However, justicias "for their own ends" had accosted them, required tribute, and prevented them from carrying weapons.[96] It was for this reason that Barranca's sons came forward with their license petition in 1666.

For the sons of Cárdenas and Barranca, as for the "chino" petitioners, the licenses were designed to instruct justicias, *ministros* (court functionaries), and vecinos to recognize that some "chinos" could legitimately carry weapons and that not all were enemies of Spaniards and colonial order. Still, such licenses accentuated the conflict between the court and those tasked with enforcing its policies. How were justicias to know which "chinos" to persecute and which to allow to bear arms? While the court attempted to mitigate ambiguities by issuing licenses, unfortunately (then, like now) the nominal aims of enforcing order and protecting the peace ultimately targeted marginalized peoples. Even those "chinos" who held weapon licenses were routinely denied their permissions to carry weapons, prevented from working, and assaulted in word and deed. The negotiation of social advancement was inherently dangerous, but "chinos" often accepted the risks for the sake of providing for their families; being exempted from paying tribute; and defending themselves, their property, and their honor.

Traveling Merchants and Traders

"Chinos" went through similar—though less rigorous—processes to acquire licenses allowing them to trade goods and provide services in the colonial Mexican commercial world. Outside of rural areas where the colonial government's power was reduced, Spanish officials often required "chinos" to hold licenses before they could legitimately pursue trades such as cutting hair and peddling products like honey, alcohol, clothing, cattle, meat, chocolate, sugar, and iron ore. Like their weapon-toting counterparts, merchants and traders often filed petitions to avoid or address justicia interference in their commercial endeavors. In these accounts, "chinos" gave oral and written testimony of discrimination and bad treatment by local officials.

Although "chino / a" was a vague category, traveling "chino" merchants and urban traders tended to cluster together in discrete communities. This section focuses on three such groups: "chino" barbers in Mexico City, traveling merchants based out of *pueblos de indios* (Indigenous towns), and urban traders, many of whom were based out of the district of San Juan Tenochtitlan in Mexico City. Legal documentation relating to members of all three groups exhibits consistent patterns of conflict with local authorities that slowed, and at times even halted, attempts at social advancement.

Mexico City was the center of trade, lawmaking, and learning in the viceroyalty. During the seventeenth century, it came to host a surprisingly large population of "chinos" practicing as barbers.[97] These specialists are often correctly cited as exemplary of the cohesiveness of "chino" communities in Mexico. This social and economic closeness may be why their history has an unusually detailed legal record. They regularly donated to the guild *cofradía* (confraternity) named Santo Cristo and even commissioned the purchase of tortoiseshell combs from transpacific traders.[98] After establishing themselves in Mexico City, "chino" barbers quickly acquired bad reputations among their Spanish counterparts for outcompeting them, employing only "chino" apprentices, and allegedly spreading illness through unsanitary bleeding practices.[99] These conflicts among competing groups of barbers resembled other ongoing disputes between Spanish and Indigenous craftsmen such as the makers of shoes, saddles, and lace. To control the market for various goods, Spaniards regularly confiscated merchandise, manipulated prices, and excluded non-Spaniards from membership in their guilds.[100]

Barbers in New Spain were responsible for performing phlebotomies, cutting hair, shaving, and even branding enslaved people.[101] The barber's art of bloodletting was highly specialized and suggests formal or informal knowledge exchange between the "chino" barbers and Mexico City's communities of healers. Bloodletting required familiarity with humoral theory and fluctuations based on the month and the time of day. Alonso López de Hinojoso wrote in 1595 that twenty-five veins were commonly used for bloodletting: "seven from the neck to the head and ten in the arms, and eight in the legs."[102] Each vein had unique uses to address different maladies and required specific techniques for safe opening. Furthermore, barbers could only bleed people with a license from a doctor.[103] If "chino" barbers operated without this direct coordination with medical authorities, they would have represented a threat to public health. However, even those who refrained from phlebotomy ran afoul of their Spanish counterparts. As early as 1625, a "chino" barber named Francisco Antonio filed an official complaint claiming that Spanish barbers had unfairly prevented him from practicing his trade, even though he never bled his clients.[104]

Rubén Carrillo Martín suggests that the flooding that inundated Mexico City from 1629 to 1634 heightened this burgeoning conflict between Spanish and "chino" barbers. Spaniards with resources fled to outlying towns, leaving contested business sectors open to those who had to stay. Attempting to reclaim their trades upon reentry, the Spanish barbers applied enough pressure to force an almost complete ban on "chinos" from practicing the trade: only twelve exceptions would be allowed by special license.[105] In the following years, a host of "chino" barbers, including Gonzalo de la Mota (1639), Silvestre Vicente (1642), and Antonio de la Cruz (1643), petitioned for these limited licenses. They insisted that, without the licenses, justicias and Spanish barbers would throw them out of their shops.[106]

However, restrictions on "chino" barbers began easing as early as 1642, when Vicente petitioned successfully for the right to have "chino" assistants. By the late 1640s, "chino" barbers had begun requesting licenses to practice without reference to the twelve-barber limit. Pedro de Asquetta (1648), Juan Agustin (1648), and Francisco Velez (1649) all emphasized their long residence in the city, marriage (in one case to a *criolla* [American-born Spaniard]), and *medias anatas* (payments to receive a privilege) to cut hair in public plazas and houses.[107] A mysterious fire that destroyed a "chino" barber's stand in the main plaza on November 16, 1658, suggests that this resurgence was not well received.[108] Setting fire to market stalls was a common form of retaliation against casta traders.[109]

By the second half of the seventeenth century, "chino" barbers were commonly operating without official licenses. A robbery case from 1667 mentioned two "chinos," Antonio Martines and Miguel Garcia, both of whom were barbers in Mexico City who practiced without licenses. The former worked out of the house of Hernando Garcia, a fellow "chino" who repaired clothes. Garcia also employed a "chino" named Lucas and a "mulato" named Juan de los Reyes as apprentices and was friends with a Spanish petty merchant named Joseph de Cuellar.[110]

Despite the increasing number of "chino" barbers allowed to practice their trade, Spaniards still found ways to persecute them. In 1650, don Fernando Gaytan de Ayala denounced a "chino" barber named Lorenzo for criminal behavior. Ayala called two Spanish witnesses to testify that Lorenzo had cut hair in the public plaza of Mexico City during the festival of San Felipe de Jesus and thus had worked on a day of rest. Perhaps Lorenzo did not know about the festival, did not recognize the danger of working on that day, or knew the danger and decided to work anyway. After all, traders sometimes participated in festivals and received payment via ecclesiastical donations.[111] Regardless of Lorenzo's intent, the court saw only a "chino" not observing Catholic customs against the backdrop of the recent barber controversies and perennial fears of unassimilated castas. The presiding judge found Lorenzo guilty and sentenced him to the archiepiscopal prison. Having the legal right to practice a trade did not protect someone from punishment for business practices deemed improper by Spanish authorities.[112]

The Lorenzo in this case may be the Lorenzo López referred to in two civil proceedings in 1634 as having outstanding debt to other "chino" barbers. By this date, "chino" barbers had acquired reputations as stable credit sources within the city.[113] In 1627, Lorenzo López (barber and vecino of Mexico City) owed Pablo Ximenez 241 pesos. Ximenez was a "chino" *maestro de barbería* (master barber) who lived in the Trinidad neighborhood and owed Juan Salvador de Baeza 180 pesos. Baeza was variously described as "chino" and "indio chino" and as a barber and a table maker. In 1629, Baeza sent an associate, an "india ladina" named Angelina Guillen, to collect on Ximenez's debt. Later that year, Ximenez paid back 70 pesos and transferred the rest of his debt to López, who still owed him 110 pesos (from the previous 241 pesos). López managed to evade this obligation for five years and found employment with another "chino" barber named Francisco de la Cruz. It seems unlikely that De la Cruz knew of López's outstanding debts when he became his financial guarantor, because Baeza promptly had De la Cruz imprisoned when the debt was transferred to him. De la Cruz soon paid the 110 pesos and hired an attorney to help him settle the matter so that he could be released from prison.[114]

Upon release, De la Cruz then had López imprisoned for the 110 pesos plus an additional 30. An alcalde released López from prison on the condition that he practice his trade in De la Cruz's shop until he paid off his debt. Apparently overwhelmed by the many years he lived in debt with no improvement to his financial circumstances, López ran away. De la Cruz waited several weeks, as was customary, and then he prosecuted him for fleeing his obligation and had two witnesses testify to what had transpired. The first witness was Juan Bravo, a Spanish weaver who likely operated an adjacent store. He noted that López had not been seen in twenty-five days. The second witness was Benito de la Cruz, a "chino" barber who worked with Domingo de Ortega, who was a "chino master barber" and *compadre* (his child's godfather or his godchild's father) to Baeza. Ortega knew López because he had attempted to collect the original 110 pesos López owed Baeza after the debt transfer from Ximenez. After hearing both witnesses, the judge ordered López found, punished with imprisonment, and eventually returned to De la Cruz to continue working off the rest of his debt.[115]

These cases elucidate the credit networks that composed, tied together, and occasionally constrained the vibrant "chino" barber community of Mexico City. The strength of this group and its members' economic success continued to threaten their Spanish counterparts and prompted further legal retaliation. In 1661, all "chino" barbers were banned from practicing their trade in the main plaza.[116] Throughout the city, over a hundred "chino" barbers were apparently cutting hair without licenses in 1667, to which Spanish authorities responded by establishing a formal commission dedicated to banning unlicensed "chino" barbers.[117] Those who continued to ply their trade would have had to do so from the periphery of the city.

The barbers of Mexico City were not the only cohesive "chino" community in central Mexico during the seventeenth century. For example, the will of Villalobos documents an active and close-knit community of "chinos" trading along the Colima-Guadalajara corridor during the early seventeenth century. In 1618, after a months-long illness, Villalobos died at age thirty-one in Zapotlán, at the home of his longtime friend and

business partner, Alonso Gutiérrez. Villalobos named Gutiérrez the executor of his will and declared his own mother—Monica Binangan, who still
lived in the Philippines—to be his heir. Both Villalobos and Gutiérrez
were Kapampangans and traveling merchants, and both were deeply integrated into the social and economic networks of both Spanish and
Indigenous societies.

Villalobos sold damask, silks, Chinese cotton, a variety of Japanese products, and cloths from Pampanga. He had "chino" connections from Acapulco
to Guadalajara, and his credit network included a few Spaniards and Afro-
Mexicans as well. In his will, he described one woman, Catalina, as his *comadre* (godchild's mother) and said that he often spent Sundays and festival
days with her. He donated forty pesos to his confraternity, Nuestra Señora
del Rosario—with which his executor was affiliated as well. He was also apparently involved in confraternities in the nearby towns of San Joseph
Tecolopa, Ixtlahuacán de los Reyes, and Tepic.[118] In addition, he employed a
criado who lived in San Joseph Tecolapa and stored some of his fabrics for
him. For most people living outside of a major urban center, the famed transpacific trade was embodied exclusively by individuals like Villalobos and
Gutiérrez, who came to their towns with rucksacks full of strange wares.

As soon as he fell ill, Villalobos went to stay with Gutiérrez—his friend,
confraternity brother, and business associate—and composed his will in
Gutiérrez's home. He eventually recovered and publicly gave a petticoat
made in Pampanga to Gutiérrez's wife as a gesture of thanks. Fabrics from
Luzon were well known, and this gift also had a sentimental meaning as it
came from his homeland.[119] When he resumed his business travels, those
who knew him considered this return to the road reckless and ill advised.
Predictably, he fell sick again, and he returned to Gutiérrez's home, staying
there seven months before finally succumbing.

Villalobos's will survives because Gutiérrez presented it to the royal
court in Guadalajara in an attempt to clear his name. He had been accused
of keeping some or all of Villalobos's estate, rather than transferring it to
the Philippines within a required period of three months. In the legal proceedings, Gutiérrez alternately described himself and Villalobos as "indio"
and "chino." When asked why he had not notified the *juzgado de bienes de
difuntos* (court of the property of the dead) that he had not heard from Villalobos's mother, Gutiérrez played on "chino" stereotypes and feigned
ignorance: "this deponent said [that] for being chino and not knowing of

lawsuits."[120] Like other petitioners, Gutiérrez tried to bolster his reputation by emphasizing his Catholic marriage (to an "india" noble named doña Mariana) and the time he had spent in Mexico (he had lived there for twenty years). Similarly, officials had typed Villalobos as a "chino," a natural of the Pampanga in the Philippines, and *chino de nación* (of the "chino" people) based on appearance. However, the court declared that four witnesses to his death were sufficient: "for [his] being indio and in a pueblo de indios, it was enough."[121] Effectively, Gutiérrez and Villalobos were both "indio" and "chino," and both Gutiérrez and Spanish officials used either or both terms depending on what was legally advantageous.

After the death of his friend, Gutiérrez painstakingly attempted to locate and catalog all items in Villalobos's will and collect all outstanding debts. In this sense, Villalobos could not have chosen a better executor, since Gutiérrez knew the pueblos de indios and trade routes that Villalobos frequented. Despite his thoroughness, Gutiérrez failed to find several items and rallied a host of witnesses to testify that his friend had sold those items during his brief recovery. One witness was Francisco Mathias, another traveling "chino" merchant. He had known Gutiérrez for twenty-six years, including in the Philippines, because "they are of the same land."[122] He traveled frequently with Gutiérrez, selling goods in Colima and nearby pueblos de indios. He had even lived in Gutiérrez's house for four years. He testified not only that Villalobos had already sold the missing items from his will but also that Gutiérrez had traveled extensively and diligently to collect all debts. Many "chinos" were unable to pay the full amount they owed Villalobos, and Gutiérrez supplied the remaining sums. Through these testimonies, Gutiérrez was finally able to convince the court that he had done everything within his power to fulfill his role as executor and that there had been no foul play. In 1622, he had transferred the remaining 420 pesos and five tomines of the Villalobos estate to Juan Viscaino, the alcalde mayor. By 1623, Viscaino still had not transferred the estate to Binangan in the Philippines, leaving him suspected of foul play. Unfortunately, the case fizzled out at this stage, and it is unlikely Villalobos's mother ever saw a single peso of his estate.

The case is an extraordinary microcosm of the strength of transpacific connections, the deployment of casta categories and stereotypes, and the forms of social integration that many Asians achieved in New Spain. Perhaps most importantly, it illustrates a vibrant and active community of "chino" traders, most of whom (like Francisco Luis, Juan Triana, and Nicolás Malanquiz) show up merely as members of Villalobos's credit network. These Asian traders, who peddled strange goods from strange lands, provided Indigenous communities with rare access to these coveted luxury goods.

During the early and middle parts of the seventeenth century, an active and well-connected group of "chino" trading communities also operated throughout central Mexico, from Puebla to San Luis Potosí. The first and longest-lasting of these collectives was based in San Juan Tenochtitlan, which consisted of four central neighborhoods (Santa María Cuepopan, San Sebastián Atzacualco, San Pablo Zoquipan, and San Juan Moyotlan) that surrounded the center of Mexico City (figure 3.3).[123] These neighborhoods housed most of the Indigenous people in the city. As opposed to the monumental thirteen square blocks of the *traza* (Spanish district), San Juan Tenochtitlan contained mostly adobe *casuchas* (shacks) and organized the Indigenous population politically through elected *cabildos* (councils) and *alcaldes* (magistrates).[124] As early as 1610, a community of "chinos" was living in San Sebastián Atzacualco, in the northeast corner of the city. There, they had their own congregation at the Jesuit College of San Gregorio. They also had an elected *alguacil* (bailiff) tasked with ensuring that they went to mass on Sundays and Catholic holidays (failure to do so could lead to imprisonment).[125] By 1655, "chinos" living in San Juan Tenochtitlan were considered constituent subjects of Indigenous governance.[126] In 1694, "chinos" joined the district's Indigenous inhabitants to found the Confraternity of the Most Holy Solitude and Agonies of Mary.[127]

For Spaniards, San Juan Tenochtitlan was known as a trading sector and useful labor pool. For example, when renovating the cathedral in January 1656, Spaniards hired two hundred "indios" of San Juan Tenochtitlan, whom the viceroy paid out of his own pocket.[128] The fires that destroyed most merchant stalls in the main plaza at the end of 1658 ultimately shifted Indigenous trading from the plaza to the market of San Juan Tenochtitlan in the southwest, reviving industries not present there since the flood of 1629.[129] The long decline of the pre-Hispanic market of Tlatelolco—which had so enchanted Hernando Cortés—endowed the flourishing San Juan market with additional novelty.[130]

However, where these multiethnic communities existed, Spanish fear was focused on them. For merchants circulating through San Juan Tenochtitlan

3.3 Appearance and Elevation of Mexico City

Juan Gómez de Trasmonte's view of Mexico City clearly depicts the well-ordered *traza* in the middle, with its grid structure and monumental edifices like the royal palace and cathedral. In stark contrast are the hovels in the outskirts, where the Indigenous population and many "chino" traders lived and conducted business. Trasmonte surely reduced the size of San Juan Tenochtitlan to emphasize the grandeur of the *traza*.

Juan Gómez de Trasmonte, *Forma y levantado de la ciudad de Mexico*, Carte di Castello 52, 1628. Reproduction courtesy of the Biblioteca Medicea Laurenziana, Florence.

and central Mexico, licenses to trade again reveal how "chinos" navigated the obstacles associated with achieving and maintaining social mobility. Eleven of the twelve "chino" licenses and license petitions for trade rights that I consulted refer to local opposition to their privileges. The consistency of *justicia* hindrance reinforces the view that these petty officials found traveling "chino" merchants inherently suspicious. The petitions of two Antonios de la Cruz are illustrative. The first Antonio de la Cruz, an "indio chino," received a license in 1639 to sell flowers, anise, cotton, and a variety of other goods so that he could pay tributes and support his wife (an "india" named Madalena Luisa) and their seven children. He testified that for thirteen years, officials had unlawfully forced the family to pay 2 percent alcabalas, although the license exempted them from those taxes "as they are natives."[131] The alcabala mattered, as paying it along with formal tribute marked him and his family as belonging to a non-Indigenous casta.[132] Despite his significant social and commercial success as a slave-owning merchant, the Puebla city council denied a second petition from him in 1648, when he requested immunity from paying a hundred pesos in alcabalas.[133] Although this large sum underscores his economic vitality, he struggled for many decades to acquire the privileges he believed he was owed, corroborating Cope's well-tested thesis that social mobility was possible for members of casta groups but increasingly difficult the higher they climbed.[134]

Similarly, the second Antonio de la Cruz, identified as a "chino" living in Mexico City, received licenses in 1653 and 1661 to practice his trade as a traveling merchant. On both occasions, he complained that justicias regularly restricted his movements and prevented him from selling his goods.[135] The fact that he raised the same grievances eight years after the first license was issued reinforces how much power the justicias had in deciding whether or not to implement court orders.

Another example comes from the license of Francisco García, an "indio chino" like the first Antonio de la Cruz. The court characterized García as a "Native of the Portuguese Indies," a vecino of Mexico City and San Juan Tenochtitlan, a married man, and a father. His physical license to sell clothing from Asia, Castille, and New Spain had come apart after four years on the road. During the interim, he had been stopped and forced to pay fines for selling without a license, prompting his return to the court and his petition for a new license in 1651.[136] García's case reveals the practical difficulties that many people faced in maintaining such a vulnerable and essential document for many years.[137]

Antonio de Silva, "chino," encountered similar difficulties in selling meat in and around Tacuba. Like many others, he conducted business so that he could pay tributes and support his family (he and his Indigenous wife, Antonia de la Cruz, had three children). Speaking about the alcalde mayor and justicias of Tacuba, he testified that "not only is he impeded but they also cause him many inconveniences and threats."[138] Although the petition does not specifically address what these threats entailed, they sufficed for the viceroy to write directly to the alcalde mayor of Tacuba and order him to prevent any harm from coming to Silva.

The 1658 case of an "indio chino" named Gonzalo Marquez de la Cruz is exceptional because here the viceroy applied a cédula from 1639 intended for the "indios" of Mérida in the Yucatan. Marquez sold fruit, vegetables, other foodstuffs, seeds, clothing, and handmade tallow candles in mule trains and on horseback. Like other petitioners before him, he had been prevented from trading. The 1639 cédula protected "indios" from Spanish officials who sought to ban them from dressing in Spanish clothing, riding horseback with bit and saddle, owning livestock, selling goods at market, and operating mule trains. Furthermore, it set the penalty for impeding "indio" merchants in these ways at two hundred pesos. This license is the only one considered here that explicitly included a clause addressing possible future Spanish misconduct.[139] Judging from the other petitions, this cédula was not widely applied to central Mexico.

The Friction of Proximity

As the license petitions make clear, geographically and socially mobile "chinos" inspired distrust throughout central Mexico. Applying for a license was an appeal to viceregal authority both for privileges categorically denied to other "chinos" and for protection from local officials. Some "chinos" like Alonso and Lima pursued social advancement by distancing themselves from the "indio" category, while others, like Marquez, benefited legally from their proximity to the "indio" status.

Notably, the Spanish suspicion that motivated these responses occasionally hindered the ability of "chinos" to integrate into local communities. Although the overwhelming trend was the formation of intimacy by proximity, there were important exceptions. Throughout the colonial period, members of castas were often formally prohibited from entering Indigenous towns for much the same reasons that "Sangleyes" were prevented from living alongside Indigenous peoples from the Philippines. Spanish concerns about spiritual backsliding, economic abuse, and unsavory influence also focused on "chinos" in Mexico, and Indigenous communities sometimes deployed this rhetoric to protect their autonomy.

For example, in 1630, the "indios" of Atlacomulco, in central Mexico, petitioned Spanish authorities to expel "chinos" for allegedly forcing them to buy their bread at high prices.[140] In 1675, one Spanish administrator considered

the possibility of forcibly segregating "indios chinos" from "indios naturales," yet another admission that "chinos" were categorically different from
"indios" of the Americas.[141] In a more enigmatic case, a "chino" named Pedro
Vázquez was elected in 1696 to be governor of the "indios" of Huitzuco,
a small town located between Mexico City and Acapulco. However, the
alcalde of nearby Iguala was ordered to remove him, since Vázquez was
discovered to be "chino and not indio."[142]

Sometimes, public suspicion of "chinos" intersected with other fears
born of both the potential dangers of spatial proximity and patriarchal ideas
of masculine honor. For example, in 1638, an "indio" baker named Sebastian
de la Cruz beat his "india" wife with an iron rod for finding her in the house
of a Francisco "chino" and sleeping with an enslaved "chino," whose name
he did not know.[143] He struck his wife five times: once on the hips, once
on her left breast, and three times on the left side of her rib cage. After
he got her home, he struck her forty more times, after which she died. Upon
hearing the beating, the "mother" (presumably of the wife) rushed into the
room, only to be violently drowned (presumably by her son-in-law).

This was not the only time that a married woman would be found in
the home of a "chino." In 1634, Francisca Tereza had a public spat with
her husband, Juan Peres, a vecino of Mexico City. After, Tereza decided to
leave Peres and told him that she was going to stay with her mother.
However, Peres soon realized that Tereza had not gone to her mother's
house but was in fact staying in the home of a "chino" barbero named
Agustin in the neighborhood of San Agustín of Mexico City. When Peres
sent several acquaintances to retrieve her from there, Tereza fled to
Tacuba, where she was ordered to return to her husband on pain of major
excommunication.[144]

On other occasions, "chinos" were the aggressors against "indios" in
criminal cases. In 1643, an enslaved "indio chino" named Gonzalo de la
Cruz, a cart driver, accosted an Indigenous man named Sebastian de Avel-
laneda in the town of San Lucas of Temascaltepec to the southwest of
Mexico City. Gonzalo yanked Sebastian's hat off his head and forced him
into an abandoned stable at knifepoint, where he robbed him of ten pesos
and six tomines. Indigenous witnesses testified that Gonzalo often mugged
"indios" who traveled through the town. However, Sebastian dropped the
charges because "honorable persons" (presumably Andres Perez de las
Mariñas, Gonzalo's enslaver) had pressured him to do so.[145]

Perhaps equally illustrative is a petition for amparo that Juan and Juana Pasquala, both "indios," submitted in a complaint against Tomas Dominguez, a "chino." They accused Dominguez of building a road through their land in 1677.[146] According to the complaint, the Pasqualas had been given the land in 1669 to sustain themselves and pay tribute, which they did in "calm and peaceful possession."[147] Eight years later, Dominguez, their neighbor, built a road through their property. He cleared the land and began construction without their consent and "with force and violence."[148] When they refused to abandon their property, Dominguez allegedly stood outside their home, making loud noises with the intent of dislodging them. This scheme reveals that Dominguez understood that Indigenous peoples' right to land in the Spanish domain was predicated on their active occupation and use of that land. In the words of Tamar Herzog, "land that was physically abandoned and left uncultivated [*inculta*] could be ceded to the first person or community who found and occupied it."[149] Thus, Dominguez's strategy resembles other similarly inventive Spanish ploys to seize Indigenous land during the same period.[150] As Spaniards began successfully justifying these land grabs with new property rights, Dominguez likely did not think of his own actions as radically different from those of other colonial elites.

During the *probanza* (evidence-gathering stage of the trial), prosecutors brought three witnesses to the court in Mexico City. All were middle-aged or elderly "indios" from Tacubaya who gave testimony through interpreters. The witnesses confirmed and condemned the abuses that Dominguez had perpetrated against the couple. If the marginalia give any indication, though, documenting the abuse was not as important as confirming the basic details of the case: that the land had been given to the Pasqualas and that Dominguez had built a road through it. Although no official statement exists that resolves the case, it exemplifies how Indigenous people used tribute obligations and records of peaceful, assimilated cultivation of land against aspiring imperial actors seeking to displace them. Their testimony contributed to an active colonial discourse propounding the danger of casta exploitation of Indigenous communities.[151]

Interestingly, at least one "chino" also used amparo to protest incursions on his land. Juan Geronimo, a Kapampangan man, was a vecino of Acayuca, 150 leagues north of Mexico City. In 1654, he alleged that many cattle from the hacienda of Rodrigo Marquez had intruded on his land and prevented

him from planting corn. This was yet another Spanish strategy developed
to prevent Indigenous people from being able to cultivate their land and
to then dispossess them of that land.[152] Geronimo requested that landowners in the jurisdiction of Guazaqualco be prevented from doing him
harm with their cattle and that they hire enough guards to ensure that none
of their animals stray onto his land. If they failed to do so, Geronimo asked
permission to shoot the cattle with bow and arrow. To support his petition, Geronimo described himself as a *principal* (chief) from the Philippines,
a married man with children, a regular tribute payer, and a certified "battalion soldier" who "has served and serves our lord the king at my own
cost with arms and horses like the other vecinos of the jurisdiction [of
Guazaqualco]."[153] He was also literate enough to sign his name to the petition. In view of Geronimo's merit and present need, the attorney who
read the document granted his request. Thus, the discomforts of proximity
reveal that "chinos" were simultaneously both dispossessors and dispos-
sessed, and accepted and rejected, in Indigenous and rural communities
of central Mexico. While most conflicts involving "chinos" occurred with
Spanish officials, local frictions signal occasional divides between "chinos"
and other non-Spaniards.

Although colonial society often failed to incorporate and support upwardly
mobile casta communities, some individuals did manage to accumulate
wealth and land and integrated themselves advantageously into colonial
settlements and cities. However, these cases are exceptional. More often,
"chinos" struggled hard to earn a living and exercise special privileges to
trade, bear arms, and not pay tributes and taxes. Like other non-Spaniards,
they strategically used their petitions to present themselves as aligned with
expectations of Hispanic behavior—a common adaptation in the face of
early modern Spanish race thinking. "Chinos" used claims of productivity,
Catholic patriarchalism, and allegiance to the crown to achieve the award
of licenses and granting of amparo. In other words, Hispanicization was
the barrier to formal privilege and protection, and Spanish perceptions of
difference mediated what social success could mean. As these cases demonstrate, even special provisions won in colonial courts could not overcome
local discrimination.

As the overlapping genres of the license and the amparo indicate, new
forms of community also resulted from attempts to scale the social ladder.

From the "chino" barbers of Mexico City to Villalobos's credit network, "chinos" collaborated with each other for mutual gain through shared trades and shared spaces like San Juan Tenochtitlan. The petitions reveal that "chinos" were deeply integrated into colonial social structures as well. The petitioners were not aimless, roving traders or temporary residents. "Chinos" often built families and communities with the goal of long-term stability in the places where they settled and worked. However, their new intimacies and proximities occasionally generated conflict with Indigenous and Spanish communities. Thus, free Asians occupied a hybrid social status that both helped and hindered them in their quest for belonging and social mobility.

Most "chinos" in the Americas found it next to impossible to achieve the forms of advancement examined in this chapter. They could not loan money, hire apprentices, apply for licenses, or purchase enslaved people—indeed, many of them were enslaved. Survival and adaptation took on an entirely different aspect for those in bondage. For "chinos" robbed of autonomy, using the rhetoric of assimilation rarely accomplished mobility. Instead, such rhetoric largely functioned as a tool to avoid punishment, for institutions like the Inquisition scourged the deviant but sometimes showed forgiveness to the penitent. For enslaved "chinos," the objective was survival. In pursuing it, they found and cultivated new constellations of social solidarity, cultural exchange, and knowledge production.

4 Contesting Enslavement in New Spain

IN 1642, THE HOSPITAL de Nuestra Señora in Mexico City refused to admit an enslaved "chino" named Manuel de la Cruz. Though face-to-face with a man dying of open sores and abscesses, the steward Alonso Díaz said that there was "no way" his institution would treat Manuel because it served neither "chinos nor slaves."[1] Forced to leave the hospital, the enslaver Antonio Freira brought Manuel to the master surgeon, Sebastián del Castillo, who provided long-term treatment to enslaved people. Sick slaves would stay at his home until they recovered or perished, and Castillo would add the cost of medicine and food to the master's bill. His remedies consisted of allowing the patient to rest, providing sustenance and medicine, and conducting phlebotomy. Open sores and abscesses were often treated with a paste made of egg and sulfate powder, as well as by cauterization in extreme cases.[2] Though the documentation of Manuel's illness left his fate unknown, it provides a brief glimpse of how a categorical, racializing exclusion brought an enslaved "chino" into a healing community that he shared with other enslaved people. This glimpse invites us to examine the racializing discourse that engendered these interactions, challenge demographic assumptions about who enslaved people were in New Spain, and explore the cultural and intellectual exchanges that characterized the communities they lived in.

Alongside enslaved Afro-Mexican and Indigenous people, "chinos" labored in bondage on plantations, in obrajes, at ports, in mule trains, alongside traders, and in wealthy households. They were not autonomous subjects afforded the privileges of vassalage under the crown but rather commodities to be bought, sold, bartered, paraded, inherited, exploited, punished, and even destroyed if that was deemed necessary. The daily realities of their subjugation shared every characteristic of Afro-Mexican and Indigenous enslavement as it had developed in colonial Mexico: the bodies of enslaved "chinos" bore the scars of colonial race making. Although a handful of free "chinos" acquired enough wealth to become enslavers, the majority of "chinos" in Mexico during the seventeenth century were enslaved.

Like the experiences of petitioners for weapon and merchant licenses, those of enslaved "chinos" sharply counter the image of New Spain as an equitably integrated colonial society populated by exceptional Asian immigrants. The growing scholarship on enslaved "chinos" implicitly demonstrates that their vulnerability to bondage eliminates the possibility of Asian exceptionalism. Nonetheless, this new field has yet to substantively examine the lives of "chinos" through the prism of early modern race making or directly question earlier scholars' optimistic view of free "chino / a" integration in New Spain (see Chapter 3). Appending race to this historiography matters deeply, as the constraints of enslavement engendered numerous Afro-Asian syntheses that have largely gone unnoticed in the scholarship on the early modern period. These cross-cultural exchanges defined the nature of life in bondage and allowed enslaved people to imagine worlds beyond their immediate circumstances.

Although Orlando Patterson's theorization of "social death" (total social alienation and dehumanization) has defined much of the traditional historiography on transatlantic enslavement, numerous studies have shown that enslaved people were not solely recipients of colonial domination.[3] Bondage did not preclude agency. According to Laurent Dubois, "We should begin from the assumption that there was an intellectual life within slave communities, and that this life involved movement between ideas and action, between the abstract and the particular, between past, present, and future."[4] Throughout the Atlantic World, enslaved people reconstituted families, forged new identities, conjured up creative imaginaries, fomented resistance, and pursued political engagement. Central Mexico was no exception. For example, Gonzalo Aguirre Beltrán and Solange Alberro have long argued that collective oppression and resistance created social intimacies and cultural exchanges between Afro-Mexican and Indigenous communities.[5] These forms of resistance and adaptation also occurred among enslaved Asians in the Americas during the early modern period, although their case has sometimes been seen as separate from that of enslaved Afro-Mexicans due to the earlier formal emancipation of "chinos" (in 1672 as opposed to 1829 for Afro-Mexicans).[6]

For many decades, both resistance to enslavement and spiritual syncretism in Mexico have been considered solely Indigenous and Afro-Mexican processes. Because studies of enslaved populations have tended to focus narrowly on one ethnic group or another, they have ultimately obscured the fact that—at the level of lived experience—convergence was the dominant trend during the seventeenth century. Convergence is both a historical occurrence, "a dynamic and dialogic process toward the meeting of minds and interests," and a methodology, a way to "decipher new, revisionary forms of agency."[7] This search for historical agency through convergence, articulated by Homi Bhabha, is aligned with the results of Giovanni Levi's melding of global and microhistory. For Levi, global microhistory foregrounds the interactions of non-Europeans, who have been categorically excluded from yet remain integral to the story of early modern global connectivity.[8] Daniel Nemser applies the concept of convergence to the multiethnic social, cultural, and sexual exchanges of *pulquerías* (maguey liquor bars) in Mexico City.[9] Laura Lewis invokes convergence in her analysis of Black *naguales* (Indigenous shape-shifting and spiritual power) in Mérida and Ometepec.[10] In fact, colonial Mexican society featured numerous convergences around specific sites (such as the *baratillo* [discount market]), cultural practices (for example, spiritual pharmacology related to the use of peyote, ololiuhqui [a morning glory seed], and *puyomate* [a type of aromatic root or mixture]), and social relationships (such as shared kinship communities).[11] One might even argue that convergence defined the emergence and fluidity of multiethnic society in New Spain during the long seventeenth century.[12] As Chapter 3 shows, free "chinos"—even those granted special privileges—participated in these convergences as well, circulating within social and religious settings with people of other ethnicities and castas. Yet while free "chinos" used convergence to increase their social mobility and integration, enslaved "chinos" deployed it to survive. For the enslaved, convergence represented the possibility of a subjecthood not entirely defined by commoditization, objectification, and alienation.

Until very recently, the historiography on the enslavement of Asian populations in Latin America focused primarily on the case of Chinese indenture in Cuba during the mid-nineteenth century, and it questioned whether convergence had occurred there on a large scale. For years, scholars have debated the nature of indenture: was it a true form of enslavement, or did it merely resemble the brutality of enslavement, since indentured laborers were technically contracted rather than being retained in perpetuity?[13] The binary of the question reflects the broader historiographical argument that indenture replaced enslavement, that the two systems were oppositional, rather than mutually constitutive. However, the case of Cuba allows us to decisively reject the "replacement narrative," since indentured Chinese workers and enslaved Afro-Cubans generally lived and labored side by side from 1847 to 1874.[14] Moreover, the institution of Chinese indenture in Cuba ended before the emancipation of Afro-Cubans (1874 versus 1886).

Still, some plantation owners indeed sought to divide the two groups based on imagined racial characteristics—believing that they were fit for different tasks and required separate living spaces.[15] For this reason, the formerly enslaved Esteban Montejo (1860–1973) expressed the still influential notion that the Chinese and Afro-Cubans had little contact during the period of indenture. Even as Montejo admired the Chinese for being "rebels from birth," he apparently said to the Cuban anthropologist Miguel Barnet that during the Sunday festivities at the Flor de Sagua plantation: "I noticed that the ones who were least involved were the Chinese. Those bastards didn't have an ear for the drums. They were standoffish. . . . Nobody paid them any mind. And folks just went on with their dances."[16] According to Barnet, Montejo remembered the barracoons as a culturally bifurcated space consisting of a dominant Afro-Cuban side rooted in West and West Central African heritage and a smaller, separate Chinese side whose occupants were unable to find common ground with the enslaved, regardless of their shared circumstances.[17]

Despite the firsthand authority of Montejo's claims, recent scholarship has contested the notion of isolated social and cultural spheres. Kathleen López notes that "Chinese coolies mostly formed common-law unions with women of African descent" and that these unions "facilitated religious syncretism."[18] Martin Tsang's work on Chinese–Afro-Cuban spiritual exchange further elaborates on the deep cultural ties binding and blending these communities. Tsang demonstrates that some Chinese laborers became spiritual specialists and joined in the syncretic practices of Santería. Others became consecrated as *babalawos* (priests) in Yoruba-derived Ifá divination. They melded the veneration of the folk hero Guangong (關公) with that of the Yoruba Changó to create new syncretic cults of "Sanfancón" devotion.[19]

López's and Tsang's innovative findings contribute to the field of Afro-Asian studies—which, for Latin American historiography, has begun offering fresh perspectives on these global encounters in colonial and postcolonial cultures.[20] Rather than focusing on discrete ethnolinguistic groups, Afro-Asian studies methodologies offer a language for examining how colonial social and labor structures, as well as racial ideologies, produced unprecedented cross-cultural, spiritual, and sexual encounters. However, the field's modern bias has kept its interventions disengaged from the scholarship on the New Spanish system of enslavement and vice versa.[21]

In central Mexico's multiethnic communities of captives, linguistic barriers, disparate customs, and distinct worldviews did not keep "chinos" from discovering that they had common ground with both Afro-Mexican and Indigenous peoples. Isolation was impossible, as "chinos" made up a relatively small percentage of the total enslaved population—meaning that they experienced enslavement within highly diverse settings. Under these circumstances, the kinds of exchanges that Aguirre Beltrán and Alberro identified among Afro-Mexican and Indigenous peoples also occurred between both of those populations and "chinos."

Colonial bureaucratic and legal documents confirm that enslaved "chinos" consistently labored in multiethnic environments and married across castas. Rubén Carrillo Martín initiated important preliminary research in this area through a quantitative study of 120 "chino / a" marriages in Puebla. For the seventeenth century, he found that enslaved "chinos" married Afro-Mexicans in 80 percent of cases, a figure signaling the close ties formed between the two groups through physical proximity and enslavement.[22] These data are far from exceptional.[23] Marrying into "local" enslaved communities was an important survival strategy for groups with low population densities in New Spain.[24] Similarly, "chinos" founded confraternities and joined existing ones that participated in colonial public life, purchased manumission for their members, and "played a crucial role in redefining the social and political roles assigned to enslaved people."[25] Consequently, "chinos" learned how to respond to the conditions of enslavement in colonial Mexico from other captives. The processes of observation, communication, and translation that facilitated these encounters epitomize the meeting of Atlantic and Pacific Worlds in New Spain.

Yet much remains unclear about the relationships and communities that enslaved "chinos" forged. In particular, very few works have considered how "chinos" joined in the cultures of resistance to enslavement and unorthodox spirituality in Mexico. For example, after studying "chino / a" encounters with the Catholic church, Tatiana Seijas concludes, "Chino slaves might well have carried their native belief systems to the New World, but the surviving historical record does not reveal non-Christian practices."[26] However, both the nature of Afro-Asian convergence and the colonial archive indicate that unorthodox beliefs and rituals played a central role in the rhythms of life in captivity.

This chapter takes seriously the bountiful evidence of integration and exchange among enslaved populations in Mexico. Ultimately, it reveals that Asian, Indigenous, and Afro-Mexican communities formed connections not only through shared social circles but also through shared reactions to Spanish colonialism and conditions of enslavement. In other words, multiethnic communities often formed in response to the harsh realities of Spanish race thinking that kept individuals in bondage.[27] In the process, these communities created and sustained alternative forms of authority, developed legal knowledge, influenced colonial power relations, and generated new forms of exchange and synthesis.[28]

Such early modern encounters make important interventions in Afro-Asian studies. Principally, they show that the Manila galleons and colonial Mexico were key sites of early multiethnic convergence, and they bear witness to the first Afro-Asian collaborations to contest bondage and colonial power in the Americas. Given the large scale of Indigenous coerced and unfree labor in New Spain, the early modern context further encourages us to consider the fundamental role of Indigeneity as a critical third point of contact on the Afro-Asian continuum. The fluidity of castas, syncretic and creolized cultures, and multiethnic intimacies, as well as the diverse nature of enslaved communities, all signal the inviolable position of Indigeneity in Afro-Asian history. In colonial Mexico, one primary anchor for collaborations among African, Asian, Indigenous, and mixed peoples was the exchange of knowledge about negotiating and contesting enslavement. Collaborations identified in the archive focus most clearly and most often on three tactics: long-term flight, blasphemy, and the formation of spiritual practices beyond that of Catholic dogma—all of which were "experiential" responses to enslavement in New Spain.[29] In acknowledging alternative authority structures in colonial Mexico, enslaved "chinos" often acted in ways that were not legally advantageous but rather due to values, traditions, and aspirations that were illegible to colonial bureaucrats and, consequently, many historians.

Runaway Chinos

Before arriving in the Americas, many sea-worn survivors of the Pacific passage had undergone multiple stages of dislocation and displacement. The people who would become the enslaved "chinos" of colonial Mexico had been captured in coastal and hinterland communities everywhere from Gujarat to Nagasaki and were often sold through interimperial networks before arriving in Spanish Manila. Most of them entered colonial Mexico via Acapulco. However, as John Chilton, an English businessman, noted in 1569, "It is evident that a part of the Asian merchandise that the Manila galleon transports is introduced inland both legally and illegally through various points of the northwestern coast."[30] For example, Domingo de la Cruz, an enslaved "chino," had entered Mexico via Salagua, north of Acapulco.[31] Clandestine entry even occurred in Acapulco. In 1594, an enslaved woman from Brunei named Catalina was disembarked during the night in an effort to avoid paying royal duties.[32]

At the port, merchants, missionaries, and administrators assigned muleteers as intermediaries to purchase enslaved people from galleon officials and sailors in Acapulco.[33] Enslaved "chinos" were then forced to travel on the camino de china to Mexico City—where, unlike free "chinos," they often lived in the traza in their enslavers' households, shops, or religious institutions.[34] In 1626, some Spanish homes held as many as eighteen enslaved Asians.[35]

This cresting wave of "chino / a" enslavement intersected with the peak of transatlantic enslavement to Mexico. During the sixteenth and seventeenth centuries, as many as 155,000 enslaved Africans are thought to have legally entered New Spain through Veracruz.[36] Both slave trades climaxed in the 1620s and 1630s and declined in mid-century as Spanish access to Portuguese channels of enslavement decreased.[37]

After arriving at an obraje in Coyoacán, a wealthy home in Mexico City, a convent in Puebla, a mine in Zacatecas, a merchant's warehouse in Tlaxcala, or a plantation in Toluca, enslaved "chinos," Indigenous peoples, and Africans alike had to come to terms with the labor-intensive nature of enslavement in the Americas. Like many of their Black and Indigenous peers, "chinos" struggled to accept the quotidian cruelties of enslaved life in New Spain. Running away was perhaps the most immediate and risky form of protesting and escaping bad treatment.[38] According to Dennis Valdés, two prominent long-term flight strategies emerged in colonial Mexico.[39] In the first, many runaways fled urban centers such as Mexico City, Puebla, and Veracruz and proceeded toward rural areas. Fugitives had to rely on social geographies of safe pueblos de indios and nearby *palenques* (maroon communities) to avoid recapture. The second, more common strategy involved flight from an urban or rural zone to a large city, after which the runaway reintegrated into colonial society with an invented identity.[40]

The Archivo General de la Nación México houses numerous *censuras* (reprobations) that provide important glimpses about those who ran away in spite of their long odds of success. A censura was meant to compel parishioners under threat of excommunication to come forward as witnesses to help recover stolen property. They "were an instrument of social control," threatening community members with spiritual punishment and damnation if they helped runaways.[41] As such, they correctly assumed that flight was close to impossible without assistance. In addition to a network of collaborators, runaways also had to rely on detailed internal cartographies garnered through years of experience and limited mobility "to get and stay lost."[42]

The censuras also imply that short-term flight was a common, even permissible, form of releasing the pressure of the system of enslavement. Enslavers would typically report a runaway to ecclesiastical authorities only after three to eight weeks of absence. For example, in 1658 doña Mariana Pérez Matamoros waited two months before submitting a request for censura for a "china" named Luisa and her twelve-year-old daughter, Juana.[43] The canon of the Mexico City cathedral, Doctor Luis de Cifuentes, received many of these requests and issued the censuras. In 1636, he reported after a month that Tomé, his own forty-year-old enslaved "chino," had escaped.[44]

Unlike short-term flight, long-term flight was rarely spontaneous and involved monumental risks, including long-distance travel, bounty hunters, exposure, hunger, and extreme punishment if caught. But runaways faced these and other challenges to escape abuses that, in Frank Proctor's formulation, exceeded the colonial norms of treatment and castigation.[45] Escape often meant leaving behind spouses, children, parents, and extended kinship and social communities, signaling the desperation inherent in the act of running away. Getting caught almost invariably resulted in flogging and other punishments like enclosure and branding. Brands often stopped repeat attempts at running away because they could immediately alert a community or a neighborhood to the presence of a runaway. Significant variations in "chino / a" skin colors led to a higher probability of branding on the face with the "S" and *clavo* (nail), marking "chinos" as *esclavos* (slaves) to eliminate any ambiguity about their status.[46] Enslaved light-skinned Afro-Mexicans were also more likely than dark-skinned Afro-Mexicans to be branded on the face.[47] In contrast, enslaved Indigenous peoples from the Americas rarely received the S and nail brand.[48]

Although Proctor notes that long-term flight was rare, a survey of twenty censuras involving enslaved "chinos" suggests that it occurred more frequently than has been thought. According to this sample, "chinas" ran away at disproportionately high rates, and a significant minority did so to free their children. The overrepresentation of women in these sources (approximately one out of four enslaved "chinos" was female, but two out of five runaway "chinos" were female) suggests a desire for their children to be born free, indicates women's double marginalization as slaves and as women, and perhaps suggests that they fled from the sex trafficking that dominated Iberian enslavement in Asia and continued on the galleons.[49]

Asian and Afro-Mexican flight often relied on multiethnic participation, sometimes even within the same family. In 1626, Martín de Bisola reported that someone "with little fear of our Lord" had freed a thirteen-year-old enslaved "chino" named Agustín. His parents, a "chino" and a "negra," could not be found, implying that they were involved in his escape.[50] In 1658, doña Margarita de Saavedra reported that four slaves had fled in rapid succession, beginning with a forty-year-old "chino" named Pedro. A few months later, a thirty-two-year-old Black woman born in her house named Juana la

Charta, then 7–8 months pregnant, escaped. A "mulato" named Manuel fled with her, leaving behind his enslaved wife and mother-in-law. Manuel's nine-year-old brother, Antonio, followed shortly thereafter. In addition to these four, Saavedra also sought to claim the children of enslaved women who had fled. She demanded the return of Juana's baby after its birth, as well as ownership of two children of another formerly enslaved Black woman named Leonor.[51] The cold possessiveness of Saavedra's petition and the consistency of flight from her household suggest her cruelty as a master. Recurrent flight also points to the strength of multiethnic runaway networks that continued to facilitate escape from what must have been an increasingly hostile environment.

To survive, runaways often stole clothing to conceal themselves or small objects that could be exchanged for sustenance and shelter. For example, in 1631 Simón of the "Sangley caste" managed to escape with forty gold pesos from his enslaver's estate in Mexico City. Simón was thirty years old, branded, and a maker of gold chains like "those that they use and make in the Philippine Islands."[52] When Angelina de la Cruz, a sixty-year-old "china," ran away in 1660, she took green and blue vestments lined in silver.[53] Similarly, when Ysabel Costarera, a forty-year-old "china," ran, she took fine green cloth, priest's clothing, and five gallons filled with silver and false gold.[54] A branded "china" who "looks mestiza" named María de la Rosa ran away in February 1660 and again in July 1661. Both times, she took with her valuable items (including silver plates; jewels; colorful Castilian cloth; green silk; and clothing with silver, gold, and flower decorations) and left behind her husband, a "chino" named Alonso Ylario. In 1661, she managed to escape after attending mass at the cathedral in Mexico City with her mistress. She was last seen in the company of a Spanish woman and had the help of a "mestiza" friend.[55] Tragically, she was eventually caught and sold to an obraje owner several years later, a common punishment for rebellious slaves.[56]

In 1637, María de la Cruz, a "negra," managed to free herself by pawning her enslaver's property to a free Black woman named Leonor de Salamanca. Over three years, María pawned cacao, achiote, clothing, and reales that collectively were worth the enormous sum of eight thousand pesos. She kept this money in a desk. One night, she hauled it out and bought her freedom. She went on to live as a free woman with the friends who had helped her, including her "chino" husband, Nicolas—ensuring that their children would be born free. Her former enslaver eventually discovered the plot, claimed that María had publicly bragged about pawning his goods, and demanded that her freedom be annulled. The paper trail ends as soon as María denied any knowledge of these claims, suggesting that the case did not proceed to a full trial or that she fled again before a trial could take place.[57]

Others were less fortunate. For example, Juan Baquero, a "chino," had been enslaved and assigned to the mines of Hostotipac (northwest of Guadalajara) with two other "chinos" under the ownership of Lucas García. García rented Juan out to Diego de Zúñiga, a miner. Juan ran from Zúñiga several times but was repeatedly caught and punished. After García died in 1654, Juan was illegally taken to Mexico City and rented out to numerous other enslavers. In 1656, he was ordered returned to the García estate.[58]

The flight from Mexico City of the twenty-two-year-old "chino" Lorenzo Álvarez, which he accomplished in 1635 with the help of a priest named Joan de Mercado, perhaps best exemplifies the collaborations that made escape possible. After a botched attempt to purchase Lorenzo, Mercado sent a friend to free him and steal from his enslaver. The list of pilfered goods is impressive, including silver plates, a Japanese silk sash, rock salt, Chinese silk socks, a green and black goat-hair dress, and numerous other valuable items.[59] After staying three nights with Mercado, Lorenzo spent thirty-five or thirty-six days with Mercado's comadre. Mercado then had a godson, Pedro Anis, disguise Lorenzo as a priest and accompany him to Anis's mother's home in Puebla. Afterward, Lorenzo traveled north to a saltpeter hacienda in Guichiapa owned by Mercado's compadre, where he stayed for two months. However, a Spanish official recognized Lorenzo when he was en route to the next hideout in Querétaro and returned him to his enslaver. The most noteworthy fact about Lorenzo's escape was that so many Spaniards in Mercado's network willingly hid a runaway for so long. Without their assistance, it would have been nearly impossible for him to attempt his long-term flight.

Such cases of Asian flight in New Spain indicate that "chinos" joined in an active social practice of running away to contest the conditions of their enslavement and escape bondage. The fact that many "chinos" chose the enormous risks of long-term flight expands Proctor's argument that cruel and unusual treatment often preceded Afro-Mexican escapes. Enslaved "chinos" quickly learned and participated in this proven technique of resisting bondage. In their approaches to running away, Asians relied heavily on local knowledge and collaborators in their extended networks. Those who succeeded in escaping sometimes built their own free communities, like the "chino" maroons who formed a palenque with Afro-Mexicans nine leagues from Acapulco and crept into town at night to ransack market stalls.[60]

Negotiating Enslavement through Blasphemy

In the Philippines, the peoples known as "chinos" in Mexico were most often identified as "indios." Since Indigenous peoples were considered neophyte Christians, they had long been exempted from formal inquisitorial inquiry. When Asians arrived in Acapulco, their legal metamorphosis from "indio / a" to "chino / a" meant that they now came under inquisitorial jurisdiction. While inquisitors in Mexico occasionally debated whether they could proceed against an "indio chino" or an "indio" from Asia, by the mid-seventeenth century, they were consistently prosecuting "chinos."[61] One of the most common types of denunciation against enslaved "chinos" accused them of speaking profanely about the Holy Trinity and the saints—in short, of committing blasphemy.

Within the labor-intensive confines of obrajes, *panaderías* (bakeries), and plantations scattered throughout New Spain, enslaved "chinos" occasionally resorted to blasphemy during moments of extreme duress. This tradition of blaspheming or threatening to blaspheme to protest brutal punishment has been well documented for cases involving enslaved Afro-Mexicans. Javier Villa-Flores argues that the enslaved used blasphemy and exposed themselves to the bureaucratic nightmare of the Inquisition to show that their severe mistreatment at the hands of their slave masters was un-Christian. In the best of cases, enslaved people could prove that enslavers had failed in their seigneurial obligation to instruct them in the Catholic faith, and the inquisitors could then force an enslaver to sell their blaspheming slaves to a new master. After all, conversion to Catholicism was a fundamental justification for slave trading in the Hispanic World.

Yet just as easily, blasphemy could increase the severity of an individual's punishment and sour their relations with both enslavers and the Inquisition. However, this was a risk that many enslaved people were willing to take during desperate moments. In a study of more than a hundred blasphemy cases, Villa-Flores concludes that "far from being an improvised utterance," blasphemy "was a socially patterned verbal act of resistance that carried within itself a legacy of usage."[62] Villa-Flores begins his essay on the infamous obraje of Melchor Días de Posadas with the story of a "Sangley" named Francisco, who participated in this established practice when he renounced God while being punished in 1659 (figure 4.1). Unfortunately, his renunciation only angered Posadas's son, who thrust a stick into Francisco's mouth and shouted: "Do you think that because you renounce God we will denounce you to the Holy Office? I have [the] permission of the Holy Office to punish you!"[63] This seemingly isolated case was in fact representative of a larger trend of Asians adopting Afro-Mexican strategies to contest their bondage.

"Chinos" accused of blasphemy also defended themselves in ways that Villa-Flores identifies with enslaved Afro-Mexicans, beginning with pleas for mercy and ending with remorse for having been compelled to renounce God to end their suffering.[64] The case of Lucas de Araujo, an enslaved "chino" (a Kapampangan from Manila), exemplifies this trend and suggests how such practices were transmitted. Lucas began work one day in 1661 as he always did, in a panadería he detested. These bakeries were notorious sites that functioned as de facto prisons for enslaved people.[65] At 1:00 a.m. that night, Lucas was still kneading dough. Frustrated, he said something "rude," and the foreman ordered that he be tied up, disrobed, and flogged. During the beating, Lucas renounced God and the saints 6–8 times, even saying that he had a demonic region on his right arm that would seek vengeance if not released, "of which the bad nature of this criminal was known."[66] Specific reference to demonic markings displayed precise knowledge of what Spaniards broadly considered to be brujería (witchcraft) and therefore worthy of denunciation.[67] According to witnesses, he did not regret saying such things, and the foreman kept him bound for fear that he might hang himself, despite his requests to be untied, now in the name of God.

Lucas's return to Christianity appeared insincere because he allegedly slept well the following night and did not admit his sins to a priest sent to hear his confession. His enslaver denounced him to the Holy Office with

4.1 Interior of an Obraje with the Protective Presence of the Holy Spirit and the Archangel Saint Michael

Though completed during the middle of the eighteenth century, this devotional ex-voto painting shows several characteristics of obrajes in the seventeenth century as well—namely, that their workforces were multiethnic and that they were spiritually vulnerable spaces in need of divine intervention and salvation.

Carlos López, *Interior de un obraje con la presencia protectora del Espíritu Santo y el Arcángel San Miguel*, 1740. Reproduction courtesy of the Museo Soumaya.

the explicit purpose of forcing Lucas to admit that he had behaved sinfully. During the initial questioning, Lucas insisted on his innocence by claiming that he had been drunk when he was tied up and had not blasphemed intentionally. Witnesses contended that "he was not drunk, but in his full judgment and depraved capacity and will" and that he frequently committed such blasphemies.[68]

After the inquisitors threatened him with major excommunication and torture, Lucas presented a very different narrative of that evening in the bakery. He stated that the whipping he received was so severe that he could not but blaspheme against God and the saints. He spoke about demons only because, after receiving more than fifty lashes, he thought that doing so might stop the beating. Tellingly, an "indio" witness at the scene had apparently cautioned him to ask for mercy from God and the Virgin—an indication of shared local knowledge about how to use blasphemy sparingly and strategically. Lucas then claimed that after invoking the love of God, he had blasphemed only four times and that he had not confessed his blasphemy earlier out of shame and fear. Despite this admission, the inquisitors condemned him to an auto de fe in which he would publicly confess his sins, receive two hundred lashes, and be returned to his enslaver. Lucas's case confirms that enslaved "chinos," like other enslaved people, often renounced the Holy Trinity during extreme punishment in an attempt to lessen its intensity. Moreover, presenting one's blasphemy to inquisitors as an involuntary response in the face of malicious maltreatment could serve as a strategy to expose the excessive nature of one's punishment. But as Lucas's penance indicates, this tactic was not always successful.

Lucas was not the only "chino" who engaged in this social practice. A denunciation launched in 1665 by Don Gabriel Garcia Moctezuma, a minister of justice in Mexico City and "protector of indios," sheds additional light on how witnesses could share ideas about blasphemy with the denounced.[69] Garcia Moctezuma had caught and chained an unnamed runaway variously described as "chino," "mulato," and "negro." The captive threatened that if he was not released, he would blaspheme in the presence of Garcia Moctezuma, his nine-year-old son, an enslaved Black doctor named Diego, a criado of the viceroy, and numerous passersby. In the end, he allegedly renounced the Virgin Mary, and the public nature of the blasphemy heightened its scandal.[70]

No witnesses corroborated Garcia Moctezuma's claim that the runaway had blasphemed. Diego only heard the captive call on the Virgin to untie him, after which he entered his own enslaver's panadería saying, "come on, man, you are crazy."[71] Santiago Bernardo de Quirós, a Spaniard who owned a shop nearby, recognized that the captive might blaspheme, given his treatment at the hands of Garcia Moctezuma, and advised him not to because a *familiar* (lay servant) of an inquisitor was present.[72] The existence of the captive's blasphemy was therefore impossible to prove. Instead of further punishment, he received a strong warning and was ordered returned to his enslaver, Diego Millán.

Perhaps the best example of how "chinos" learned the social practice of strategic blasphemy comes through a denunciation in 1626 at Gaspar de Herrera's obraje in Puebla. One day, an enslaved "chino" named Luis de Peña was made to punish an enslaved Black man named Manuel. (Slaves often had to punish one another at the behest of enslavers and their foremen in obrajes.)[73] In the presence of several enslaved Black men, Luis gave Manuel five lashes, whereupon he renounced God and the Virgin Mary. Luis then gave him two more lashes, and Manuel renounced them a second time. The punishment then ceased. Shortly afterward, at the same obraje an enslaved man named Jusepe de Tierra Mala similarly blasphemed twice when punished "because they also stopped whipping him" after he did so.[74] All three enslaved witnesses to the blasphemy, including an elderly enslaved man named Juan Mandinga, covered for Manuel and Jusepe. They insisted that the men had blasphemed only to prevent further punishment and so should be forgiven.

These blasphemies present a blueprint for cultural transmission. After seeing how Manuel avoided receiving more lashes, Jusepe had clearly copied his strategy. It is easy to imagine that if faced with similar punishment, the enslaved Luis might have considered blaspheming as well. After all, Manuel's blasphemy had given Luis an excuse to prematurely stop the punishment. Just like Lucas's interactions with the unnamed "indio" and the unnamed captive's interactions with the Black doctor and Spanish shop owner, Luis's experience suggests a world teeming with the transmission of vernacular knowledge.

Flight, blasphemy, and other forms of self-advocacy in New Spain's race-conscious society ultimately hint at the conversations, friendships, collaborations, and learning that colonial archives suggest but rarely, if ever, identify directly. Yet as Ivor Miller has argued, the fact that such acts were ignored in archival formation or were historically considered illegal does not mean they did not happen or were not fundamental to knowledge transmission and identity formation.[75] An awareness of these absences allows us to better understand cases with few details, like that of an enslaved "chino" named Tomás, who blasphemed in 1663 on the sugar plantation of Santiago Tenextepango in the vicinity of Cuernavaca. Though the denunciation is brief, tellingly, Tomás worked alongside a "mestizo" and two slaves (presumably Afro-Mexican), who may have supplied useful information on how to contest the conditions of enslavement.[76] When enslaved people like Tomás filled the air with blasphemous utterances, they created a documentary record of protest against the brutalities of bondage designed to remind inquisitors and enslavers that fair treatment was not only prudent, but also a religious obligation.

Nondogmatic Spirituality

Like runaways and blasphemers, Asian spiritualists in Mexico negotiated enslavement with knowledge and creativity. They drew on nondogmatic practices originating from all over the world to gain recognition and resources and to form new communities. Asian practitioners of nondogmatic spiritual traditions have not been studied in detail, but they most clearly exemplify the process of convergence. Undoubtedly, the best-known example of an enslaved Asian spiritual authority in colonial Mexico is Catarina de San Juan. Contrary to popular belief, Catarina was not only known for exemplary Catholic behavior during her lifetime. Spaniards frequently cursed her as a *hechicera* (sorceress) because of her miraculous powers, which she often used to transcend the limitations of her material surroundings and even her own body.[77]

By all accounts, Catarina was deeply traumatized by her captivity. Even at the end of her life, Joseph del Castillo Graxeda knew her to say (in his allegedly accurate transcription of her speech), "Look, father, when they captured to me, they made slave; many anxieties, much work, only the divine Majesty knows what I went through."[78] Her ascetic Catholicism provided a reprieve from life in bondage, but her spiritual powers frequently exceeded Catholic norms of miraculous occurrences. They were a way for her to return home, since "for this virgin the memory of the Mughal [country] was very pleasant."[79] The comment surely understated her terrible longing for a distant land, a lost family, and a life before captivity and free from abuse.

Catarina was known to travel or "bilocate" in her visions, both geographically and between worlds.[80] Bilocating allowed her to escape the physical duress of her daily life—including her violent and unconsummated marriage of fourteen years with Domingo Suárez, a "chino" she freed from captivity—and contribute to the Catholic mission in other parts of the world, particularly Asia.[81] She allegedly told her confessor, Alonso Ramos, that "what I have seen most frequently is my parents in purgatory . . . until in one of these years, I saw them come in the company of the *nao* [ship] of the Philippines to the port of Acapulco, from where, on their knees, they came into my presence."[82] Catarina's spiritual visions allowed her to see what enslavement had taken away: her parents, the embodied manifestations of a lost home. Consequently, the Spanish and New Spanish Inquisitions censored Ramos's hagiography and its attestation of Catarina's extraordinary power in 1692 and 1696, respectively.[83]

Despite the threat of inquisitorial backlash, by the mid-seventeenth century, dynamic, multiethnic traditions of magic and healing defined the rhythms, controversies, and remedies of colonial daily life in Mexico. The scholarship on colonial *curanderismo* (healing) and *hechicería* (magic) recognizes both the enduring presence of Indigenous and West / West Central African spiritualities and their confluence, exchange, and creolization.[84] As Joan Bristol writes, "orthodox Christian practice and unorthodox ritual practices, as defined by the Spanish church, coexisted at every level of society."[85] Late sixteenth-century books of common antidotes and local healing in New Spain demonstrate the highly mixed nature of these traditions.[86] In the accusatory language of Hernando Ruiz de Alarcón in 1629, "those who deal frequently with the Indians easily become infected with their customs and superstitions, especially if they are base people."[87] However, the demand for folk remedies was nearly universal, as hechicería and brujería could offer solutions that eclipsed the therapeutic capacities of Catholic doctrine.

For example, in 1656, Alonso de Arsegueren, a clergyman, made a series of denunciations based on rumors and stories he had heard in Mexico City. He had been staying with a friend of his, the silversmith Francisco de

Ybarra, when Ybarra's son, a sixteen-year-old student named Antonio, told him a strange story. Antonio apparently knew an enslaved "chino" named Manuel del Rosario who found a stolen silver plate after drinking peyote. The word *peyote* comes from the Nahuatl word *peyotl,* meaning "a thing that glimmers, glows." It is a small, flowering cactus that produces a fruit with hallucinogenic properties.[88]

While peyote had numerous medicinal uses commonly prescribed by a *ticitl* (Nahua doctor), its ceremonial use in divinatory cults resulted in an inquisitorial ban on its consumption in 1620.[89] To the authors of the ban, the devil entered the spiritual world of "indios" through divination with peyote and undermined the Catholic faith throughout the Americas and even as far as the Philippines.[90] When Arsegueren threatened to denounce Manuel for doing precisely what the Inquisition had banned, Antonio's mother interceded, insisting that the "chino" was a known liar and that this story had to be another of his fabrications. Later, when the mother was not present, Arsegueren approached Antonio once more and asked for details. Arsegueren learned that a "mulato" had paid Manuel five pesos to find a stolen silver plate. With the five pesos, the "chino" bought peyote gendered as male and female, which he gave to a virgin to grind up. Thus, Manuel was following an established procedure to achieve clairvoyance through peyote consumption.[91] Peyote-drinking rituals often required a virgin's intercession to ensure that the plant's divine powers were uncontaminated.[92] The "mulato" drank of the concoction three times and then successfully located the plate. Nothing came of this denunciation or Arsegueren's later denunciations, one of which recounted how a renowned "mulato" dance master told him a story of a "mulata" who drank peyote and lost her mind.[93]

In the story of Manuel, both mother and son—although they disagreed on what happened—projected common Spanish stereotypes of castas. According to the mother, the "chino" was simply a liar who fabricated stories for personal gain. According to the son, the "chino" practiced strange rituals that granted inexplicable powers. The clergyman considered these rituals to be a religious offense punishable by major excommunication. For our purposes, this story elucidates the "chino" Manuel's leadership in the cult of peyote consumption in Mexico City. Prior to Arsegueren's denunciation, Manuel must have participated in and practiced these rituals with either Indigenous or Afro-Mexican specialists numerous times. Using peyote had seemingly become a reliable source of additional coin as well, which he could one day use to purchase his freedom. Manuel then taught the "mulato" the secrets of its ritual consumption, exemplifying the multiethnic demand for solutions that peyote could provide. Though peyote had pre-Columbian roots in Indigenous cosmologies, the practice had broad appeal during the colonial period, and Afro-Mexicans had participated in these cults since at least the late sixteenth century.[94] Therefore, practitioners like Manuel were fundamental to the adaptations that enabled the survival of this persecuted Indigenous practice during the colonial period.

As unusual as finding a silver plate for money may seem, it was not uncommon for people to consume pharmacological hallucinogens like ololiuhqui or peyote to find "stolen, lost, or misplaced" objects.[95] Robert Schwaller uncovered a case from 1570 of a "mulata" from Spain named Barbola de Zamora who was living in Zacatecas and drank peyote and charged Indigenous "Chichimecas" to find lost objects.[96] Similarly, in 1675 in Puebla, the "chino" Diego Palomino and his five-year-old daughter, Teresa, were accused of finding lost objects for money through clairvoyance. A "mestiza" named Juana had apparently lost her son, Miguel (then two and a half years old), and her friend, a "mestiza" named Josepha, recommended that she use a *zahorina* (female clairvoyant) to find him. Juana decided to approach Palomino and Teresa about her lost son. Apparently, the two "chinos" had established their divinatory reputation by successfully finding a wedding mantle for six pesos. Palomino told Juana that Teresa had gained her power from God and that she could perform her miraculous feats only for money. Juana refused to pay and later found her son in someone else's home. In the end, inquisitors ordered Palomino and Teresa to stop claiming divine power under threat of severe punishment, and they also commanded Palomino to raise his daughter to be a good Catholic.[97] In addition to providing a fleeting glimpse of "china" girlhood and the believability (or lack thereof) of her powers, the case demonstrates that "chinos" like Palomino recognized that the appropriation and manipulation of supernatural remedies were viable and popular ways to quickly earn money.[98]

At least one "chino" facilitated the practice of divination as an enslaver. Pedro Elen, a "chino," worked as a drummer in the garrison of Acapulco's Fort of San Diego. During the late 1610s, he requested that Madalena, an enslaved "mulata" whom he owned, take ololiuhqui to divine the location of the galleons expected to reach Acapulco in a given year. She responded that two were coming. This was not an isolated incident. Madalena was one of the most important galleon seers of a cohort of mostly free Afro-Mexican women in Acapulco who practiced divination and love magic. Madalena was their ololiuhqui specialist, and she frequently used Elen's house as the site where she worshipped ololiuhqui and made predictions with it.[99]

According to the ever-vigilant Ruiz de Alarcón, "The so-called *ololiuhqui* is a seed like lentils or lentil vetch which, when drunk, deprives one of judgment. And the faith that these unhappy natives have in this seed is amazing, since, by drinking it, they consult it like an oracle for everything whatever that they want to know, even those things which are beyond human knowledge."[100] The ololiuhqui seeds were typically stored in baskets and later ground up and mixed into alcoholic drinks. Unlike the consumption of peyote, ceremonies involving ololiuhqui tended to be private and could last for days at a time. Ceremonies of consumption involved offering incense and flowers to it on an altar, reciting specific incantations, sweeping the area where the plant grew, and watering the plant.[101] When taken properly, ololiuhqui made it possible to communicate directly with gods, saints, and ancestors. The timing of Elen's request places Madalena as one of the first Black women in New Spain to learn the ritual consumption of ololiuhqui. Her "chino" enslaver's involvement hints at prior experiences and exchanges with Indigenous populations in and around the transpacific port that retained these practices.

An inquisitorial denunciation from 1628 elucidates how these forms of multiethnic knowledge transfer may have occurred. An obraje owner named Jacome Basalle forced an enslaved "chino," Francisco Lopez, to ask the Holy Office for forgiveness for casting the cut-off head of a cat into the street. Francisco had been enslaved in Bengala and brought to Manila at the age of seven. There he was baptized, learned Spanish, and lived for 8–10 years. A barber named Alonso Balderrama traded him across the Pacific, and after a year in Acapulco, Francisco marched to Mexico City in the mule train of a ship's captain from Peru (whose name he could not later recall). In the capital, Francisco was incarcerated for wounding a Black man. Basalle bought Francisco from the public prison and put him to work in his obraje in Texcoco. Francisco reported that Basalle would punish him without cause and had locked him in a room for over a year to prevent him from running away.

While imprisoned in Mexico City, Francisco had met several detained "mulato" vaqueros of the central Mexican hinterlands who taught him how to free himself from any confinement. Since the sixteenth century, multi-ethnic vaqueros had acquired reputations for practicing and developing numerous mixed nondogmatic rituals.[102] For Ruiz de Alarcón, the vaqueros' belief in the "divine" qualities of a certain root demonstrated that the devil "does not miss a chance to introduce a heathen superstition." Empowered pouches containing this root were said to protect the vaqueros from falling off their mounts and suffering other forms of bodily harm.[103]

The vaqueros told Francisco that to free himself he had to place the head of a black cat in a hole and, before the head, call on a god (which Spaniards assumed to be the devil); the god would then come and free him. Their advice echoed various Indigenous Tonal rituals (in which a small animal like a cat, dog, or toad was killed to influence the physical world) that were practiced in a wide territory between Durango to the north and Puebla to the south. What they recommended to Francisco also resembled numerous West Central African rites of animal sacrifice. Such practices often included sewing materials or food into an animal or burying it alive to produce a desired effect in a person.[104]

While detained in Texcoco, Francisco managed to find a dark cat, catch it, and decapitate it. He then placed the severed head between two rafters in his room. Tellingly, he reported that at the prospect of calling on the devil, a great fear overcame him, and he hurled the cat's head into the street, inadvertently alerting passersby to his heresy. Although Francisco had not hesitated to kill and decapitate the cat, his claim of an about-face before the point of no return was fundamental to his confession and stated desire "to live and to die in the holy Catholic faith of our redeemer Jesus Christ."[105] This strategic appeal to Catholic redemption worked well: Francisco left the inquisitorial audience with only a warning and, even better, with an order for Basalle to treat him better to avoid any future temptation to offend God. In other words, the inquisitors held the enslaver partially responsible for Francisco's transgressions. Not only had Francisco learned an Afro-Mexican technique of resistance from the detained "mulatos," but he had also managed to manipulate the inquisitorial process in his favor to improve his treatment by Basalle. Perhaps the ritual had worked.

Another example of shared knowledge comes from an enslaved "chino" named Antonio, who traveled to San Marcos (north of Acapulco) to purchase *polvos de solimán* (poisonous powders) for his enslaver. He asked a local *bruja* (witch), a "mulata" named Leonor de Ontiveros, where to find such powders. She directed Antonio to an herbalist in the plaza who was an Indigenous woman. Antonio bought the powders, but rather than deliver them to his enslaver, he decided to use them for his own purposes. He poisoned the husband of an Indigenous woman named Mariana, with whom he had *mala amistad* (extramarital sexual relations). After the husband's death, Antonio married Mariana.[106] This union ensured that Antonio's children would be born free, gave him the possibility of living away from his enslaver, and increased his chances of being free later in life. Antonio's actions demonstrate that "chinos" also participated in colonial Mexico's energetic cultures of love magic, which often subverted the sacrament of Catholic marriage by using substances and rituals from both Indigenous and Afro-diasporic traditions.

The example par excellence of an enslaved "chino" spiritualist is that of Antón, who in 1652 was accused of palm reading and divination (including finding a silver plate). In Jacinto da Silva's obrajes (first in Tlaxcala and later in Coyoacán), Antón was known as *el sabio* (the wise one). In his testimony before the inquisitors, he recounted a dizzying series of sales and dislocations from Kochi to Melaka, Makassar, Manila, Acapulco, Veracruz, Tlaxcala, and finally to Coyoacán. He was the son of a Malabari scribe named Chone, was literate in the local Brahmic script, had been married in his homeland to a woman named Tirimala, and had made a living as a spice trader. In 1622, he boarded a Portuguese vessel with nine other South Asian traders. When they awoke, they found that they had been enslaved and were en route to be sold in Melaka. Antón was then thirty-five years old. By the time of his denunciation, he had spent thirty years in captivity.

To mitigate the difficulties of life in Silva's obrajes, Antón performed palm readings for the thirty-five enslaved Afro-Mexicans working alongside him.[107] A spike in enslaved labor in obrajes during the mid-seventeenth century meant that for the first time the mills were a predominantly Afro-Mexican space: Black people represented 59 percent of the workforce in obrajes in Coyoacán by 1650.[108] Like Afro-Mexican healers and diviners, Antón quickly acquired a reputation as a gifted expert. He served a multi-ethnic clientele, some of whom often traveled a full day from Mexico City specifically for his readings.[109] He told clients if they would find love, when a baby would be born, if a woman would become a nun, and so on. Since he could not speak Spanish or Nahuatl well, he relied on a couple of weavers (of unknown origin) for translation and split his earnings with them. He confessed to performing dozens of palm readings, for which he charged 1–4 reales per prognostication. He even made predictions at the behest of his enslaver, who would have profited from the readings as well. When pressed, Antón claimed that he only wanted to make some money to buy chocolate, tobacco, and pulque for himself and the others laboring in the obraje.

In Coyoacán, he was widely known as a *zahorí* (clairvoyant), and he even claimed that he had been trained as one before becoming a Christian.[110] The word *zahorí* comes from the Arabic *zuharí,* which referred to a geomancer who could read the earth—specifically, "lines drawn in the earth."[111] Beginning in the sixteenth century, Spanish scholars frequently debated the secular (natural) or diabolic (unnatural) origins of a zahorí's powers.[112] In Spain, zahoríes were clairvoyants whose sight penetrated the soil to discover underground sources of water, veins of metal, and buried bodies. Several philosophers and theologians (for example, Alphonsus Gutiérrez de Veracruz, Martín del Río, and Juan Eusebio Nieremberg) considered it possible to attain some of these abilities without diabolic intervention.[113] The ambiguous nature of divining the earth through its surface similarly extended to divining the future through the body (as in chiromancy, for example), which was also not always considered diabolic.[114] Therefore, admitting to practicing chiromancy and emphasizing his training as a zahorí in Kochi all worked in Antón's favor. Seijas notes that Antón exhibited additional knowledge of inquisitorial inquiries when he mentioned his heritage from a "land of gentiles, not of Muslims or Jews."[115] In so doing, Antón also tapped into the conflicts of the Malabar Rites Controversy of 1610, which sought to differentiate the secular cultural customs of the Malabari elite from transgressive religious idolatry.[116]

Despite the severity of the accusations against Antón—which included that he had made a pact with a demon and claimed to have received his power from God—he managed to provide mundane explanations for his supernatural abilities, a common defensive tactic among the accused. He claimed that he had made up predictions as a joke, that others found objects for him, and that he worked with an enslaved Burmese man who acted as an informant. Even the sabio moniker came from the obraje's majordomo, who apparently gave all of the obraje's enslaved chinos a nickname. Antón's defense, the ambiguity of a zahorí's abilities, and his gestures of Christianity (including the ability to recite the Ave Maria and Pater Noster) merited clemency. After he had spent 245 days in prison, the inquisitors ordered that he be loaded on a mule while wearing a miter and holding a green wax candle in his hands, and ordered him to both announce his crimes in the streets and abstain from divination in the future. Although Antón was quick to deny any religious infraction, the spiritual practices unearthed during this trial resemble practices carried out among Afro-diasporic therapeutic communities, aimed at both elevating non-dogmatic forms of authority and providing immediate responses to life's troubles through practices derived from a range of spiritual traditions across the Atlantic World.[117]

The case ends there, but Antón's story might not. In the meticulous diary of Gregorio Martín de Guijo, there is a curious entry for Monday, June 4, 1657, five years after Antón's penance. Guijo wrote that in the central plaza of Mexico City, six people received criminal punishment. Among them were an Indigenous woman who sold pulque and an "old chino" condemned for participating in a theft.[118] Each of the latter two received two hundred lashes, and they were sold to an obraje for the next six years. Antón could have been the "old chino": he would have been seventy then. The alleged crime fits his penchant for collaborating with Indigenous and Afro-Mexican people, and "theft" was a secular term that Antón used during his trial to explain how he divined the location of lost objects. Guijo's diary entry opens the possibility that Antón was determined to continue being el sabio, the educated merchant of Malabar, regardless of the consequences.

Finally, the denunciations against Antonio Rosado and María Juana—in 1651 and 1686, respectively—are perhaps the most explicit examples of Afro-Asian convergence in Mexico. Described variously as a "mulato" and "of the chino caste," Antonio had been born in Goa to a father of mixed Portuguese and East African heritage from Mozambique and a mother from Ternate.[119] A free man in the employ of Franciscan missionaries, Antonio had been unjustly enslaved and sold in Manila. At the age of seventy in 1651, he still labored in an obraje in Mexico City. During mass, Antonio declared that God and the Virgin Mary had abandoned him.[120] Although inquisitors sentenced him to receive two hundred lashes, they berated his enslaver for treating him badly and recommended selling him to prevent future blasphemies, which the enslaver subsequently did.[121] Antonio's case clearly demonstrates that "chinos" could be both Asian- and Afro-diasporic and that convergence in the Indian Ocean World had melded with a new form of Afro-Asian convergence in enslaved communities in New Spain.

Similarly, María Juana was a *mulata achinada* (Asian-looking "mulata") from the Philippines who was a domestic servant to Madre Damiana de San Cristobal of the Convent of San Bernardo in Mexico City.[122] San Cristobal accused María Juana of being a bad Christian since she had said that she loved the devil more than God and had made a pact with the devil, and she had claimed that she had seen him and considered him very beautiful. Experiencing sexual temptation through the devil was known to be a way in which early modern women manifested sexual desire that did not conform to the expectations of Catholic marriage.[123] San Cristobal testified, "I give all that my powers can do to subdue the *mal natural* [bad nature] of that china."[124] Her language implicitly compares the sexually deviant "bad nature" of a "china" (conflated with "mulata achinada") to the behavior and habits of an assimilated Christian, parroting stereotypes that framed mixed Afro-descended women as sexually unrestrained.[125] Although the inquisitors were prepared to excommunicate María Juana, San Cristobal convinced them to issue a significantly lighter sentence: giving María Juana a stern warning and requiring her to confess her sins and otherwise demonstrate her penitence. Ultimately, San Cristobal believed that punishment would suffice to bring María Juana back to good behavior and that excommunication (which would have meant giving up on her potential transformation) would have been too harsh and unfair. At the end of the case, María Juana was in tears and begged for mercy.

Antonio's and María Juana's cases reveal that the two poles of the Afro-Asian binary in New Spain could not be neatly disentangled. "Chinos" and Afro-Mexicans lived side by side and had similar experiences of racialization, economic disenfranchisement, and cultural dislocation, but these were not the only reasons why they responded to such conditions in remarkably similar ways. Just as important, they were often categorized in overlapping ways within the casta system. In the words of Norah Gharala, "chinos could also be negros," and "the concept of Indo-Pacific *chinos* or *indios* who were also *negros* fit into early modern imaginations in New Spain."[126] Indeed, "chinos" could be *amulatados* ("mulato"-looking), "negros," and *prietos* (dark-skinned), often for the sake of justifying enslavement, and Afro-Mexicans could also be "achinados."[127] At times, their ethnicities also overlapped—as in the case of Antonio, who was Portuguese, East African, and from Ternate.

Much as Afro-Mexicans did, enslaved "chinos" ran away, blasphemed, and created therapeutic communities that blurred and transgressed the rigid bounds of Catholic spirituality. Confronting their own dislocation and disenfranchisement in New Spain, enslaved Asians, Afro-Mexicans, and Indigenous people engaged in cultural and intellectual exchanges of uncommon diversity in world history as they sought to improve their material and spiritual lives.

5 TRAJECTORIES BEYOND CENTRAL MEXICO

WHEN THE SEVENTY-TWO-YEAR-OLD Alonso Coronel denounced himself to the Inquisition in Durango in 1693, he described himself as an "indio native and resident of the city of Lima."[1] However, the inquisitors had already discovered that Coronel was born in Lima to Kapampangan parents from Macabebe. And witnesses stated that "[he is a] chino [and] *apparently* native *that says* he is from the city of Lima."[2] Inquisitors in Mexico failed to see Coronel for what he said he was, an Indigenous person born in the Americas. To them, he would always be only a "chino," since he had the "color and eyes that those who are called chinos in Mexico City usually have."[3] Phenotypical traits had transformed Coronel from a Peruvian "indio" to a member of the casta of most other Asians in Mexico.

The case of Coronel indicates several trends of critical importance to the historiography of the "chinos" of New Spain. Although most Asians who came to the Americas in the early modern period disembarked and remained in Mexico, Asian mobility clearly extended beyond the viceregal core. For over a thousand men, women, and children, Acapulco became a point of departure to more distant lands. It should be no surprise that Coronel was born in Lima, for the Viceroyalty of Peru hosted a substantial population of both free and enslaved Asians. During the long seventeenth century, Asian servants, petitioners, traders, artisans, and enslaved people reached nearly every corner of the Spanish empire. Scattered records document their presence virtually everywhere Spanish ships sailed: as far north as present-day California and Oregon, as far south as Lima, and even across the Atlantic to Spain.

Due to the relative dearth of records from this period on Asians in the Americas beyond central Mexico, as well as to the newness of their study, these regions have received little or no scholarly attention. The new historiography of early modern Asian mobility to and through the Americas— pioneered by Edward Slack, Melba Falck Reyes, Héctor Palacios, Déborah Oropeza, Tatiana Seijas, and Rubén Carrillo Martín—focuses exclusively on central Mexico and its wealth of extant documentation. In 2015, Carrillo Martín concluded that "the exploration of the Peruvian case remains unresolved and [so do those] of other colonial enclaves beyond the North American viceroyalty."[4] While the works of Leo Garofalo (2020), Lucío de Sousa (2019), Mariano Bonialian (2015), and Michelle McKinley (2012) have begun to fill the gaps in our knowledge of early Asian experiences in Peru, some regions (like Guatemala and Oregon) remain almost entirely untouched. No study has yet examined the full scope of early modern Asian dispersion throughout the hemisphere.

This chapter uses case studies from the full expanse of the Viceroyalty of New Spain, Peru, and Spain not only to demonstrate that the Asian presence in the early modern Hispanic World was far wider ranging than previously thought, but also to show that the racialization of Asians took on local characteristics in various parts of the Spanish empire. For example, colonial officials in Peru and Spain often did not uphold the Mexican paradigm of chino-genesis established in Acapulco. As the case of Coronel suggests, as distance from central Mexico increased, so too did the instability of the "chino / a" marker. Asians often tried to leave the "chino / a" label behind as they departed from New Spanish shores. Some succeeded in becoming "indio / a" again, as they had been in the Philippines or the Indian Ocean World. Others, like Coronel, were unable to shake their "chino / a" identification in Mexico despite their insistence on being "indios."

As Chapters 3 and 4 demonstrate, the formation of the "chino / a" category in Acapulco had an immediate effect throughout central Mexico. Other regions that maintained close contact with the viceregal core tended to mirror these patterns of chino-genesis. In Guatemala, for example, Spanish officials who had previous experience in Mexico continued to use "chino / a" to refer to Asian people, particularly in legal settings when they prosecuted Asians for aberrant behavior. In contrast, the term "chino / a" was used only sporadically in Lima throughout the seventeenth century. For example, a Peruvian tribute register for 1613–1614 recorded 114 Asian "indios" in Lima, only a handful of whom were also "chinos." And official records in Lima generally categorized Asians using the fluid terms common in Acapulco's treasury records from 1590 to 1615, before that port adopted "chino / a" as the primary legal designation for Asian subjects. Mexico's path to chino-genesis thus was not fully replicated in Peru, owing in large part to the distance between the two viceroyalties: nautical travel along the Pacific coast was often limited or banned, and when it did occur, the journey from Acapulco to Lima's port of Callao lasted many weeks. Comparably, the "chino / a" label rarely survived the transatlantic journey to Spain. On the Iberian Peninsula, "indio / a" retained its broader signification, referring to any Indigenous vassal subject of the empire from the Americas to Asia. "Chino / a" referred solely to the denizens of the Kingdom of China, and the Mexican use of "chino / a" generally appeared only in correspondence from the Americas addressed to recipients in Spain. For example, Pedro de Vergara Gaviria (in Mexico) called the Japanese Juan Antonio a "chino" in a letter to King Felipe IV in 1623, an identification that likely caused some confusion in the royal court.[5]

Even when the "chino / a" label did not travel, however, Asians often found themselves relegated to a similar, second-class-subject position as "indios." The institutions of colonial power to which "chinos" responded in Mexico—enslavement, the *audiencias* (courts), and the Catholic church—existed throughout the Hispanic World. For this reason, Asians elsewhere in the Americas often continued to contest colonial stereotypes of behavior, petitioning for special privileges, and engaging in cultural exchanges in ways that had characterized "chino / a" experiences in central Mexico. This was not a coincidence, since like the "chinos" of New Spain, Asians in Peru (for example) had often lived for years in Manila and survived the Pacific passage. Moreover, many of them had either stopped over at or settled in Mexico before traveling south. The patterns of "chino / a" communal cohesion, intermarriage, and mutual assistance that developed in Mexico also appeared in Lima, due in part to the fact that there were more than 114 Asians there during the early seventeenth century. Though the overall scale of Asian presence in Peru was considerably less than that in Mexico during this period, the concentration of Asians in Lima was high enough to produce documentable convergences among them.

In contrast, the low numbers of Asians in Seville greatly exacerbated their social isolation and their dependence on local communities in ways that, with a few exceptions, largely eliminated the possibility of intra-Asian contact or family formation. Asians generally arrived on the Iberian Peninsula in diplomatic delegations, to petition for royal favor based on past service, and in the retinues of officials or missionaries as either enslaved subjects or "free" servants. As petitioners for the opening of new trade routes, the receipt of pensions, or protection from abuse, Asians in Spain used legal language to portray themselves as subjects worthy of royal intervention. Their goals and immediate circumstances often differed from those of "chinos" in Mexico, but their manipulation of legal rhetoric and Spanish expectations of behavior resembled similar strategies on the other side of the Atlantic.

Although they ended up thousands of miles apart, Asians who journeyed beyond central Mexico continued to be linked through their approaches to negotiating their hybrid subject statuses in the colonial world. Whether they had been denounced to the Inquisition in Guatemala, awarded freedom in Lima, or abandoned by a missionary in Seville, Asians across the Hispanic World confronted the politics of their surroundings as they sought to eke out an existence in societies still coming to terms with the new demographic realities of global empire.

Early Expeditions to California and Oregon

As we have seen, the Viceroyalty of New Spain stretched from Mexico to the Philippines. In the Americas, it also had jurisdiction over an enormous territory that included Spanish North America, Central America, and the Caribbean. The earliest documentation of Asians in the Americas outside of Mexico resulted from early Spanish expeditions to gain more knowledge about the still poorly charted seas and lands of New Spain. The true size of the Pacific Ocean remained unknown, and frequent sightings of Californian shores inspired curiosity as to what lay beyond them. These expeditions were often explicitly intended to investigate rumors of legendary deposits of gold or to locate safe harbors for the galleons at higher latitudes than Mexico.

One such voyage, that of Pedro de Unamuno from Macau to Acapulco in 1587, is responsible for the first recorded Asian presence in Las Californias (present-day California) and, therefore, in what is now part of the United States. Before arriving in Mexico, Unamuno's men studied the Cal-

ifornian coast with a contingent of eight "Luzon indios," who were warriors, scouts, and "spies."[6] Assuming that "indios" from one land (the Philippines) would serve as useful intermediaries with "indios" from another
(California), Unamuno deployed his Philippine auxiliaries in accordance
with well-established Spanish military protocol in both Asia and the Americas. In so doing, Indigenous peoples from the Philippines became entangled for the first time in the Spanish incursions attributed to the invasion
of the Americas. Initially, they did so as "indios" from the Philippines, since
their presence preceded chino-genesis in Acapulco.

Unamuno named the first point of disembarkation San Lucas (a site
known today as Morro Bay) in accordance with the liturgical calendar, as
was customary.[7] For several days, the landing party tracked signs of human
activity by following footpaths, searching abandoned farms and huts, and
trekking toward distant fires. When the group became lost, the Philippine
auxiliaries found high ground to reorient the expedition. After a fruitless
search, the men turned back to their launch and promptly stumbled into
an ambush. Native warriors wounded three Spaniards with arrows and fire-
hardened spears. One Spaniard who was not wearing armor died after
being struck through the chest by a lance. The attack also killed one of the
Philippine auxiliaries, who had attempted to protect the wounded with his
shield.[8] With a volley of gunfire, the Spanish and Philippine landing party
managed to escape.

Several days later, the Spaniards and auxiliaries disembarked further
south to wash their clothes and acquire fresh water. There, they spotted
another band of Native warriors. As a gesture of peace, a Spaniard and a
Philippine auxiliary gave the Natives some bizcocho. However, after a fu-
tile attempt at communication, the meeting ended in a brief exchange of
arrows and gunfire before both sides retreated.[9] Unamuno and the rest of
his expedition then rushed south to Acapulco to seek treatment for the
wounded.

In the following years, several more voyages to the Californian coast departed from Manila and Acapulco in search of the Northwest Passage and
the Bering Strait (*el estrecho de Anian*), though with similar results.[10] Sebastián
Vizcaíno's expedition to map the North American coast left the clearest
record of Asian involvement. Vizcaíno assembled the crews of his three
ships—the *San Diego, Santo Tomás,* and *Tres Reyes*—in Acapulco on February
28, 1602, in advance of their departure on May 5. This mustering period

benefited from the presence of idle galleon sailors who had arrived at the port during the trade season. Unsurprisingly, some of the crew members were Asian sailors recovering from the brutal Pacific passage. The crew of the *San Diego* included a diver (*buzo*) named Anton Thomas, who was described as an "indio" of Malabar and paid fifteen pesos per month.[11] Antonio Bengala ("indio") and Francisco Miguel ("japón") are listed among the grumetes and were paid the elevated rate of ten pesos per month. Christoual Catoya ("chino") was hired as both a grumete and a skilled carpenter. He received sixteen pesos, five tomines, and four granos per month. Two "chinos" were listed as pages: Agustin Longalo and Lucas Cate.[12] The use of these forms of categorization ("indio," "japón," and "chino") was typical of pre-1615 labeling practices in Acapulco. Miguel received a specific designation as Japanese, signaling his perceived difference from both "indios" and "chinos." Both South Asians, Thomas and Bengala, were labeled "indios." The "chinos" were of ambiguous ethnicities, but the trade of one of them (carpenter) and their surnames suggest that they were from the Philippines.

Vizcaíno's expedition succeeded at charting the coast but not much else. The *Santo Tomás* turned back early, with forty sailors sick. Treasury records document the onboard deaths of three enslaved Africans who served as grumetes.[13] After being blown off course at Cape Mendocino, *San Diego*, the flagship, reached as high as 42 degrees latitude and named what they found there Cape Sebastian (in what is now southern Oregon). In view of snowy, forested mountains Vizcaíno ordered their return to Acapulco, given that "there are not three [healthy] sailors [left] that can serve to furl the main topsail."[14] The crew suffered from acute scurvy and hunger until the ship dropped south to the Mazatlán Islands, where they sustained themselves by eating prickly pears.[15] Meanwhile, the *Tres Reyes* reached 43 degrees and found a river that the surviving crew erroneously thought to be the entrance to "Anian" (the straits to Asia).[16]

When the *San Diego* lurched back into the protected Bay of Acapulco, only half of its crew still lived. Forty-eight crew members had died during the voyage. Amazingly, Thomas, Bengala, Miguel, Cate, and Longalo were all among the living. Only Catoya, the carpenter, was not listed as a survivor, but an Agustin Sao ("chino grumete") who did not appear in the ship's initial roster figured among the survivors.[17] Vizcaíno's voyage proved costly in terms of both the lives of the crew and money with little to show in profit. The newly appointed viceroy, Juan de Mendoza y Luna, looked unfavorably on the prospect of future expeditions and eliminated their funding. While they lasted, these voyages were markers not only of early Spanish interest in the West Coast of North America, but also of unusual imperial trajectories that historicize the earliest Asian encounters with lands that are now part of the United States. Incentivized by higher pay, Asians participated in these quests to extend Spanish control in North America, since Asian ports and Acapulco remained the primary zones of recruitment for sailors for such ventures. The ways in which Asians were identified on these voyages echoed the prevailing forms of categorization in Acapulco during the same period.

Guatemala and the Farthest Reaches of New Spain

During the sixteenth century, the Kingdom of Guatemala developed early connections to the emerging Spanish Pacific World. Diego García de Palacio, a judge of the Real Audiencia in Santiago de Guatemala, entered the young business of constructing transpacific galleons (supervising the building of the *Santa Ana* and *San Martín*) in 1578. In the same year, he penned an ambitious letter to King Felipe II, proposing to lead an armada from Guatemala to invade China. To accomplish such a feat, García de Palacio proposed a new Pacific-Atlantic connector via the Puerto Caballos y Fonseca to replace the emerging Acapulco-Veracruz route.[18] Although his plan was never carried out and the Kingdom of Guatemala never became a great center of transpacific exchange, its westward orientation generated a limited Asian presence within it during the seventeenth century.[19]

Treasury records from Acapulco indicate that "chinos" were deeply involved in Pacific coast trading into the Maya regions of New Spain, and it is likely that Asians arrived in Central America via these involvements, as well as with the ubiquitous overland mule trains.[20] The confessions to the Inquisition of Joseph Fernández de Isla ("mulato") in 1648 affirm that "chinos" were not only present in Guatemala but also engaged in nondogmatic spiritual practices similar to those practiced by Asians in Mexico. At the age of seventeen or eighteen, Fernández de Isla traveled from Mexico to Santiago de Guatemala for an unknown reason. There, he encountered a woman named Antonia, whom he described as a "china." Fernández de Isla's use of the word indicates his familiarity with it in the central Mexican context and his assumption of its applicability to a person in Guatemala.

Antonia was a freed woman who had once been enslaved by a Captain Caraba. She allegedly told Fernández de Isla that she could give him an herb that would aid him in his next quarrel if he said, "Now is the time, Lucifer. Help me."[21] She also informed him that she had given two live worms wrapped in *cañuela* (fescue grass) to another "mulato" from Spain for courage. Together, Fernández de Isla and Antonia walked a league beyond Santiago de Guatemala in search of such herbs. Antonia found three suitable types. On picking the final variety, she flicked the leaves. As the plant folded inward, she said, "close it, old whore."[22] Fernández de Isla watched Antonia and then mimicked her actions and words.

After returning to the city, Fernández de Isla decided to conduct a test. He called on Lucifer for help with the herbs in his possession and waited to see if using them invigorated him. When nothing happened, he threw the herbs out and denounced Antonia to the Inquisition. Although brief, Fernández de Isla's testimony provides tantalizing evidence of a "china" being active in Indigenous and Afro-descendant spiritual communities in ways that echo patterns present in central Mexico.

Most "chinos" like Antonia had arrived in the Kingdom of Guatemala with their enslavers. An enslaved "chino" named Mateo de la Torre and his legal representative used evidence of travel to the Kingdom of Guatemala in his enslaver's company to prove a record of faithful service during his first manumission trial, in 1639.[23] This pattern of travel through bonded labor also applies to an enslaved man named Diego de la Cruz, who had run away and was captured in Santiago de Guatemala in 1659.

According to the records about Diego's case, in the early hours of July 10, an Indigenous Kaqchikel Maya woman named María Setina rushed down the road called Aguas Calientes in the neighborhood of Espíritu Santo. She roused the *alguacil mayor* (chief constable) and his two assistants, all Indigenous men, from their slumbers and reported that someone had robbed her home of all the family's clothing. Not even a shirt for her two daughters remained. At approximately 4:00 a.m., the men discovered someone sleeping on a bench next to a suspiciously large bundle of clothes.[24] These officials would later describe the man as "mulato," a common marker of ambiguous otherness.[25] They woke him, forced a confession out of him, and escorted him to the public jail before sunrise.

The next day, a scribe recorded the culprit's testimony. The man told the scribe that his name was Diego de la Cruz and that he had been born into enslavement in Manila. His enslaver, Diego Ruiz, had embarked with him on the *Nuestra Señora de la Victoria* in July 1656. By March 1657, after an excruciating eight-month crossing, the derelict ship had drifted past Acapulco to the port of Amapala (in present-day Honduras) with only a handful of survivors. Amapala was a quiet fishing port known for shipping pitch up and down the coast.[26] The arrival of a deathly silent Manila galleon filled with bodies would have been a bizarre, otherworldly occurrence.

Ruiz was one of the many people who had died during the passage. After the survivors landed, a small band of free and enslaved people fled into the countryside. Diego had been on the run for two years when he was finally apprehended, alone, in the outskirts of Santiago de Guatemala.[27] It was not until his formal sentencing to fifty lashes and sale for 225 pesos that officials of the royal court referred to the captive as a "chino."[28]

The case is telling, for Diego's categorization depended on who was describing him. The Indigenous officials felt that Diego conformed to local stereotypes of "mulato" deviancy. The Spanish officials, who had the benefit of the captive's testimony, drew on the Mexican colonial lexicon to identify him as a "chino." This dissonance between the observations of Indigenous and Spanish officials reveals that they racialized Diego (who was perceived as physically ambiguous) using Afro-descendant and Asian identifiers. At the same time, the cases of Antonia and Diego reinforce the view that chino-genesis extended beyond central Mexico in the labeling practices of people with a link to the viceregal core. Therefore, the precedent of Acapulco informed but did not always determine how Asians were identified elsewhere. Yet no matter where they lived, "chinos" remained deeply engaged in the processes of colonial contestation and exchange that were fundamental to Afro-Asian convergences in central Mexico.

Transpacific Lima in the Seventeenth Century

As distance from the viceregal core increased, the "chino / a" label became increasingly fluid. Outside of Mexico, the largest Asian population in the Americas during this period resided in Lima, in the Viceroyalty of Peru. When free and enslaved Asians disembarked at the port of Callao, they entered the Andean World having already experienced multiple continental displacements, which often included at least one trans-American journey from Acapulco. In contrast to Mexico, in Peru there was no Odyssean overland journey to the metropolis, given the short distance between Callao and Lima. Few Asians had any reason or opportunity to leave Lima after arriving there.

As in Mexico, in Peru the demand for Asian merchandise fostered the movement of people. Limeño elites owed their access to Asian products and labor in part to the long history of Andean-Pacific connections that preceded Spanish arrival. Indeed, Andean-Pacific contact predated the Spanish invasion by over half a century. One of the principal sources for this history is Pedro Sarmiento de Gamboa's provocative 1572 manuscript titled "Historia de los Inca."[29] Sarmiento was a Spanish navigator and intellectual who had traveled widely in the Viceroyalty of Peru to gather oral testimonies and documents pertaining to pre-Hispanic Andean histories. He structured his manuscript as a biographic chronicle of Inca kings (complete with Inca origin mythology), leading up to the Spanish invasion.

The manuscript recounts that during the reign of Pachacuti Inca Yupanqui (1418–1471), one of his sons, Tupac Inca Yupanqui, received strange visitors from across the sea as the son and his troops invaded the Pacific coasts of present-day northern Peru and southern Ecuador.[30] The visitors were merchants who had arrived in a town called Tumbes on wooden ships with sails. They claimed to be from two islands far to the west, whose names were translated into Quechua as Auachumbi (outer island) and Ninachumbe (fire island), "where there were many people and gold."[31]

Tupac Inca resolved to find these distant islands. He ordered the construction of a great number of ships, commanded a monumental force of twenty thousand men to accompany him, and named his brother, Tilca Yupanqui, admiral of the fleet. After nearly a year at sea, they were all believed dead. But Tupac Inca finally returned from the islands and entered Cuzco "with the biggest, most solemn, and most rich triumph that any Inca had entered [with] in the House of the Sun."[32]

Sarmiento believed Auachumbi and Ninachumbe to have been the Solomon Islands. He and Álvaro de Mendaña had sailed to the Solomons in 1567, and according to their measurements, the island chain lay about two hundred leagues west of Lima.[33] In fact, it was Sarmiento's awareness of Tupac Inca's oceanic feats that motivated his proposing a follow-up expedition to the governor of Peru.[34] Moreover, Sarmiento was not the only Spaniard to hear stories of Pacific encounters from Andeans or to find evidence of Andean navigation of the Pacific. Pedro Cieza de León (1553) and Pedro Pizarro (1571) both paid special attention to Andean experiences with and knowledge of the world's largest ocean.[35]

Andean-Pacific encounters increased Spanish interest in maintaining Pacific connections with the Viceroyalty of Peru. Due to Sarmiento's and others' budding interest in Pacific exploration from Callao, colonial Peru nearly became a new frontier of transpacific galleon trade. Its residents had a formidable demand for East and Southeast Asian products, fueled by a booming extraction economy from Potosí—an Andean silver "mountain" located in present-day Bolivia.[36]

However, for New Spanish traders and Atlantic-based investors Peru was the source of possible unwanted competition with established trade routes across both the Atlantic and the Pacific. Against their wishes, the crown's initially unregulated stance on transpacific trade had allowed two galleons to travel directly between Cavite and Callao during the early 1580s. Then in 1582, royal orders and local laws formally prohibited transpacific trade between the two ports and sought to severely limit communication between Callao and Acapulco as well. Nonetheless, two more ships sailed directly from Asia to Peru, illicitly bypassing New Spain and arriving in 1589 and 1590.[37] The last ship to leave Callao for Asia during this period was the *Nuestra Señora del Rosario,* whose 1591 departure led to a decisive ban on further transpacific trade missions from the Viceroyalty of Peru in 1593.[38]

To circumvent these prohibitions, Limeño merchants continued to conduct trade through the two ships permitted to travel along the American coast between Callao and Acapulco. They also employed contraband trafficking, intermediary ports, and representatives with established networks through Central America to increase their access to the Manila galleons' wares.[39] Sustaining this trade was no small feat, since traveling south from Panama required months of tacking against the wind (the return journey took only three weeks).[40] The decks of the southbound ships had to be relatively clear, "without any kind of superstructure," to decrease the adverse effect of the winds. As a result, "the passengers, no matter who they are, must remain uncovered day and night throughout the voyage," exposed to the elements.[41]

By the beginning of the seventeenth century, Limeño elites were systematically investing in transpacific trade, and they continued to do so despite increasing prohibitions. Roughly half the cargo of ships sailing from

Acapulco to Callao during this period consisted of Asian goods. These products were cheap, selling them was profitable, and Bonialian argues that they also made it more viable to acquire highly coveted Spanish goods from Acapulco than from nearby Portobelo. During the early seventeenth century, the Pacific Mexico-Peru trade corridor even eclipsed that of the Atlantic Seville-Portobelo corridor in terms of volume and profit. By 1620, several merchants on the Calle de los Mercaderes (Merchant Street) in Lima were regularly selling goods imported from Asia via Acapulco.[42] Pedro de León Portocarrero, a traveling Portuguese converso, reported seeing numerous Asian peoples in Lima in 1607–1615.[43]

Indeed, these enduring networks had produced a distinct community of Asians in Lima, most of whom were enslaved. The Pacific coast boasted an active slave trading network from Perico, in Panama, down "to markets in Guayaquil, Paita, or Piura, as well as Trujillo before reaching Callao, Lima's port."[44] Ships traveling that route and stopping at its ports relied primarily on both free and enslaved Africans and Afro-descendants for sailing and dock labor. However, there is some evidence that Asian sailors joined Black crews for the journey south from Acapulco. On a journey to Lima in 1607, three of the San Francisco's five grumetes (Lope Adal, Juan Bagio, and Andres Tacotan) were "indios chinos."[45] These circuits distributed Asian sailors and captives along the Pacific coast. Those who ended up at Lima, the southern terminus, left an impression on the archival record.

For scholars of Asians in early colonial Peru, the Lima padrón of 1613–1614 is an essential source. The padrón was a tribute register that cataloged personal details relevant to present and future tax collection to give the crown "recourse in the event of resistance to payment."[46] Juan de Mendoza y Luna instituted this form of census when he became viceroy, to increase tribute revenue.[47] For him, the padrón functioned as a tool that could be used to verify the tribute obligations of various "indios" and their original pueblos in the context of a highly mobile and rapidly urbanizing population. The viceroy charged Miguel de Contreras with implementing the padrón, requiring him—with the help of collaborating clergy, alcaldes, and caciques (Indigenous nobles)—to go to each of Lima's 3,163 houses. The officials asked Indigenous residents their name, age, occupation, origin, and how many years they had resided in the city, as well as the names of their cacique and the encomendero to whom they owed tribute.[48]

It is likewise important to note that the census did not record "indios" in the nearby populous district of Cercado and that many Indigenous people fled Lima to avoid being recorded in the census, a common response.[49] After four months spent accumulating information, the *visita* (inspection) ended on January 28, 1614. Despite these gaps in the padrón, Noble David Cook found that the inspection had been rigorously executed and argued that the padrón's information had few errors.[50] For Cook, what made the census historically valuable—in addition to its mere survival and its thoroughness—was its snapshot of a population that had recently arrived in Lima to labor: most of the "indios" were single young men.

Surprisingly, the end of the padrón records a population of 114 "indios and indias of Asia [*la china*], Japan, and Portuguese India."[51] They made up 5.5 percent of the "indio / a" population in Lima and 5.6 percent of the laboring "indios" in the city, at a time when Lima's "indios" constituted roughly 8.0 percent of the city's population.[52] McKinley considers the conflation of Asians and Andean peoples into "indios" to be the result of a broadened definition of the "indio / a" category in Peru, which established their subordinate position as colonial subjects.[53] Identifying Asians, most of whom were enslaved, as "indios" rather than as "chinos" also had an economic function: it inflated the number of subjects used to calculate the tribute obligations of Indigenous leaders to encomenderos and the royal treasury.

A relatively high share (42 percent) of the 114 Asians were women, and approximately half of the 114 were enslaved.[54] Thirty-eight claimed to be— or were identified as—from Asia ("la china"), fifty-six from the Portuguese Indies, and twenty from Japan. In addition to these broad regional designations, some individuals mentioned a specific provenance. For example, fourteen "indios" of "la china" listed Manila as their birthplace, three (one from "la china" and two from the Portuguese Indies) mentioned Macau, and nine (two from "la china" and seven from the Portuguese Indies) mentioned Melaka. Other locations in "la china" included Xagua (mentioned by three Asians), Vonbon (Ambon; one), Pampanga (one), and Penaqui (identified as close to Manila; one).[55] "Indios" from the Portuguese Indies mentioned other specific sites: Geba (Java; one), Lisboa (Lisbon; one), Pigo (Pegu; one), Xaguay (one), casta Mancasa (Makassar; one), Mengala (Bengala; one), Xaguo (two), Busarate (Gujarat; one), Chauli (Chaul; one), Camboxa (Cambodia; one), Cuchi (Kochi; one), and Salao (possibly in Laos; one).

Of the Japanese, one came from Nagasaki, and two had been born in Goa. One person from Macau in the Portuguese Indies was "mestizo": his father was Spanish and his mother was baptized and Japanese. Many (both children and adults) did not know how old they were or where they were from, since they had been enslaved and displaced at a young age.

Significantly, only 3 of the 114 total identified themselves as "chino": Andres Chino (from Melaka, in the Portuguese Indies), Melchior Chino (Java), and Geronimo Chino (the Portuguese Indies). They were all named "Chino" but did not use the word when describing where they were from. The varied geographic origins of those who called themselves "Chino" reflect the emerging formation of the "chino / a" label in Acapulco as a socially constructed, rather than an ethnolinguistic, category. Clearly, "Chino" had a similarly broad range of meanings in Lima during the same period, albeit on a far smaller scale. Interestingly, the padrón also labeled five Asians as "indios chinos" and two as "chinos," even though none of them used those terms to describe themselves. The two "chinos" were Francisco Manila and Juan Alvarez (both from Manila), and the "indios chinos" were Andres Pérez, Juan del Campo, Esperanza (Juan del Campo's wife), Isabel Mexia, and an unnamed shop owner.[56] In contrast to those who called themselves "Chino," those labeled "chinos" and "indios chinos" were all from Manila. Although this evidence is limited, the discrepancy in origins between those who named themselves Chino and those described by others as "chinos" or "indios chinos" suggests that some officials in Lima thought of the two categories as including only people indigenous to the Philippines.

Since most Asians in Lima had arrived from Mexico, where they were likely called "chino / a" or "indio / a chino / a," the register was clearly inconsistent in applying these labels. For example, Diego Matigon, Elena, and Susana, had arrived in Lima from Mexico City nine months earlier but were not categorized as "chino / a."[57] Thus, the "chino / a" precedent in Acapulco seldom informed what categories Asians were assigned to in the 1613–1614 padrón. At the same time, this document did not deliver the final word on official identifications of Asians in Lima. For example, McKinley found that Francisco Ximenez "de la china" (of Asia) later appeared as a "chino" in a Lima marriage record, along with his children of "chino" and "morena" description.[58]

Given the padrón's general lack of direct references to people's previous histories in Mexico, as well as its inconsistent use of "chino," it is possible that a few Asians recorded there had arrived directly from Asia on one of the four galleons that docked in Callao from 1580 to 1590. In so doing, these Asians would have bypassed the process of chino-genesis geographically and also preceded it in time. However, the majority of Asians had arrived in Lima within the previous ten years. The use and significance of "chino / a" in Lima, therefore, can likely be traced back to Acapulco and not to linguistic traditions native to Peru (for example, the use of "china" to mean "servant girl" in Quechua). The preference in Peru for "indio / a" to describe Asians resembled earlier practices in Mexico and those in the Philippines. However, in the Peruvian case being identified as "indio / a" was hardly a protection from enslavement. For example, the padrón listed fourteen Asian "indios" as branded (like Pedro Andrés, who had been branded on the face) and / or enslaved at a young age (such as Antonio, who had been captured at the age of six and had served his enslaver for thirteen years).[59] Being from the Portuguese Indies, having been branded on the face, and having been captured in a so-called just war all characterized what was considered to be legitimate enslavement throughout the Hispanic World, despite the formal protections for members of the "indio / a" category inscribed in the New Laws of 1542.

Whether they were categorized as "indios" or "chinos," Asian people adapted to colonial Peru's social hierarchies and colonial institutions much as they did in Mexico, though on a smaller scale. Of the 114 Asians in the padrón, 41 were married, and 24 of those people had chosen other Asians as spouses. Only a few of these couples identified themselves as being of the same ethnolinguistic group, indicating that patterns of pan-Asian communal formations in Peru were comparable to "chino / a" marriage and godparentage in Mexico. Such communal formations are even more significant in the Peruvian case, however, given that there were far fewer available Asian partners than was the case in Mexico. The remaining seventeen of the forty-one married Asians in the padrón had wed "indios" from Peru (four), New Granada (two), and New Spain (one); free or enslaved "negros" (four); "mestizos" (two); a "mulato" (one); a "morena" (one); and someone of unknown casta category (two). The presence of early marriages among Asians, Andeans, and Afro-Andeans broadens Rachel O'Toole's claim that "enslaved and indigenous people relied on each other for the necessities of daily life" in Peru.[60]

The household of Juan del Campo, a carpenter, further suggests the close ties within Lima's Asian community. After spending eight years in Lima, Juan del Campo married Esperanza (as noted above), a woman who, like him, was from Manila. They had a son named Jusepe, who was one and a half at the time of the padrón. They decided to adopt another boy— an orphan named Geronimo, whose father (Diego Banero, also from Manila) had died. This adoption, which would have been a costly commitment, is an important example of how people with shared origins protected each other in a distant land.[61]

The Asian population in Lima also demonstrated a notable integration with other non-Spaniards in their communities. For example, Juan Álvarez, an "indio of la china" and *abridor de cuellos* (ruff opener; a type of artisan), employed a thirteen-year-old "indio" apprentice named Juan Agustín, who had come from Guamanga.[62] Juan López, another abridor de cuellos, provides a further example: he married Juana López, a "negra criolla" of Lima, whom he freed from enslavement.[63]

The padrón also recorded the protest of an unnamed Japanese man from Nagasaki. When asked for the names of his cacique and encomendero, he responded only that in his homeland "there are no caciques or encomenderos since all the indios are free [*libres*]." He had married Andrea "de casta Mancasa" (from Makassar in the Portuguese Indies) and purchased her freedom for three hundred pesos.[64]

While the padrón remains a key source of information about early modern Asian mobility to and through the Americas, it provides an incomplete record. With its narrow focus on Lima's "indios," it missed an unknown number of Asians residing outside the city in places like Callao and those who evaded categorization as "indio / a" altogether. For example, from 1608 to 1610, four "indios chinos," one Japanese man, and a "chino" joined a multiethnic labor force to construct a bridge renowned in Lima for its six arches. The bridge crossed the Rimac River and connected the center of Lima to its San Lázaro district.[65] These laborers appeared in the will of Juan de Corral, the bridge's architect, as Phelipe Mata, Diego Choa, Andres Tagotan, and Bartolomé Guidal (the four "indios chinos"); Miguel de Silva ("japón"); and Alonso Leal ("chino").[66]

Only one of these people, Andres Tacotan, appears in the padrón, where he was listed as an "indio" from Manila.[67] Tacotan had worked as a grumete aboard the *San Francisco,* which had sailed from Acapulco to Callao in 1607. Like Corral's will, the treasury record from Acapulco identified him as an "indio chino." The fact that Tacotan had been an "indio chino" in Acapulco in 1607 and again in 1610 in Lima suggests that the wide range of categories used in Acapulco before 1615 may have been more influential to the identification of Asians in Peru beyond the context of the padrón. By 1614, Tacotan (now an "indio," according to the padrón) had found employment in the store of a man named Simon Diaz as an abridor de cuellos and *soletero* (darner) on the Calle de las Descalzas. An unnamed "indio" from Penaqui also "comes and goes" from Tacotan's house to the district of Surco to work as a stonemason (both were single men).[68]

The sparse information available about other laborers gives a sense of the socioeconomic difficulties that many Asians in Peru endured. Juan de Baeza, a Japanese man in Callao, left a will in 1625 that revealed he was both single and poor and had worked as a soletero. He was buried in the main church of Callao, and he had no money to pay for any masses in his name. Similarly, Juana Xapona, a Japanese woman, served the wife of a lawyer of the royal court of Lima for two years and received a paltry twelve pesos per year for her labor.[69]

Although most Asians in early modern Lima were enslaved or lived among the urban poor, at least one acquired a moderate social standing. In a will dated 1644, Leonor Alvarez of the East Indies included four enslaved people in her estate and left two hundred pesos for her burial, masses, and candles.[70] She had lived in Lima for at least twelve years (likely longer), was the widow of Hernando Gutiérrez ("nación chino"), and had no children.[71] With no blood relatives to inherit her estate, she left everything to an enslaved woman, Isabel de la Cruz—a "china" of Canton whom she freed along with Isabel's daughter, Gracia de la Ascension, because "even though both were my slaves, I have raised them and had them as my companions."[72] Along with Isabel, Alvarez named Tomas de Aquino, an Indigenous Philippine man from Manila, as her executors. She urged them to take care of Isabel's son, Marcos, "given that the boy turned out somewhat naughty . . . so that he did not end up in jail or punished."[73] Although Alvarez had granted them freedom via manumission after her death, the fact that she had not done so earlier problematizes the affective, maternalistic language of the will. Slave ownership differentiated Alvarez, as a non-European woman, from those in bondage and allowed her to participate in Lima's social life as a member of the lower rank of the elite.[74] The fact that Alvarez called herself a person from the "East Indies" and not a "china" reinforced her social distance from enslaved people.

Alvarez's manumission of Isabel coincided with a larger push to free "indios" in Peru during the same period, and according to the jurist Juan de Solórzano Pereira, this movement included "indios" of the "East Indies" as well.[75] Solórzano Pereira was a leading writer on the legitimacy of Spanish rule in the Americas and the rights of Indigenous peoples under the colonial system.[76] In the first volume of *Política Indiana* (1648), he challenged the enslavement of Asians who had been captured in the Portuguese sphere once they crossed into the Hispanic World. He wrote that the Real Audiencia of Lima had zealously applied royal orders aimed at freeing Indigenous peoples in the Americas to Asians "who the Portuguese trade through the route between the Philippines and Mexico."[77] It is probable that the court began to liberate Asians in Lima while Solórzano Pereira was a judge there (from 1609 to 1627).[78] Perhaps the infrequent use of the "chino" label in Peru facilitated the inclusion of Asians in the category of "indios" who deserved freedom. This early effort to emancipate Asians alongside other "indios" in Peru marks the first instance in which the enslavability of Asians was collectively challenged in the Americas. However, the enslavement of the "chinos" of New Spain would not be substantially contested under these terms until the 1670s, nearly two decades after Solórzano Pereira's death in 1655 (see Chapter 6).

There are only sparse records about the second generation of Asians born in Lima, like the abovementioned Gracia de la Ascension. The case of Coronel, which opened this chapter, is a significant exception. Coronel's self-denunciation before the New Spanish Inquisition in 1693 exemplified the clash between the fluid Asian identifications in Peru and the more rigid use of "chino / a" in central Mexico. In positioning himself as an "indio," rather than a "chino," Coronel certainly sought to mitigate the possibility of inquisitorial punishment.

Although he called himself an "indio," witnesses and inquisitors in Mexico consistently rejected his self-fashioning. One physical description in the Inquisition's records is particularly revealing: "the said Alonso Coronel is of medium stature, wide face, of color and eyes that those who are called chinos in Mexico City normally have, hair and lips all black, and some gray hair in his sparse beard. His dress is wool clothes."[79] Owing to his physical appearance, Coronel was definitively identified as a "chino" in New Spain.

Although Coronel initially denied knowledge of his parents and their origins, he later admitted that his father was Xptobal Peres of Macabebe. At a young age, Coronel had left Peru for New Spain, then traveled to Spain, and eventually returned to central Mexico. In his early sixties, he settled in Petatlán, forty leagues north of Acapulco—the port where his parents had landed many decades before.[80] In Petatlán, he had married Leonor de Hinojosa, an enslaved "mulata," on a cacao plantation, and they had had two children, María and Joseph. Leonor's enslaver, Juan Martin de Hinojosa, described the children as "mulatillos."[81] According to Hinojosa's testimony, during these years Coronel ran a mule train from Petatlán to Michoacán, selling agricultural products. After two or nine years (depending on the witness), Leonor fell ill. Rather than help her recover, Coronel abandoned the family, gave his wife up for dead, and stole 172 pesos from Hinojosa. In 1693, the daughter, María, was either sixteen or eighteen and remained enslaved. The son, Joseph, had died at the age of four, and Hinojosa testified that Leonor had succumbed to disease in 1688.

A man with picaresque wanderlust, Coronel reached the far northern Súchil Valley near Durango and the mines of Sombrerete several years later. A mining boom from 1630 to 1680 had created great interest in the distant silver outposts of Mexico, especially Parral. As the boom depleted local Indigenous populations, mining entrepreneurs recruited free and enslaved laborers from further afield, including members of the Yaqui Indigenous group, Pueblos, Afro-Mexicans, and even "chinos."[82]

In the Súchil Valley, Coronel quickly immersed himself in the mixed social circles of these mining communities and acquired a reputation for befriending "mestizos" and "chinos." At the age of seventy-one he married a woman named Ana María Cano, whom he claimed to have known for five years. In the record, she appears as originally from San Luis Potosí and as both a "morisca" and a "mestiza" who had a "white face."[83] Coronel's self-denunciation occurred after just one year of this marriage. The inquisitors of Durango imprisoned him as punishment for having married a second time without knowing whether or not his first wife was still alive. Since Leonor had, in fact, been interred for four years before the second marriage, Coronel received an official ratification of his union with Cano.

Although the decision to denounce oneself may initially seem strange, there are several reasons why Coronel might have chosen to do so. First, he claimed that the desire to save his soul at the end of his life compelled him to come forward. If this statement was true, it reflected a second-generation mind-set that had absorbed the Hispanic and Catholic rhetoric of guilt for sinful behavior. Second, self-denunciation was a common way to appeal to the inquisitor's Catholic sense of clemency in the hope of mitigating punishment. Coronel may have opted for this approach if he believed that someone (perhaps his wife or one of her relatives) was on the verge of denouncing him anyway. Third, by initiating the case, Coronel confirmed Leonor's death and the survival of his daughter, María. If Cano had learned of Coronel's first marriage and pressured him to confirm his former wife's state, then the inquisitorial procedure allowed Coronel (then an elderly man) to access that information without having to travel hundreds of miles through dangerous territory.

Coronel's wayward story sheds light on the forms of mobility available to American-born free Asians, as well as on the stereotypes of foreignness that they encountered throughout the empire based on their physical appearance. It further highlights how some second-generation Asians in the Americas sought to claim local Indigeneity to shed categories that emphasized their overseas heritage. By 1636, only twenty-two enslaved Asians appeared in a list of the population of the archbishopric of Lima. It is safe to assume that diminishing contact with Acapulco during the mid-seventeenth century translated to lower numbers of Asian entries into Peru through Callao.[84] The padrón of 1613–1614 represented a high point in the presence of Asians in Peru that was not surpassed until the period of indenture in the nineteenth century. Sporadic contact with Acapulco after 1615 until the late seventeenth century meant that use of the "chino / a" label had spread unevenly across the Viceroyalty of Peru. Yet the realities of galleon travel, enslavement, and colonial racialization—whether as "indios," "indios chinos," and / or "chinos"—continued to produce pan-Asian, Asian-Indigenous, and Afro-Asian convergences comparable to those found in central Mexico.

Spain, the Other Side of the World

In the early years of the seventeenth century, a man from the Philippines named Gregorio Moreno accompanied a Spanish official traveling from Acapulco to Callao. After the journey, Moreno desired to return to his homeland across the Pacific. In Peru, a chaplain named Francisco Luis promised Moreno sponsorship on a Manila galleon if Moreno would serve him on the voyage back up the coast to Acapulco. Luis did not keep his promise. Instead, he coerced Moreno into serving him on the journey to Spain and abandoned him in Madrid in 1607 with no resources. Although officials of the Casa de Contratación (House of Trade) in Seville granted Moreno's petition for a hundred *ducados* to pay for the return journey to the Philippines, he complained eight months later that he had not received any funds.[85]

Moreno's story of service, abandonment, and delayed justice from Spanish institutions reveals the contours of early modern Asian dispersion from the Americas to Spain. Asians often served in the retinues of missionaries, enslavers, and officials on the Pacific crossing, and the same was true of the transatlantic journey to Spain. Sometimes, Asians accompanied the same sponsors from their journeys on the Manila galleons, or like Moreno, they found new sponsors in the Americas to serve on the ships to Spain. Once in Seville, these sponsors frequently abandoned their charges, who had no means of surviving in that strange and distant land, leading them to petition for assistance from Spanish institutions like the Casa de Contratación. While some transatlantic Asian travelers arrived at Spanish ports in relative comfort, the majority did so in conditions that resembled those of Moreno, or they were outright enslaved.

However, long before Asian subjects like Moreno traveled across the Atlantic to the Iberian Peninsula, Asians—particularly the enslaved—had been coming, going, and settling with their enslavers in both Spain and Portugal via the Cape of Good Hope. Nancy van Deusen and Juan Gil have initiated important work on the porousness of Iberian imperial spaces that generated a significant Asian population on the peninsula during the mid-sixteenth century.[86] These Asians were almost never called "chinos." In Spain, the colonial lexicon relied on a longer history of parading people claimed as "indio / a" vassals through the seat of empire. Indigeneity indicated displacement and vulnerability and connoted a paternalistic obligation to protect people from abuse.

Beginning in the early sixteenth century, Portuguese officials and merchants returning to the peninsula from the Indian Ocean often transported enslaved people in their retinues for service and sale.[87] Ships headed to the peninsula from India could carry as many as 200–300 captives.[88] Enslaved Asians and East Africans who had been punished by the inquisitorial tribunal in Goa were also often sold to merchants in Portugal. Some of these captives served the royal court. For example, Catherine of Austria, the queen of Portugal during the early to mid-sixteenth century, owned an enslaved Chinese man named António and seven other people from India.[89]

From Portugal, Andalusian merchants purchased some of these early captives, creating new intrapeninsular networks of Asian enslavement. According to Gil, most of those who were trafficked in the early sixteenth century were young boys from Malabar. This trade even occasionally extended to the Americas before the 1565 opening of the Pacific.[90] The best-known case of an early transatlantic Asian crossing is that of Juan Núñez, an enslaved cook from Calicut in the service of Juan de Zumárraga, the first bishop of Mexico. Juan arrived in Mexico in 1528 or 1534 and was likely the first Asian man to live in the colonial Americas. He received his freedom in Zumárraga's will in 1548.[91]

Although few of the approximately 650,000 displaced and relocated "indios" throughout the Spanish empire during the sixteenth century originated in Asia, their steadily increasing numbers on the Iberian Peninsula, along with the influx of luxury goods there, rapidly expanded Spanish curiosity about Asia and its peoples.[92] Van Deusen argues that "indio / a" domestic laborers in Castile shaped Spaniards' conceptions of the broader world and were "integral to the development of understandings of self in relation to other and to the formation of social and cultural governance as European contacts throughout the globe expanded."[93] This growing contact between the peninsula and the "indio / a" inhabitants of the empire rapidly expanded Spanish understanding of "indio / a" subjecthood and personhood. As in the Americas, Asians in Spain were involved in legal disputes determining the legitimacy of "indio / a" enslavement. For example, enslavers in Carmona, Andalusia, coerced four enslaved Calicut witnesses in 1562 to testify that Felipa, an "india," was from Calicut, not Mexico, and could therefore legally be kept in bondage as someone who came from the Portuguese Indies.[94]

The opening of the Pacific in 1565 further transformed peninsular awareness about and interest in distant regions. As Asians began arriving in Mexico in larger numbers, a few of them began departing from Veracruz in the companies of enslavers and missionaries and traveling across the Atlantic to the peninsula, often after stopping in Cuba.[95] This unprecedented transpacific-to-transatlantic channel consequently created new possibilities for diplomatic contact between the peninsula and Asian polities—namely, Japan.[96]

The first delegation to the peninsula from Japan, the Tenshō embassy, landed in Lisbon in 1584. Organized by the Jesuit Alessandro Valignano to bolster support for his order in Asia, the delegation featured two ambassadors (Mansho Ito and Miguel Chijiwa), two nobles (Julian Nakaura and Martino Hara), two servants (their names are not known), and two Japanese Jesuits (Costantino Dourado and Jorge de Loyola). From Lisbon, they went to Madrid and Rome. Christina Lee argues that despite the spectacle of their arrival, they did not inspire lasting curiosity about the Japanese "as a distinct people" in Spain and that "the treatment [of] and interest in the Japanese were mainly determined by the social standing and public reputation of their spokesmen (within Spanish society)."[97]

Marco Musillo has demonstrated that the delegation was not treated so dismissively when it arrived in the Italian kingdoms to visit Pope Gregory XIII. He argues that not only did the Japanese receive support as a ploy to bolster Medici political power in the region, but they also won widespread acclaim thanks to their own efforts. The Japanese joined in Italian court traditions and demonstrated their nobility in ways that would have been recognizable to their aristocratic audiences. In the town of Imola, they left a gift of calligraphy, which has been retained to this day as an enduring message of friendship.[98] Among the Catholic kingdoms, therefore, Spanish Castile was an outlier in that its reception of Japanese embassies rarely matched the respect and solemnity apparent in its neighbors' reception.

The Keichō embassy of Hasekura Rokuemon Tsunenaga to Europe (1614–1617) received an even less enthusiastic welcome in Spain (figures 5.1 and 5.2).[99] According to Lee, Hasekura's poor reception was evidence that Spaniards failed to make direct associations between his group and the

5.1 Statue of Hasekura Rokuemon Tsunenaga in Old Havana

Hasekura's brief stop in Havana, Cuba, has been commemorated on
the eastern side of the old city. Funded by the Sendai Ikuei Gakuen
school in 2005, the monument preserves and expands the historical
memory of the embassy. The site also includes a Japanese garden
(where members of the local wushu school often train), pieces of the
wall of Sendai Castle, and markers pointing east and west toward
Sendai and Rome (11,850 and 8,700 kilometers away, respectively).

Photo courtesy of the author.

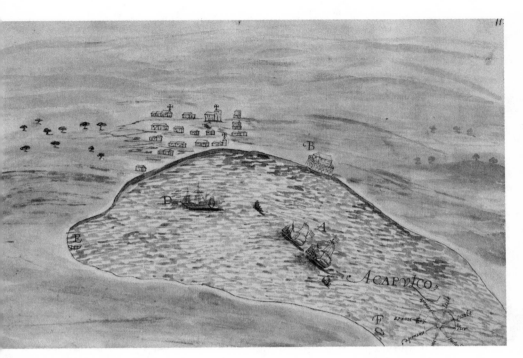

5.2 The Bay of Acapulco

Nicolas de Cardona drew a map of Acapulco during his stay in 1615 before heading up the Mexican and Californian coasts. "D" shows the location of "a ship that had come from Japan" (*una nao que auia venido del japon*), a clear reference to the *San Juan Bautista* that had transported Hasekura and approximately 120 other Japanese merchants across the Pacific from 1613 to 1614.

Nicolas de Cardona, "Descripciones geográphicas e hydrográphicas de muchas tierras y mares del Norte y Sur en las Indias, en especial del descubrimiento del Reino de la California," 1632. Reproduction courtesy of the Biblioteca Nacional de España.

earlier Tenshō embassy. They did not extend the initial interest they had shown Valignano's delegation to that of Luis Sotelo, a Franciscan friar in Hasekura's embassy with a reputation for being an avaricious social climber. King Felipe III rejected most of Sotelo's petitions, including those referring to a trade treaty with Masamune Date (the daimyo [local lord] who had sent the ambassadors), a promotion to the rank of bishop for Sotelo, and a knighthood of the Order of Santiago for Hasekura "for being of a gentile nation."[100]

By the end of their stay in Spain, the Japanese and Sotelo had been asked numerous times to leave the peninsula. They had even been robbed and forced out of the Franciscan convent in Madrid that had housed them. Hasekura eventually received the discriminatory moniker of "el japón" ("the Japanese one"), with no accompanying title.[101] One member of the entourage, don Tomás Felipe Japón (also called don Tomás de la Puente Japón), was even illegally branded as a slave in 1622. In 1623 he petitioned to return to the Philippines through the province of Honduras.[102] A handful of Japanese stayed behind voluntarily, though, and settled in Spain at Coria del Rio, near Seville. They married local women, generating a population with the surname "Japón" that persists to this day.[103] Even more Japanese members of this delegation remained in Mexico, and by 1629 Mexico City had a "Barrio de los Japones" (Japantown).[104] One member of the embassy, Luis Sasanda, settled temporarily in Michoacán and is a rare case of a non-European becoming a Franciscan friar. He was martyred in Japan with Sotelo, his old sponsor, in 1624 and beatified in 1867.[105]

These Japanese delegations were not the only examples of Asians traveling to Spain to seek royal favor. A Chinese gunsmith from the Philippines named Antonio Perez traveled to the court of King Felipe III in 1608 to petition for privilege based on merit. He claimed to have been impoverished by his twelve years of service in Spanish expeditions from Cambodia to the Chinese coast. He must have been one of the very few "Sangleyes" in the Spanish military in Asia at the time of the 1603 uprising. In battle, he had been shot several times, and an exploding powder keg had mutilated his arm.[106] To earn a living, he requested employment as a Chinese translator in Manila at the rank of alguacil mayor. Although this request was denied, Perez's fortunes would soon improve.

The same year that Perez arrived in Spain, Hernando de los Ríos Coronel had requested updated information on artillery makers in the Philippines, since the only ones he knew had begun work decades earlier, in 1587 and 1593. The surprising response from one official was that Perez was the only person who still practiced this trade. Coronel's reply expressed the familiar dilemma at the heart of colonial social politics in Manila, whether to be governed by pragmatic need or racialized stereotypes: "I am informed that [Perez] is a very good manufacturer of gunpowder and that he knows about fireworks. If it is not an impediment [his] being Chinese to do it, he is suitable."[107] Since no other skilled gunsmiths resided in Manila, Perez was hired for a substantial four hundred pesos per year. Though Spanish master gunsmiths could expect to receive six hundred pesos per year and Perez's predecessor had made five hundred pesos per year, Perez stood to do quite well.

When petitioning to be able to return to the Philippines in 1610, Perez excised his ethnicity from the documentation. Doing so made him less threatening to colonial authorities—who, even in Spain, may have been wary of "Sangleyes" with military experience and influence after the devastation of 1603. Perez described himself as an "indio from the city of Manila" and a "citizen of Manila."[108] Only his witnesses, Diego Aduarte and Pedro Matias, commented that Perez was originally from either Macau or Guangdong province. However, the officials of the Casa de Contratación in Seville simply concluded that he was an "indio from the city of Manila."[109] The physical description of Perez accompanying his travel license reinforced this ambiguity, noting that he was "of little beard, hairless, dark [*parda*] in color due to extreme pockmarks on the face."[110] It is likely that he survived the return voyage and successfully took up his new post.

Similarly, don Diego Dimarocot, the son of one of the two Philippine war heroes of 1603 (see Chapter 1), traveled to Spain via Mexico to petition for royal favor in 1623. His father, don Guillermo Dimarocot, had died without receiving royal compensation despite the extraordinary services he had rendered. The son had risen to the rank of *sargento mayor* (third in command) after numerous campaigns in the Spice Islands. He arrived at the court of King Felipe IV after surviving the Pacific passage, traveling overland through Mexico, and sailing across the Atlantic to Spain. Based on his own merits—as well as the merits of his father and the fact of his brother's death in Ternate—don Diego petitioned to be awarded the *encomienda* of Guagua, his hometown in Pampanga. Collectively, his family had fought the Zambales, the "Negrillos," Pangasinan rebels, "Sangleyes," the Dutch, Japanese pirates, and Malukans, in addition to disarming their own people after 1603 at Spanish insistence. To his petition, don Diego appended the praise of his commanding officers, who described him and his father as "honored," "virtuous," and "valiant."[111] He also demonstrated that, instead of receiving just reward for their loyalty, soldiers from the Philippines were often treated "[as] if they were slaves" and given excessive work while on campaigns.[112]

Don Diego's displays of valor and clear Hispanicization conformed to discourses of honor and meritorious service. His full petition asked for the encomienda of Guagua with its two thousand tribute-paying residents, a pension of eleven hundred *escudos* per year, and five hundred ducados for the return trip to the Philippines.[113] After deliberation, the Council of the Indies refused the encomienda request but did award don Diego a considerable pension of five hundred ducados per year and a one-time payment of the same amount for his return to the Philippines. While far short of what don Diego felt that he and his family were owed, this reward formally represented the crown's recognition of the military services of Philippine soldiers and their merit at court.

Shortly after don Diego's departure, however, the king ordered the governor of the Philippines to ban "indios" from traveling to Spain.[114] Like many royal proclamations, this one proved ineffectual. Don Nicolás de los Ángeles, the nephew of don Ventura de Mendoza (the other hero of 1603), arrived in Spain in 1630 to request an encomienda as well. Although his initial petition was unsuccessful, he finally received an encomienda in 1652 after fighting against "Sangleyes" during their uprising in Manila in 1639.[115] Similarly, don Geronimo de Lugay traveled to Spain and petitioned for (and eventually received) an encomienda based on the merits of his father, who had fought in numerous military campaigns from 1606 to 1647.[116]

However, the experiences of the Tenshō and Keichō embassies, the gunsmith Antonio Perez, and war heroes like don Diego Dimarocot were exceptional. Most Asians arriving on the Iberian Peninsula did not travel in delegations with official sponsors, never attended court, and were in no position to ask for encomiendas or other coveted forms of social advancement. They had more in common with people like Moreno. They arrived as servants or in enslaved retinues accompanying Spanish officials, missionaries, merchants, and nobles. The experiences of two Kapampangan men from the town of Apali—Lucas Luis and Diego Farfán—are indicative of the difficulties Asians often faced on the Peninsula.

Although they arrived in Spain three years apart (in 1606 and 1609, respectively), Luis and Farfán had grown up together and traveled to Seville in the service of Augustinian missionaries, who had presided over the conversion of many Indigenous people in the Philippines. In 1612, both Luis and Farfán lodged petitions with the Casa de Contratación to return to "their homeland" in the Philippines after having been abandoned abroad.[117] Farfán's patron, Fray Juan Gutiérrez, had left him to travel to Madrid and Toledo. Luis's sponsor, Fray Juan de Pineda, had also gone to Toledo and had then died. Without the friars, these men had no resources or means of sustenance "for being in a strange land."[118] Together, they sought aid at the Augustinian convent in Seville and managed to enlist the help of a man named Fray Miguel, whom they both had met in the Philippines in 1601. During their court appearances in 1612, they presented Fray Miguel and each other as witnesses to affirm that they "went about helpless, suffering hardship and lack of religious instruction" and needed to return home.[119] By then, the Casa de Contratación had developed special protections for "indios" abandoned on the Iberian Peninsula and sponsored them with licenses for a return journey.[120] Luis departed in 1612, and Farfán left in 1614 after recovering from an illness. Their experiences demonstrate the great dependency of such people on the missionaries or other officials in whose service they traveled. Desperate, these two men successfully mobilized the rhetoric of "indio / a" vulnerability to obtain permits to return to the Philippines.

The Japanese Juan Antonio's later journey in 1623 had some similarities with those of Luis and Farfán. Having lost his father, mother, and two brothers "in defense of the Catholic faith" (it is possible that they were martyred in Japan), Antonio had left the Philippines and spent two years in Mexico City.[121] There, his knowledge of Japanese furniture caught the attention of a judge named Pedro de Vergara Gaviria. Gaviria hired Antonio to assemble a Japanese bed that he had purchased as a gift to the recently crowned Felipe IV. Antonio sailed from Mexico across the Atlantic to Spain and arrived at the royal palace in 1623. There, he successfully assembled the bed before the king. He carried a letter from Gaviria, which stated that Antonio could repair the bed if it had arrived damaged and noted that "this chino also knows how to repair *biombos* [Japanese screen panels] and everything of his land that is damaged." Gaviria also mentioned that Antonio might need financial assistance because "he is poor and very humble."[122]

Shortly thereafter, Antonio submitted a petition to the crown for employment as a soldier because he had "spent all he had for the route being so long, and he suffers extreme hardship for being where he has no familiarity with no one that can help him."[123] The king ordered Juan Ruíz de

Contreras to send a letter to Gaviria, asking whether any assistance had been given or was forthcoming from his estate in Mexico City. Gaviria's brother, Diego, responded, saying that Antonio had gone to Spain voluntarily and that Gaviria had already given him three hundred pesos for the journey out of goodwill, not because he was obliged to do so. Whether or not this was true, Diego had effectively freed Gaviria of further responsibility.

In the following months, Antonio filed two more increasingly desperate petitions to the crown. In the first, he asked for work as an interpreter "because he is a man familiar with the languages of those parts [Asia] and he knows them very well." He also requested an appointment as a consul with a salary "that is usually given to those who have similar offices."[124] In his next petition, submitted just two days later, Antonio had already abandoned his quest to be an interpreter. Instead, he asked to serve as a soldier in the fleet leaving for San Juan and then for Mexico "because he has no other means of traveling for his great [financial] need."[125] A brief response from the Council of the Indies allowed "that he be given license to return."[126]

Antonio's case—like those of Luis and Farfán—reinforces the common theme of Asian dependency in Spain on official assistance and sponsorship. It also reveals that for Gaviria, the "chino" Antonio was merely a disposable accessory to his gift to the king. Once Antonio carried out his task, Gaviria absolved himself of any responsibility for Antonio's well-being. Material fascination with Asian goods was never removed from the colonial management of Asian bodies. Antonio had to rely on the pious deaths of his family members and appeals to patriarchal sympathy in multiple petitions simply to be allowed to return across the Atlantic, months after his initial request.

Worse still were the experiences of enslaved "indios" from Asia, as a 1655 petition to the Council of the Indies by Pedro de Mendoza reveals. Mendoza had been captured and enslaved at the age of six during Governor Sebastián Hurtado de Corcuera's war against Jolo in 1635. Pedro's godfather, don Pedro Díaz de Mendoza (from whom he received his Christian name), told him that his parents were "moros" from Jolo. After Mendoza was captured, Corcuera sold him to doña María de Francia, who took him to New Spain. She died shortly afterward, and Corcuera then brought Pedro to Spain. Pedro testified that Corcuera was a brutal master, giving him *mala vida* (a bad life or lifestyle), so he escaped in Toledo and made his way to Seville, where he was recaptured, beaten, and branded. Pedro sought legal recourse and argued that all "indios" in Spain had been freed by royal order. He challenged Corcuera to produce documentation that he had been legitimately enslaved.

In response, Corcuera recounted a lengthy tale of his conquests in Mindanao and Jolo and asserted that all "moros" captured in just war were legitimate slaves. Therefore, he argued that Pedro was not a protected "indio" but a vulnerable Muslim captive. Corcuera then claimed that he treated all of his captives "with love and teachings as if they were children" and that the men petitioning for freedom (Pedro and another enslaved man from Ternate) were "ingrates." He also sought to discredit Pedro's character by alleging that he had robbed the castellan of Toledo, don Matheo Varona, of silver and had a history of flight.[127] Corcuera interpreted Pedro's escape as evidence that he feared punishment for theft, rather than that he had been badly treated by his enslaver. In the end, Corcuera said that "if the Council were to judge . . . that [his slaves] should be made free . . . he would deliver and send them . . . with very good will because they are of greater expense than service."[128] In the end, the council sided with Corcuera because of Pedro's Muslim background and history of flight and theft. Council members merely encouraged Pedro to seek assistance from the *procurador de pobres* (attorney of the poor).

In contrast, the case of Juan Castelín Dala in 1632 was straightforward. Born in the Philippines, Dala had been enslaved and brought to Spain by a galleon's master of artillery, Juan Baptista de Molina, who later sold him to don Antonio de Mendoza. In response to recent crown orders to send "indios" to their homelands, Mendoza had granted Dala his freedom to return to the Philippines "where he has his parents."[129] Unlike for Pedro, the rhetoric of "indios" in need of protection was occasionally a path to freedom for enslaved Asians in Spain like Dala who had no alleged Muslim background and were not captured in just war.

As these cases show, for most Asians who crossed the Atlantic, the Spanish provinces and royal court were exclusionary, prohibitively costly, and often outright hostile. Although the Council of the Indies was more likely (though not guaranteed) to enforce liberatory royal decrees than were governors in the colonies, Asian "indios" in Spain remained plagued by hardship. Moreover, because of their transience they only rarely formed the kinds of multiethnic communal ties that their counterparts developed in the Americas.

These cases also demonstrate that the "chino / a" label rarely survived the Atlantic crossing. Its deployment was usually limited to documents written and sent abroad by Spaniards in Mexico, like Gaviria's description of the Japanese Juan Antonio. Though most Asians arriving on the Iberian Peninsula had passed through Mexico, where they became "chinos," in Spain they reasserted their claims to the rights afforded to "indios" that had been categorically obliterated in Acapulco.

In this respect, Spain offers perhaps the most extreme example of a pattern also visible in other parts of the empire: chino-genesis sometimes informed but rarely determined how Asians were legally identified beyond New Spain. As distance from the viceregal core increased, the use of "chino / a" became less consistent. Asians who traveled beyond New Spain often identified themselves as "indios" to claim protections that they had lost in Acapulco. Far from their homelands, many Asians preferred to disappear into the protection of larger groups rather than reclaim an identification with places that existed only on the lips of travelers or in a fading memory of a world that was now distant and perhaps unfamiliar.

6 THE ELUSIVE EIGHTEENTH CENTURY

IN 1746, ALEXANDRO Mauricio de Arabo—"de nación china" (Asian) and "de nación Philipino" (from the Philippines)—died alone of an unspecified illness at the inn of Juana de Azebedo in Matanchén, Mexico.[1] The town is just east of San Blas, a port in the present-day state of Nayarit. At San Blas, the Manila galleons could stop and restock on supplies on their way south to Acapulco. Mauricio was traveling northwest from Guadalajara, where he was a citizen and worked as a cigar maker and barber. He clearly had not anticipated dying on this trip, as he left no will. The subsequent investigation into his possessions included interviews with various merchants who knew basic details about his life. He had been married with a son, but both his wife and child had already died. He had raised his wife's cousin, Juan Ygnacio Auriel, who still lived in Guadalajara. Mauricio had offered these details to his colleagues but had never spoken of his parents or life before arriving in New Spain. Although he barely owned enough to cover the expenses of his funeral, what he did possess reveals his participation in the transpacific trade that crept up the northern coast during the eighteenth century. Mauricio owned "three pairs of socks from China," "a pair of new stockings from China," "four fine plates from China," "two chocolate bowls from China," and other Asian goods. He was literate enough to keep his own account books and even owned "seventy-two *cartillas* [small books] from Asia," likely in Chinese characters.[2]

One of the most striking aspects of Mauricio's story is the year in which he made his final trip, 1746. As Tatiana Seijas accurately states, the study of Asians in the Americas in the late colonial period is a "historiographical vacuum."[3] A couple of articles and scattered notations in other texts broach the subject, but the question of how Asians in New Spain adapted to life in the last century of colonial rule remains unanswered. This shortage of scholarship on the topic has supported a common historiographical argument that Asians faded from the colonial Mexican archive during the eighteenth century. These claims center on the notion that the term "chino / a" ceased to refer to Asians over time and that, consequently, it is now nearly impossible to track Asian peoples in Mexican archival records from the late colonial period.[4] Yet Mauricio's story and others like it indicate that Asians did not vanish from the New Spanish core in the eighteenth century, nor did they stop being "chinos." The "vacuum" of the late colonial period is therefore more a problem of historical study than a dearth of archival material.

The narrative of Asian disappearance may be due most prominently to the visually striking colonial genre of art known as the casta paintings. This genre became popular in Mexico during the mid-eighteenth century, and many such paintings were designated for the export market. They exhaustively categorized permutations of colonial *mestizaje* (racial mixing) and often exemplified Bourbon-era bewilderment about the diversity and customs of colonial Mexico's masses.

Typically, each painting depicts a father, mother, and child and assigns a casta to each. Collectively, the images of families in the paintings illustrate the process of ethnogenesis: they create a visual way to racially classify which people originated from which combination of parents. The paintings' intimate depictions of family life are often pastoral and suggest the emergence of creolized cultures structured around racialized hierarchies of power and heredity.

According to these paintings and the discourses underlying them, "chinos" descended from castas already present in New Spain, not people from Asia. The casta combinations that could produce "chino / a" people were largely Afro-Indigenous and included "mulato" and "india," *barcino* (spotted animal) and "mulata," *lobo* (wolf) and "india," "lobo" and "negra," "coyote" and "mulata," "español" and "morisca," and *chamicoyote* (combination of chamizo [another Afro-Indigenous category] and coyote) and "india."[5] In particular, a 1777 casta painting by Ignacio María Barreda offers one of the clearest visual interpretations of non-Asian "chino / a" identity and its permutations in Mexico during the eighteenth century (figure 6.1).

6.1 Castes of New Spain

Casta paintings expressed a profound anxiety about the mixing of castas over time and the gradual dissolution of Spanish blood in families in the Americas.

Ignacio María Barreda, *Castas de Nueba España*, 1777. Reproduction courtesy of the Real Academia Española de la Lengua.

The painting's depiction of mestizaje unfolds across sixteen generations. It begins with the classic union of a Spanish man and an Indigenous woman, who have a "mestizo" child. At the end of the first row, a Spanish woman (the great granddaughter of the first Spaniard) interrupts her predecessors' return to whiteness by having a "mulato" child with a "negro." From this point on, Blackness defines the lineage. Three generations later, two phenotypically white parents have a *tornatras* (throwback) "negro" child, and this moment signals the definitive end of whiteness in the family. The final panel in the bottom row depicts a child called "hold yourself in the air" (*tente en el aire*) because he or she is "neither less nor more than his or her [Black] parents."[6] The painting is thus a warning of how a Spanish family line could end with Black descendants.

On the path to this final panel, the third row traces how "chino" personhood could influence casta categorization. In the first panel, an "indio" and a "loba" have a "chino" child. In the second, the "chino" has a "zambaiga" child with an "india." In the third, the "zambaiga" finds a "chino" partner, and they have a *cambujo* (chicken or dark-skinned person).[7] Finally, a "cambuja" and a "chino" have a *genizara* (a word referring to a captive Indigenous person of the northern Mexican frontier).[8] The first panel of the fourth row is the culmination of this process: "From Chino and Genizara. Albarazado."[9] In the image, the husband and wife grab each other's hair, and the "chino" holds a rock in his left hand as if to dash the wife's brains out. Such is the result, in Barreda's view, of generations of mixing with "chinos." Nowhere does Barreda suggest that these "chinos" could be Asian.

In the early nineteenth century, Alexander von Humboldt confirmed the widespread nature of the non-Asian "chino / a" casta during his travels to the Spanish Americas: "The descendants of negroes and Indian women bear at Mexico, Lima, and even at the Havannah, the strange name of *Chino*, Chinese."[10] These "chinos" were entirely separate from his racial taxonomy of "the men of mixed extraction" who lived in Mexico. The latter consisted of "Europeans, Africans, American Indians, and Malays; for from the frequent communication between Acapulco and the Philippine islands, many individuals of Asiatic origin, both Chinese and Malays have settled in New Spain."[11] In natural histories, paintings, and new ethnographic discourses from the mid-eighteenth to the early nineteenth centuries, "chinos" had ceased to be Asian—even though Humboldt made crystal clear that

Asians remained a significant demographic group in New Spain until the end of the colonial period.

Accompanying these categorical changes in the eighteenth century, a strong disconnect emerged between what had become fluid definitions of the "chino / a" casta in the Americas and the word's definition in Spanish-language dictionaries published in Spain. The *Diccionario de autoridades* (1729) was among the first to define "chino," and it did so as follows: "a type of dog that has no hair and has the shape of a small hound, extremely cold and useful for [treating] kidney stones [*el mal de ijada*], applying it to that part. It was given this name because the first ones came from Asia [*la China*]."[12] According to Eliette Soulier, this species of dog arrived in the Americas via the Manila galleons, as the dogs were known for hunting rats on the ships. The use of "chino" to denote a dog—in a period when the word still referred both colloquially and legally to people throughout the Hispanic World—aligns the word with other derogatory casta labels that conflated mixed people and animals, like "lobo," "mulato" (from *mula* [mule]), and "coyote." Formal definitions from both Spain and the Americas did not use "chino / a" to refer to Asian people for most of the eighteenth century: the identification of "chinos" with the "kingdom of China" did not appear in Spanish dictionaries until 1780.[13]

In seeking an explanation for this semantic shift, Edward Slack and Rubén Carrillo Martín have proposed that the "chino / a" category became "Africanized" during the eighteenth century. According to them, "chino / a" gradually lost its association with Asian populations and, as indicated by the casta paintings, became a vague marker of mixed Indigenous and Afro-Mexican heritage. Carrillo Martín explains the disappearance of Asians from the "chino / a" category as a process hastened by multiple factors: Asian claims of "indio / a" status to escape enslavement toward the end of the seventeenth century; a reduction in galleon travel during the same period, which lowered the number of Asians arriving in Mexico; persistent intermarriage patterns between Asians and Afro-Mexicans; and the ravaging of Asian populations in Mexico by tropical diseases.[14] The notion that "chino / a" became an Afro-Indigenous category remains an important and dominant claim in the scholarship on this period.[15]

As the Africanization thesis suggests, the notion that Asians disappeared—either demographically or simply from archival records—in colonial Mexico during the eighteenth century is closely tied to the evolution of the "chino / a"

label. The example of the family of Juan de Páez, a Japanese man in Guadalajara, demonstrates the difficulty of tracking Asian individuals using
the colonial lexicon after more than one or two generations. In 1635 or
1636, Páez married Margarita de Encío, the daughter of a Japanese man
named Luis de Encío (colloquially called "Luis the chino") and an Indigenous woman named Catalina de Silva.[16] They had nine children between
1637 and 1660 and thirteen grandchildren between 1659 and 1682.[17] Though
Páez maintained that he was a "native of the city of Osaka in the Kingdoms
of Japan" when he died in 1675, his mixed children and grandchildren
did not claim Japanese heritage in legal settings.[18] Generational mixing
and economic security allowed members of the Páez clan to shed their
markers of Asian heritage over time.[19] Similarly, the half-Japanese Barranca
children in Veracruz in 1666 did not carry casta descriptors in their petition for a license to bear arms (see Chapter 3).

The difficulty of tracing second- and third-generation Asians through
the archives extends to other parts of Central and South America, including
Peru and Guatemala, where Asian populations were much smaller to begin
with. While long-range Asian migration from central Mexico proliferated
during the seventeenth century, its archival imprint in Central and South
America had diminished significantly by the eighteenth century. The image
of the elderly, Lima-born Alonso Coronel (see Chapter 5) calling himself
"indio" in the far northern frontier of Mexico in the late seventeenth
century aptly embodies the latter trend. For these reasons, the task of
tracking Asians outside of Mexico in the late colonial period is extraordi-
narily difficult. Because there was significant variation in how second- and
third-generation Asians categorized themselves, only areas that had direct
access to transpacific trading routes over the longue durée could maintain
traceable Asian populations over time. Therefore, it is difficult to determine
the extent to which Asians continued their hemispheric circuits during the
eighteenth century, using the extant records.

Despite these challenges, and even though the "chino / a" category acquired new meanings during the late colonial period, archival documents reveal that Asians in Mexico continued to call themselves and were
called "chinos" throughout the eighteenth century. Asian "chinos" never
disappeared: instead, they remained prominent in colonial social and legal
imaginaries. Overreliance on the export-oriented casta paintings and their
accompanying discourses has confounded the search for crucial Bour-

bon-era adaptations and continuities in Asian populations.[20] Although "chino / a" became a more contested category in the eighteenth century, its legal and vernacular uses then remained consistent in many ways with those of earlier periods.

What did change to a greater degree during the eighteenth century were patterns of Asian spatial and social mobility. For example, in the half-century after the emancipation of "chinos" in 1672, the number of enslaved Asians dropped significantly in Mexico. The subsequent end of the transpacific slave trade in Asian captives significantly reduced the overall numbers of Asians arriving in Acapulco, especially the number of Asian women—almost all of whom had been enslaved. However, the natural increase in second- and third-generation Asian populations in Mexico meant that a larger number of Asian and Asian-descended women now lived in the Americas than ever before. Late eighteenth century parish records from the Pacific coast provinces demonstrate that reality.[21]

Furthermore, the transition to Bourbon rule after the War of Spanish Succession (1701–1714) and subsequent reforms to colonial trade policies affected the distribution of Asian communities along Mexico's Pacific coast. As Mauricio's story demonstrates, Asian populations slowly migrated north as an adaptation to new initiatives that began to reroute trade from the old centers of Acapulco and Veracruz to smaller ports. This migratory pattern brought new commercial prospects to regional centers like Guadalajara.

Despite these structural changes, much also stayed the same. Both transient and migratory Asian individuals and communities remained highly visible in Mexico in the late colonial period. Asian sailors continued coming and going with the seasonal arrival and departure of the Manila galleons. They still regularly deserted, married members of local populations, and developed the plantation economies of the Pacific coast. Concurrently, pious inquisitors remained wary of Asians who participated in and contributed to non-Catholic spiritual and sexual practices.

Still, the study of "chinos" during the late colonial period requires a careful consideration of what Ben Vinson calls "caste pluralism," or the fluid state of drifting among several casta categories simultaneously.[22] Frequently, officials used multiple labels, such as "chino or lobo," to identify colonial subjects whom they found racially ambiguous.[23] Today, our ability to ascertain whether these subjects were Afro-Indigenous or Asian remains rooted in other markers connected to nación, *naturaleza* (essence), geographic context, and physical description.[24] For this reason, I have prioritized the use of sources that contain these more direct references to the Asian provenance of a "chino / a." Even when we conservatively exclude cases that do not contain qualifying descriptors beyond "chino / a," the archive reveals not only the long-term presence of Asians in the Americas but also a wide range of continuities—and some changes—in patterns of geographic concentration, inquisitorial denunciation, and labor hierarchies.

By the Wars of Mexican Independence (1810–1821), the decline of the Manila galleons had overlapped with the emergence of new forms of Asian displacement and diaspora to the Americas via indenture (1806–1917). After the Manila galleons finally collapsed, along with New Spain itself, other European powers dominated the new era of Asian mobility to the Americas. Thus, this chapter covers the period from the end of the seventeenth to the early nineteenth century to address the "historiographical vacuum" that Seijas identifies—and to populate it with people who did not "disappear" but lived fully, much as their predecessors had in previous centuries.[25]

The Old and the New in the Eighteenth Century

During the sixteenth and seventeenth centuries, "chinos" were highly mobile Asian subjects who created new forms of multiethnic community in the Americas with Indigenous and Afro-Mexican populations. These patterns remained consistent into the eighteenth century. Galleon trade had declined in the mid-seventeenth century, owing to the Qing invasion of Ming China and stagnating silver production in the Americas. However, shipping volume increased again in the 1680s and remained at its highest levels until 1740.[26] A boost in silver output in the Americas, a stabilization in the Chinese demand for silver, and rising populations worldwide fueled the revitalization of transpacific trade.[27] Over several decades, many "chinos" gravitated to coastal regions north of Acapulco to profit from these strengthened mercantile connections.

Yet daily life in colonial Mexico did not change dramatically with the arrival of the new century. Antonio de Robles's *Diarios de sucesos notables (1665–1703)* describes many seasonal rhythms during the first years of the eighteenth century that were the same as those during the last years of the seventeenth. On Sunday, January 17, 1700, news of the Manila galleon's anchorage in Acapulco reached Mexico City, almost exactly a year to the day since it had last arrived.[28] Undoubtedly, the year's most noteworthy event for the colony had transpired in Madrid, thousands of miles away. King Carlos II, known as "el Hechizado" (the bewitched), died without an heir in November 1700, ending Hapsburg rule in Spain. The War of Spanish Succession (1701–1714) would soon follow, and the Peace of Utrecht that marked the war's end confined Spanish rule in Europe to the Iberian Peninsula and confirmed the Bourbon inheritance of the Spanish Crown. The first of these monarchs, King Felipe V, initiated a series of administrative reforms (known to historians as the Bourbon Reforms) that his successors would expand to centralize power, entrench colonial rule, and maximize overseas revenue.

But news of the Bourbon succession would not arrive in Mexico until March 1701, five months after King Carlos's death.[29] The previous year was an unexceptional one for most denizens of the Viceroyalty of New Spain. "Chinos" continued to be mistreated with impunity. For example, Robles's diary mentions an incident in which an unnamed "chino" coachman was shot dead with a blunderbuss on Monday, October 18. Five days later, the murderer, called only "the captain" and identified as the son of a man named Pascual Rodríguez, mortally wounded a "mulato" coachman who had only asked not to be splashed in the street.[30] Until the end of the diary, Robles commented on the comings and goings of the Manila galleons, the dangers of the route they took, and contraband trade. He ended his diary with a lament that since no galleon had arrived in 1703, "all goods have risen to very elevated prices."[31] Also in 1703, a "chino" named Sebastian de Gusman, a clock repairman and shop owner in Zacatecas, had insulted the *corregidor* (chief magistrate) by claiming that he had been a servant in the corregidor's household. Gusman apparently did so to avoid paying taxes, but his action prompted the corregidor to send out bounty hunters to imprison Gusman. He took shelter in the Convent of San Agustín.[32] Great changes had begun to occur in Spain, but daily life in Mexico was business as usual at the onset of the eighteenth century.

What had changed significantly for "chinos" by the end of the seventeenth century was their status as enslaveable subjects. Although some "chinos" had petitioned for manumission on the basis of unlawful enslavement, their occasional successes were determined only case by case.[33] Many "chinos" argued that they had not been captured in just war, that they had been taken from their families as children, and that they belonged to groups that were supposed to be protected from enslavement. However, convincing cases of unjust capture or enslavers' verbal promises of freedom upon their deaths could be subverted through the intervention of powerful Spaniards. For example, Mateo de la Torre, an enslaved "chino" from the Bay of Bengal, opened a second bid for freedom in 1647 (he had failed previously in 1639) with a request for eight years of backpay. The case's result depended less on Mateo and his assigned lawyer's arguments for freedom and more on the derailing influence of the executor of the will of Mateo's former enslaver. The executor, Juan de Ontiberas Barrera, had petitioned successfully to append the "voluminous" documentation of a "totally independent" case to Mateo's manumission proceedings to flood the trial with paperwork.[34] Ontiberas also argued that Mateo had brought his petition before the wrong court, such that Mateo "has to recognize to whom the knowledge of his case pertains."[35] These maneuvers resulted in Mateo being "justly fearful to litigate" against someone "so favored and powerful" as Ontiberas.[36] Meanwhile, Mateo's new enslaver tried to smuggle him away so that he could not appear in court, and one year later, Mateo was still enslaved and confined in an obraje that Ontiberas owned. The case for manumission was dropped.

However, the fates of many enslaved "chinos" would soon change. Fernando de Haro y Monterroso, a Spanish prosecutor who arrived in Guadalajara in 1670, became the leader of a movement to end the enslavement of "chinos."[37] When he took up his post, Haro y Monterroso was largely unknown and even unimportant. But soon thereafter, he began speaking out and writing letters against various injustices he observed in Guadalajara and the greater region of New Galicia. On July 17, 1671, he joined an ongoing legal denunciation of the president of the Real Audiencia of Guadalajara, Antonio Álvarez de Castro, for his rampant abuse of Indigenous people for "personal services."[38] These services were often thinly disguised forms of de facto enslavement. They consisted primarily of such tasks as providing agricultural labor, working on construction projects, looking after children, and cooking for a household.[39] This imbroglio resulted in the removal of Álvarez de Castro from his position.

Haro y Monterroso's vision of justice extended beyond this controversy. In 1671, he reopened a discussion on the emancipation of Indigenous

"Chichimecas" that had been tabled in 1659. Tapping into the earliest arguments against slave trading in the Americas, he maintained that enslavement hindered conversion and unlawfully split up families.[40] Crucially, he believed that enslaved "chinos" deserved freedom along with enslaved Indigenous "Chichimecas," Indigenous Sinaloas, and Indigenous peoples of New Mexico and the New Kingdom of Leon.[41] Adding the emancipation of "chinos" to that of "indios" effectively expanded the arguments for freedom that Juan de Solórzano Pereira had considered in the Peruvian case, which had appeared in his *Política Indiana* over two decades before.[42]

Haro y Monterroso wrote that in Mexico City "there are a great number of these chinos . . . taken for slaves and the women chinas too and their children without any difference."[43] Then on October 9, 1671, at Haro y Monterroso's encouragement, the Real Audiencia of Guadalajara made a historic pronouncement: it ruled that the slave trade in "indios chinos" must cease and "all women of any age and all of the sons younger than fourteen at the time they were taken in just war be declared free."[44] This ruling was intended to free all subsequent generations of "chinos," since they would be born to free mothers. Moreover, all other enslaved "chinos" would have the legitimacy of their enslavement checked. Despite the broad applicability of this order, only six "chinos" received their freedom. These liberated "chinos" were to be deported to Asia on the next galleons to leave Acapulco.[45]

Early in 1672, Haro y Monterroso continued his bold reforms by attacking the encomendero elites: he petitioned the Real Audencia of Guadalajara to dissolve the remnants of the encomienda and repartimiento systems and to give back pay to all Indigenous laborers at a rate of two reales per day of work.[46] The Audiencia soon issued a sweeping order to free all "indios" and "indias" of New Vizcaya.[47] What Haro y Monterroso lacked in station and experience, he compensated for in ambition.

On March 20, 1672, Queen Regent Mariana of Austria discussed the merits of Haro y Monterroso's arguments in the Council of the Indies, and on April 7, she confirmed the Real Audiencia's order to liberate the "indios chinos." She thanked Haro y Monterroso for his "zeal" and concluded that "it is so just and proper to leave the indios with their freedom."[48] On December 23, she expanded the order to apply to all Indigenous peoples (including all "chinos") throughout Mexico.[49] Only those whose enslavement could be proven to be the result of a "just war" would remain in bondage.[50]

With great enthusiasm, Haro y Monterroso carried out her decree in Guadalajara.

However, the reception to emancipation in Mexico City was hostile. In 1673, the prosecutor Martín de Solís Miranda questioned who the order applied to. Suddenly, there was great interest in determining who exactly "chinos" and "indios chinos" were. Did the queen regent's order mean that all Asians were free or only those from certain regions? How could an enslaved person's origins be proven? By making freedom a technical and academic issue, Miranda delayed emancipation. Meanwhile, a report from 1674 noted that enslavers in Mexico City "took [chinos] away to obrajes and mining settlements with the intention of hiding them so that they cannot reach justice."[51]

In 1675, Miranda declared that the liberated "indios filipenses" (Philippian indios) and "enslaved Orientals (called chinos)" were "very different from the docility and sincerity of the native indios of this kingdom for their being cleverer and of not as good inclinations and customs."[52] He proposed to segregate these populations from the city's Indigenous people by giving them either land outside the city or a special district within its borders. Further, he argued that the emancipation order would unjustly free members of enslaved communities whose parents or grandparents had been in servitude (implying that their bondage was legitimate). Allegedly, the decree would also scandalize the viceroyalty by freeing enslaved Muslims, give enslaved Afro-Mexicans cause for revolt out of jealousy, and impoverish nobles who kept enslaved people as wealth.[53] He added that "although this matter was easy to implement in the Audiencia of Guadalajara for the number of these slaves not reaching twenty in the entire district, here it is recognized as very damaging and dangerous."[54]

In response to Miranda, Haro y Monterroso confessed that he had shared some of the same doubts about categories and cases of legitimate enslavement in his initial letter to the crown. The emancipation orders would necessarily violate colonial precedent. Nonetheless, he wrote that "the goal of Her Majesty is not in gaining vassals [through slavery] but to increase the guild of the church, and slavery is in opposition [to this goal]."[55] The royal order held.

Miranda's resistance, as well as that of other enslavers, meant that awards of freedom came slowly and at great personal risk to "chinos."[56] Robles recorded that three years after the queen regent's proclamation, the Real

Audiencia of Mexico City relented and freed thirty-one "chinos."[57] However, enslavers who presented "legitimate" titles of ownership were permitted to keep their enslaved people.[58] In 1676, the crown reprimanded the Real Audiencia for delaying the emancipation of "chinos" and instructed its judges to implement the order of 1672.[59] Such intransigence meant that enslavement would persist for decades after formal abolition.[60] For example, a parish register of Petatlán, near the contraband port of Zihuatanejo, recorded the presence of twenty-five enslaved "chinos" in 1681, nine years after emancipation. These twenty-five people even outnumbered the district's thirteen free "chinos." Ten of the twenty-five enslaved people lived in the town itself, while the other fifteen toiled on nearby estates.[61]

Enslaved litigants who fought to receive an audience at court cited the new rulings and had some success. For example, Domingo de la Cruz petitioned for and received freedom in Zapotlán in 1678 on the basis that all "chinos" were free.[62] Since he was Indigenous to the Philippines, he was a "chino" and therefore free. Perhaps more telling is the case of Inés Rodríguez, whose husband, an Indigenous man from Tepic named Marcos Xil, managed to successfully litigate for her freedom in 1683. She was the daughter of Agustina Castellanos—a "china" born out of wedlock in New Spain who was the daughter of María, a "china" from the Philippines. Castellanos's brother had also been ruled free as a "chino," and on the basis that all members of the family were "chinos," Rodríguez received freedom from bondage.[63] After three generations of enslavement in Mexico, her family was now free. In the decades following the emancipation orders, their enforcement and cases of individual litigation succeeded in liberating hundreds of enslaved Asians throughout the viceroyalty.[64]

Still, the rhetoric justifying the enslavement of Asians persisted. It pervaded the hagiographies of Catarina de San Juan, composed after her death in 1688–1692. The authors of these texts repeatedly argued that enslavement, despite its unquestionable traumas, had brought Catarina to the Catholic church. In the words of Alonso Ramos, "It cannot be doubted that among the extremely serious sorrows that this innocent virgin suffered in such miserable captivity, especially in the repeated and almost continuous risks of death, the greatest [sorrow] would be not being baptized."[65] The implication was that it was better to be an enslaved convert than to be a free pagan. This rhetoric echoes Solórzano Pereira's notion that (in the paraphrasing of James Muldoon) the sufferings of the enslaved "were

minimal in comparison to the political and spiritual freedom they obtained as a consequence of coming under Christian domination."[66]

These hagiographies even depicted Catarina as a willing slave after she
landed in Mexico. Even though Miguel de Sosa allegedly tried to treat her
like a daughter, Catarina offered her voluntary submission when she told
him "not to treat her like a woman, nor like a daughter, but like a slave."[67]
After receiving her freedom upon his death, Catarina repeatedly belittled
herself before the Virgin Mary, Jesus, God, and Santa Ana by proclaiming
herself a "slave of your slaves."[68] Although her efforts to manumit other
enslaved men and women make it clear that she abhorred enslavement,
her alleged humility as a voluntary slave of God was meant to exemplify
her holiness. In other words, Catarina's hagiographers used her subjection
to regimes of bondage to uplift the church. Catarina's piety as an enslaved
person fueled the hope of placing Asia under Catholic hegemony, and in
her visions, she bore witness to the global spread of Catholic fervor.[69] Although the legitimacy of Asians' enslavement could now be contested in
court, such hagiographic representations suggest that even among those
who most admired Catarina, her "willful" submission to enslavement and
her Catholic piety remained popular justifications for her bondage.

Royal edicts from 1700 reveal that although the enslavement of "chinos"
in Mexico had formally ended, the transpacific slave trade had not. The
Nuestra Señora del Rosario, which landed in Acapulco in 1699, had an "excessive" number of enslaved passengers and amount of contraband.[70] According to one of the edicts, the principal reason for the crown's desire to
limit the flow of enslaved people across the Pacific to Mexico was that
"many profess the Muslim faith."[71] Because enslaved Asians could no longer
legally be traded across the Pacific, most captives were now East African.
An enslaved man from Mozambique named Antonio was probably a passenger on the 1699 crossing. Sold in Manila on November 8, 1698, his ownership was transferred to Antonio del Pozo to clear a debt in Acapulco. This
enslaver then sold him in Antequera to Antonio Martínez in 1703.[72]

One of the last enslaved Asians brought across the Pacific was also
ensnared in these continuing circuits of enslavement. In December 1710,
Joseph Moret of Malabar arrived in Acapulco in bondage on the *Nuestra
Señora del Rosario.* A *cirujano* (surgeon) by trade, he was declared free in
March 1711, although he remained in the service of his former enslaver, don
Francisco Moret, in Mexico.[73] After 1710, Asians do not appear in the ros-

ters of the enslaved on the galleons. For example, when it arrived in Acapulco in 1714, the *Nuestra Señora de Begoña* carried at least ten enslaved Africans, five of whom remained on board for the return journey to the Philippines, but no enslaved Asians were recorded as passengers on this voyage.[74] It is not known exactly how long the transpacific slave trade in Africans continued, but enslaved Africans (who were often sold on the island of Mozambique and elsewhere in the Indian Ocean World) appear in New Spanish records through the end of the colonial period.[75] Africans and Afro-descendants also continued serving on the galleons at least through the end of the eighteenth century.

In 1718, more than four decades after "chinos" had been declared free of enslavement, Juan de Balenzuela petitioned for manumission from Fernando de Balenzuela in Mexico. Juan was labeled as a "chino" and described as having the "appearance [of] being native to those islands [the Philippines] or Pampango."[76] Witnesses had assumed he was free in the Philippines and during the galleon crossing "because all of the chinos of said islands enjoy liberty."[77] In the absence of any documentation of his enslaved status, he was ruled free. In the eighteenth century, rather than marking his vulnerability to enslavement, his "chino" appearance had become a marker of freedom.[78]

But this was not always the case. Danielle Terrazas Williams located a handful of sales of enslaved "chinos" and "chinas" in and around Xalapa in 1736 and 1738.[79] Although the transpacific slave trade in Asian captives had been outlawed, some "chinos" clearly still lived in bondage in colonial Mexico well into the eighteenth century. While these "chinos" may have been Afro-descendants, rather than Asians, their continued enslavement proves that the emancipation orders of the late seventeenth century failed to fully eradicate slave trading in "chino / a" captives. If the Africanization of the "chino / a" label began during this period, it may well have been because some Afro-Mexicans (and / or the mixed children of "chinos" and Afro-Mexicans) chose to pass as "chinos" to try to avoid enslavement. The physical ambiguity of "chinos" likely facilitated this exchange of castas.

Decades after their initial promulgation, the emancipation orders issued at Haro y Monterroso's insistence gradually ended the nefarious transpacific slave trade in Asian captives that had lasted for over a hundred years. Demographically, the end of the trade significantly reduced the total number of Asians entering the viceroyalty. It also limited the ethnic and

gender diversity of Asian populations reaching the Americas. Newly arriving "chinos" were almost exclusively Asian sailors and merchants and,
therefore, predominantly from the Philippines and male. Asian women in
the Americas during the eighteenth century, who were now present in
larger numbers than ever before, were almost always second- or third-
generation descendants of people from Asia.

However, the legacy of transpacific enslavement would continue to
haunt "chinos" in Mexico through the end of the colonial period. In 1810,
Viceroy don Francisco Xavier Venegas republished a royal decree from 1803
forbidding *blancos* (white people) from marrying people who "had a near
or distant origin to slaves."[80] Included in the list of castas covered by this
totalizing law were "chinos," and the measure was specifically designated
to be read aloud in Acapulco, as well as a few other urban centers. Although
this order was largely unenforced, it conjured up a historical imaginary of
"chinos"—both Asian and Afro-Indigenous—as enslaved people almost
150 years after they had been formally emancipated.[81] While the decrees
promulgating the end of "chino / a" enslavement are sometimes thought
to signal the end (or nearly the end) of the Asian presence in New Spain,
the existence of free and newly freed Asians over the next few decades, particularly along the Pacific coast, proves that this was not the case.

"Chino" Mobility and Bourbon Reform

In the mid-eighteenth century, free and freed "chinos" in Mexico continued
to live in coastal communities and expanded trade routes to new sites along
the northern coast. Writing about Acapulco in 1746, Joseph Antonio de
Villa-Señor y Sánchez noted that "indios do not live in this city but in the
towns of its jurisdiction, and in it alone, close to four hundred families of
chinos, mulatos, and negros vecinos are found" with "barely . . . eight families of Spaniards."[82] Furthermore, Acapulco had three militia companies:
"one of chinos, the other of negros, and the third of mulatos, [they are]
those that do their watches in continual lookout in the patrols at the port
as well as on both coasts."[83] In 1743, Francisco de Solano wrote that the garrison of the Fort of San Diego belonged to a confraternity that sponsored
masses every Tuesday and buried its brothers with a holy shroud called that
of San Francisco.[84] The garrison and militias were well disciplined and re-

ported to the fort every month for military drills and exercise. When fully mustered from Acapulco and the surrounding lands, they could contain as many as 609 troops.[85] Definitively, "chinos" remained prominent and essential citizens of the port as the militias expanded during the eighteenth century.[86]

A journey north of a day and a half was Coyuca, which consisted of the town proper and two larger nearby pueblos de indios. One of these settlements was San Nicolás Obispo, also known as San Nicolás de los Chinos. Villa-Señor y Sánchez noted in 1746 that it was home to 120 families of "chinos," or seven families more than three years earlier.[87] Significantly, this number was larger than the 100 Indigenous families residing in the town center and in the other settlement (San Agustín Tixtlanzingo).[88]

The "chino / a" community in Coyuca was fairly tight knit and dated back to at least the early seventeenth century.[89] Free "chinos" settled in Coyuca most visibly in 1643, when four "chinos" purchased a caballería. As the free population grew, it consisted primarily (in the words of Solano) of "Philippine indios of Luzon vulgarly called chinos."[90] Many of them married Indigenous women, though Solano noted that some of Coyuca's "chinos" appeared to be "pardo."[91] These "chinos" labored at nearby plantations, repaired the galleons in Acapulco, served as shore sentinels and militiamen, and "ferried people across Coyuca lagoon on their boats."[92] They enjoyed relative political autonomy, with their own town alguacil and alcalde. They also founded their own parish, which encompassed outlying townships like San Agustín Tixtlanzingo and nearby haciendas.[93] In defense of their right to the land and exemption from a proposed tax, the alcalde of San Nicolás, a "chino criollo" named Pedro Zúñiga, recounted in 1744 that "our neighborhood of San Nicolás was founded since ancient times by the Philippine indios who came yearly from Manila" and married Indigenous women, "giving the population the size that it has today."[94]

On April 21, 1766, a devastating earthquake hit Acapulco, and many survivors fled northward. The seismic shock destroyed the venerable Fort of San Diego and damaged every home in the city. The residents erected makeshift shelters in the plazas, but many decided to move away rather than rebuild. This outward migration from Acapulco likely contributed to the long-term vitality of "chino / a" communities in nearby towns.[95] A parish register from 1777 recorded 388 "chinos" living in Coyuca, a clear example of this demographic continuity.[96] This number even surpassed the 121 "chinos" (63 men and 58 women) recorded in Acapulco for the same year.[97]

The Bourbon Reforms accounted for some of this mobility as well.[98] One key piece of the reforms was an effort to revitalize the Iberian Peninsula by increasing tax revenue and undermining the old Hapsburgian trade monopolies and institutions.[99] Through a mastery of colonial commerce, the Bourbons sought to stabilize Spanish finances, in large part to fund new wars and expansion in Europe and elsewhere.[100] In the words of D. A. Brading, "by the close of the century New Spain had emerged as a source of revenue second only to the metropolis itself."[101] During the eighteenth century, colonial Mexican tax revenue under Bourbon rule increased from three million pesos to over twenty million.[102] By 1800, Mexico was responsible for 66 percent of the world's silver production.[103]

Central to this economic "revolution" was the establishment of trade routes with *navíos de perimso* (register ships), beginning shortly after the Bourbon succession. This change from the previous fleet system sought to increase the efficiency of trade and end the contraband trafficking that flourished during and after the succession. Although these early efforts largely failed to achieve the latter goal, they began to stimulate mercantile interest and activity in coasts and ports that had been considered far-flung backwaters for most of the colonial period.[104]

For example, the new policies drew fresh metropolitan interest to sites like Guadalajara and further north to San Blas.[105] As a result Guadalajara expanded rapidly, along with the rest of urban Mexico during the eighteenth century. It was transformed from a "modest, desolate city" to a "handsome urban center."[106] Its population increased sixfold, to over thirty thousand people—a surge largely driven by migration from other regions.[107] Similarly, the diocese of Michoacán, north of Acapulco, had contained 11 percent of colonial Mexico's population in 1742 but held 19 percent by 1810.[108]

Undoubtedly, this population growth also encompasses the renewed northern movement of Asians from Acapulco. As Jaime Olveda demonstrates, numerous marriage records attest to this trajectory, as well as a rare 1728 license to a Philippine man named Pedro Pérez that permitted him to fish for pearls along the seaboard.[109] Parish registers from Atoyac, just south of Guadalajara, provide decisive evidence of northward Asian mobility. One register from 1770 documented that 148 "chinos" (a considerable number) lived in its jurisdiction, primarily in the small towns of Monte Obscuro (home to 28 men and 40 women) and San Juan Chiquito (33 men and 19 women).[110] By comparison, a parish register of Atoyac and its environs from 1683 listed only 62 "chinos" living in the neighborhood of San Francisco and on two farms.[111] Therefore, the population of "chino / a" parishioners in Atoyac increased by roughly 138 percent over an eighty-seven-year period.

Alexandro Mauricio de Arabo, whose story opened this chapter, was one Philippine merchant who adapted his trade activities to serve the Guadalajara–San Blas corridor. As Spanish reformers began searching for alternatives to the Manila galleon route in the second half of the eighteenth century, San Blas emerged as an important shipyard for the galleons, in part due to its connection to Guadalajara. There, galleon officials began to make a habit of exchanging trade goods for ship repairs.[112] In 1784, the writer Agustín Íñigo Abbad y Lasierra proposed a new transpacific alternative to Acapulco centered on San Blas.[113] "Chinos" with connections to Guadalajara helped actualize Abbad y Lasierra's vision by rerouting Pacific coast trading into San Blas, and they participated in this trade until at least 1818, when the "unparalleled prosperity" of this new route peaked.[114] One "chino" merchant was Miguel Sales, a "Native of the Kingdom of Manila" who worked in the import sector.[115] In 1811, rebel "insurgents" captured him and stole two saddles—including one with silver garnish—as he escorted a group of five Spanish merchants to Guadalajara.[116] Eventually, the thieves either returned the saddles to him or gave him their approximate value.

There are only sparse records from this period of Asian "chinos" scattered throughout the viceroyalty's core, away from the coast.[117] As migration northwest from Acapulco increased, the number of Asians in the central highlands dropped. Using primarily matrimonial records, Carrillo Martín located cases pertaining to eleven Philippine Natives in Mexico City, Puebla, Toluca, and Otumba from 1752 to 1803.[118] In 1753, twenty "chinos" and "indios chinos" were counted among the population of foreigners in Mexico City.[119] In 1811, a census recorded only two "chinos" of ambiguous provenance in Mexico City, out of a total population of more than 168,000 people.[120] Although it is difficult, if not impossible, to know precisely why so few "chinos" appear in these records, these numbers undoubtedly are due to several overlapping factors: the ambiguous meanings of "chino / a,"

mestizaje, increased movement to the coast, the general decline of the galleon route, and spikes in death rates due to disease at the beginning of the
nineteenth century.[121] When combined with the contemporaneous counts
of "chinos" in coastal areas, these data from the highlands cannot indicate
that Asians disappeared from Mexico during this period.

Eighteenth-Century Convergences

Although population counts are useful tools for tracking the movement
of "chinos" in Mexico, they can only imply how "chinos" adapted to life
in New Spain during the eighteenth century. Inquisition records from this
period signal both important continuities in collaborative spiritual practices
and manifestations of racialization in the late colonial period. During the
seventeenth century, as noted in Chapter 4, "chinos" adopted a diverse array
of spiritual practices common in multiethnic communities to mitigate the
harsh realities of enslavement, make money, and resist colonial authority.
Doing so meant engaging in intellectual exchanges and knowledge production with Indigenous, African, and Afro-descendant spiritual and pharmacological experts. These convergences continued during the Bourbon era
long after the emancipation of "chinos." Asians navigated the Holy Office
under Bourbon rule much as their predecessors had during the Hapsburg
period. Early eighteenth-century denunciations resemble those of the previous centuries and reveal that Asian people continued to display similar
inclinations toward creolization, spiritual leadership, and multiethnic
convergence.

Late colonial Bourbon rulers had not only transformed colonial eco-
nomics but had also sought to reform religious governance in Spain and
its colonies by reducing the power of the Catholic Church through measures
that Brading has called an outright "assault" on Baroque Catholicism.
Across the Hispanic World, the mendicant orders lost control of parishes;
popular spiritual practices and confraternities were suppressed; religious
festivals were canceled or reduced in size; the Jesuits were expelled from
the colonies; and ecclesiastical property was confiscated, among other ag-
gressive policies.[122]

The move toward secularism and reduced church influence affected the
Inquisition as well. By the late eighteenth century, the Holy Office had
largely become a political tool for policing not religious faith but royalist

sentiment. Although zealous parish priests and concerned citizens continued denouncing unorthodoxy, fewer spiritual infractions merited the trouble of a full trial or the spectacle of punishment.[123] While some clergymen and inquisitors continued to undermine the large-scale popular devotions of Baroque festivals, top-down efforts to suppress vernacular religiosity proved largely unable to unseat the old ways.[124]

Nondogmatic practices survived alongside Baroque devotions as well. For example, in 1719 in Acapulco, an "indio or chino" from the Philippines advised José de la Asención, a "free mulato," on how to attract women.[125] He told Ascención to give some tobacco mixed with three human hairs to the woman he sought to seduce. Tobacco smoke was a sacred, purifying element in Indigenous communities in central Mexico, and numerous West Central African spiritual practices that appeared in colonial Mexico used human body parts like hair and bones for many rituals.[126] Ascención allegedly followed the instructions, but the procedure failed to produce results—which led him to denounce his erstwhile adviser. The denunciation also referred to a broader community of "indios or chinos" of the Philippines in Acapulco who regularly practiced various enchantments to seduce women.[127] Given the transience of Asian sailors in Acapulco, these seduction rituals were often intended to swiftly initiate sexual relations between sailors and members of local groups.

In a similar vein, denunciations in the late eighteenth century against Asian husbands who had abandoned their spouses in one region before settling in another region and marrying someone else resulted in less severe punishments than during earlier periods.[128] The continued mobility of "chinos" throughout Mexico meant that bigamy was almost too common to prosecute. One of the most complete cases involving this cohort of bigamist husbands is that of Nicolas Soza. He appeared before an inquisitorial tribunal in 1772 after having been accused of marrying women in both Cavite and Cuernavaca. The case is significant for the careful attention that the inquisitors paid to both Soza's racial categories and their own jurisdiction to prosecute him.

Soza identified himself to the inquisitors as a "Sangley mestizo," a reference to the descendants in the Philippines of "Sangley" men and Philippine women. Unlike "Sangleyes," "Sangley" mestizos had acquired a reputation for being loyal to the crown, Hispanicized, and stalwart defenders of Manila. Despite Soza's self-identification, the scribe depicted him as follows: "he is tall and thin, small eyes, like a Sangley, snub-nosed, chino colored, and short black hair, and uses a biretta."[129] This observer deployed stereotypes about the appearance of both "Sangleyes" and "chinos" (such as eye shape and skin color) to describe Soza's physical appearance. In this way, he discounted Soza's claim to be part of a privileged group, associating him instead with the "chino / a" casta and the legal vulnerabilities that this designation still carried. Importantly, this description indicates that some Spanish officials during the late eighteenth century still understood both "Sangley" and "chino" to indicate specific physical features associated with Asians in Mexico.

However, when Soza was asked to describe his origins, he undermined these constructions of racial difference to his benefit. He said that he was a shoemaker from Santa Cruz, Manila, and that his *calidad* (overall quality) was that of a "Sangley mestizo." Since "mestizo" in central Mexico referred most often to the descendants of Spanish men and Indigenous women, the inquisitors asked Soza if he had any Spanish ancestors. Soza replied that his parents were "Sangley mestizos" and not Spaniards "*nor any other casta.*"[130] In his testimony, therefore, Soza refused to divide his heritage between "Sangley" and "mestizo." He could not be reduced to two halves but was a pure "Sangley mestizo," which the inquisitors conflated with "pure chino."[131] Soza's self-presentation confused the inquisitors, who concluded that they did not have jurisdiction to pursue the case—despite Soza's confession that he had gotten married in both Cavite and Cuernavaca.[132] Echoing numerous earlier cases in which "chinos" had rhetorically manipulated racial categories to their benefit, Soza crafted a careful testimony that successfully evaded inquisitorial punishment. He may also have benefited from the Bourbon-era movement in the Inquisition away from individual denunciations and toward the persecution of those using Baroque Catholic practices and of uncertain political allegiance.

During this period, change came to the viceregal capital as well. In 1769, a canon named Manuel Joachin Barrientos Lomelin y Cervantes had jurisdiction over the Tribunal (*provisorato*) of Indios and Chinos in Mexico City. In an inflammatory pronouncement against apostasy, Lomelin y Cervantes described those "commonly called Chinos" as "those of the Philippines, who reside in their district."[133] In addition to their tendency toward bigamy, "chinos" and "indios" alike were supposedly likely to commit blasphemy, participate in superstitious curing, consume peyote, suck myrtle, take *pipitzitzintli* (a hallucinogen), experience ecstasy and miracles, profess that they had had revelations, use divinatory dolls, give offerings to spirits, light incense in caves, bathe together, and more. The punishment for committing these crimes was fifty lashes and imprisonment.[134] However, if the extant documentation is any indication, Lomelin y Cervantes's fervor did not snare offending "chinos." The existence and pronouncements of the Tribunal of Indios and Chinos in Mexico City testify to the continuity of Afro-Asian-Indigenous convergences described in Chapter 4. Despite the zealotry of individual officials like Lomelin y Cervantes, the reforms that reduced the power of the Catholic Church made these deeply entrenched practices less worthy of a full trial and castigation than they had been in previous centuries.

Eighteenth-Century Galleons and Transient Communities

After devastating the southern Chinese coast during its southward invasion against the last Ming holdouts, the Qing dynasty gradually restabilized the Chinese market for foreign goods by the late seventeenth century. The ensuing peace led to a renewal in the demand for silver, which revitalized the Manila galleons. The period from 1680 to 1740 is known as a golden age of transpacific shipping.[135] However, the increased volume of merchandise in cargo holds and the favorable profit margins for merchants on both sides of the Pacific did not greatly affect the migratory rates of free people after the emancipation of "chinos." Asian migration during this period owed its stability simply to the annual coming and going of the galleons. Sailors still regularly abandoned the sea for life in central Mexico, despite the now institutionalized punishment of up to ten years in the galleys if they were caught.[136] For example, in 1790 port officials in Acapulco found that twenty-one crew members had failed to board the *San Andrés* for its return to the Philippines due to sickness (three people) or desertion (eighteen).[137]

By the middle of the eighteenth century, the Bourbon movement toward large-scale economic reform had intersected with a series of practical setbacks for the galleons: the system of registered ships undermined the existing commercial system, Chinese trade to Manila began to falter again, and continual war with the British was punctuated by George Anson's dramatic capture of the Manila galleon *Nuestra Señora de Covadonga* in 1743. Drastic financial losses for the crown ensued.[138]

Yet during this period of imperiled transpacific shipping, the lives of crew members on the ships broadly resembled the experiences of crews in the sixteenth and seventeenth centuries. Poorly paid wage laborers continued to perform most of the work in Cavite and at sea. Of the Philippine port, the German Johann Christian Sinapius wrote in 1763 that "generally, all of the ships that are required for the trade with Acapulco are there. Here one can see constantly between two hundred and three hundred Natives, at times up to six hundred, that work loading the warships and Spanish galleons."[139] These labor patterns had been in place for generations.

An exhaustive review of the crew of La Santísima Trinidad y Nuestra Señora del Buen Fin in 1751 also reveals that the composition of galleon crews in the eighteenth century had some similarities with that of crews in earlier centuries, with a few important discrepancies (see the appendix).[140] Nicknamed either the Poderoso or the Filipino, this enormous vessel displaced two thousand tons and was the largest Manila galleon to sail the Pacific route. It made its maiden voyage from Manila to Acapulco in 1751, arrived in good order, and set sail for the return voyage in April 1752. From 1751 to 1762, it was the only full-sized galleon to sail between the Philippines and Mexico.

The review is exceptional for its abundance of details about most members of the crew. Galleon crew lists typically recorded only names and shipboard jobs. In contrast, entries in this review provide details including the crew member's hometown, age, marital status, identifying physical features, and father's name. These details invite a closer examination of how place of birth and role on the ship were aligned.

According to the review, there were 407 crew members and officials, 297 of whom had recorded hometowns. Of those 297, 222 (75 percent) listed an Asian locale (most often Cavite) as their place of birth. While we cannot be certain that an Asian hometown always indicated Asian ethnicity, the review implies a strong correlation between the two. For example, it identifies Eujenio del Rosario, a sailor and battalion drummer, as a "criollo" of Manila, meaning that the other crew members from Manila (or elsewhere in the Philippines) were likely Indigenous. Even if we make a small allowance for variance between hometown and ethnicity, this document demonstrates definitively that galleon crews remained overwhelmingly Asian during the eighteenth century. It also shows that Asians achieved greater social mobility on the galleons during the decades following the emancipation of "chinos."

During the seventeenth century, Asian sailors had served almost exclusively as grumetes, the lowest-ranking position on board except for enslaved laborers. The only exceptions were a handful of marineros, guardianejos, and Cagayan carpenters. After emancipation, ship rosters demonstrate that Asians came to occupy a wider variety of better paying positions.[141] Significantly, the Spanish grumete positions were no longer for Spaniards alone. Sixteen of the thirty-one Spanish grumetes on the 1751 crossing listed an Asian hometown.[142]

The title of Spanish grumete had once allowed ship captains to distinguish higher-paid Spaniards from lower-paid Asian grumetes performing similar tasks. In 1751, experienced Spanish and Asian grumetes could earn the same title and receive the same pay. Unlike in the seventeenth century, many sailors of Asian provenance were listed as full sailors and artillerymen and in more specialized roles as well. For example, don Andres de Sarrate was from Manila and held the rank of captain (distinct from the ship's "general" or overall commander) and the position of pilotage master.

Of the 221 crew members in the review with a confirmed Asian hometown (not counting the Spanish "criollos"), the overall breakdown is as follows: Cavite (140), Manila (56), Cagayan (8), Bulacan (4), Macau (3), Cebu (2), Pangasinan (2), Pampanga (1), Philippines unspecified (1), Siam (1), Ilocos (1), Camarines (1), and Marianas (1). Thus, all but five of those with Asian origins hailed from the Philippines. Ninety-nine crew members listed as Asian were married. This shows that despite the promise of months and years away from a spouse, many married sailors still labored on the galleons, and it provides an important context for the continuity of bigamy cases against Asians in New Spain. Lorenzo Theodoro was one bigamous sailor who, during the 1770s, received inquisitorial punishment for having married both Dorotea la Colorada in Mexico and Dominga Gerbacia in Manila.[143] Many non-Asian sailors also clearly had established kinship ties through marriage in the Philippines: twelve non-Asian crew members in the review had been married in Manila (seven) or Cavite (five). Only four non-Asians had been married outside of the Philippines.

Undoubtedly, this cohort of crew members and sailors was a diverse and eclectic group. The physical descriptions note with startling frequency the presence of facial and bodily scarring: these rough-and-tumble men were veterans of a brutal oceanic world.[144] Perhaps most significant, though, is a clustering of words used to describe Asian men that conformed broadly to racialized and gendered stereotypes: yellowish skin (often referred to elsewhere as "quince-colored" or in the review as *trigueño* [wheat-colored]) and beardlessness. The review uses "wheat-colored" for thirty-two individuals identified as having Asian origins and *lampiño* (beardless) for sixteen.[145] These descriptors were assigned to European- and American-born crew members at significantly lower rates (only nine of these people were referred to as "wheat-colored" and five as "beardless"). Furthermore, seventeen crew members of European or American origin were described as *cerrado de barba* (full-bearded), versus only seven of Asian birth. In colonial ethnography, the presence or absence of facial and bodily hair was a core indication of masculinity and a sure method of distinguishing Spanish from non-Spanish people.[146] The prevalence of these tropes in relation to Asian crew members expresses long-standing Spanish stereotypes of Asian and Indigenous men as physically nonnormative and effeminate.[147]

Although the level of description of the review of *La Santísima Trinidad y Nuestra Señora del Buen Fin* is exceptional, the ship's crew demographics are representative of broader maritime labor patterns in the region during the eighteenth century.[148] While the availability of experienced sailors in the Philippines had generally declined during the seventeenth century, these labor pools had slowly begun to recover on Luzon as Indigenous populations stabilized after decades of demographic collapse. By the eighteenth century, numerous imperial powers sought to hire Philippine mariners who were renowned as skilled and reliable sailors.

In 1762, Spain entered the Seven Years' War as an ally of France and an opponent of Britain. This intervention led almost immediately to Spain's devastating losses of both Havana and Manila, which permanently affected its transatlantic and transpacific trades for the remainder of the colonial period. When the British captured Manila, they managed to seize *La Santísima Trinidad y Nuestra Señora del Buen Fin*. The ship's loss was a catastrophe, representing the Spanish forfeiture of millions of pesos.[149] Some of the younger men in the 1751 crew list likely witnessed this defeat. After the British victory, no full-sized Spanish galleon would ever again navigate the Pacific passage. From 1762 to 1815, the Manila galleons were actually frigates and smaller vessels.[150]

With this enormous amount of plunder, the British held onto Manila until 1764, relinquishing control of it only at the conclusion of the war. The conflict's aftermath permanently altered the Iberian Peninsula's economic relationship to the Philippine archipelago in ways that further undermined the Manila galleons. In 1765, some warships and trading vessels began sailing directly from the Philippines to the Peninsula instead of across the Pacific to Mexico. According to Mariano Bonialian, "until at least 1784, the peninsular position was that of intervening in the Philippine route and trying to displace the New Spaniards from the business of trafficking Asian goods in New Spain."[151] This move provided unprecedented opportunities to peninsular elites and decisively undercut the dominance of the transpacific galleons through the formation of new trade companies that had direct contact with the Philippines, such as La Real Compañía de Filipinas (the Royal Philippines Company).[152] Though the Company declined after a couple of decades in operation, it decisively fortified the direct connection between Spain and the Philippines, promoted archipelagic economic development, and even created new avenues for the introduction of Asian goods to Mexico—all of which reduced the viability of the Manila galleons.[153]

Asian sailors, primarily from the Philippines, served as crew members on the fifteen vessels that sailed this new route around the Cape of Good Hope.[154] The *Santa Rosa de Lima* arrived in Manila from Acapulco in 1768, and in 1770, it sailed from Manila to Cádiz, entering the harbor on August 11.[155] There, it unloaded crate after crate of Asian merchandise destined for direct consumption on the Peninsula without the mediation of New Spain.[156] At least ninety-nine "chino" sailors helped operate the ship.[157] These crew members remained in Cádiz and worked in local shipping until 1772. Realizing that they had no way to return to the Philippines on their own (and perhaps wanting them gone), Spanish officials devised a plan to "return them to Manila, their homeland."[158] The ninety-nine sailors would embark on three separate ships headed for Veracruz: the *Urca Peregrina,* the *San Juan,* and the *San Carlos.* When they arrived in Mexico, they were to be given half their pay in wine and twenty pesos to pay for the overland "march" to Acapulco.[159] There, they would board a Manila galleon that would finally return them to the Philippines, which would complete their Odyssean circumnavigation—probably in 1774. The list of the ninety-nine "chinos" demonstrates that Asian crew members were dominant on the new Cavite-Cádiz route and that a greater proportion of them served as full sailors than their counterparts had on the Manila galleon route during the long seventeenth century.[160] Six of the "chinos" were artillerymen, a military role that Spanish and Afro-descendant soldiers typically held during the seventeenth century.[161]

Like any notarial record, crew lists provide just enough information to remind us of how much we do not know about the people listed and their lives, friendships, rivalries, memories, and hopes. However, the lists do indicate that galleon crews crossing both the Pacific and the Atlantic remained dynamic, global communities including Asians through the late colonial period. Even as the Manila galleon route began to decline, men (most of whom were from the Philippines) continued practicing their maritime trades on alternative routes, no longer restricted to the old Cavite-Acapulco line. By the end of the eighteenth century, they also served in increasing numbers on ships flying the flags of other European empires.[162]

The End of the Galleon Line

From 1565 to 1740, the Manila galleons had monopolized transpacific trade. Only the rare privateering venture and the environmental hazards of the route undermined their dominance.[163] However, by the middle of the eighteenth century, significant British, French, and Dutch penetration into the Pacific Ocean challenged Spanish hegemony. Although scholars like Warren Cook and Rainer Buschmann have demonstrated that Spaniards remained active and relevant in the eighteenth-century rush to claim the Pacific, the ocean had ceased to be a "Spanish Lake"—if it ever had been one.[164]

Several related developments precipitated the shrinking influence of the Manila galleons. The War of Jenkins' Ear (1739–1748) and the Seven Years' War (1756–1763) had dealt major blows to galleon commerce in the Philippines. In particular, the British seizure of Manila generated uprisings against the Spanish in Guagua, Cagayan, Ilocos, Laguna, Batangas, Tayabas, Cavite, Samar, Panay, Cebu, and Zamboanga.[165] In addition, steeply rising prices of Chinese and Indian goods reduced demand for and thus commercial interest in such products in Acapulco, leading to an overall reduction in the flow of bullion from the Americas in Asian markets.[166] Unsurprisingly, the concurrent expulsions of Chinese from Manila in 1755 and 1766 did little to reduce this decline.[167]

Edicts legalizing *comercio libre* (free trade) between specific territories in 1765 and 1778 further undermined the Cavite-Acapulco monopoly on transpacific shipping and opened the possibility for new, alternative routes across the Pacific that could respond more flexibly to market demand.[168] In 1770, a French ship sailed from Bengal to Callao, carrying goods worth 3–4 million pesos. Another arrived in Buenos Aires in 1782 with Asian merchandise worth 22,000 pesos.[169] These edicts simultaneously facilitated the entry of Asian sailors, primarily from the Philippines, into all major Western maritime ventures. For example, Philippine Natives became prominent on US whaling vessels sailing out of New Bedford, Massachusetts, and they would eventually establish the fishing village of St. Malô outside of New Orleans during the early nineteenth century.[170]

While the transfer of trading power from the Cavite-Acapulco line to other, transimperial commercial routes had already fundamentally altered the nature of transpacific trade, the Wars of Mexican Independence (1810–1821) marked the definitive end of the Manila galleons. In 1810, a parish priest named Miguel Hidalgo y Costilla inaugurated the famous rebellion against "bad government" with a speech, the Grito de Dolores (Cry of Dolores). He assembled a large but untrained force that began its war against New Spain by seizing the city of Guanajuato and its mines.[171] The insurgency "broke silver capitalism" and definitively ended the use of the Cavite-Acapulco route when José María Morelos and his revolutionary forces captured and burned Acapulco in 1813.[172] The *Magallanes, San Carlos,* and *San Antonio* sailed to Acapulco in 1811, 1812, and 1813, respectively, but were unable to unload and sell their cargo there. Trade was redirected up the coast with the help of "chino" merchants in San Blas. The *Magallanes* was forced to sell its merchandise at low prices and returned to Cavite in 1815 with only a small profit. On April 13 of that year, the crown finally decreed a formal end to the transpacific trade between the Philippines and Acapulco. The Manila galleons were no more.[173] Silver exports plummeted from an all-time high in 1809, and this shock wave disrupted economies from the Americas to East and South Asia. British manufacturers filled this market vacuum by positioning themselves "to adapt to a world without silver."[174]

Nevertheless, a handful of ships from the Philippines continued to arrive in San Blas and other trading towns on the Mexican Pacific coast until the early 1820s. They made little money for their trouble.[175] The man who would become the first emperor of a free Mexico, Agustín de Iturbide, confiscated the large sum of 525,000 pesos from a vessel that arrived in Acapulco in 1820 to purchase wares from Mexico City. In 1822, *El Feliz* arrived from the Philippines to request reparations for this loss. Iturbide's refusal to pay signaled the beginning of a long-term break in contact between the Spanish Philippines and the newly independent Mexico.[176] The transpacific migratory channels that had sent Asians to Mexico's Pacific coast for over 250 years had finally ground to a halt. The end had come slowly but definitively.

Yet even in these final moments, Iturbide's and the rebel commander Vicente Guerrero's declaration of independence for Mexico, the "Plan de Iguala," began with an inclusive vision of *americanos* (Americans) that indicates the demographic influence of both the Atlantic and Pacific on the new nation.[177] Iturbide announced that americanos were "not only those born in America, but also the Europeans, Africans, *and Asians* [asiáticos] who reside there."[178] Iturbide clearly appropriated the radical language of earlier leaders in the fight for independence like Morelos (against whom Iturbide had once fought), but this broad appeal was still an important and rare acknowledgment of the transoceanic heritage of newly independent americanos, no matter who articulated it.[179]

The interimperial competition that contributed to the end of the Manila galleon line simultaneously facilitated a new wave of nineteenth-century Asian movement to the Americas via indenture. As Lisa Yun and Richard Allen have argued, Dutch and British experiments in forced labor regimes and displacement in the Indian Ocean World (and, to a lesser extent, in the Americas) began as early as the seventeenth century.[180] Sites of forced displacement included Batavia (1619–1740), Virginia (1635), the Cape Colony (1652), Southern Sulawesi (1653–1682), and Nootka Sound (1788).[181] These initiatives redirected Iberian circuits of labor exploitation in Asia away from the Manila galleons and toward British and Dutch imperial channels worldwide. These many colonial experiments—which had varying gradations of forced labor, from outright enslavement to seasonal servitude—inspired and legitimized the large-scale displacements of the period of indenture. From 1806 to 1917, over 700,000 Chinese and South Asians arrived in the Americas as conscripted laborers or indentured servants under coercive contracts.[182]

When the British Lieutenant William Layman proposed to ship Chinese laborers to Trinidad in 1802, he had already accumulated considerable colonial experience in the Indian Ocean World, and he even cited examples of Chinese productivity and industriousness in Indonesia as precedents for his plan. Robert T. Farquhar implemented the plan in 1806, and he had also already experimented with displacing Chinese artisans in the Maluku Islands, Penang, and Borneo.[183] The result was a shipment of 200 Chinese laborers to Port of Spain, where the 192 who had survived the journey disembarked in 1806. Their arrival in the Caribbean occurred at a time when Manila galleons crewed by Asian sailors were still coming and going from Acapulco.

While the Trinidad experiment was eventually abandoned (only seven Chinese remained by 1834), it marked the beginning of a new wave of Asian mobility to the Americas. These transnational circuits would profoundly influence the language and process of abolition, as well as the relational racialization of both Asian- and Afro-diasporic peoples in the Americas.[184] The contracts that supposedly differentiated the labor of indentured Asians from that of enslaved Africans were often mere fiction despite promises of fair treatment. These new regimes of exploitative labor defined the emergence of modern Asian diasporas in the Americas. They originated during the final years of the Manila galleons and grew from the geopolitical processes contributing to the ships' decline. Still, a few Philippines Natives remained visible as "chinos" in early national Mexico even as the first Chinese began appearing in records in Trinidad (1806), Brazil (1810), and Cuba (1830s).[185] Migratory channels in the early modern and modern periods were contiguous for a brief time, and multiple meanings of "chino / a" as Asian, Afro-Indigenous, and Chinese proliferated simultaneously.

From 1847 to 1874, an overlapping web of British, US, French, Spanish, and Portuguese interests conspired to coerce 125,000 Chinese laborers to sign contracts that landed them in the brutal sugar plantation economy of Cuba.[186] Cutting cane and enduring a cloistered existence in the barracoons, new Chinese arrivals lamented that they had become de facto slaves. One indentured Chinese laborer, Xian Zuobang, reported, "No matter what status one had in China, one will become a slave [in Cuba]."[187] His compatriot Li Zhaochun mourned, "We didn't know that we were sold to Cuba to be slaves for the rest of our lives and suffer so much that we would hope to die soon, but our hope has not been granted."[188] Similarly, beginning in 1849, 100,000 Chinese were shipped to Peru to work in the plantations and guano mines.[189] New waves of Chinese migrants were contracted for work in the United States, Mexico, and Central America as well, initially on a small scale. The Treaty of Guadalupe Hidalgo in 1848 forced Mexico to cede a third of its land to the United States, and Chinese indentured laborers, prospectors, and merchants soon arrived in the newly occupied California territory. On land that many still imagined as Mexican, 325 Chinese arrived in 1849, "followed by 450 in 1850, 2,176 in 1851, and, suddenly, 20,026 in 1852."[190] Farther south, in 1855, forty-five Chinese arrived in Puntarenas, Costa Rica, to labor as servants and on plantations.[191] Chinese railroad workers landed in Mexico as early as 1864. Larger numbers would not arrive until after 1880 "as a solution for labor shortages" under the regime of Porfirio Díaz, president of Mexico in 1876–1880 and 1884–1911.[192] A little over four decades after the end of Spanish galleon contact with the Mexican Pacific coast, new imperialisms had produced migratory channels propelling Asian populations to the old centers of transpacific trade. By the beginning of the twentieth century, Chinese laborers (and the new waves of Japanese and Korean migrants who joined them) would again be labeled "chinos" irrespective of their origin.[193] Whether intentionally or not, this new pattern of identification echoed the old colonial usage of the term and carried many of its orientalizing stereotypes. The migratory modernity of Díaz's Mexico, it turned out, was just a "trick of time."[194]

Ultimately, the temporal "vacuum" that Seijas identified as a central problem in the historiography of Asians in the Americas is what connects two major migratory periods: one centered in the long seventeenth century, and the other in the nineteenth. Instead of compartmentalizing the early modern and the modern periods, we should see them as overlapping and interconnected. By the nineteenth century, the Americas had been receiving galleon-confined Asians for nearly 250 years. These trajectories never fully ceased but were rerouted through transimperial networks. The forms of racialization that justified large-scale Chinese and South Asian dislocation to the Americas during the period of indenture had already been consolidated hundreds of years before, during Spanish and Portuguese circuits in Asia. In the Americas during the early colonial period, we also find the historical antecedents of displacement, labor migration, and knowledge production that were manifested during the nineteenth century. While nineteenth-century Asian migration occurred on a much larger scale, what enabled these modern diasporas was a reinvention and expansion of a nearly forgotten Baroque precedent.

CONCLUSION

TODAY, THE BUILDING in Puebla where Catarina de San Juan supposedly lived is a boutique hotel called the Casona de la China Poblana (Noble House of the China Poblana). Across the street is the Jesuit Templo del Espíritu Santo (Temple of the Holy Spirit) where Catarina was interred in 1688. The luxurious Casona features an intimate courtyard, vibrant interiors, and a statue of the China Poblana herself. She greets all her guests with an alluring smile, wearing an elegant version of the attire that bears the same name (see the Introduction). Antonio Carrión speculated that "maybe the *zangalejo* [buckram clothing] or *castor* of the China of Puebla has an origin in the dress of Catarina de San Juan, as they used to say."[1] Many commentators have taken Carrión's "maybe" to indicate a definitive connection.[2]

The hotel features ten suites that heighten its exotic, pseudohistorical appeal. They bear names like "The Grand Mughal," "Samarkand," "Agra," "Mirra," "The Ship," and "Akbar." A stay in the hotel, then, is a journey both in time and to distant places. However, the hotel's delicate touches and ornate orientalisms would have been quite foreign to Catarina, who led an ascetic life. According to Joseph del Castillo Graxeda, she "lived in various places [in Puebla], and in them she always lived in gloomy little rooms, filled with filthy creatures, the floors deserted of any refinement, and covered with some cold cobbles that came with them."[3] Catarina sought to imitate the model and suffering of Christ by eschewing all earthly pleasures.

She lived on alms alone and never wore the elaborate style of dress now attributed to her. In fact, Castillo Graxeda described her vestments as "fleeing from the delicacy of silk."[4] Far from influencing the fashion of colonial Mexico, she wore only secondhand clothes and "always the crudest, the coarsest."[5] She died with only five reales (less than one peso) to her name. According to Castillo Graxeda, she once said, "I eat the breads that they give for the dogs because I, what am I but [a] china dog baptized on two legs."[6]

Despite Catarina's abject poverty and extreme humility, Castillo Graxeda and her other hagiographers maintained that she lived with dignity and did not tolerate abuse. She once accepted a peso from a confessor who responded, "Who does this china think she is, as if [she were] holy." To this, she responded, "Take your peso. How holy or china? I do not need [a] peso. There I have my redeemer, who takes care of me."[7] Catarina withstood endless abuse and earthly hardship to exercise her material and spiritual freedom. How ironic, then, that the place where she supposedly spent her last days of pious suffering unabashedly commodifies and misconstrues her legacy.

The Jesuits who knew her and clamored for her beatification have long gone, but through their writings, the blurred image of a holy woman who escaped enslavement and chose austerity remains. What do we do with these fragments and the fleeting glimpses of others who crossed the Pacific, who lived and died in the central Mexican highlands, or by the coast, or in the cities, mines, and mills—in the Andes? What do we do with the mountain of names and stories that accompanies Catarina's (each of which is worthy of remembrance) and that together constitute a new canon about a new people who populate and reshape a once familiar history?

I offer this book as evidence that these names represent the historical predecessors—the diasporic ancestors, in the broadest sense—of every person of Asian descent who has made a home in the Western Hemisphere. Though they lived and died hundreds of years ago, their example inspires us to turn difference into empathy, division into solidarity, and a fragmented past into a shared historical heritage.[8] In the thousands, they transformed the colonial world, from Mexico's hot Pacific lowlands to its northern frontier. In small towns and urban centers, they articulated new modes of self-fashioning both within and distinct from those of the "chino / a" monolith. They contributed to and led vibrant spiritual cultures that converged with Indigenous, European, and Afro-diasporic traditions. Improbably, they persisted through generations and remained visible even when the last

Manila galleon left Mexican shores forever and when the clamor for independence shook the decaying bastions of colonial rule.

Yet in the land that was once the heart of a vast, transpacific empire, little remains to remind its denizens of the early Asian presence there. Except for the fading plaque on Catarina's tomb, the Museo Histórico de Acapulco (housed in the rebuilt Fort of San Diego), the tuba still consumed on Mexico's Pacific coast, and the colonial-era Asian furniture and art in the Museo Franz Mayer and a couple of other institutions, the imprint of the "chinos" of New Spain has seemingly faded away. The focus on modern migratory waves from the late nineteenth century on has occluded the remembrance of a diverse Baroque past.

But the new need not take away from the old. On May 17, 2021, President António Manuel López Obrador of Mexico issued a formal apology for the "little genocide" of 303 Chinese residents in Torreón, Coahuila, during the Mexican Revolution.[9] From May 13 to May 15, 1911, insurgent forces and bitter locals attacked Chinese residents and, as had happened in Manila in 1603, looted and appropriated their property. On behalf of the Office of the President of the Republic, Donají Morales Pérez organized a conference (held on September 8–10, 2021) to commemorate the "memories of the Chinese community in Mexico." This gathering not only was an opportunity to celebrate the cultural contributions of Chinese Mexicans to the nation, but it also created space to recognize the long-term Asian presence in New Spain as a diasporic precursor to contemporary Chinese Mexican history. These proceedings signaled that the discourses of mestizaje, so emblematic of the Mexican national narrative, have blocked out the historical legacies of Asian peoples in Mexico from the sixteenth century to the present. The generations of Asians and Asian descendants who settled on the Pacific coast left an indelible mark that scientific methods are only beginning to confirm. A preliminary genetic study has found heterogeneous Asian DNA at higher rates in the population in Acapulco (5–14.5 percent East Asian and Melanesian ancestry in some individuals) than elsewhere in Mexico, and that DNA has been present for thirteen generations (since approximately 1620).[10] The descendants of the first Asians in the Americas are still here.

The notion that the experiences of Asian peoples in Mexico have any connection to Asian peoples elsewhere in the hemisphere has not been much discussed. Although a handful of scholars have been thinking about transnational Asian networks that include Latin America, the study of Asian diasporic populations in the Americas remains startlingly bound to specific nations.[11] Nowhere is this nation-centric approach more apparent than in the United States, the birthplace of the Asian American. As Asian American studies turns back to its radical origins, however, a path toward transnational inclusivity opens.

The political project of establishing "Asian America" and "Asian American" consciousness owes its origins to the student strikes at San Francisco State University in 1968–1969.[12] Young educated Asian Americans found commonalities that cut across ethnic lines through decolonial advocacy, the movement against the Vietnam War, and the fight for civil rights for Black Americans. Many Asian Americans expressed broad solidarity with all oppressed peoples against "the twin chains of Babylon—racism and imperialism."[13] These radical (often Afro-Asian) connections always represented strong counterarguments to the racist motifs of the model minority myth that viewed Asians as perpetually foreign overachievers. Asian American studies emerged out of the strikers' call for an education that would reflect the diversity of the student body and for a new canon neither invested in romanticizing the so-called Far East nor obsessed with the Cold War's domino theory in Southeast Asia and Indochina.

Asian American histories examine what it means to be diasporic in the United States, and one of the central features of the diasporic condition is the act of searching or yearning for an origin, beginning, or first. Publications in this field offer new firsts that hammer yet more nails into the coffin of the old canon. The list of these publications' topics includes Afong Moy, the first Chinese woman to reach the United States (in 1834); St. Malô, the first Philippine town established in the United States (early 1840s); and Miyo Iwakoshi and her family, the first Japanese immigrants to settle in Oregon (1880).[14] We long to know where and who we came from. Who were the pathfinders, those who endured hardship so that later generations could live better? As timelines lengthen and firsts multiply to accommodate new findings, the United States inevitably loses its monumental status as the proprietor of Asian American histories. The term *America* becomes unfixed from the megalithic *United States* and returns to its true meaning, referring broadly to two continents and the islands between them.

The early modern period contained many firsts, and the fact that they were firsts matters. By the end of the sixteenth century, Asians were coming, going, and settling in the Americas via central Mexico. Philippine crew members on a Spanish ship landed in California on the way to Acapulco twenty years before the founding of Jamestown, in Virginia. A multiethnic Asian crew accompanied Sebastián Vizcaíno on the 1602 voyage that named Oregon's Cape Sebastian in 1603. In 1613–1614, 114 Asians originating in places from Goa to Japan appeared in a tribute register in Lima. These stories and others like them hold enormous potential to unseat the nation-state—the United States, in particular—as the arbiter of historical memory, and they deserve to have an inviolable position in the annals of Asian American history.

Strikingly, the experiences of Asians in the Americas during the early modern period provide some of the earliest instances of panethnic solidarity that are at the heart of Asian American political consciousness. Consider, for example, the numerous ways in which enslaved Asian, Indigenous, and Afro-Mexican people collaborated to negotiate the conditions of bondage. Asians in the Spanish Americas consistently created social, economic, and cultural communities that transcended the boundaries of ethnic kinship. Or consider how the Pacific passage engendered multiethnic communication and collaboration that "chinos" would replicate in Mexico. Transpacific movement via the Manila galleons inaugurated a new era in global history that directly speaks to the political, social, cultural, and pedagogical aspirations of Asian American studies today.

But settling the issue of Asian origins in the hemisphere with a nod to the sixteenth century is to arrive at a false summit. Uncovering the first "first" is not the final objective. Asian American literature has long confronted the disorienting difficulty of trying to unearth a corroded past that dissolves at a touch, for the geographic journey from continent to continent is also ephemeral. It is more remembered than embodied, more inherited than lived. Thi Bui communicates this reality in her masterful graphic novel, *The Best We Could Do: An Illustrated Memoir* (2018). For her, the idea of a fixed origin fades into past traumas whose echo reverberates through the generations. She asks, "How did we get to such a lonely place? We live so close to each other and yet feel so far apart. I keep looking toward the past . . . tracing our journey in reverse . . . over the ocean, through the war, seeking an origin story that will set everything right."[15] The illustrated panels of Bui's novel depict empty sidewalks, power lines, a shadow, and a two-page spread of her watching her father navigate tumultuous seas in a flat bottom fishing boat as they fled Vietnam. Yet for her, the impossibility of a settled origin is not paralyzing: the act of searching convalesces and fulfills.

Bui's quest recalls the legendary Cuban writer Alejo Carpentier's *Viaje a la semilla* (Journey to the source), a narrative told in reverse, where the beginning and end are both themselves and each other.[16] For Carpentier, it is not the protagonists of Spanish descent but an enslaved Afro-Cuban man who controls the flow of time forward and backward. How can the stories of colonized people be anything but their own? In the exchange of past and present, the archival records of peoples long gone come alive as they lift off from tattered pages and alight in our minds. Thus, the search for the first Asians in the Americas should not end when we gaze at a sprawling archival cemetery spread across several continents or when we stand before the locked vault of Catarina. Rather, the quest reaches a new plateau when we direct our attention inward and allow these archival phantasms to stimulate a new historical consciousness—one that is sensitive to silences, empathetic toward difference, and radical in its search for new ways of being in the world.

Prophetically, the last stanza of the Jesuit Joseph de Tapia's funerary poem in honor of Catarina reads:

> The eternity to which she flew competes:
> That lying on the pyre bearing Catarina,
> The eagle lives on, [while] the phoenix may resurrect.[17]

Whether we believe that Catarina became the undying eagle or the phoenix awaiting rebirth, each of these spectral paths immortalizes her and others like her who once lived and never truly departed. When we choose to follow them, these paths reward our flight to worlds far beyond our surroundings, time, and spiritual horizons.

APPENDIX

NOTES

SELECTED BIBLIOGRAPHY

ACKNOWLEDGMENTS

INDEX

Appendix

The 1751 Review of the Crew of *La Santísima Trinidad y Nuestra Señora del Buen Fin*

La Santísima Trinidad y Nuestra Señora del Buen Fin was the largest galleon to sail on the Pacific route from 1565 to 1815. It had 407 crew members on its maiden voyage in 1751, from Manila to Acapulco. The ship was captured by the British in 1762.

Name in the order of appearance	Position	Origin or casta	Age	Marital status	Father's name	Identifying features
Don Francisco Urtariz	Shipboard general					
Don Pedro Jurado	Chaplain					
Don Juan de Araneta	Master of silver					
Don Faustino Matienso	Chief navigator					
Don Simón Buteo	Second navigator					
Don Francisco Fonz Serrada	Third navigator					
Don Manuel Viejo Marquez	Boatswain					
Valentino Andres de San Miguel	Carpenter					
Nicolas de la Rosa	Caulker					
Andres Lujardo	Diver					
Don Estevan Mairineire	Artilleryman, sergeant major	Genoa	45	Single	Don Francisco	Full beard
Don Luis del Castillo	Artilleryman, battalion captain	Kingdom of Murcía	40	Single		Short body, somewhat wheat-colored
Don Cassimiro de Norsagaria	Artilleryman, shipboard lieutenant captain	Province of Alaba, dominion de Vizcaya	32		Don Francisco	With a scar on the forehead, short body

(continued)

Name in the order of appearance	Position	Origin or casta	Age	Marital status	Father's name	Identifying features
Don Juan de Galban	Artilleryman, shipboard lieutenant captain	Kingdom of New Spain	22	Single	Don Juan Eusevio	With a scar on the right side of the forehead, short body
Don Andres de Sarrate	Artilleryman, captain, pilotage master	Manila	30		Don Juan Ygnacio	With a mole on the right side of the neck
Don Estevan de Acuña	Artilleryman and lieutenant	Galicia in the Kingdom of Castille	35	Single	Don Estevan	With a scar on the bottom lip
Don Joseph Nabarro	Artilleryman, cadet	Manila	23	Single	Don Andres	Tall body and pockmarked
Don Vicente Quiroga	Artilleryman, cadet	Manila	28	Single		Short body and with a scar on top of the left hand
Don Andres Cauiedes	Artilleryman, cadet	Native of these islands [Philippines]	21	Single	Domingo Joseph	With a scar on top of the middle finger of the right hand
Don Pedro Abadia	Artilleryman, first constable	San Juan de Luz, province of Guipúzcoa	35	Married in Manila	Don Salomon	Freckled with pockmarks with scar on the forehead
Don Francisco de Salinas	Artilleryman, second constable	Barcelona	40	Married in Manila	Don Juan	Freckled, blue eyes, short body
Don Juan Thomas de Erazo	Brigade artilleryman	The town of Arruazo, Kingdom of Navarre	30	Single	Don Domingo	Full-bodied, ginger, with a mole on the left cheek
Joachin Barreiro	Brigade artilleryman	Santiago [de Compostela] of Galicia	25	Single	Domingo	With a scar next to the right side of the lip
Joseph Lazaro del Pino	Brigade artilleryman	Port of Veracruz	29	Single	Venito	With a scar on the right hand and a mole on the nose
Francisco de la Rosa	Brigade artilleryman	Aramonte in Andalucía	24	Married in Manila	Juan	With a big scar on the forehead
Don Pablo Guimpines	Artilleryman, second boatswain	Mallorca	38	Married in the port of Cavite	Jaime	With a scar on the left cheek
Don Marttin de Calizondo	Artilleryman, second guardian [subordinate boatswain]	Yrun in Guipuzcoa	40	Single	Don Mun	Short body with a scar on the forehead

Name in the order of appearance	Position	Origin or casta	Age	Marital status	Father's name	Identifying features
Mattheo Sarmiento	Artilleryman, first cooper	Cavite	30	Married	Matheo	With a scar on top of the middle finger of the right hand
Antonio Cardeño	Artilleryman, battalion sergeant	Kingdom of New Spain				Wheat-colored, of medium stature with a scar, drooping right eye
Don Miguel de Prada	Artilleryman, battalion sergeant	Monicillo in Andalucía, Kingdom of Castille	45	Single	Don Miguel	With a scar on the left side of the forehead
Don Joseph de Acuña y Alencastre	[Assume same as above]	Town and court of Madrid	40	Married in Manila	Don Joseph	With a scar above the upper lip next to the nose, raised eyes
Don Ygnacio Tera	Artilleryman, rigging master	Cavite	35	Married	Don Francisco	With a scar on the right eyebrow
Rovertto Carlos Palomé y Vara	Artilleryman, chief of water	Scotland	29	Single	Rovertto	Ginger, blue eyes, with a scar on top of the right hand
Thomas Francisco	Artilleryman	Cavite	38	Married	Antonio	Pockmarked, full-bodied
Domingo de Campos	Artilleryman	Cavite	38	Married	Antonio	Scar on the eyebrow
Francisco de Medras	Artilleryman	Barcelona	36	Single	Joseph	With a scar between the two eyebrows, full beard
Miguel Guia	Artilleryman	Mallorca	40	Single	Guillermo	Full beard
Andres Guzman	Artilleryman	Cavite	39	Married	Juan	With a scar on the forehead
Diego de Achica	Artilleryman	Bilbao in the Kingdom of Castille	40	Single	Andres	Full beard
Pedro Palacios	Artilleryman	Cavite	36	Married	Julian	With a scar on the beard
Francisco de Vallesterte	Artilleryman	Mallorca	40	Married in Cavite	Miguel	Full beard, skinny
Gregorio Vidan	Artilleryman	Estella of Navarre	31	Single	Silas	Pockmarked
Ysidro Marques	Artilleryman	Cataluña	35	Married in Cavite	Benito	Full beard
Miguel de Aguilar	Artilleryman	Mallorca	32	Married in Cavite	Miguel	Full beard

(continued)

Name in the order of appearance	Position	Origin or casta	Age	Marital status	Father's name	Identifying features
Jeorje Gras	Artilleryman	[Illegible]	28	Married in Manila	Jorje	Full beard
Alexandro Pavon	Artilleryman	San Lucar de Barrameda	33	Single	Alejandro	Wheat-colored, full-bodied
Anttonio Luque	Artilleryman	Mallorca	42	Single	Anttonio	Pockmarked, full beard
Joseph Medrano	Artilleryman	Cavite	36	Married	Joseph	Beardless, full-bodied
Joseph de la Peña Mendiraua	Artilleryman	Cavite	50	Single	Joseph	Branded on the chin
Ramon de Cardenas	Artilleryman	Cavite	30	Married	Lorenzo	Wheat-colored and branded on the chin
Juan Pabon	Artilleryman	Jerez de la Frontera	35	Single	Juan	Wheat-colored and frizzy hair
Joseph Francisco	Artilleryman	Cavite	36	Married	Juan Antonio	With a heart-shaped mark on the bottom side of the left hand
Mariano Fernandez	Artilleryman	Cavite	30		Mariano, Spanish-born	Pockmarked
Augustin Villegas	Artilleryman	Resident in Cavite, Basque	51	Married in Cavite	Augustin	Beardless
Joseph Uttado	Artilleryman	Macao	28	Single	Joseph	With a mole on the cheek
Pedro de Aguilar	Artilleryman	Cavite	42	Married	Agn	With a cross-shaped mark on the bottom side of the left hand
Juan Carlos Noveda	Artilleryman	Lisbon	35	Single	Juan	Full beard and short body
Juan Herrnandez	Artilleryman	Daroca in the Kingdom of Aragon	31	Single	Juan	Full beard
Estevan Carlos	Artilleryman	Genovese	48	Single	Estevan	Full-bodied and full beard
Bernardo Diaz	Artilleryman	Principality of Asturias	25	Single	Bernardo	Cleft chin
Phelipe Gabitan	Artilleryman	Cavite	25	Married	Juan	With a scar above the eyes
Juan de Flores	Artilleryman	Havana	49	Married in Manila	Juan	Full beard
Xtoval Cardillo	Artilleryman	City of Seville	25	Single	Pedro	With a mole on the left cheek
Theodocio Marquez	Artilleryman	Macao	53	Married	Manuel	Short body and snub-nosed

Name in the order of appearance	Position	Origin or casta	Age	Marital status	Father's name	Identifying features
Gregorio Esteban	Artilleryman	European	25	Single	Gregorio	With a scar on the forehead
Francisco del Rosario	Artilleryman	Cavite	42	Married	Vicente	With a scar on the nose
Joseph de la Cruz de San Roque	Artilleryman	Cavite	37	Married	Juan	Wheat-colored
Miguel de Silva	Artilleryman	Cavite	40		Augn	With a scar on the forehead
Anttonio Bernaval	Artilleryman	Zaragoza	48	Married in Cavite	Francisco	Pockmarked
Fray Pheliciano Leal	Sailor, surgeon	Manila	34		Don Diego	With a deformed cross on the left hand and a scar on the right hand
Geronimo de la Cruz	Sailor, second cooper	Cavite	20	Single	Geronimo	Freckled with pockmarks and a scar on the right side of the forehead
Joseph de Castro	Sailor, battalion squad corporal	Mexico	22		Joseph	Eyebrows together with a scar on the left one
Balentin Arraos	Sailor, battalion squad corporal	Manila	38		Captain Don Juan Baptista	Full-bodied, little beard, white and round face
Juan Baptista de San Miguel	Sailor, messenger	Cebu			Don Nicolas	Full-bodied and missing one finger on the right hand
[Illegible] Salcedo	Sailor, messenger	Of this city [Manila]	32		Juan	Of medium stature, wheat-colored, and beardless
Francisco Garcia Pacheco	Sailor, messenger	Bulacan	33		Eugenio	With two holes in the left cheek
Salvador Yjaino	Sailor, messenger	Of this city [Manila], "mestizo"				Of medium stature, with a mole on the left cheek, raised nose
Eujenio del Rosario	Sailor, battalion drummer	Criollo, native of Manila				
Thomas de Vargas	Sailor, soldier	Marianas	30		Miguel	With a mole on top of the left side of the nose
Agustin de Leon	Sailor	Manila, Spanish "mestizo"	31		Joseph	Turned up nose with a mole above the chin
Alejandro Albaro	Sailor	Manila	41		Ygnacio	With a scar on the forehead

(continued)

Name in the order of appearance	Position	Origin or casta	Age	Marital status	Father's name	Identifying features
Juan Joseph Sanchez	Sailor	Peru	30			Short body, black and full beard
Pedro Capracio	Sailor	Manila	41		Pedro	Tall and smaller stature
Domingo Amador	Sailor	Of this city [Manila]	30		Joseph Antonio	Of medium stature and little beard
Dionisio Perea	Sailor	Manila	22		Antonio	With a mole on the left eyebrow
Joseph Estevan Rodriguez	Sailor	Manila	30		Bernave	Full-bodied, white, beardless, small eyes, small and stocky, and black hair
Pedro de los Reies	Sailor	Manila	41		Blas	With a scar on the right side of the nose
Abdon Ygnacio de Rivera	Sailor	Mexico	21		Antonio	Full-bodied, beardless, black eyes and hair
Thadeo Silino	Sailor	Toluca	20		Juan	Medium stature, wheat-colored
Joseph de Tavaletta	Sailor	Mexico	41			Medium stature, pockmarked
Vicencio Constantino	Sailor	Of this city [Manila]	30		Joseph	
Manuel de Silba	Sailor	Manila	31		Manuel	With ten moles on the right cheek
Pheliciano Thorralbo	Sailor	Manila	26			Wheat-colored, gaunt, of good appearance
Juan Joseph Rodriguez	Sailor	Manila	41		Simon	With a mole underneath the right side of the jaw
Thomas Gomendio	Sailor	Mexico				Medium stature, white, ginger, and skinny
Ygnacio de Riuera	Sailor	Manila, "mestizo"				Gaunt and somewhat pockmarked
Joseph de Rojas	Sailor	New Spain	25		Manuel	With a scar on the right eyebrow
Salbador Carmona	Sailor	Manila	32		Francisco	With a scar next to the left eyebrow and a mole on the forehead
Joseph de Vargas	Sailor	Manila, "mestizo"	30			Wheat-colored, short body, beardless

Name in the order of appearance	Position	Origin or casta	Age	Marital status	Father's name	Identifying features
Agustin Ximenez	Sailor	Manila	33		Lucas	Medium stature
Andres de Castro	Sailor	Cavite	32	Married	Carlos	Pockmarked
Raphael Marques	Sailor	Cavite, Spanish "mestizo"	35		Manuel	With a mole below the nose
Andre Hernandez	Sailor	Cavite	30	Married	Joseph	With a mole on the forehead
Juan de los Santos	Sailor	Cavite	25	Single	Francisco	Wheat-colored
Francisco Jiron	Sailor	Cavite	30	Married	Nicolas	With a mole on the chin
Valerio Casales	Sailor	Cavite	26	Single	Joseph	With a scar on the lip
Don Merejildo Phelipe	Sailor	Cavite	25	Married	Juan	With a mole above the eyebrows
Lorenzo Castro	Sailor	Cavite	47		Estevan	With a mole on the left side of the tongue
Martin de Flores	Sailor	Manila	20	Married	Juan	With a scar on the right hand
Antonio Augustin	Sailor	Cavite	38	Single	Antonio	Wheat-colored
Diego de la Cruz Rivera	Sailor	Cavite	37	Married	Juan	With a pointed nose
Lucas Henrriquez	Sailor	Cavite	37	Married	Augustin	Snub-nosed
Lorenzo Medina	Sailor	Manila	38	Married	Salvador	With a scar on the tongue
Francisco Marcos	Sailor	Cavite	40	Married	Juan	Indio with a broken finger
Balentino Culalio	Sailor	Pangasinan	30	Single	Christoval	With a scar on the forehead
Athanasio de Chaves	Sailor	Cavite	37	Married	Manuel	Pockmarked
Manuel Morales	Sailor	Cavite	20	Single	Manuel	With a scar on the tongue
Joseph Camachilo	Sailor	Cavite	29	Married	Ygnacio	Wheat-colored
Miguel Mendoza	Sailor	Cavite	30	Married	Matheo	Beardless and wheat-colored
Alejandro Flores	Sailor	Cavite	32	Married	Carlos	With a scar on the chin
Juan Lucas del Rosario	Sailor	Cavite	32	Married	Diego	With a scar on the face
Juan de Austria	Sailor	Pangasinan	31	Married	Juan	With a scar on the forehead
Romualdo Daual	Sailor	Cavite	20	Single	Phelipe	Beardless
Bernardo Garcia	Sailor	Cavite	30	Married	Pasqual	Wheat-colored
Juan Manalili	Sailor	Cavite	50	Married	Mathias	With a scar on the lip
Juan Lopez Zabaleta	Sailor	Cavite	25	Single	Juan	With a scar on the nose
Augustin Dato	Sailor	Cavite	32	Married	Juan	Wheat-colored
Augustin Clemente	Sailor	Cavite	25	Married	Andres	With a mole inside the eye

(continued)

Name in the order of appearance	Position	Origin or casta	Age	Marital status	Father's name	Identifying features
Thomas de los Reyes	Sailor	Cavite	30	Married	Joseph	With a mole next to the nose
Santiago de Aguilar	Sailor	Cavite	30	Married	Thomas	With a scar on the forehead
Pasqual Medrano	Sailor	Cavite	30	Single	Juan	Pockmarked
Luis Medina	Sailor	Mexico	30	Married	Joseph	Full beard
Francisco Manis	Sailor	Cavite	31	Married	Francisco	Pockmarked
Juan Eusebio Guebara	Sailor	Cavite	29	Single	Matheo	With a mole on the right cheek
Francisco de la Trinidad	Sailor	Manila	36	Married	Juan	With a mole on the lip
Francisco Samaniego	Sailor	Cavite	30	Married	Salvador	Pockmarked
Salvador Geronimo	Sailor	Cavite	27	Married	Francisco	With a mole on the lip
Domingo Esponde Yriatte	Sailor	Spanish of the town of Vera	23		Bernardo	With a cut on the cheek
Alonso de los Reyes	Sailor, leader of those who work with augers	Cavite	33	Married	Miguel	Wheat-colored
Bernardo Ledeño	Sailor, sharpener	Cavite	33	Married	Francisco	Pockmarked
Juan Niego	Sailor	Manila	35	Married	Tomas	With a scar on the thumb
Juan de la Cruz	Sailor	Cavite	30	Married	Jacinto	With a mole on the chin
Bernardino de Ocampo	Sailor, second caulker	Cavite	30	Married	Pasqual	With a wart on the cheek
Gregorio Samaniego	Sailor	Cavite	37	Married	Joseph	Beardless
Nicolas de Santa Maria	Sailor	Cagayan	30	Married	Tomas	Wheat-colored
Juan Grande	Sailor	Ilocos	29	Single	Pedro	Wheat-colored
Jacinto Lopez	Sailor	Cagayan	30	Married	Pedro	Wheat-colored
Manuel de la Cruz	Sailor	Cagayan	45	Married	Tomas	With a mole above the nose
Pedro Joseph	Sailor	Cagayan	30	Married	Andres	Wheat-colored
Juan Anttonio Berroa	Sailor	Havana	20		Angel	With a mole on the thumb, wheat-colored
Joseph Faba	Sailor	Genova	46		Anttonio	With a cut nose
Augustin Bobadilla	Sailor	Cavite	40	Married	Ygnacio	With a wart on the cheek
Simon Alonso	Sailor	Cavite	30	Married	Francisco	With a mole on the nose
Joseph Miguel de Thomas	Sailor	Cavite	36	Single	Miguel	With a scar on the forehead

Name in the order of appearance	Position	Origin or casta	Age	Marital status	Father's name	Identifying features
Juan Marcos	Sailor	Bulacan	34	Married	Nicolas	With a wart on the lip
Ignacio Vicente Perez	Sailor	Cavite	31	Single	Manuel	Pockmarked
Santiago de Guevara	Sailor	Cavite	30	Married	Manuel	Pockmarked
Candido de Campos	Sailor	Cavite	35	Single	Juan	Tall body and wheat-colored
Sebastian Romero	Sailor	Antequera	34	Single	Juan	Pockmarked
Francisco Benite	Sailor	Cavite	36	Single	Augustin	With a mole on the eyebrow
Joseph Torralba	Sailor	Manila	20	Single	Miguel	One-eyed
Vicente Aguilar	Sailor	Cavite	37	Married	Joseph	With a wart on the eyebrow
Roque Phelipe de Vega	Sailor	Cavite	20	Married	Juan	With a mole on the chin
Eusevio Lopez	Sailor	Cavite	35	Married	Fausto	With a mole on the ear
Francisco de Guia	Sailor	Cavite	23	Single	Francisco	Pointed nose
Juan Toral	Sailor	Zamora in Castilla	40	Single	Matheo	Short body, wheat-colored, and big eyes
Phelipe Theran	Sailor	Cavite	25	Married	Geronimo	Pockmarked
Joseph Cruzalaegui	Sailor	Cavite	25	Married	Salbador	Little body
Joseph Sanchez Garcia	Sailor	Cavite	27	Married	Matheo	Pockmarked
Manuel de Acosta	Sailor	Cavite	25	Married	Francisco	Full beard
Reymundo de los Santos el Mozo	Sailor	Cavite	26	Single	Phelipe	With a mole on the chin
Martin de Sena	Sailor	Cavite	27	Single	Santiago	With a mole next to the nose
Juan Pedro Callejas	Sailor	Cavite	27	Married	Diego	With a mole on the throat
Thomas Aranzamendy	Sailor	Cavite	25	Married	Francisco	Pockmarked
Lucas Faxardo	Sailor	Cavite	37	Married	Alonzo	Pockmarked
Pablo Aldaco	Sailor	Mexico	21	Single	Pablo	Pockmarked
Luis Rodriguez	Sailor	Macao	39		Capetano	Full beard
Nicolas de Castro	Sailor	Cavite	26	Married	Candido	Full beard and wheat-colored
Manuel Roman	Sailor	Cavite	36	Married	Juan	Full beard
Domingo Roman	Sailor	Cavite	26	Married	Juan	Full beard
Diego Jiron	Sailor	Cavite	25	Married	Nicolas	With a scar mark next to the eye
Bernardo Zalzedo	Sailor	Cavite	24	Single	Gregorio	Pockmarked
Joseph Diaz	Sailor	Cavite	33	Married	Domingo	Pockmarked
Andres Miguel	Sailor	Kingdom of Castille	27		Simon	Full-bodied, with a mole on the right cheek

(continued)

Name in the order of appearance	Position	Origin or casta	Age	Marital status	Father's name	Identifying features
Andres Henriquez	Sailor	Cavite	25	Married	Santiago	With a mole on the left side of the neck
Laurencio Anastacio	Sailor	Cavite	37	Single	Diego	With a scar in an eye
Seuastian del Castillo	Sailor	Cavite	30	Married	Alonzo	Pockmarked
Reymundo Lagos	Sailor	Siam, Portuguese "mestizo"	32	Married	Antonio	Full beard
Matheo Mariano	Sailor	Cavite	30	Married	Nicolas	Pockmarked
Juan Joseph de Esquibel	Sailor	Cavite	25	Married	Juan	With a scar on the forehead
Antonio de los Reyes Valencia	Sailor	Cavite	25	Married	Manuel	Wheat-colored
Vicente Monterrubia	Sailor	Mexico	28	Married	Thomas	Full beard
Lucas Pangilinan	Sailor	Cavite	38	Single	Roque	Wheat-colored
Carlos Gutierrez	Sailor	Cavite	50	Married	Gaspar	With a wart above an eyebrow
Francisco Apalit	Sailor	Cavite	25	Married	Juan	Wheat-colored
Paulino de la Cruz	Sailor	Manila	32	Single	Juan	Full beard
Alonso Olavides	Sailor	Cavite	30	Married	Gregorio	With a mole on the right cheek
Santiago Narzisso	Sailor	Cavite	39	Single	Salbador	With a mole above the nose
Nicolas Morales	Sailor	Manila	24	Single	Juan	Skinny
Bernardo Lopez Calderon	Spanish grumete, soldier	Mexico	34		Alonzo	Tall and freckled with pockmarks
Pedro Alcantara Salinas	Spanish grumete	Manila	36		Santiago	Big eyes with a mole in the nose
Miguel Carmona	Spanish grumete	Cavite			Francisco	With two scars on both sides of the mouth
Joseph Gomez	Spanish grumete	New Spain	20		Joseph	Full-bodied, full beard
Miguel Benavidez	Spanish grumete	Mexico	22		Alonzo	Big eyes, turned up nose, with a scar on the forehead
Anastacio Sanchez	Spanish grumete		23		Francisco	Full-bodied, wheat-colored, and little beard
Nicolas Ortega	Spanish grumete	Manila	25		Francisco	With a mole on the face, next to the left ear
Francisco Antonio Siguenza	Spanish grumete	Manila	22		Manuel	Beardless
Lazaro de la Cruz	Spanish grumete	Manila	49		Lazaro	Tall and wheat-colored

Name in the order of appearance	Position	Origin or casta	Age	Marital status	Father's name	Identifying features
Manuel Pasqual	Spanish grumete	Manila	28		Basilio	With two moles on the left side of the upper lip and a scar on the cheek
Joseph Joachin Contreras	Spanish grumete	Mexico	26		Francisco	Tall, little beard, and black eyes
Joseph Ysidro	Spanish grumete	Moreno, Mexico			Bernardo	Full-bodied, beardless, blue eyes
Domingo Hernandez	Spanish grumete	Cagayan	24		Domingo	Spotted face
Saturnino Gabriel Andres	Spanish grumete	Cavite	18			Beardless, pockmarked
Diego de los Reyes	Spanish grumete	Manila	41		Lorenzo	With a scar on the left cheek
Manuel Yslaba	Spanish grumete	Mexico	21		Thomas	White, black eyes, snub-nosed
Joseph Barbaseda	Spanish grumete	Manila	21		Roque	With a mole on the right temple
Andres Alberto	Spanish grumete	Manila	22			Little body, beardless, pockmarked
Joseph Benito de Torres	Spanish grumete	Mexico	27		Bartholome	With a mole on the right cheek
Andres de Salinas	Spanish grumete	Manila	23		Santiago	Full-bodied, white
Martin de Tapia	Spanish grumete	Royal mines of Pachuca	39		Juan Antonio	Pockmarked, full-bodied
Domingo Miguel	Spanish grumete	Cagayan	32		Andres	With a mole next to the left side of the nose
Joseph Rivera	Spanish grumete	New Spain	33			Full-bodied, black and full beard
Juan Antonio Sintado	Spanish grumete	New Spain	34			Tall body, skinny, wheat-colored
Manuel de Arze	Spanish grumete	Mexico	27		Pedro	With a big hole on the left cheek
Felix Joseph Xauier	Spanish grumete	Cebu	31		Lorenzo	Freckled with pockmarks
Pablo de Miranda	Spanish grumete	Cagayan				Full-bodied and cross-eyed
Joseph Echavarria	Spanish grumete	Mexico	25		Juan	Full beard and black eyes
Mariano Antonio de Murcia	Spanish grumete	Mexico	22		Sabador	Wheat-colored; beardless; black eyes, eyebrows, and nose
Domingo Rodriguez	Spanish grumete	Mexico	21		Domingo	White, pockmarked, and blue eyes

(continued)

Name in the order of appearance	Position	Origin or casta	Age	Marital status	Father's name	Identifying features
Luis Mariano Hernandez	Spanish grumete	Manila	36		Luis	With a mole on the thumb of the right hand
Miguel Gonzalez Jonas	Spanish grumete	Cavite	29	Married	Juan	With a wart on the cheek
Lorenzo Miguel de Quiros	Spanish grumete	Manila	30	Married	Domingo	Wheat-colored
Salbador de Campo	Spanish grumete	Cavite	19	Single	Antonio	Pockmarked
Antonio Diaz	Spanish grumete	Cavite	30	Married	Domingo	Wheat-colored
Manuel Hernandez Ramos	Spanish grumete	Cavite	25	Married	Francisco	With a scar above the eyes
Juan Francisco Aristorena	Spanish grumete	Nueva España	33	Married in Manila	Juan	Frizzy hair
Carpio Vicente	Spanish grumete	Cavite	25	Married	Mathias	Wheat-colored
Alberto Nicolas	Spanish grumete	Cavite	24	Single	Juan	Wheat-colored
Joseph Phelipe	Spanish grumete	Cavite	46	Single	Augustin	With a scar on the eyebrow
Mathias Bauptista	Spanish grumete	Cavite	30	Married	Francisco	With a scar on the eyebrow
Jacinto de la Concepcion	Spanish grumete	Cagayan	32	Married	Thomas	With a wart above the nose
Miguel Ramirez	Spanish grumete	Cavite	35			With a mole on the forehead
Vicente Pulido	Spanish grumete	Cavite	40	Married	Juan	With a scar on the eyebrow
Marin de Bargas	Spanish grumete	Cavite	26	Married	Juan	With a scar on the chest
Simon de los Santos	Spanish grumete	Cavite	48	Single	Andres	With a scar on the forehead
Carlos Gutierrez	Spanish grumete	Cavite	30	Married	Andres	With a wart next to the nose
Manuel Domingo	Spanish grumete	Manila	18	Single	Roque	Pockmarked
Pedro del Rosario	Spanish grumete	Cavite	32	Single	Domingo	With a mole next to the right eye
Faustino Mayoral	Spanish grumete	Cavite	29	Single	Joseph	Pockmarked
Pedro de la Rossa	Spanish grumete	Bulacan	30	Married	Feliciano	With a mole on the upper lip
Pedro Fausto	Spanish grumete	Manila	31	Single		Indio, with a mole next to the eye
Exmeregildo Herman	Spanish grumete	Manila	28	Single	Andres	Indio, with a mole next to the nose
Juan Matheo	Spanish grumete	Bulacan	25	Married	Miguel	With a scar on the forehead
Juan Luna	Spanish grumete	Manila	21	Single	Miguel	With a mole on the cheek
Balthasar de Robles	Spanish grumete		40	Married	Pedro	With a scar on the chin
Clemente Panbalan	Spanish grumete	Manila	20	Single	Juan	With a scar on the nose

Name in the order of appearance	Position	Origin or casta	Age	Marital status	Father's name	Identifying features
Hernando Calderon	Spanish grumete, works with augers	Cavite	20	Single	Pedro	Pockmarked
Blas de la Cruz	Spanish grumete, works with augers	Cavite	25	Married	Juan	Spotted face
Miguel Sigua	Spanish grumete, works with augers	Cavite	26	Single	Pedro	With a scar on the chin
Alonzo de los Santos	Spanish grumete, works with augers	Cavite	23	Single		With a wart next to the nose
Simon de Mendoza	Spanish grumete, *panday* (blacksmith)	Cavite	25	Married	Juan	With a mole on the cheek
Secundino Bernardo	Spanish grumete, panday	Cavite	19	Single	Alonzo	With a mole next to the chin
Joseph Endaya	Spanish grumete, panday	Cavite	21	Single	Ventura	With a mole on the jaw
Faustino Martin	Spanish grumete, panday	Cavite	23	Single	Ventura	Little body
Antonio de los Reyes	Spanish grumete, panday	Cavite	25	Single	Santiago	With a mole above the nose
Francisco de la Cruz	Spanish grumete, panday	Cavite	25	Single	Miguel	With a mole on the cheek
Francisco de la Cruz	Spanish grumete, panday	Cavite	26	Married	Juan	With a scar next to the eye
Santiago de los Reyes	Spanish grumete, panday	Cavite	23	Married	Carlos	With a mole on the face
Gabriel Augustin	Spanish grumete, caulker	Cavite	26	Married	Manuel	With a scar on the lip
Juan Candelaria	Spanish grumete, caulker	Cavite	22	Single	Augustin	With a mole above the lip
Juan de Ocampo	Spanish grumete, caulker	Cavite	26	Single	Ventura	With a mole on the face
Joseph de Cantabrana	Spanish grumete	Mexico	20	Single	Joseph	Beardless
Roque de Espiritu	Spanish grumete	Cavite			Roque	Beardless and wheat-colored
Joseph Dimaracut	Spanish grumete	Cavite	28	Single	Francisco	Pockmarked
Juan Baptista Ragel	Spanish grumete	Cavite	21	Married	Thomas	With a mole on the chin
Nicolas Faxardo	Spanish grumete	Cavite	19	Single	Augustin	With a mole next to the eye
Juan Marcos	Spanish grumete	"Negro"	22	Married	Ramon	Full beard
Carlos Villegas	Spanish grumete	Cavite	29	Married	Carlos	With a mole on the neck
Thomas Francisco Aldana	Spanish grumete	Cavite	17	Single	Augustin	With a scar on the eyebrow

(*continued*)

Name in the order of appearance	Position	Origin or casta	Age	Marital status	Father's name	Identifying features
Victorio Guicoano	Spanish grumete	Cavite	24	Single	Joseph	With a scar next to the nose
Miguel de los Reyes	Spanish grumete	Cavite	26	Single	Roque	Wheat-colored face, big eyes
Phelipe Baluyut	Spanish grumete	Cavite	23	Single	Juan	Medium stature, beardless, with a scar on the face
Dionicio Bastidas	Spanish grumete	Cavite	30	Married	Theodoro	With a folded ear
Andres de la Cruz Bagatao	Spanish grumete	Cavite	28	Single	Andres	Skinny body
Vicente Garzia	Spanish grumete	Manila	20	Single	Juan	With a mole on the chest
Juan Catalan	Spanish grumete	Cavite	25	Single	Juan	With a mole next to the lip
Juan Pasqual de Arze	Spanish grumete	Cavite	22	Married	Nicolas	With a scar next to the eye
Sebastian Barron	Spanish grumete	Manila	25	Single	Miguel	With a mole next to the eye
Carpio de la Cruz	Spanish grumete	Cavite	27	Married	Juan	With a mole on the chest
Joseph Osorio	Spanish grumete	Lima	40		Pedro	Black
Andres Manuel de los Santos	Spanish grumete	Manila	24		Juan	Beardless and pockmarked
Bartholome Villegas	Spanish grumete	Cavite	20	Single	Manuel	With a mole on the chin
Joachin Madriaga	Spanish grumete	Cavite	22	Single	Nicolas	With a scar on the face
Acasio Aguilar	Spanish grumete	Cavite	18	Single	Xptoual	With a mole on the neck
Diego Bauptista	Spanish grumete	Camarines		Single	Pedro	With a scar above the eyebrow
Luxardo Flores	Spanish grumete	Manila	22	Single	Domingo	With a mole on the cheek
Eusevio Bauptista	Spanish grumete	Cavite	22	Single	Augustin	With a scar on the tongue
Bernardo Seleigue	Spanish grumete	Cavite			Bernardo	Wheat-colored and beardless
Pedro Gregorio de Pessa	Simple grumete,[a] soldier	Manila	30		Nicolas	With a scar on the left cheek
Joseph Cedillo	Simple grumete	Mexico	19		Antonio	Medium stature, little beard, and big eyebrows
Marcos Sanxines de Tapia	Simple grumete	Manila	58		Pedro	Wheat-colored and beardless
Francisco Diaz	Simple grumete	Mexico	29		Farrelino	Full-bodied, with a scar on the cheek
Domingo de Pino	Simple grumete	New Spain	22		Luis	With a scar on the left side of the forehead

Name in the order of appearance	Position	Origin or casta	Age	Marital status	Father's name	Identifying features
Francisco Vazques Correa	Simple grumete	Kingdom of Galicia	40		Francisco	With a scar on the left cheek
Martin de Herrera	Simple grumete	Manila	21		Joseph	Of good stature, with a scar on the forehead
Luis de Torres	Simple grumete	Manila	38		Juan	Wheat-colored, beardless, big eyes, and a mole on the cheek
Pedro Ambrocio de la Trinidad	Simple grumete	Manila	38			Of medium stature with little beard
Miguel de la Cruz	Simple grumete		28		Nicolas	Wheat-colored, beardless, of medium stature
Juan Jardinero	Simple grumete		48		Thomas	Full-bodied, blue eyes
Joseph de Castro	Simple grumete	Manila			Luis	With a mole next to the right eyebrow
Domingo de Pessa	Simple grumete	Pampanga	22		Alonzo	With a mole below the left side of the chin
Manuel Vicente de Tapia	Simple grumete	Manila, Spanish "mestizo"	40			Wheat-colored, little beard, and a wart on the nose
Francisco de Santa Anna	Simple grumete					
Pedro Patricio	Simple grumete					
Manuel Endaya	Simple grumete					
Juan Joseph Gutierrez	Simple grumete					
Seuastian Madlanbayan	Simple grumete					
Estevan Ferrer	Simple grumete					
Bernardo Guillermo	Simple grumete					
Eusevio Gutierrez	Simple grumete					
Santiago Romero	Simple grumete					
Thomas Francisco Aldana	Simple grumete					
Manuel de Santa Anna	Simple grumete					
Bartolomé Añesco	Simple grumete					
Francisco de la Cruz	Simple grumete					
Phelipe Domingo	Simple grumete					
Juan Alberto	Simple grumete					
Ignacio Fernandez	Simple grumete					
Juan Pandanan	Simple grumete					
Jacinto Bigmalan	Simple grumete					
Juan de Leon	Simple grumete					
Joseph Garcia	Simple grumete					

(*continued*)

Name in the order of appearance	Position	Origin or casta	Age	Marital status	Father's name	Identifying features
Phelipe Fulgencio	Simple grumete					
Fernando Morante	Simple grumete					
Domingo Diaz	Simple grumete					
Ventura Cadal	Simple grumete					
Juan Otilario	Simple grumete					
Andres Pacudan	Simple grumete					
Juan Butet	Simple grumete					
Nicolas Henriquez	Simple grumete					
Miguel de los Santos	Simple grumete					
Pedro de la Cruz	Simple grumete					
Pablo de la Fuente	Simple grumete					
Francisco Evangelista	Simple grumete					
Pablo de la Cruz	Simple grumete					
Eugenio de la Cruz	Simple grumete					
Antonio Carac	Simple grumete					
Salbador de los Reyes	Simple grumete					
Pasqual de los Vantos	Simple grumete					
Nicolas Tolentino de San Roque	Simple grumete					
Juan Francisco	Simple grumete					
Augustin Silberio	Simple grumete					
Bartolome Mariano	Simple grumete					
Mathias Suarez	Simple grumete					
Pedro Alcantara	Simple grumete					
Estevan Ferrer	Simple grumete					
Pedro Pundalan	Simple grumete					
Manuel Salgado	Simple grumete					
Manuel Joseph Diaz	Simple grumete					
Juan del Rosario	Simple grumete					
Joseph Martinez	Simple grumete					
Pablo Fuentes	Simple grumete					
Manuel Solis	Simple grumete					
Juan Manabat	Simple grumete					
Acacio Pingol	Simple grumete					
Alexo Ordoñes	Simple grumete					
Estevan Ferrer	Simple grumete					
Ysidro Oliba	Simple grumete					
Basilio de Guzman	Simple grumete					
Juan de Dios	Simple grumete					
Joseph Diaz	Simple grumete					
Domingo Natic	Simple grumete					
Juan Marcos	Simple grumete					
Luis Resio	Simple grumete					
Juan Francisco	Simple grumete					
Pasqual de los Reyes	Simple grumete					

Name in the order of appearance	Position	Origin or casta	Age	Marital status	Father's name	Identifying features
Pedro Pablo Domingo	Simple grumete					
Thomas de la Cruz de San Roque	Simple grumete					
Alexandro Faustino	Simple grumete					
Salbador de Acuña	Simple grumete					
Vizente Mariano	Simple grumete					
Juan Augustin	Simple grumete					
Pedro de la Cruz	Simple grumete					
Lorenzo de Herrera	Simple grumete					
Thomas Recio	Simple grumete					
Joseph de los Santos	Simple grumete					
Juan Mariano	Simple grumete					
Guillermo de Torres	Simple grumete					
Pedro Pablo	Simple grumete					
Manuel de Miranda	Simple grumete					
Vicente Garzés	Simple grumete					
Marzelo Nabarro	Simple grumete					
Luis de la Cruz	Simple grumete					
Nicolas Faxardo	Simple grumete					
Juan Nicolas	Simple grumete					
Juan Sabino	Simple grumete					
Nicolas Ramirez	Simple grumete					
Martin Silberio	Simple grumete					
Juan de Guebara	Simple grumete					
Lucas Madlanbayan	Simple grumete					
Domingo Sican	Simple grumete					
Luis de Sossa	Simple grumete					
Ygnacio de los Santos	Simple grumete					
Pedro Bingao	Simple grumete					
Joseph Antonio Vergara	Simple grumete					
Gregorio Mariano Escobal	Simple grumete					
Thomas de Leon	Simple grumete					

Source: "Expediente sobre tripulaciones y caja de ahorros," 1753–1755, Archivo General de Indias, Filipinas, 157, N.1, fols. 97–145.

Note: Empty cells in the table indicate that there is no information in the record.

ª On the difference between the pay of the simple grumete and that of the Spanish grumete, see Chapter 6, note 142.

NOTES

Abbreviations

AGI   Archivo General de Indias, Seville, Spain
AGN   Archivo General de la Nación México, Mexico City, Mexico
ARANG Archivo de la Real Audiencia de la Nueva Galicia, Guadalajara, Mexico
AUST   Archives of the University of Santo Tomas, Manila, Philippines
JCBL   John Carter Brown Library, Providence, RI

A Note on Terminology

1. For a discussion of both Indigenous and Spanish meanings of "Filipino," see William Henry Scott, *Barangay: Sixteenth-Century Philippine Culture and Society* (Quezon City: Ateneo de Manila University Press, 1994), 6–7; Damon L. Woods, *The Myth of the Barangay and Other Silenced Histories* (Quezon City: University of the Philippines Press, 2017), 2–3.

2. Dana Murillo, *Urban Indians in a Silver City: Zacatecas, Mexico, 1546–1810* (Stanford, CA: Stanford University Press, 2016), 4.

3. Nicole von Germeten, "Paula de Eguiluz, Seventeenth-Century Puerto Rico, Cuba, and New Granada (Colombia)," in *As If She Were Free: A Collective Biography of Women and Emancipation in the Americas,* ed. Erica L. Ball, Tatiana Seijas, and Terri L. Snyder (New York: Cambridge University Press, 2020), 44n3.

Introduction

1. Joseph del Castillo Graxeda, *Compendio de la vida, y virtudes de la venerable Catharina de San Juan* (Puebla, Mexico: Imprenta de Diego Fernandez de Leon, 1692), 133.

2. "Tuviese en muerte mas decente lugar" (Castillo Graxeda, *Compendio de la vida,* 134). Wherever possible, I have sought to maintain the original orthography of early modern Spanish language. All translations are mine unless otherwise noted.

3. Alonso Ramos, *Los prodigios de la Omnipotencia y milagros de la gracia en la vida de la venerable sierva de Dios Catarina de San Juan,* ed. Gisela von Wobeser (Mexico City:

Universidad Nacional Autónoma de México-Instituto de Investigaciones Históricas, 2017), 3:153; Francisco de Aguilera, *Sermon que en las honras de la Venerable Madre Catharina de San Juan predicó* (1688), 9r, Biblioteca de la Universidad de Sevilla.

4. Ramos, *Los prodigios*, 3:154.

5. "Una iglesia en jueves santo, donde entra y sale el concurso de toda una ciudad que anda las estaciones" (Ramos, *Los prodigios*, 3:154).

6. Aguilera, *Sermon*, 20v.

7. "No es explicable el numeroso gentío que concurrió y asistió al entierro . . . hasta por las azoteas, balcones y ventanas de las casas que corresponden a las puertas del templo de nuestro colegio del Espíritu Santo, se asomaban una multitud de hombres y mujeres" (Ramos, *Los prodigios*, 3:156).

8. "A robarle los pocos adornos que le habían quedado a la difunta" (Ramos, *Los prodigios*, 3:158).

9. "Quanto adora el mundo por mas precioso, lo consigue por santa, sin pretenderlo, ni buscarlo una China pobrecita, esclava, estrangera, que nos haze llenar las lenguas de sus elogios, los corazones de Jubilos, y aun los ojos de lagrimas" (Aguilera, *Sermon*, 22r).

10. "Fue Catharina natural de el Reyno de el Mogor: el lugar donde nacio, no se sabe, ni ella lo supo, por tener tan poca edad, quando se aparto de el" (Castillo Graxeda, *Compendio de la vida*, 7).

11. Rubén Carrillo Martín, *Las gentes del mar Sangley* (Mexico City: Palabra de Clío, 2015), 79–80; Charles Ralph Boxer, *Women in Iberian Expansion Overseas, 1415–1815: Some Facts, Fancies, and Personalities* (New York: Oxford University Press, 1975), 42–43.

12. Interestingly, the Nobel Prize–winning Mexican writer, Octavio Paz, would also later describe "orientals" (*orientales*)—comprising "Chinese, Hindus, and Arabs"—as "secretive [*herméticos*] and indecipherable [*indescifrables*]." Octavio Paz, *El laberinto de la soledad* (Mexico City: Fondo de Cultura Económica, 1992), 27.

13. "Aquí de china, me veis / el color; por dentro el oro / guardo del mejor tesoro, / que escondido aquí hallaréis. / Aunque más vueltas le deis / a la llave, no abrirá, ninguno la entenderá; / que la cifra sólo Dios / la sabe, mas para vos / a su tiempo lo dirá" (quoted in Ramos, *Los prodigios*, 3:162).

14. Antonio Carrión, *Historia de la ciudad de Puebla de los Angeles (Puebla de Zaragoza)* (Puebla, Mexico: Tipografía de las Escuelas Salesianas de Artes y Oficios, 1897); Carrillo Martín, *Las gentes,* 70; Blacke Seana Locklin, "Orientalism and Mexican Nationalism: Catarina de San Juan as the China Poblana's Asian Mother," in *Orientalism and Identity in Latin America: Fashioning Self and Other from the (Post)Colonial Margin,* ed. Erik Camayd-Freixas (Tucson: University of Arizona Press, 2013), 65.

15. "La *China* como le decían por cariño" (Carrión, *Historia,* 1:183).

16. Héctor M. Medina, "'Charros' and Bullfights on Both Sides of the Atlantic Ocean: Folkloric Stereotypes and Traditional Festivals between Myth and History," *Folklore* 126, no. 1 (2015): 78. On the dress of the "china" and the representation of "chinas" in Mexican art from the nineteenth century as a "mestiza" national symbol, see Beatriz de Alba-Koch, "*Celestina* and Agustín Arrieta's *China Poblana:* Mexico's Female Icon Revisited," in *A Companion to Celestina,* ed. Enrique Fernandez (Leiden, the Netherlands: Brill, 2017), 339–361.

17. Catarina de San Juan was not the only non-Spanish woman to be transformed into a legend after her death. For the case of the "Mulata de Córdoba," see Danielle Terrazas Williams, *The Capital of Free Women: Race, Legitimacy, and Liberty in Colonial Mexico* (New Haven, CT: Yale University Press, 2022), 2–3 and 219–220.

18. Tatiana Seijas, *Asian Slaves in Colonial Mexico: From Chinos to Indians* (New York: Cambridge University Press, 2014), 21–22; Stuart B. Schwartz, *All Can Be Saved: Religious Tolerance and Salvation in the Iberian Atlantic World* (New Haven, CT: Yale University Press, 2008), 21–24.

19. Quoted in Kathleen Ann Myers, *Neither Saints nor Sinners: Writing the Lives of Women in Spanish America* (New York: Oxford University Press, 2003), 59.

20. "Por contenerse en él revelaciones, visiones, y apariciones inútiles, inverosímiles, llenas de contradicciones y comparaciones impropias, indecentes y temerarias y que *sapiunt blasphemiam* (que saben o que casi son blasfemias)" (quoted in Kate Risse, "Catarina de San Juan and the China Poblana: From Spiritual Humility to Civil Obedience," *Confluencia* 18, no. 1 [2002]: 74).

21. Gauvin Alexander Bailey, "A Mughal Princess in Baroque New Spain: Catarina de San Juan (1606–1688), the China Poblana," *Anales del instituto de investigaciones estéticas* 71 (1997): 39.

22. Myers, *Neither Saints nor Sinners*, 46.

23. Gisela von Wobeser, "Estudio introductorio," in Ramos, *Los prodigios*, 1:68–69.

24. Risse, "Catarina de San Juan," 75.

25. Seijas, *Asian Slaves*, 1–4.

26. For the clearest articulation of this imperative, see Rainer F. Buschmann, Edward R. Slack Jr., and James B. Tueller, *Navigating the Spanish Lake: The Pacific in the Iberian World, 1521–1898* (Honolulu: University of Hawai'i Press, 2014).

27. I have drawn these data from "Categoría: Galeón de Manila," Historia Naval de España, February 27, 2021, https://todoavante.es/index.php?title=Categor%C3%ADa%3AGale %C3%B3n_de_Manila&fbclid=IwAR37f4PMmuSevf3ZsInSzEUCosh3xWoTenE1pKqTLe8 UKVIxDnlvIKeQlNE. Any errors in these total counts are my own and not those of the online item.

28. Guillermo de Bañuelos y Carrillo, *Tratado del estado de las islas Philipinas, y de sus conueniencias* (Mexico City: En la imprenta de Bernardo Calderon, 1638), 18r; Buschmann, Slack, and Tueller, *Navigating the Spanish Lake*, 24.

29. Déborah Oropeza, *La migración asiática en el virreinato de la Nueva España: Un proceso de globalización (1565–1700)* (Mexico City: El Colegio de México, 2020), 17.

30. Christina Lee and Ricardo Padrón, introduction to *The Spanish Pacific, 1521–1815: A Reader of Primary Sources,* ed. Christina Lee and Ricardo Padrón (Amsterdam: Amsterdam University Press, 2020), 11.

31. For a few standout examples, see Bernard Bailyn, *Atlantic History: Concept and Contours* (Cambridge, MA: Harvard University Press, 2005); David Armitage, "Three Concepts of Atlantic History," in *The British Atlantic World, 1500–1800,* ed. David Armitage and Michael J. Braddick (New York: Palgrave Macmillan, 2002), 11–27; Jorge Cañizares-Esguerra, *Entangled Empires: The Anglo-Iberian Atlantic, 1500–1830* (Philadelphia: University of Pennsylvania

Press, 2022); Roquinaldo Ferreira, *Cross-Cultural Exchange in the Atlantic World: Angola and Brazil during the Era of the Slave Trade* (New York: Cambridge University Press, 2012); Alison Games, "Atlantic History: Definitions, Challenges, and Opportunities," *American Historical Review* 111, no. 3 (2006): 741–757; Stephanie E. Smallwood, *Saltwater Slavery: A Middle Passage from Africa to American Diaspora* (Cambridge, MA: Harvard University Press, 2008).

32. Buschmann, Slack, and Tueller, *Navigating the Spanish Lake,* 4–5.

33. Emma Helen Blair and James Alexander Robertson, eds., *The Philippine Islands, 1493–1898,* 55 vols. (Cleveland, OH: Arthur H. Clark, 1903–1909). On the problems of using these volumes today, see Lee and Padrón, introduction, 12–13.

34. Roscoe R. Hill, "Dr. James Alexander Robertson, 1873–1939. Editor: 1918–1939," *Hispanic American Historical Review* 19, no. 2 (1939): 127–129.

35. William Lytle Schurz, *The Manila Galleon: Illustrated with Maps* (New York: E. P. Dutton, 1939).

36. Pierre Chaunu, "Le Galion de Manilla. Grandeur et decadence d'une route de la sole," *Annales: Economies, Sociétés, Civilisations* 6, no. 4 (1951): 447–462; Pierre Chaunu, *Las Filipinas y el Pacífico de los Ibéricos siglos XVI-XVII-XVIII* (Mexico City: Instituto Mexicano de Comercio Exterior, 1974); Katharine Bjork, "The Link That Kept the Philippines Spanish: Mexican Merchant Interests and the Manila Trade, 1571–1815," *Journal of World History* 9, no. 1 (1998): 25–50; Dennis O. Flynn, Arturo Giráldez, and James Sobredo, eds., *European Entry into the Pacific: Spain and the Acapulco-Manila Galleons* (New York: Routledge, 2001). See also Christian G. De Vito, "Towards the Global Spanish Pacific," *International Review of Social History* 60, no. 3 (2015): 449–462.

37. See Buschmann, Slack, and Tueller, *Navigating the Spanish Lake;* Lee and Padrón, introduction; Ryan Dominic Crewe, "Connecting the Indies: The Hispano-Asian Pacific World in Early Modern Global History," *Estudos Históricos* 30, no. 60 (2017): 18–34; Christina Lee, *Saints of Resistance: Devotions in the Philippines under Early Spanish Rule* (New York: Oxford University Press, 2021); Ricardo Padrón, *The Indies of the Setting Sun: How Early Modern Spain Mapped the Far East as the Transpacific West* (Chicago: University of Chicago Press, 2020); Arturo Giráldez, *The Age of Trade: The Manila Galleons and the Dawn of the Global Economy* (Lanham, MD: Rowman and Littlefield, 2015); Andrés Reséndez, *Conquering the Pacific: An Unknown Mariner and the Final Great Voyage of the Age of Discovery* (Boston: Houghton Mifflin Harcourt, 2021); Norah L. A. Gharala, "'From Mozambique in Indies of Portugal': Locating East Africans in New Spain," *Journal of Global History* 7, no. 3 (2022): 243–281; Kristie Patricia Flannery, "Can the Devil Cross the Deep Blue Sea? Imagining the Spanish Pacific and Vast Early America from Below," *William and Mary Quarterly* 79, no. 1 (2022): 31–60.

38. Lee and Padrón, introduction, 16.

39. "Si no se considera a la población asiática que integró a la sociedad novohispana, nuestra visión de la Nueva España es incompleta" (Oropeza, *La migración asiática,* 26); Déborah Oropeza Keresey, "La esclavitud asiática en el virreinato de la Nueva España, 1565–1673," *Historia Mexicana* 61, no. 1 (2011): 49.

40. Ricardo Padrón, *The Indies,* 235, and "A Sea of Denial: The Early Modern Spanish Invention of the Pacific Rim," *Hispanic Review* 77, no. 1 (2009): 15.

41. Padrón, *The Indies*, 34–38.

42. Padrón, "A Sea of Denial," 15–18, and *The Indies*, 240–247.

43. Padrón, "A Sea of Denial," 19.

44. Antonio de Herrera y Tordesillas, *Historia general de los hechos de los castellanos en las islas i Tierra Firme del Mar Oceano* (Madrid: En la Emprenta Real, 1601), 4:1–2.

45. "De Poniente, respecto de Castilla" (Herrera y Tordesillas, *Historia general*, 4:2, 6).

46. On constructions of the Spanish Pacific "from below," see Flannery, "Can the Devil Cross the Deep Blue Sea?," 34.

47. Buschmann, Slack, and Tueller, *Navigating the Spanish Lake*, 7.

48. Lee and Padrón, introduction, 16.

49. Crewe, "Connecting the Indies," 20.

50. Oropeza, *La migración asiática*, 146 and 214.

51. See Edward R. Slack Jr., "The Chinos in New Spain: A Corrective Lens for a Distorted Image," *Journal of World History* 20, no. 1 (2009): 35–67; Melba Falck Reyes and Héctor Palacios, *El japonés que conquistó Guadalajara: La historia de Juan de Páez en la Guadalajara del siglo XVII* (Guadalajara, Mexico: Universidad de Guadalajara, 2009); Oropeza Keresey, "La esclavitud asiática"; Oropeza, *La migración asiática;* Seijas, *Asian Slaves;* Martín, *Las gentes.* Possibly the earliest writings in this tradition are Ángel Núñez Ortega, *Noticia histórica de las relaciones políticas y comerciales entre México y el Japón, durante el siglo XVII* (Mexico City: Imprenta del gobierno, 1879), and Homer H. Dubs and Robert S. Smith, "Chinese in Mexico City in 1635," *Far Eastern Quarterly* 1, no. 4 (1942): 387–389.

52. See James H. Sweet, *Domingos Álvares, African Healing, and the Intellectual History of the Atlantic World* (Chapel Hill: University of North Carolina Press, 2011); Ferreira, *Cross-Cultural Exchange;* Smallwood, *Saltwater Slavery.*

53. Crewe, "Connecting the Indies," 20; Ryan Dominic Crewe, "Transpacific Mestizo: Religion and Caste in the Worlds of a Moluccan Prisoner of the Mexican Inquisition," *Itinerario* 39, no. 3 (2015): 464.

54. John-Paul A. Ghobrial, "Introduction: Seeing the World like a Microhistorian," *Past & Present* 242, no. 14 (2019): 15, "The Secret Life of Elias of Babylon and the Uses of Global Microhistory," *Past & Present,* no. 222 (2014): 59, and "Moving Stories and What They Tell Us: Early Modern Mobility between Microhistory and Global History," *Past & Present* 242, no. 14 (2019): 249. See also Sebouh David Aslanian et al., "*AHR* Conversation: How Size Matters: The Question of Scale in History," *American Historical Review* 118, no. 5 (2013): 1445; Tonio Andrade, "A Chinese Farmer, Two African Boys, and a Warlord: Toward a Global Microhistory," *Journal of World History* 21, no. 4 (2010): 573–591; Giovanni Levi, "Frail Frontiers?," *Past & Present* 242, no. 14 (2019): 46.

55. Matt Matsuda, *Pacific Worlds: A History of Seas, Peoples, and Cultures* (New York: Cambridge University Press, 2012), 5. See also Matt Matsuda, "Afterword: Pacific Crosscurrents," in *Pacific Histories: Ocean, Land, People,* ed. David Armitage and Alison Bashford (Basingstoke, UK: Palgrave Macmillan, 2014), 326.

56. Oropeza, *La migración asiática*, 157; Edward R. Slack Jr., "Sinifying New Spain: Cathay's Influence on Colonial Mexico via the *Nao de China*," *Journal of Chinese Overseas* 5, no. 1 (2009): 6–7. See also Rubén Carrillo Martín, "Asians to New Spain: Asian Cultural and

Migratory Flows in Mexico in the Early Stages of 'Globalization' (1565–1816)," PhD diss., Universitat Oberta de Catalunya, 2015, 7.

57. Edward R. Slack Jr., "Orientalizing New Spain: Perspectives on Asian Influence in Colonial Mexico," *México y la Cuenca del Pacífico* 15, no. 43 (2012): 99.

58. Seijas, *Asian Slaves*, 84.

59. Oropeza undercounts the number of Manila galleon voyages to Mexico during this period (*La migración asiática*, 151–152).

60. Rogers Brubaker, "The 'Diaspora' Diaspora," *Ethnic and Racial Studies* 28, no. 1 (2005): 5–6; Regina Lee, "Theorizing Diasporas: Three Types of Consciousness," in *Asian Diasporas: Culture, Identities, Representations*, ed. Robbie B. H. Goh and Shawn Wong (Hong Kong: Hong Kong University Press, 2004), 53–54.

61. Stéphane Dufoix, *Diasporas*, trans. William Rodarmor (Berkeley: University of California Press, 2008), 11–33; Ien Ang, "To Be or Not to Be Chinese: Diaspora, Culture and Postmodern Ethnicity," *Southeast Asian Journal of Social Science* 21, no. 1 (1993): 5–14; Hem Raj Kafle, "Diaspora Studies: Roots and Critical Dimensions," *Bodhi* 4, no. 1 (2010): 144.

62. For a timeless study of silences and archives, see Michel-Rolph Trouillot, *Silencing the Past: Power and the Production of History* (Boston: Beacon, 1995).

63. See Saidiya Hartman, "Venus in Two Acts," *Small Axe* 12, no. 2 (2008): 1–14.

64. "Bienes de difuntos: Domingo de Villalobos," 1621–1622, Archivo General de Indias (AGI), Contratación, 520, N.2, R.14.

65. For older interpretations of "chino / a," see Dubs and Smith, "Chinese in Mexico City in 1635," and P. J. Bakewell, *Silver Mining and Society in Colonial Mexico: Zacatecas 1546–1700* (New York: Cambridge University Press, 1971), 123–124.

66. Martín, *Las gentes*, 21–22.

67. Dana Murillo, *Urban Indians in a Silver City: Zacatecas, Mexico, 1546–1810* (Stanford, CA: Stanford University Press, 2016), 5.

68. "Juan Alonso," 1591, Archivo General de la Nación México (AGN), Indios, vol. 6a, exp. 1200.

69. Oropeza, *La migración asiática*, 224.

70. Martín, *Las gentes*, 110–124; Giovanni Francesco Gemelli Careri, *Viaje a Nueva España*, trans. Francisca Perujo (Mexico City: Universidad Nacional Autónoma de México, 1983), 73; Matthew J. Furlong, "Peasants, Servants, and Sojourners: Itinerant Asians in Colonial New Spain, 1571–1720," PhD diss., University of Arizona, 2014, 613–615.

71. Gayatri Chakravorty Spivak coined the term *strategic essentialism* in an interview from 1984. Mridula Nath Chakraborty, "Everybody's Afraid of Gayatri Chakravorty Spivak: Reading Interviews with the Public Intellectual and Postcolonial Critic," *Journal of Women in Culture and Society* 35, no. 3 [2010], 621. See also Elisabeth Eide, "Strategic Essentialism," in *The Wiley Blackwell Encyclopedia of Gender and Sexuality Studies*, ed. Nancy A. Naples (Malden, MA: Wiley-Blackwell, 2016); Ang, "To Be or Not to Be Chinese," 14.

72. Murillo, *Urban Indians*, 11.

73. James Clifford, "Diasporas," *Cultural Anthropology* 9, no. 3 (1994): 306; Jana Evans Braziel and Anita Mannur, "Nation, Migration, Globalization: Points of Contention in

Diaspora Studies," in *Theorizing Diaspora: A Reader,* ed. Jana Evans Braziel and Anita Mannur (Malden, MA: Blackwell, 2003), 6–7.

74. Dominic Yang, *The Great Exodus from China: Trauma, Memory, and Identity in Modern Taiwan* (New York: Cambridge University Press, 2020), 10. See also Brubaker, "The 'Diaspora' Diaspora," 13.

75. David B. Ruderman, *Early Modern Jewry: A New Cultural History* (Princeton, NJ: Princeton University Press, 2010), 12.

76. Stuart B. Schwartz, *Blood and Boundaries: The Limits of Religious and Racial Exclusion in Early Modern Latin America* (Waltham, MA: Brandeis University Press, 2020), 5.

77. Geraldine Heng, *The Invention of Race in the European Middle Ages* (New York: Cambridge University Press, 2018), 4–5; Cord J. Whitaker, "Race-ing the Dragon: The Middle Ages, Race and Trippin' into the Future," *Postmedieval* 6, no. 1 (2015): 7.

78. Rebecca Earle, *The Body of the Conquistador* (Cambridge: Cambridge University Press, 2012), 215.

79. María Eugenia Chaves, "Race and Caste: Other Words and Other Worlds," in *Race and Blood in the Iberian World,* ed. Max-Sebastián Hering Torres, María Elena Martínez, and David Nirenberg (Berlin: Deutsche Nationalbibliothek, 2012), 53. Compare to Tamar Herzog, "Beyond Race: Exclusion in Early Modern Spain and Spanish America," in *Race and Blood in the Iberian World,* 153.

80. Robert C. Schwaller, *Géneros de Gente in Early Colonial Mexico: Defining Racial Difference* (Norman: University of Oklahoma Press, 2016), 6.

81. Francisco Bethencourt, *Racisms: From the Crusades to the Twentieth Century* (Princeton, NJ: Princeton University Press, 2015), 2.

82. Earle, *The Body of the Conquistador,* 214.

83. For the foundational text, see Michael Omi and Howard Winant, *Racial Formation in the United States,* 3rd ed. (New York: Routledge, 2014). Omi and Winant have had an enormous influence on the field of ethnic studies and scholars seeking to examine race in historical contexts beyond the United States in the twentieth century.

84. David Nirenberg, *Neighboring Faiths: Christianity, Islam, and Judaism in the Middle Ages and Today* (Chicago: University of Chicago Press, 2014), 173. Compare to María Elena Martínez, *Genealogical Fictions: Limpieza de Sangre, Religion, and Gender in Colonial Mexico* (Stanford, CA: Stanford University Press, 2008), 11.

85. Heng, *The Invention of Race,* 27. I removed the italics from the original.

86. Irene Silverblatt writes: "'Race thinking' cuts a wider swath than 'race' because it moves us behind and beyond racism's narrow, nineteenth-century origins. . . . It represents a potential way of sensing, understanding, and being in the world, a cultural possibility that can become part of social identities and social practices" (*Modern Inquisitions: Peru and the Colonial Origins of the Civilized World* [Durham, NC: Duke University Press, 2004], 17–18). Compare to Bethencourt, *Racisms,* 1–8; Omi and Winant, *Racial Formation,* x.

87. See David Eltis, "Europeans and the Rise and Fall of African Slavery in the Americas: An Interpretation," *American Historical Review* 98, no. 5 (1993): 1399–1423. However, Spaniards were sometimes enslaved when captured in the Mediterranean World. See Daniel

Hershenzon, *The Captive Sea: Slavery, Communication, and Commerce in Early Modern Spain and the Mediterranean* (Philadelphia: University of Pennsylvania Press, 2018).

88. Matthew Restall, *When Montezuma Met Cortés: The True Story of the Meeting That Changed History* (New York: HarperCollins, 2018), 326–328.

89. Antonio Feros, *Speaking of Spain: The Evolution of Race and Nation in the Hispanic World* (Cambridge, MA: Harvard University Press, 2017), 76.

90. Jorge Cañizares-Esguerra, "New World, New Stars: Patriotic Astrology and the Invention of Indian and Creole Bodies in Colonial Spanish America, 1600–1650," *American Historical Review* 104, no. 1 (1999): 37.

91. Miguel A. Valerio, *Sovereign Joy: Afro-Mexican Kings and Queens, 1539–1640* (New York: Cambridge University Press, 2022), 84; see also 88–89.

92. Ann Twinam, *Purchasing Whiteness: Pardos, Mulattos, and the Quest for Social Mobility in the Spanish Indies* (Stanford, CA: Stanford University Press, 2015), 42–43.

93. "Y si esta gente [Zambales and Chinos] tan brava la poblaran y ataran con leyes y policía, vinieran con el tiempo a perder aquel soberbio natural y hacerse de diferentes costumbres; porque si los animales incapaces de razón se domestican con el trato y pierden su fuerza mucho mejor harán esto hombres capaces de razón. El ejemplo tenemos con los negros, que con ser una gente que parece que es la escoria del mundo, tan bozales cuando los traen, que aun parecen mayores bestias que las que realmente lo son, al fin, tratando con gente política, vienen a aprender acciones de hombres; pues ¿Cuánto mejor hicieran esto los indios de estas islas [Filipinas] en quienes se ha descubierto mucho ingenio para todo lo que se les quisiera enseñar?" (Juan de Medina, *Historia de los sucesos de la Orden de N. Gran P. S. Agustín de estas islas Filipinas, desde que se descubrieron y se poblaron por los españoles, con las noticias memorables* [Manila: Tipo-Litografía de Chofré y Comp., 1893], 132).

94. Daniel Martinez HoSang and Natalia Molina, "Introduction: Toward a Relational Consciousness of Race," in *Relational Formations of Race: Theory, Method, and Practice*, ed. Natalia Molina, Daniel Martinez HoSang, and Ramón A. Gutiérrez (Oakland: University of California Press, 2019), 8.

95. Daniel Nemser, *Infrastructures of Race: Concentration and Biopolitics in Colonial Mexico* (Austin: University of Texas Press, 2017), 41 and 63.

96. Kris Manjapra, *Colonialism in Global Perspective* (New York: Cambridge University Press, 2020), 10.

97. See Paul H. Freeman, *Out of the East: Spices and the Medieval Imagination* (New Haven, CT: Yale University Press, 2008).

98. Nemser, *Infrastructures of Race*, 26.

1. The Fragile Convivencia of Colonial Manila

1. Parian comes from the Tagalog *pali-an* (a place of bargaining). See Miguel Rodríguez Maldonado, *Relacion verdadera del levantamiento de los sangleyes en las Filipinas, y el milagroso castigo de su rebelion: Con otros sucessos de aquellas Islas* (Seville, Spain: Clemente Hidalgo, 1606), 4; Robert Ronald Reed, *Colonial Manila: The Context of Hispanic Urbanism*

and Process of Morphogenesis (Berkeley: University of California Press, 1978); Ethan P. Hawkley, "The Birth of Globalization: The World and the Beginnings of Philippines Sovereignty, 1565–1610," PhD diss., Northeastern University, 2014, 201.

2. "Sangley" comes from a Tagalog pronunciation of the Hokkien *sionglai* (常来; "[those who] come frequently"). See Edward R. Slack Jr., "New Perspectives on Manila's Chinese Community at the Turn of the Eighteenth Century: The Forgotten Case of Pedro Barredo, Alcalde Mayor of the Parián 1701–1704," *Journal of Chinese Overseas* 17 (2021): 121; Christina Lee, *Saints of Resistance: Devotions in the Philippines under Early Spanish Rule* (New York: Oxford University Press, 2021), 44.

3. "Alzamiento de los sangleyes," 1606, Archivo General de Indias (AGI), Patronato, 25, R.63.

4. William Lytle Schurz, *The Manila Galleon: Illustrated with Maps* (New York: E. P. Dutton, 1939), 89.

5. Schurz, *The Manila Galleon*, 89.

6. Michelle A. McKinley, "The Unbearable Lightness of Being (Black): Legal and Cultural Constructions of Race and Nation in Colonial Latin America," in *Racial Formation in the Twenty-First Century*, ed. Daniel Martínez Hosang, Oneka LaBennett, and Laura Pulido (Berkeley: University of California Press, 2012), 135.

7. "La justicia Divina mostraua, que semejantes pecados, como alli se cometian, eran merecedores de semejante pena" (Maldonado, *Relacion verdadera*, 5).

8. Luciano Santiago, "The Filipino Indios Encomenderos (ca. 1620–1711)," *Philippine Quarterly of Culture and Society* 18, no. 3 (1990): 167.

9. "Perss[on]a ajil y de confianza" ("Petición de Diego de Maracot de encomienda en Guagua," 1623, AGI, Filipinas, 39, N.20, fol. 22).

10. "Pelearon mui bien con los sangleyes y con mucha fidelidad y gusto" ("Petición del procurador Ríos Coronel sobre varios asuntos," 1607, AGI, Filipinas, 27, N.51, fols. 321v–322r).

11. Edward R. Slack Jr., "Orientalizing New Spain: Perspectives on Asian Influence in Colonial Mexico," *México y la Cuenca del Pacífico* 15, no. 43 (2012): 99–100; Tatiana Seijas, *Asian Slaves in Colonial Mexico: From Chinos to Indians* (New York: Cambridge University Press, 2014), 73–108; Lucío de Sousa, *The Portuguese Slave Trade in Early Modern Japan: Merchants, Jesuits and Japanese, Chinese and Korean Slaves* (Boston: Brill, 2019), 439–456.

12. Schurz, *The Manila Galleon*, 91.

13. Schurz, *The Manila Galleon*, 38.

14. Compare to Teofilo F. Ruiz, *Spanish Society, 1400–1600* (repr.; New York: Routledge, 2014), 57.

15. Francisco Colín, *Labor evangélica, ministerios apostólicos de los obreros de la Compañia de Iesvs, fvndacion, y progresos de sv provincia en las islas Filipinas* (Madrid: por Ioseph Fernandez de Buendia, 1663), John Carter Brown Library (JCBL), 19–20.

16. Ubaldo Iaccarino, "The 'Galleon System' and Chinese Trade in Manila at the Turn of the 16th Century," *Ming Qing Yanjiu* 16 (2011): 112.

17. Pedro de Medina, *Libro de grandezas y cosas memorables de España* (Seville: En casa de Dominico de Robertis, 1549), JCBL, 51r.

18. For an overview of the total volume of trade from China to Manila, see Arturo Giráldez, *The Age of Trade: The Manila Galleons and the Dawn of the Global Economy* (Lanham, MD: Rowman and Littlefield, 2015), 34–37; C. Lee, *Saints of Resistance*, 46.

19. Guillermo Ruiz-Stovel, "Chinese Merchants, Silver Galleons, and Ethnic Violence in Spanish Manila, 1603–1686," *México y la cuenca del Pacífico* 12, no. 36 (2009): 47.

20. See Evelyn Hu-DeHart, "Spanish Manila: A Transpacific Maritime Enterprise and America's First Chinatown," in *Oceanic Archives, Indigenous Epistemologies, and Transpacific American Studies,* ed. Yuan Shu, Otto Heim, and Kendall Johnson (Hong Kong: Hong Kong University Press, 2019), 49–61.

21. Juan Gil, *Los chinos en Manila: Siglox XVI y XVII* (Lisbon: Centro Científico e Cultural de Macau, 2011), 19–20; Giráldez, *The Age of Trade*, 27; William Henry Scott, *Prehispanic Source Materials for the Study of Philippine History* (Quezon City: New Day, 1989), 65–73. The first recorded Chinese-Philippine contacts date to the tenth century.

22. On the global importance of New World silver, see John Tutino, *Making a New World: Founding Capitalism in the Bajío and Spanish North America* (Durham, NC: Duke University Press, 2011), 7 and 77–78.

23. Birgit Tremml-Werner, *Spain, China, and Japan in Manila, 1571–1644: Local Comparisons and Global Connections* (Amsterdam: Amsterdam University Press, 2015), 271.

24. "Cada nación ha formado una jerigonza por donde se entienden . . . los chinos, para decir 'alcalde,' 'español' y 'indio,' dice así: *alicaya, cancia, juania*" (quoted in Gil, *Los chinos en Manila,* 342).

25. Antonio García-Abásolo, "La audiencia de Manila y los chinos de Filipinas: Casos de integración en el delito," in *Homenaje a Alberto de la Hera,* ed. José Luis Soberanes Fernández and Rosa María Martínez de Codes (Mexico City: UNAM, Instituto de Investigaciones Jurídicas, 2008), 341, "Los chinos y el modelo colonial español en Filipinas," *Cuadernos de Historia Moderna* 10 (2011): 227, and "La difícil convivencia entre españoles y chinos en Filipinas," in *Élites urbanas en Hispanoamérica,* ed. Luis Navarro García (Seville, Spain: Secretariado de Publicaciones de la Universidad de Sevilla, 2005), 493; Ryan Dominic Crewe, "Pacific Purgatory: Spanish Dominicans, Chinese Sangleys, and the Entanglement of Mission and Commerce in Manila, 1580–1640," *Journal of Early Modern History* 19 (2015): 360–364, and "Occult Cosmopolitanism: Convivencia and Ethno-Religious Exclusion in Manila, 1590–1650," in *Philippine Confluence: Iberian, Chinese and Islamic Currents, c. 1500–1800,* ed. Jos Gommans and Ariel Lopez (Leiden, the Netherlands: Leiden University Press, 2020), 57; José Antonio Cervera, *Cartas del Parián: Los chinos de Manila a finales del siglo XVI a través de los ojos de Juan Cobo y Domingo de Salazar* (Mexico City: Palabra de Clío, 2015), 164–173. See also Atsuko Hirayama, "¿Convivencia beneficiosa o cohabitación hostil? Españoles y chinos en Manila en la primera época de la colonización española de las islas Filipinas (1565–c. 1650)," in *Nueva España: Puerta americana al Pacífico asiático,* ed. Carmen Yuste López (Mexico City: Universidad Nacional Autónoma de México, 2019), 92–93.

26. David Nirenberg, *Communities of Violence: Persecution of Minorities in the Middle Ages,* 2nd ed. (Princeton, NJ: Princeton University Press, 2015), 245.

27. Nirenberg, *Communities of Violence,* 38.

28. Francisco Bethencourt, *Racisms: From the Crusades to the Twentieth Century* (Princeton, NJ: Princeton University Press, 2015), 139; Antonio Feros, *Speaking of Spain: The*

Evolution of Race and Nation in the Hispanic World (Cambridge, MA: Harvard University Press, 2017), 107.

29. See Ethan P. Hawkley, "Reviving the Reconquista in Southeast Asia: Moros and the Making of the Philippines, 1565–1662," *Journal of World History* 25, nos. 2–3 (2014): 285–310.

30. "Carta de Domingo de Salazar sobre conflicto jurisdiccional con Diego de Mújica," 1581, AGI, Filipinas, 84, N.24, fols. 11 and 15–22.

31. "Carta de Domingo de Salazar sobre agravios a indios.," 1582, AGI, Filipinas, 84, N.36.

32. Hawkley, "The Birth of Globalization," 126.

33. There were two types of "slaves" (*alipin*): the *namamahay* and the *saguiguilid*. The Franciscan ethnographer Juan de Plasencia wrote in 1589 that the namamahay were *pecheros* (workers) but that the saguiguilid could be likened to people enslaved according to Spanish norms. Juan de Plasencia, *Las costumbres de los tagalos en Filipinas según el Padre Plasencia*, ed. Trinidad H. Pardo de Tavera (Madrid: Tipografía de Manuel Ginés Hernández, 1892), 12. *Guilir* (the root of saguiguilid) meant "entrance to the house" in Tagalog, indicating that the enslaved did not have the right to live in the house. Instead, they dwelled among the *nipa* (palm) stilts underneath the house with the animals and field tools. Plasencia, *Las costumbres de los tagalos*, 13; Antonio de Morga, *Svcesos de las islas Filipinas* (Mexico City: En Casa de Geronymo Balli, 1609), 141v–142v; Vicente Rafael, *Contracting Colonialism: Translation and Christian Conversion in Tagalog Society under Early Spanish Rule* (Quezon City: Ateneo de Manila University Press, 2017), 146; William Henry Scott, *Barangay: Sixteenth-Century Philippine Culture and Society* (Quezon City: Ateneo de Manila University Press, 1994), 225–228; Seijas, *Asian Slaves*, 46.

34. Linda A. Newson, *Conquest and Pestilence in the Early Spanish Philippines* (Honolulu: University of Hawai'i Press, 2009), 24–37.

35. Sousa, *The Portuguese Slave Trade*, 54.

36. Morga, *Svcesos de las islas Filipinas*, 142v. For this reason, two Kapampangan elites, don Juan de Manila and Nicolas Mananguete, had raised arms against the Spaniards in protest in 1585. The latter was defeated and surrendered, and the former died in battle. See "Carta del dominico Cristóbal de Salvatierra sobre varios asuntos," 1585, AGI, Filipinas, 84, N. 47.

37. Déborah Oropeza, *La migración asiática en el virreinato de la Nueva España: Un proceso de globalización (1565–1700)* (Mexico City: El Colegio de México, 2020), 136.

38. Manuel Castillo Martos, *Bartolomé de Medina y el siglo XVI* (Santander, Spain: Universidad de Cantabria, 2006), 152; Sousa, *The Portuguese Slave Trade*, 439.

39. Hawkley, "The Birth of Globalization," 155.

40. "Carta de la Audiencia de Manila sobre sublevaciones, etc.," 1589, AGI, Filipinas, 18A, R.7, N.47.

41. Cristina E. Barrón Soto, "La migración filipina en México," in *Destino México: Un estudio de las migraciones asiáticas a México, siglos XIX y XX*, ed. María Elena Ota Mishima (Mexico City: El Colegio de México, 1997), 377; Sousa, *The Portuguese Slave Trade*, 439.

42. Tonio Andrade, *Lost Colony: The Untold Story of China's First Great Victory over the West* (Princeton, NJ: Princeton University Press, 2013), 21–22.

43. Scott, *Prehispanic Source Materials*, 75–77; Giráldez, *The Age of Trade*, 27.

44. See Kenneth Pomeranz, *The Great Divergence: China, Europe, and the Making of the Modern World Economy* (Princeton, NJ: Princeton University Press, 2000), 171–174.

45. Gil, *Los chinos en Manila*, 35.

46. "Ques vergüenza dezirlo" (Domingo de Salazar, "Carta de Salazar sobre relación con China y sangleyes," 1590, AGI, Filipinas, 74, N.38, fol. 186r). Also see Cervera, *Cartas del Parián*.

47. Stephen Greenblatt, *Marvelous Possessions: The Wonder of the New World* (Chicago: University of Chicago Press, 1991), 14.

48. Juan González de Mendoza, *Historia de las cosas mas notables, ritos y costumbres, del gran reyno dela china* (Rome: Vincentio Accolti, 1585), JCBL.

49. Ricardo Padrón, *The Indies of the Setting Sun: How Early Modern Spain Mapped the Far East as the Transpacific West* (Chicago: University of Chicago Press, 2020), 1; Donald F. Lach, *Asia in the Making of Europe* (Chicago: University of Chicago Press, 1977), 1.2:742–750.

50. Mendoza, *Historia de las cosas*, 28 and 34.

51. For one of the most evocative accounts of a Chinese Christian wedding, see Miguel Martínez, "Manila's Sangleyes and a Chinese Wedding (1625)," in *The Spanish Pacific, 1521–1815: A Reader of Primary Sources*, ed. Christina Lee and Ricardo Padrón (Amsterdam: Amsterdam University Press, 2020), 73–90.

52. John N. Crossley, "Juan Cobo, el Códice Boxer y los sangleyes de Manila," in *El Códice Boxer*, 98–105.

53. "Sangley cristiano antiguo en la tierra . . . rico y muy favorecido de los españoles, temido y respetado de los sangleyes . . . y tenia muchos ahijados, y dependientes, que este era muy españolado y brioso" (Morga, *Svcesos de las islas Filipinas*, 108r).

54. Oropeza, *La migración asiática*, 107–108 and 112.

55. "Testimonio de las escrituras de Navotas, Malabon, Cotcot y Salinas," 1599–1644, Archives of the University of Santo Tomas, Becerros 32 and 22.

56. C. Lee, *Saints of Resistance*, 46.

57. "Ban mescladas supresticiones e ydolatrias" and "todo lo qual es en gran escandalo de los nueuos xpianos" (Cristobal de Salvatierra, "Auto de Cristóbal de Salvatierra sobre representar comedias," 1592, AGI, Filipinas, 6, R.7, N.90).

58. "Sobre las ceremonias de los chinos en Filipinas," 1594, Archivo General de la Nación México (AGN), Inquisición, vol. 223, exp. 36, fol. 434r.

59. Bartolomé Leonardo de Argensola, *Conqvista delas islas Malvcas* (Madrid: Alonso Martín, 1609), 200–203.

60. Christina Lee, "Hair and Personhood in the Spanish Philippines of Early Modernity" (presentation, Renaissance Refugees, Indiana University, Bloomington, September 22, 2017).

61. C. Lee, *Saints of Resistance*, 49.

62. Quoted in Berthold Laufer, "The Relations of the Chinese to the Philippine Islands," *Smithsonian Miscellaneous Collections* 50, no. 1789 (1908): 262.

63. "Con ferocidad mas que barbara" (Argensola, *Conqvista delas islas Malvcas*, 206).

64. Argensola, *Conqvista delas islas Malvcas,* 211–215. A similar turn to prayers and offerings to folk deities during desperate situations at sea appears in a separate occasion in 1579 discussed by Mendoza's writing (*Historia de las cosas,* 337–338), which is a possible referent for Argensola. On Argensola as a Golden Age poet and historian, see Otis H. Green, "Bartolomé Leonardo de Argensola y el reino de Aragón," *Archivo de Filología Aragonesa* 4 (1952): 51; El Conde de la Viñaza, ed., *Obras sueltas de Lupercio y Bartolomé Leonardo de Argensola* (Madrid: M. Tello, 1889), 2:276.

65. "Puso horror y enbidia a los dos Christianos" (Argensola, *Conqvista delas islas Malvcas,* 210). Compare to Francisco López de Gómara, *La conquista de Mexico* (Zaragoza, Spain: Miguel Capila, 1553), fol. 1.

66. Joan-Pau Rubiés, "El Códice Boxer como enigma: En búsqueda de la voz de un autor," in *El Códice Boxer,* 82.

67. Jonathan Gebhardt, "Global Cities, Incoherent Communities: Communication, Coexistence, and Conflict in Macau and Manila, 1550–1700," PhD diss., Yale University, 2015, 75.

68. Gil, *Los chinos en Manila,* 282–283.

69. "El ser estos sangleis gente condicciossisima y tan manosa y traidora quanto se a spirimentado y visto" (Luis Pérez Dasmariñas, "Carta de L. P. Mariñas sobre convivencia con sangleyes," 1597, AGI, Filipinas, 18B, R.7, N.72, fol. 2; emphasis added).

70. "Un pecado avominable y nefando" (Luis Pérez Dasmariñas, "Carta de L. P. Mariñas sobre convivencia con sangleyes," 1597, AGI, Filipinas, 18B, R.7, N.72, fol. 2). Sodomy could refer to any same-sex sexual behavior, from flirtation to penetration. Same-sex relations were common in Fujian at the time and served to form alliances between older mentors and younger men. See also Zeb Tortorici, *Sins against Nature: Sex & Archives in Colonial New Spain* (Durham, NC: Duke University Press, 2018), 74 and 87–88; Andrade, *Lost Colony,* 25; Hawkley, "The Birth of Globalization," 262.

71. "Tan costosso lastimosso y dapnosso y que ynpidio tanto bien y servicio de dios y de v magd" (Luis Pérez Dasmariñas, "Carta de L. P. Mariñas sobre convivencia con sangleyes," 1597, AGI, Filipinas, 18B, R.7, N.72, fol. 2).

72. "Gente tan ruyn atrevida viciossa y desvergonzada" (Luis Pérez Dasmariñas, "Carta de L. P. Mariñas sobre convivencia con sangleyes," 1597, AGI, Filipinas, 18B, R.7, N.72, fol. 2).

73. "Todos los demás sangleis ynfieles destas islas se recojan y enbarquen y enbien a sus tierras con mucho cuidado rigor y puntualidad" (Luis Pérez Dasmariñas, "Carta de L. P. Mariñas sobre convivencia con sangleyes," 1597, AGI, Filipinas, 18B, R.7, N.72, fol. 5).

74. Andrés Reséndez estimates that a *legua* was a measurement of distance that averaged nearly six kilometers (*The Other Slavery: The Uncovered Story of Indian Enslavement in America* [Boston: Houghton Mifflin Harcourt, 2016], 202).

75. Luis Pérez Dasmariñas, "Carta de L. P. Mariñas sobre convivencia con sangleyes," 1597, AGI, Filipinas, 18B, R.7, N.72, fols. 5–6.

76. My sincerest thanks to Ryan Crewe for sharing James Chin's able translation of the Chinese letter.

77. Miguel de Benavides, "Carta del obispo de Nueva Segovia Miguel de Benavides sobre quejas de los chinos," 1598, AGI, Filipinas, 76, N.41, fol. 6.

78. Padrón, *The Indies of the Setting Sun,* 266.

79. Timothy Brook, *Vermeer's Hat: The Seventeenth Century and the Dawn of the Global World* (New York: Bloomsbury Press, 2008), 168.

80. "Todos estan espantados de ver que un barbaro haga justicia en tierra del rey nro señor" ("Carta e información sobre tres mandarines chinos," 1603, AGI, Filipinas, 59, N.45, fol. 12).

81. "Si quereys que esto sea oro será lo pero si no quereis que lo sea no lo será la que yo digo es que cortéis las cabezas a los indios de esta tierra y todo el cuello le hallareis lleno de caderillas y gargantillas de oro y este es el oro que yo digo" (Miguel de Benavides, "Carta de Benavides sobre incursión a Mindanao, oro de Cavite," 1603, AGI, Filipinas, 74, N.47, fol. 309w).

82. Morga later cast doubt on the legitimacy of this fear and reported that not everyone believed an invasion was likely (*Svcesos de las islas Filipinas,* 99v). See also Laufer, "The Relations of the Chinese," 269.

83. C. Lee, *Saints of Resistance,* 50.

84. "Eecharon de un golpe todos los moros y judíos de hespana y eso tomaron por su blason y no piense v magd que solo están esta gente en Manila o junto a Manila sino por toda la tierra . . . y derramando esta diablura y otros vicios por toda ella" (Miguel de Benavides, "Carta de Benavides sobre incursión a Mindanao, oro de Cavite," 1603, AGI, Filipinas, 74, N.47, fol. 311r).

85. "Caja de Filipinas. Cuentas," 1603, AGI, Contaduría, 1206, fol. 383v; "Alzamiento de los sangleyes," 1606, AGI, Patronato, 25, R.63; José Eugenio Borao Mateo, "The Massacre of 1603: Chinese Perception of the Spanish in the Philippines," *Itinerario* 22, no. 1 (1998): 7.

86. "Estauamos todos con los cuchillos a las gargantas" (Juan de Garrovillas, "Carta del franciscano Juan de Garrovillas sobre alzamiento de sangleyes," 1603, AGI, Filipinas, 84, N.122, fol. 1).

87. "Tras esto la gente de menos capacidad los mirava [a los sangleyes] ya como enemigos, y los tratava muy mal, con lo qual ellos andavan ynquietos, y temerosos" (Diego Aduarte, *Historia de la provincia del Sancto Rosario de la Orden de Predicadores en Philippinas, Iapon y China* [Manila: Luis Beltrán, 1640], 1:290).

88. Morga, *Svcesos de las islas Filipinas,* 107v.

89. Argensola, *Conqvista delas islas Malvcas,* 319; Morga, *Svcesos de las islas Filipinas,* 108r.

90. "Fingida lealtad" (Argensola, *Conqvista delas islas Malvcas,* 319); "rico y muy favorecido de los españoles" and "haciendo del ladron fiel" (Morga, *Svcesos de las islas Filipinas,* 108r–v).

91. "Que por el passo en que estaua, no deuia aquella muerte, y que siempre auia sido vasallo leal de su Magestad y que Dios sauia lo que tenia en su pecho, y lleuaua en su corazon" (Maldonado, *Relacion verdadera,* 7).

92. "Que que gallina le auia cantado al oydo? Que le siguiessen, que con veynte y cinco soldados bastaua para toda la China" (Argensola, *Conqvista delas islas Malvcas,* 321).

93. "Le dio tal priessa, que lo molieron, y quebraron las piernas. Y que de rodillas peleó gran rato, hasta que le desatinaron a palos, sin que le defendiesse un morrión fuerte"

(Argensola, *Conqvista delas islas Malvcas*, 322). See also Padrón, *The Indies of the Setting Sun*, 270–271.

94. "Monstruos" and "Aunque seria de menos cuydado el matarlos todos, o intentarlo, no parecia justo hazer castigo en gente, de cuyo delito no se tenia certeza" (Argensola, *Conqvista delas islas Malvcas*, 324).

95. "Carnizeros" ("Carta de Juan de Bustamante sobre la sublevación de los sangleyes," 1603, AGI, Filipinas, 35, N.68, fol. 1069v); Argensola, *Conqvista delas islas Malvcas*, 328. See also Padrón, *The Indies of the Setting Sun*, 270. For the equivalent shifting of the burden of guilt in the case of Tenochtitlan, see Inga Clendinnen, "'Fierce and Unnatural Cruelty': Cortés and the Conquest of Mexico," *Representations* 33 (1991): 91–94.

96. The reinforcements had come from the provinces of Pampanga, Bulacan, Laguna de Bay, Tondo, Bombon, and Calisaya, noted for having "people with more reason and more wealth and civility than the other indios for being close to the city of Manila and showing more love to the Spaniards and also for their being of greater energy and resolve (es gente de mas razon y de mas caudal y pulicia que los demás indios por estar cerca desta ciudad de Manila y mostrar mas amor alos hespañoles y tambien por ser ellos de mas animo y brio ["Carta de Acuña sobre sublevación de sangleyes, galeras," 1603, AGI, Filipinas, 7, R.1, N.12, fol. 7]).

97. "Acudiendo siempre a los puestos mas peligrosos y de mas riesgo" ("Petición de Diego de Maracot de encomienda en Guagua," 1623, AGI, Filipinas, 39, N.20, fol. 26).

98. Argensola, *Conqvista delas islas Malvcas*, 332.

99. "Petición de Diego de Maracot de encomienda en Guagua," 1623, AGI, Filipinas, 39, N.20, fols. 35–36.

100. "Petición de Diego de Maracot de encomienda en Guagua," fols. 36–37.

101. "Caja de Filipinas. Cuentas," 1603–5, AGI, Contaduría, 1206, fols. 270r–279r; Hawkley, "The Birth of Globalization," 255.

102. "Carta de Acuña sobre sublevación de sangleyes, galeras," 1603, AGI, Filipinas, 7, R.1, N.12, fol. 3.

103. Gil, *Los chinos en Manila*, 487.

104. "Testimonio de las escrituras de Navotas, Malabon, Cotcot y Salinas," 32, 16–39, and 244.

105. Gebhardt, "Global Cities, Incoherent Communities," 144.

106. Kerilyn Schewel, "Understanding Immobility: Moving beyond the Mobility Bias in Migration Studies," *International Migration Review* 54, no. 2 (2019): 337.

107. Crewe, "Occult Cosmopolitanism," 56.

108. Gil, *Los chinos en Manila*, 487.

109. "Daño yrreparable" (Pedro de Acuña, "Carta de Acuña sobre sublevación de sangleyes, galeras," 1603, AGI, Filipinas, 7, R.1, N.12, fol. 4).

110. Spaniards owed the return of the "Sangleyes" to three veteran Chinese ship captains named Guansan, Sinu, and Guanchan, who encouraged their compatriots to sail once more for the Philippines to trade and settle there. Gil, *Los chinos en Manila*, 484.

111. "Testimonio de las escrituras de Navotas, Malabon, Cotcot y Salinas," 32 and 16–39.

112. Newson, *Conquest and Pestilence*, 126–130 and 143–146; Reséndez, *The Other Slavery*, 17.

113. C. Lee, *Saints of Resistance,* 5.

114. "Carta de Juan de Artiz enviando cuentas," 1605, AGI, Filipinas, 35, N.76.

115. Miguel de Benavides, "Carta de Benavides sobre sublevación de los sangleyes," 1603, AGI, Filipinas, 74, N.54, fol. 373v.

116. "Carta de Juan de Artiz enviando cuentas," 1605, AGI, Filipinas, 35, N.76, fol. 1160r.

117. "Testimonio del número de sangleyes que entran en Manila," 1606, AGI, Filipinas, 35, N.82, fols. 1226v–1227r.

118. Gil, *Los chinos en Manila,* 388; Sousa, *The Portuguese Slave Trade,* 192; Borao Mateo, "The Massacre of 1603," 10.

119. Tatiana Seijas, "Portuguese Slave Trade to Spanish Manila: 1580–1640," *Itinerario* 32, no. 1 (2008): 24; Sousa, *The Portuguese Slave Trade,* 27, 35, and 261–284; Déborah Oropeza Keresey, "La esclavitud asiática en el virreinato de la Nueva España, 1565–1673," *Historia Mexicana* 61, no. 1 (2011): 22.

120. C. Lee, *Saints of Resistance,* 36.

121. Sousa, *The Portuguese Slave Trade,* 6.

122. Quoted in Sousa, *The Portuguese Slave Trade,* 61.

123. Gary P. Leupp, *Servants, Shophands, and Laborers in the Cities of Tokugawa Japan* (Princeton, NJ: Princeton University Press, 1992), 17.

124. Sousa, *The Portuguese Slave Trade,* 66 and 180–181.

125. Sanjay Subrahmanyam, *The Portuguese Empire in Asia, 1500–1700: A Political and Economic History,* 2nd ed. (West Sussex, UK: Wiley-Blackwell, 2012), 65; Seijas, "Portuguese Slave Trade," 25.

126. Joseph del Castillo Graxeda, *Compendio de la vida, y virtudes de la venerable Catharina de San Juan* (Puebla, Mexico: Imprenta de Diego Fernandez de Leon, 1692), 7.

127. "Todas las furias de el infierno," and "providencia" (Alonso Ramos, *Los prodigios de la Omnipotencia y milagros de la gracia en la vida de la venerable sierva de Dios Catarina de San Juan,* ed. Gisela von Wobeser [Mexico City: Universidad Nacional Autónoma de México-Instituto de Investigaciones Históricas, 2017], 1:68). See also Castillo Graxeda, *Compendio de la vida,* 18.

128. Stephanie Hassell, "Inquisition Records from Goa as Sources for the Study of Slavery in the Eastern Domains of the Portuguese Empire," *History in Africa* 42 (2015): 411–412.

129. Subrahmanyam, *The Portuguese Empire in Asia,* 240.

130. Mauro Escobar Gamboa, ed., *Padrón de los indios de Lima en 1613* (Lima: Universidad Nacional Mayor de San Marcos, 1968), 541.

131. Hugo Cardoso, "The African Slave Population of Portuguese India: Demographics and Impact on Indo-Portuguese," *Journal of Pidgin and Creole Languages* 25, no. 1 (2010): 9; Richard B. Allen, "Satisfying the 'Want for Labouring People': European Slave Trading in the Indian Ocean, 1500–1850," *Journal of World History* 21, no. 1 (2010): 57.

132. "Proceso contra Anton chino, por hechicero y adivinador," 1659, AGN, Inquisición, vol. 456, exp. 2, fols. 55–98.

133. Markus Vink, "'The World's Oldest Trade': Dutch Slavery and Slave Trade in the Indian Ocean in the Seventeenth Century," *Journal of World History* 14, no. 2 (2003): 140; Subrahmanyam, *The Portuguese Empire in Asia,* 176; Seijas, "Portuguese Slave Trade," 24.

134. "Mateo de la Torre," 1648, AGN, Procesos Civiles, Caja 79, exp. 2855.

135. Oropeza Keresey, "La esclavitud asiática," 26.

136. Sousa, *The Portuguese Slave Trade,* 54.

137. António Manuel Hespanha, *Filhos da terra: Identidades mestiças nos confins da expansão portuguesa* (Lisbon: Tinta-da-china, 2019), 152.

138. Hespanha, *Filhos da terra,* 288.

139. Norah L. A. Gharala, "'From Mozambique in Indies of Portugal': Locating East Africans in New Spain," *Journal of Global History* 7, no. 3 (2022): 244; Sousa, *The Portuguese Slave Trade,* 8 and 424.

140. Omar H. Ali, *Malik Ambar: Power and Slavery across the Indian Ocean* (New York: Oxford University Press, 2016), 30; Hespanha, *Filhos da terra,* 288.

141. Diego Javier Luis, "The Deportation of Free Black People from Manila in the Seventeenth Century," in *The Spanish Pacific, 1521–1815: A Reader of Primary Sources,* vol. 2, ed. Christina Lee and Ricardo Padrón (Amsterdam: Amsterdam University Press, forthcoming).

142. Sousa, *The Portuguese Slave Trade,* 183–184; Seijas, *Asian Slaves,* 37–38.

143. Reséndez, *The Other Slavery,* 57.

144. Juan de Solórzano Pereira, *Política Indiana* (Madrid: Diego Díaz de la Carrera, 1648), 1:69.

145. The Koreans listed here had likely been captured during the Imjin War and sold to the Portuguese in Nagasaki. "Petición de Sancho Bravo de Acuña de bienes y sueldo de Pedro de Acuña," 1613, AGI, Filipinas, 36, N. 78, fols. 957r, 961r, and 964v–965r; Sousa, *The Portuguese Slave Trade,* 92–129.

146. "Venta de esclava china en Manila," 1627, AGN, Indiferente Virreinal, Caja 2440, exp. 021 (Civil Caja 2440). Despite what we know about the numbers of slaves entering Manila, there has been surprisingly little work on enslaved communities or slave owners in the Philippines in the early modern period.

147. "Carta del comisario de Acapulco avisando la salida de las naos y acompañando una obligacion de Lorenzo de Lisballo, por presos. Manila. Acapulco," 1643, AGN, Inquisición, vol. 416, exp. 21, fols. 262r–v. "Casta baeilan" could be a reference to Ceylon.

148. Sousa, *The Portuguese Slave Trade,* 189 and 200–209.

149. Seijas, *Asian Slaves,* 60.

150. Tatiana Seijas puts the total count at ten thousand during the 1620s (*Asian Slaves,* 35). See also Oropeza Keresey, "La esclavitud asiática," 26.

151. "Caja de Filipinas. Cuentas," 1637–1638, AGI, Contaduría, 1218, fols. 59r–v and 82r–v; Tatiana Seijas, "Slaving and the Global Reach of the Moro Wars in the Seventeenth Century," in *Philippine Confluence,* 298.

152. Oropeza, *La migración asiática,* 238.

153. "Autos sobre libertad promovidos por Domingo de la Cruz, chino y esclavo natural de Manila, contra Juan Sánchez Bañales vecino de Zapotlán," 1678, Archivo de la Real Audiencia de la Nueva Galicia (ARANG), Caja 9, Exp. 9, Prog. 124, fol. 1r.

154. Oropeza, *La migración asiática,* 144–145.

155. Ben Vinson III, *Before Mestizaje: The Frontiers of Race and Caste in Colonial Mexico* (New York: Cambridge University Press, 2017), 250.

156. "Por tener tan poca edad, quando se aparto de el" (Castillo Graxeda, *Compendio de la vida, 7*).

157. Seijas, *Asian Slaves*, 88–89.

158. Oropeza, *La migración asiática*, 148.

159. Seijas, *Asian Slaves*, 95–98; Oropeza, *La migración asiática*, 144–145 and 156.

160. Seijas, *Asian Slaves*, 89.

161. "Caja de Acapulco," 1637, AGI, Contaduría, 905A, fols. 363r–83r.

162. "Caja de Acapulco," 1640, AGI, Contaduría, 905A, fols. 453r–459v.

163. "Caja de Acapulco," 1645–1646, AGI, Contaduría, 905A, fols. 832r–835v and 907r–909v.

164. Oropeza Keresey, "La esclavitud asiática," 9–10; Seijas, *Asian Slaves*, 90 and 94–95.

165. Oropeza, *La migración asiática*, 151.

166. One peso was worth eight tomines, and each tomín was worth twelve granos. Woodrow Borah and Sherburne F. Cook, *Price Trends of Some Basic Commodities in Central Mexico, 1531–1570* (Berkeley: University of California Press, 1958), 9; "Caja de Acapulco," 1618, AGI, Contaduría, 903.

167. Seijas, *Asian Slaves*, 74–75 and 107.

168. "Informe sobre comercio de esclavos de las islas Chamures," AGI, Filipinas, 6, R. 10, N. 188, fol. 1.

169. Seijas, *Asian Slaves*, 98–107.

170. Santiago, "The Filipino Indios Encomenderos," 166.

171. José Eugenio Borao Mateo, "Contextualizing the Pampangos (and Gagayano) Soldiers in the Spanish Fortress in Taiwan (1626–1642)," *Anuario de Estudios Americanos* 70, no. 2 (2013): 587. See also Augusto V. de Viana, "The Pampangos in the Mariana Mission, 1668–1684," *Micronesian Journal of the Humanities and Social Sciences* 4, no. 1 (2005): 1–16.

172. "Caja de Filipinas. Cuentas," 1630–1631, AGI, Contaduría, 1212.

173. Juan de Medina, *Historia de los sucesos de la Orden de N. Gran P. S. Agustín de estas islas Filipinas, desde que se descubrieron y se poblaron por los españoles, con las noticias memorables* (Manila: Tipo-Litografía de Chofré y Comp., 1893), 128.

174. Matthew J. Furlong, "Peasants, Servants, and Sojourners: Itinerant Asians in Colonial New Spain, 1571–1720," PhD diss. University of Arizona, 2014, 136.

175. Seijas, "Slaving and the Global Reach of the Moro Wars," 290.

176. Newson, *Conquest and Pestilence*.

177. Furlong, "Peasants, Servants, and Sojourners," 303–305 and 321–322.

178. Eight silver reales were worth one gold peso. Borah and Cook, *Price Trends*, 10.

179. "Caja de Filipinas. Cuentas," 1609–1610, AGI, Contaduría, 1209.

180. A few isolated cases exist of Philippine grumetes making as little as one or two pesos per month. Furlong, "Peasants, Servants, and Sojourners," 290 and 302; Giráldez, *The Age of Trade*, 141.

181. "Caja de Acapulco," 1606–1615, AGI, Contaduría, 902.

182. Borah and Cook, *Price Trends*, 45.

183. Edward R. Slack Jr., "The Chinos in New Spain: A Corrective Lens for a Distorted Image," *Journal of World History* 20, no. 1 (2009): 39.

184. On the perennial threat of the "Sangleyes," see Guillermo de Bañuelos y Carrillo, *Tratado del estado de las islas Philipinas, y de sus conueniencias* (Mexico City: En la imprenta de Bernardo Calderon, 1638), 3v–7v.

185. See Newson, *Conquest and Pestilence*, appendix B.

186. Newson, *Conquest and Pestilence*, 254–255.

187. C. Lee, *Saints of Resistance*, 92–93.

188. Bañuelos y Carrillo, *Tratado del estado de las islas Philipinas*, 17r.

189. "Cágome en toda Manila" (quoted in Gil, *Los chinos en Manila*, 201).

190. "Carta de Morga pidiendo plaza en México o Perú," 1598, AGI, Filipinas, 18B, R.8, N.98; "Carta de Morga pidiendo traslado a México o Perú," 1599, AGI, Filipinas, 18B, R.9, N.119; "Peticiones de Morga de traslado y ayuda de costa," 1601, AGI, Filipinas, 19, R.2, N.10; "Carta de Morga para que se le deje salir de Filipinas," 1602, AGI, Filipinas, 19, R.3, N.42.

191. Oropeza, *La migración asiática*, 207.

192. "Á un chino que le servía, y de quien parece tenía más confidencia; y á otro chino 19 reales . . . por cariño que le tenía, por haberlo criado. A los demás chinos (que su familia se componía de sólo ellos y eran muchos), dejó en recomendación á su albacea. Dió libertad á sus esclavos, que parece que eran ocho" ("Relación del tumulto acaecido en México, el año de 1692, por un testigo presencial anónimo," in *Documentos inéditos ó muy raros para la historia de México*, ed. Genaro García [Mexico City: Vda. de Ch. Bouret, 1907], 233).

193. Dahpon David Ho, "The Burning Shore: Fujian and the Coastal Depopulation, 1661–1683," in *Sea Rovers, Silver, and Samurai: Maritime East Asia in Global History, 1550–1700*, ed. Tonio Andrade and Xing Hang (Honolulu: University of Hawai'i Press, 2016), 260; Brook, *Vermeer's Hat*, 177–178.

194. Crewe, "Pacific Purgatory," 365.

2. The Pacific Passage

1. Andrés Reséndez, *Conquering the Pacific: An Unknown Mariner and the Final Great Voyage of the Age of Discovery* (Boston: Houghton Mifflin Harcourt, 2021), 5.

2. William Lytle Schurz, *The Manila Galleon: Illustrated with Maps* (New York: E. P. Dutton, 1939), 15.

3. Arturo Giráldez, *The Age of Trade: The Manila Galleons and the Dawn of the Global Economy* (Lanham, MD: Rowman and Littlefield, 2015), 133.

4. In theory, "indio / a" could refer to any vassal subject indigenous to overseas lands claimed by the Spanish or Portuguese empires (with the exception of Africa).

5. Robert C. Schwaller, *Géneros de Gente in Early Colonial Mexico: Defining Racial Difference* (Norman: University of Oklahoma Press, 2016), 226; Joanne Rappaport, "'Asi lo paresçe por su aspecto': Physiognomy and the Construction of Difference in Colonial Bogotá," *Hispanic American Historical Review* 91, no. 4 (2011): 605.

6. Marie Louise Pratt writes, "I use [contact zones] to refer to social spaces where cultures meet, clash, and grapple with each other, often in contexts of highly asymmetrical relations of power, such as colonialism, slavery, or their aftermaths as they are lived out in many parts of the world today" ("Arts of the Contact Zone," *Profession* [1991]: 34).

7. Pablo E. Pérez-Mallaína, *Spain's Men of the Sea: Daily Life on the Indies Fleets in the Sixteenth Century* (Baltimore, MD: Johns Hopkins University Press, 1998), 135.

8. Sebastián de Pineda counted an average of 1,400 Indigenous carpenters per galleon constructed in the Philippines. Sebastián de Pineda, "Petición de Sebastián de Pineda de puesto en la armada que va a Filipinas," 1619, Archivo General de Indias [AGI], Filipinas, 38, N.12.

9. Linda A. Newson, *Conquest and Pestilence in the Early Spanish Philippines* (Honolulu: University of Hawai'i Press, 2009), 28–30.

10. "Caja de Filipinas. Cuentas de Real Hacienda," 1609, AGI, Contaduría, 1209, fols. 98r–v.

11. Other parts of the galleons came from further afield: the rigging and sails from the Ilocos, metal from East and South Asia, and specialized parts from Veracruz overland and across the Pacific. Mariano Bonialian, "Acapulco: Puerta abierta del Pacífico, válvula secreta del Atlántico," in *Relaciones intercoloniales: Nueva España y Filipinas*, ed. Jaime Olveda (Zapopan, Mexico: El Colegio de Jalisco, 2017), 130–131; James S. Cummins and Nicholas Cushner, "Labor in the Colonial Philippines: The Discurso Parenético of Gómez de Espinoza," *Philippine Studies* 22, nos. 1–2 (1974): 121.

12. Christina Lee, *Saints of Resistance: Devotions in the Philippines under Early Spanish Rule* (New York: Oxford University Press, 2021), 119.

13. The rice ration was supposed to amount to a "half-celemín" (just over two liters) of grain per day ("Caja de Filipinas. Cuentas de Real Hacienda," 1609, AGI, Contaduría, 1209, fol. 94v). See also Sebastián de Pineda, "Petición de Sebastián de Pineda de puesto en la armada que va a Filipinas," 1619, AGI, Filipinas, 38, N.12.

14. The Dominican Domingo Fernández Navarrete believed that the cost of ships in Acapulco was four times higher than in Asia (*Tratados historicos, politicos, ethicos, y religiosos de la monarchia de china* [Madrid: Imprenta Real, 1676], 301). See also Rubén Carrillo Martín, *Las gentes del mar Sangley* (Mexico City: Palabra de Clío, 2015), 54.

15. Sebastián de Pineda, "Petición de Sebastián de Pineda de puesto en la armada que va a Filipinas," 1619, AGI, Filipinas, 38, N.12.

16. The English privateer Captain Woodes Rogers considered a hull made of lanang to be impenetrable after firing cannons on a Manila galleon during an attack on December 27, 1709. David Cordingly, *Pirate Hunter of the Caribbean: The Adventurous Life of Captain Woodes Rogers* (New York: Random House, 2011), 85. See also Andrew Peterson, "What Really Made the World Go Around? *Indio* Contributions to the Acapulco-Manila Galleon Trade," *Explorations* 11, no. 1 (2011): 7.

17. Giráldez, *The Age of Trade*, 124; Sebastán de Pineda, "Petición de Sebastián de Pineda de puesto en la armada que va a Filipinas," 1619, AGI, Filipinas, 38, N.12.

18. "Caja de Filipinas. Cuentas de Real Hacienda," 1609, AGI, Contaduría, 1209, fol. 93r.

19. "Carta de la Audiencia de Manila sobre el galeón Santo Cristo de Burgos," 1695, AGI, Filipinas, 26, R.4, N.18, fol. 73v.

20. Matthew J. Furlong, "Peasants, Servants, and Sojourners: Itinerant Asians in Colonial New Spain, 1571–1720," PhD diss. University of Arizona, 2014, 290 and 302.

21. Tatiana Seijas, *Asian Slaves in Colonial Mexico: From Chinos to Indians* (New York: Cambridge University Press, 2014), 84.

22. Pérez-Mallaína, *Spain's Men of the Sea*, 66. In the middle of the eighteenth century, George Anson, a British admiral, wrote, "It is well known to those who are acquainted with the *Spanish* customs in the *South-Seas,* that their water is preserved on shipboard not in casks but in earthen jars, which in some sort resemble the large oil jars we often see in *Europe.* When the *Manila* ship first puts to sea, she takes on board a much greater quantity of water than can be stowed between decks, and the jars which contain it are hung all about the shrouds and stays, so as to exhibit at a distance a very odd appearance . . . their only method of recruiting their water is by the rains, which they meet with between the latitudes of 30 and 40° North, and which they are always prepared to catch. For this purpose they take to sea with them a great number of mats, which, whenever the rain descends, they range slopingly against the gunwale, from one end of the ship to the other, their lower edges resting on a large split bamboe; whence all the water which falls on the mats, drains into the bamboe, and by this, as a trough is conveyed into a jar. And this method of furnishing themselves with water, however accidental and extraordinary it may at first sight appear, hath never been known to fail them, but it hath been common for them, when their voyage is a little longer than usual, to fill all their water jars several times over" (*A Voyage round the World in the Years MDCCXL, I, II, III, IV* [London: John and Paul Knapton, 1749], 240–241).

23. Reséndez, *Conquering the Pacific,* 73.

24. Reséndez, *Conquering the Pacific,* 51.

25. Kuroshio in Japanese means "'Black Current,' owing to its characteristic cobalt-blue color" (Reséndez, *Conquering the Pacific,* 142 and 151).

26. Reséndez, *Conquering the Pacific,* 145 and 150.

27. Navidad was of great importance in the history of transpacific expeditions, as Miguel de Legazpi's fleet departed from there in 1564. Reséndez, *Conquering the Pacific,* 17 and 80; Martín, *Las gentes del mar Sangley,* 56.

28. Reséndez, *Conquering the Pacific,* 145.

29. "Propuesta de nueva ruta de Filipinas a Nueva España," 1613, AGI, Filipinas, 329, L.2, fol. 170r.

30. Pérez-Mallaína, *Spain's Men of the Sea,* 171; Giráldez, *The Age of Trade,* 140.

31. Pedro Manuel de Arandia y Santestevan, *Ordenanzas de marina, para los navios del rey, de las islas Philipinas, que en Guerra, y con reales permissos hacen viages al Reyno de la Nueva España, ù otro destino del Real servicio* (Manila: Imprenta de la Compañiia de Jesús, 1757), 49.

32. Reséndez, *Conquering the Pacific,* 165.

33. Giráldez, *The Age of Trade,* 141.

34. Furlong, "Peasants, Servants, and Sojourners," 309.

35. Martín, *Las gentes del mar Sangley,* 56.

36. Diego García de Palacio, *Instrucion nauthica: Para el buen vso, y regimiento de las naos, su traça, y y [sic] gouierno conforme à la altura de Mexico* (Mexico City: En casa de Pedro Ocharte, 1587), 119–120.

37. Furlong, "Peasants, Servants, and Sojourners," 316–317.

38. "Caja de Acapulco," 1635, AGI, Contaduría, 905A, fols. 202r–205v.

39. Furlong, "Peasants, Servants, and Sojourners," 305–306.

40. Sebastián de Pineda, "Petición de Sebastián de Pineda de puesto en la armada que va a Filipinas," 1619, AGI, Filipinas, 38, N.12.

41. "Caja de Acapulco," 1610, AGI, Contaduría, 902.

42. Déborah Oropeza writes that at least two enslaved Asians threw themselves overboard at Ticao, in the Visayas, to avoid the Pacific crossing (*La migración asiática en el virreinato de la Nueva España: Un proceso de globalización [1565–1700]* [Mexico City: El Colegio de México, 2020], 152–153).

43. "Especialmente los indios grumetes" (Hernando de los Ríos Coronel, "Petición del procurador Ríos Coronel sobre varios asuntos," 1605, AGI, Filipinas, 27, N.51, fol. 216r).

44. Giráldez, *The Age of Trade*, 134.

45. "Cosa ordinaria en esta carrera" (Francisco Colín, *Labor evangélica, ministerios apostólicos de los obreros de la Compañía de Iesvs, fvndacion, y progresos de sv provincia en las islas Filipinas* [Madrid: por Ioseph Fernandez de Buendia, 1663], 205).

46. Cameron La Follette, Douglas Deur, and Esther González, "The Galleon's Final Journey: Accounts of Ship, Crew, and Passengers in the Colonial Archives," *Oregon Historical Quarterly* 119, no. 2 (2018): 225.

47. Francesco Carletti, *My Voyage around the World: The Chronicles of a 16th Century Florentine Merchant*, trans. Herbert Weinstock (New York: Pantheon Books, 1964), 79.

48. "Los entretendra y divertirá con buenas palabras" ("Carta de la Audiencia de Manila sobre el galeón Santo Cristo de Burgos," 1695, AGI, Filipinas, 26, R.4, N.18, fol. 17r).

49. "Todos los que vienen tocados del Berben, o mal de Loanda, que son los achaques mas pestíferos, que dan en aquella nauegacion, y luego Disenteria, raro es el que escapa" (Pedro Cubero Sebastián, *Peregrinacion del Mvndo* [Naples: Carlos Porfile, 1682], 386).

50. Jaime Olveda, "El Puerto de la Navidad," in *Relaciones intercoloniales*, 114; Schurz, *The Manila Galleon*, 128.

51. Gregorio Martín de Guijo, *Gregorio M. de Guijo, diario, 1648–1664*, ed. Manuel Romero de Terreros (Mexico City: Editorial Porrúa, 1952), 2:76; "Bienes de difuntos: Diego Ruiz," 1671, AGI, Contratación, N.2, R.3, fols. 12r–13v.

52. Thomas Gage, *A New Survey of the West-Indies: Or, The English American His Travel by Sea and Land* (London: E. Cotes, 1655), 20.

53. "Y auiendo salido de tierra caliente muere mucha gente y se les pudieren las encías y se les caen los dientes" (Hernando de los Ríos Coronel, "Petición del procurador Ríos Coronel sobre varios asuntos," 1605, AGI, Filipinas, 27, N.51, fol. 314v).

54. Don Alonso de Arellano, quoted in Reséndez, *Conquering the Pacific*, 153.

55. "Eran estos vientos tan frios, que hubo quien mariesse [*sic;* muriesse?] elado, sin otra enfermedad mas que el frio, con el qual se juntava el encapillar muchas veces las olas la nao, y mojar a los que no tenían abrigo (que eran casi todos) con que crecia el frio grandemente, y aviendo salido de un templo tan cálido como el de esta tierra, y entrar como repentinamente en otro tan frio, no puedo [*sic;* puede?] dexar de causar muchas enfermedades, y assi murieron en este viaje muchos, y entre ellos el general, y el maestre, y vn mercader rico. (Diego Aduarte, *Historia de la provincia del Sancto Rosario de la Orden de Predicadores en Philippinas, Iapon y China* [Manila: Luis Beltrán, 1640], 2:400).

56. "Ni los nacidos, y criados en [las Filipinas] pueden deponer de vista de que color sea la nieue, ni de que calidad el hielo" (Colín, *Labor evangélica*, 45).

57. "Orden sobre buen trato a los indios grumetes," 1608, AGI, Filipinas, 340, L.3, fols. 36v–37r; "Orden sobre trato a pasajeros y marineros en las naos," 1620, AGI, Filipinas, 340, L.3, fols. 256r–v.

58. Giráldez, *The Age of Trade*, 128.

59. Seijas, *Asian Slaves*, 82.

60. Juan de Silva, "Petición de Juan de Silva sobre su viaje," 1607, AGI, Filipinas, 20, R.1, N.15.

61. "Carta de la Audiencia de Manila sobre el galeón Santo Cristo de Burgos," 1695, AGI, Filipinas, 26, R.4, N.18, fol. 15v.

62. "Orden de evitar ofensas al llevar esclavas en las naos," 1608, AGI, Filipinas, 340, L.3, fols. 41v–42r.

63. Seijas, *Asian Slaves*, 79.

64. "Algunas esclavas de buen parecer" (Joseph del Castillo Graxeda, *Compendio de la vida, y virtudes de la venerable Catharina de San Juan* [Puebla, Mexico: Imprenta de Diego Fernandez de Leon, 1692], 18–19).

65. Castillo Graxeda, *Compendio de la vida*, 19.

66. Pérez-Mallaína, *Spain's Men of the Sea*, 164.

67. Francisco de Aguilera, *Sermon que en las honras de la Venerable Madre Catharina de San Juan predicó* (Biblioteca de la Universidad de Sevilla, 1688), 6r; Seijas, *Asian Slaves*, 15.

68. Alonso Ramos, *Los prodigios de la Omnipotencia y milagros de la gracia en la vida de la venerable sierva de Dios Catarina de San Juan*, ed. Gisela von Wobeser (Mexico City: Universidad Nacional Autónoma de México-Instituto de Investigaciones Históricas, 2017), 1:315.

69. "Caja de Acapulco," 1643–1646, AGI, Contaduría 405A, fols. 697v and 908v.

70. Seijas, *Asian Slaves*, 16.

71. Oropeza, *La migración asiática*, 143; Pablo Sierra Silva, *Urban Slavery in Colonial Mexico: Puebla de los Ángeles, 1531–1706* (Cambridge: Cambridge University Press, 2018), 134.

72. Pérez-Mallaína, *Spain's Men of the Sea*, 237 and 244.

73. Oropeza, *La migración asiática*, 270.

74. Martin Austin Nesvig, *Ideology and Inquisition: The World of the Censors in Early Mexico* (New Haven, CT: Yale University Press, 2009), 105; Hans-Jürgen Prien, *Christianity in Latin America*, trans. Stephen Buckwalter, rev. and expanded ed. (Leiden, the Netherlands: Koninklijke Brill, 2013), 65.

75. John Blanco, "Idolatry and Apostasy in the 1633 Jesuit Annual Letter," in *The Spanish Pacific, 1521–1815: A Reader of Primary Sources*, ed. Christina H. Lee and Ricardo Padrón (Amsterdam: Amsterdam University Press, 2020), 117–118.

76. Pedro Chirino, *Relacion de las islas Filipinas i de lo que en ellas an trabaiado los padres de la Compañía de Iesvs* (Rome: Esteban Paulino, 1604), 76–77.

77. "Parece avian negado ambos su nacion, porque ni en ella se hallava la doblez, y brio colerico de los Iapones, ni en ella [*sic*] cudicia, y bachilleria de los Chinos" (Aduarte, *Historia de la provincia*, 1:109).

78. John Leddy Phelan, *The Hispanization of the Philippines: Spanish Aims and Filipino Responses, 1565–1700* (Madison: University of Wisconsin Press, 1959), 49.

79. John N. Crossley, "Juan Cobo, el Códice Boxer y los sangleyes de Manila," in *El Códice Boxer: Etnografía colonial e hibridismo cultural en las islas Filipinas,* ed. Manel Ollé and Joan-Pau Rubiés (Barcelona: Edicions de la Universitat de Barcelona, 2019), 94; Phelan, *The Hispanization of the Philippines,* 50.

80. "Soy una nao de China / que una china desembarcó, / Acapulco es poco barco / para abarcar esta china. / Es mi nombre Catarina, / mi rumbo sin barlovento: / Espíritu Santo el viento / san Ignacio el capitán; / sus pilotos me pondrán / en tierra de salvamento" (quoted in Ramos, *Los prodigios,* 3:160). See also Seijas, *Asian Slaves,* 27.

81. Unfortunately, the image does not survive.

82. Ramos, *Los prodigios,* 3:160. I thank Leland Grigoli for his assistance with the grammatic subtleties of Latin.

83. "Se confiesen y comulgen cumpliendo con la obligación de christiano" ("Carta de la Audiencia de Manila sobre el galeón Santo Cristo de Burgos," 1695, AGI, Filipinas, 26, R.4, N.18, fol. 15r).

84. Seijas, *Asian Slaves,* 80; Giráldez, *The Age of Trade,* 136.

85. The devotion to this image later became localized in Antipolo and blended with Indigenous devotional practices during the late seventeenth century. C. Lee, *Saints of Resistance,* 108 and 122.

86. Giráldez, *The Age of Trade,* 127–128.

87. Quoted in C. Lee, *Saints of Resistance,* 110.

88. Giráldez, *The Age of Trade,* 120.

89. Giráldez, *The Age of Trade,* 138.

90. Pérez-Mallaína, *Spain's Men of the Sea,* 238.

91. "Los dias que el t.po diere lugar se dira missa y la salue por las tardes con la reverencia de vida y devosion posible que haciendolo assi se conseguira muy buen viage y feliz sucesos" ("Carta de la Audiencia de Manila sobre el galeón Santo Cristo de Burgos," 1695, AGI, Filipinas, 26, R.4, N.18, fols. 15r–v). See also La Follette, Deur, and González, "The Galleon's Final Journey," 225.

92. "Serà de su cuydado à que se hagan con toda reverencia los rezos establecidos, en los sitios, y à las horas acostumbradas, en alta voz. Y los dias de Domingo, y de otras Fiestas, de dar lugar el tiempo, y con acuerdo del Capitan del Navio, podrà explicar la Doctrina, y Oraciones a los Gurumetes [sic; grumetes], y demas Gente de Mar, como à la Tripulacion, y Guarnicion, y que todos acudan alternativamente à estos actos de devocion, y religion; y de los que faltaren, sin legitima causa, ò por malicia, seràn castigados" (Arandia y Santestevan, *Ordenanzas de marina,* 95).

93. "Por no afligir a los de la nao: Señor Padre, muchas mares he nauegado: pero en mi vida he visto tal temporal y baxo deshecho" (quoted in Cubero Sebastián, *Peregrinacion del Mvndo,* 383).

94. Cubero Sebastián, *Peregrinacion del Mvndo,* 384.

95. Colín, *Labor evangélica,* 637.

96. Seijas, *Asian Slaves,* 80.

97. "[Todos] dizen en alta voz, como si se echaran casi a morir: En vuestras manos, Señor, nos encomendamos: cuidado vuestro ha de ser esta misera barquilla, que se expone a nauegar este tan dilatado Archipelago, y todos a una voz dizen: Assi lo esperamos: y dando la vela a los vientos, comienzan a nauegar . . . no se ve otra cosa . . . hasta llegar a reconocer estas señas que parece, que la diuina prouidencia alli las depara, para que el galeon no se pierda" (Cubero Sebastián, *Peregrinacion del Mvndo*, 385).

98. "Sargazo gigante, *Marcrocystis pyrifera*, un alga típica del litoral pacífico americano" (Martín, *Las gentes del mar Sangley*, 58).

99. Schurz, *The Manila Galleon*, 239.

100. "Y por mis mismos ojos los vi" (Cubero Sebastián, *Peregrinacion del Mvndo*, 386).

101. "Pescado a manera de monillos" (Cubero Sebastián, *Peregrinacion del Mvndo*, 386).

102. Morga, *Svcesos de las islas Filipinas*, 172r; "Las focas y los leones y los elefantes marinos" (Martín, *Las gentes del mar Sangley*, 58).

103. Pilots calculated latitude by measuring the distance from the sun at noon to the horizon using declination tables. Reséndez, *Conquering the Pacific*, 31–32.

104. "Los marineros vestidos ridículamente, hazen vn Tribunal, y traen presos a toda la gente de mas importancia del galleon, comenzando desde el General, y a cada uno le toman su residencia de lo que ha pasado: y haziendole cargo, le echan la condenacion, segun la persona, con que es vn dia para todos de mucha fiesta: al General le acumulauan, que no queria dar licencia, para que se abriesse el escotillon para sacar agua, con que los auia echo perecer de sed. Al Sargento mayor (que tambien era Doctor) que auia derramado mucha sangre humana, porque auian hecho sangrar mas de ducientas personas. Al Piloto que siempre andaua a pleitos con el sol. A mi, que sentado en vna silla siempre les andaua reprehendiendo: y que era el Lazarillo de la muerte, porque al que baxaua a visitar entre puentes debaxo la cubierta, al otro dia le echauan por la banda: con que luego nos condenauan y sentenciauan: vna, que diesse chocolate, otro vizcocho, otro dulces, otro otras cosas diferentes" (Cubero Sebastián, *Peregrinacion del Mvndo*, 387).

105. Pérez-Mallaína, *Spain's Men of the Sea*, 161.

106. "Libros de pasat[iem]po y devocion," "libros de cauallerias y la ystoria pontifical y oras en que rrezan" ("Visita a la nao *Nuestra Sra. de la Asuncion* llegada a Acapulco el 14 de marzo de 1590," 1590, Archivo General de la Nación México [AGN], Inquisición, vol. 172, exp. 1, fol. 8).

107. "Carta de Corcuera sobre marineros de Cavite," 1636, AGI, Filipinas, 8, R.3, N.47.

108. Giráldez, *The Age of Trade*, 139.

109. "Orden de prohibir el juego en las naos de Filipinas," 1679, AGI, Filipinas, 331, L.7, fols. 293r–v; Pérez-Mallaína, *Spain's Men of the Sea*, 156.

110. "El sancto nombre de dios en bano ni de su bendita madre ni ofender la mag.d diu.a castigando al que lo contraviniere" ("Carta de la Audiencia de Manila sobre el galeón Santo Cristo de Burgos," 1695, AGI, Filipinas, 26, R.4, N.18, fol. 15v).

111. "Dios hazia mucho contra la dicha nao," "padre dita [*sic*; dicta?] alla tu salve que si boy al infierno trauajo tiene todos" and "encomienda tambien las que estan en el infierno" (quoted in "Denuncia contra Martin Costa, contramaestre de una nao de China, por palabras," 1608, AGN, Inquisición, vol. 283, exp. 15, fols. 94–97).

112. See Javier Villa-Flores, "'To Lose One's Soul': Blasphemy and Slavery in New Spain, 1596–1669," *Hispanic American Historical Review* 82, no. 3 (2002): 435–468.

113. Kristen Block, *Ordinary Lives in the Early Caribbean: Religion, Colonial Competition, and the Politics of Profit* (Athens: University of Georgia Press, 2012), 36.

114. Alex R. Mayfield, "Galleons from the 'Mouth of Hell': Empire and Religion in Seventeenth Century Acapulco," *Journal of Early Modern Christianity* 5, no. 2 (2018): 238.

115. "Ni bien era de día, ni bien era de noche" (Aguilera, *Sermon*, 6v).

116. "Ni el confesor adivina / lo que ella dice" (quoted in Ramos, *Los prodigios*, 3:163).

117. See Norah L. A. Gharala, "'From Mozambique in Indies of Portugal': Locating East Africans in New Spain," *Journal of Global History* 7, no. 3 (2022): 267.

118. "Antonio Geronimo y Agueda de la Cruz indios chinos," 1611, AGN, Matrimonios, vol. 262, exp. 49.

119. Oropeza, *La migración asiática*, 224.

120. Martín, *Las gentes del mar Sangley*, 110 and 114.

121. See Seijas, *Asian Slaves*, 152–153.

122. Ignacio Muñoz, "Derroteros de los mares de Marruecos, Canarias, América y Filipinas, y otros documentos," Biblioteca Nacional de España, Mss / 7119, c. late 1600s, fols. 291v–292r. See also Oropeza, *La migración asiática*, 88. For more on Muñoz, see José María Moreno Madrid, "A Seventeenth-Century Collection of Rutters: *Derroteros de los mares de Maruecos, Canarias, América y Filipinas, y otros documentos*, compiled by Ignacio Muñoz," *Rutter Technical Notes* 5 (2021): 4–24.

123. Oropeza, *La migración asiática*, 126.

124. "Libro de recibo y gasto del hermano Andrés de Aldana," 1612–1616, AGN, Caja 0487, exp. 005.

125. "Caja de Acapulco," 1595, AGI, Contaduría, 900.

126. "La casa del dho ospital de manera que si no se cubría antes de las aguas no se podía vivir ni abitar" (quoted in "Caja de Acapulco," 1616, AGI, Contaduría, 904, fol. 480).

127. Pérez-Mallaína, *Spain's Men of the Sea*, 147.

128. "[Los marineros] temen el llegar a los puertos por los executores de los r[eale]s derechos que a las tempestades de la mar y es gran dolor que después de siete meses y mas de navegación llegando al puerto donde piensas allar refigerio y descanso de tanto trauaxo hallan que todas desde el menor al mayor parece están conjurados contra ellos" ("Orden de dar buen trato a marineros," 1660, AGI, Filipinas, 341, L.6, fols. 240v–241v).

129. Schurz, *The Manila Galleon*, 181.

130. Herlinda Ruiz Martínez, "Entre proyectos de ingeniería militar e Inquisición. Adrián Boot en Nueva España (1615–1640)," *Boletín del Archivo General de la Nación* 7 (2021): 203.

131. Timothy Brook, *Vermeer's Hat: The Seventeenth Century and the Dawn of the Global World* (New York: Bloomsbury, 2008), 176.

132. "Caja de Acapulco," 1616, AGI, Contaduría, 904, fol. 480.

133. Pérez-Mallaína, *Spain's Men of the Sea*, 105.

134. "Orden de limitar el equipaje de los marineros en las naos," 1608, AGI, Filipinas, 340, L.3, fols. 42v–43r.

135. "Carta de Corcuera sobre visita obispo, naos a Acapulco," 1636, AGI, Filipinas, 8, R.3, N.37.

136. "Capítulo de carta del virrey sobre derechos en naos," 1639, AGI, Filipinas, 8, R.4, N.115.

137. "Orden sobre trato a marineros en Acapulco," 1678, AGI, Filipinas, 341, L.7, fols. 309v–310v.

138. "Estrema necesidad" ("Orden de pagar a marineros y pilotos," 1660, AGI, Filipinas, 341, L.6, fols. 239r–240v).

139. "Llega la persecui[ci]on de los puertos aun a los difuntos" ("Orden de pagar a marineros y pilotos," 1660, AGI, Filipinas, 341, L.6, fols. 239r–240v). See also "Orden de pagar a marineros de las naos de Filipinas, 1677, AGI, Filipinas, 341, L.7, fols. 231v–233r.

140. Giovanni Francesco Gemelli Careri, *Viaje a Nueva España*, trans. Francisca Perujo (Mexico City: Universidad Nacional Autónoma de México, 1983), 8. This official salary is probably an underestimate.

141. Navarrete, *Tratados*, 298. Alex Mayfield has since shown that, in Nahuatl, it means "where the reeds were destroyed or washed away" ("Galleons from the 'Mouth of Hell,'" 221–222).

142. "Una fuentecilla muy tenue, que apenas echa un hilo de agua, que le llaman el Chorrillo, que para llenar vna botija, es menester dos horas" (Cubero Sebastián, *Peregrinacion del Mvndo*, 389).

143. "Esto es lo que tiene el celebrado puerto de Acapulco" (Cubero Sebastián, *Peregrinacion del Mvndo*, 389).

144. "En cuanto a la ciudad de Acapulco, me parece que debiera dársele más bien el nombre de humilde aldea de pescadores (tan bajas y ruines son sus casas, hechas de madera, barro y paja) que el engañoso de primer emporio del mar del Sur y escala de la China" (Careri, *Viaje a Nueva España*, 7).

145. Carletti, *My Voyage around the World*, 56.

146. On desertion and mutiny in the Spanish Pacific, see Stephanie Mawson, "Rebellion and Mutiny in the Mariana Islands, 1680–1690," *Journal of Pacific History* 50, no. 2 (2015): 129–130.

147. "Se desaniman de todo punto para no volver" ("Orden sobre vejaciones en Acapulco a gente de Filipinas," 1633, AGI, Filipinas, 340, L.3, fols. 460v–461v).

148. Furlong, "Peasants, Servants, and Sojourners," 313.

149. "Caja de Acapulco," 1606, AGI, Contaduría, 902.

150. Olveda, "El Puerto de la Navidad," 120; Edward R. Slack Jr., "The Chinos in New Spain: A Corrective Lens for a Distorted Image," *Journal of World History* 20, no. 1 (2009): 39–40; Oropeza, *La migración asiática*, 168 and 172; Sebastián de Pineda, "Petición de Sebastián de Pineda de puesto en la armada que va a Filipinas," 1619, AGI, Filipinas, 38, N.12.

151. Oropeza, *La migración asiática*, 169 and 171.

152. "Lo apetecen mas que el bino que ba de españa" (Sebastián de Pineda, "Petición de Sebastián de Pineda de puesto en la armada que va a Filipinas," 1619, AGI, Filipinas, 38, N.12).

153. "Los enbarquen y buelban a ellas y que los palmares . . . con que hace esto se queme = y las palmas se corten" (Sebastián de Pineda, "Petición de Sebastián de Pineda de puesto en la armada que va a Filipinas," 1619, AGI, Filipinas, 38, N.12).

154. Alberto Carrillo Cázares, *Partidos y padrones del obispado de Michoacán: 1680–1685* (Zamora, Spain: El Colegio de Michoacán, 1996), 381; Oropeza, *La migración asiática*, 13.

155. Oropeza, *La migración asiática*, 177–178.

156. "Sube de chino en las palmas" (quoted in Oropeza, *La migración asiática*, 184).

157. Claudia Paulina Machuca Chávez, "Cabildo, negociación y vino de cocos: El caso de la villa de Colima en el siglo XVII," *Anuario de Estudios Americanos* 66, no. 1 (2009): 177 and 184–185; Cázares, *Partidos y padrones*, 336–390.

158. "Orden sobre trato a pasajeros y marineros en las naos," 1620, AGI, Filipinas, 340, L.3, fols. 256r–v; "Orden sobre trato a marineros y pasajeros en las naos," 1620, AGI, Filipinas, 340, L.3, fols. 268r–v.

159. "Petición del Cabildo secular de Manila sobre mal trato a pasajeros," 1633, AGI, Filipinas, 27, N.158; "Petición del Cabildo secular de Manila sobre dar buen trato a marineros," AGI, Filipinas, 27, N.166; "Orden de favorecer marineros de la carrera de Filipinas," 1638, AGI, Filipinas, 340, L.4, fols. 138v–140v; Giráldez, *The Age of Trade*, 140.

160. "Capítulo de carta del virrey sobre derechos en naos," 1639, AGI, Filipinas, 8, R.4, N. 115.

161. Giráldez, *The Age of Trade*, 142.

162. "Se experimentan los mismos perjuicios," AGI, Filipinas, 28, N.91, fol. 733r.

163. See James Lockhart, *We People Here: Nahuatl Accounts of the Conquest of Mexico* (Berkeley: University of California Press, 1993).

164. Matthew Restall, *When Montezuma Met Cortés: The True Story of the Meeting That Changed History* (New York: HarperCollins, 2018), 273–274.

165. Restall, *When Montezuma Met Cortés*, 275–276.

166. One of the most unusual and elaborate plans to conquer China would have had troops departing from Guatemala in the 1580s. See José Antonio Cervera, "Los planes españoles para conquistar China a través de Nueva España y Centroamérica en el siglo XVI," *Cuadernos de Intercambio sobre Centroamérica y el Caribe* 10, no. 12 (2013): 207–234; François Chevalier, *Land and Society in Colonial Mexico: The Great Hacienda*, trans. Alvin Eustis (Berkeley: University of California Press, 1963), 38; Oropeza, *La migración asiática*, 14–15.

167. Reséndez, *Conquering the Pacific*, 40.

168. Reséndez, *Conquering the Pacific*, 140, 159, and 162; Salvador Bernabéu and José María García Redondo, "Mapas trastornados: Análisis histórico-visual de los derroteros del galeón de Manila en el siglo XVIII," in *Nueva España, puerta americana al Pacífico asiático*, ed. Carmen Yuste López (Mexico City: Universidad Nacional Autónoma de México, 2019), 159–160.

169. Andrés Reséndez, *The Other Slavery: The Uncovered Story of Indian Enslavement in America* (Boston: Houghton Mifflin Harcourt, 2016), 13–17, 99, and 100–115.

170. Schwaller, *Géneros de Gente*, 18.

171. Stuart B. Schwartz, *Blood and Boundaries: The Limits of Religious and Racial Exclusion in Early Modern Latin America* (Waltham, MA: Brandeis University Press, 2020), 9.

172. Schwartz, *Blood and Boundaries*, 82.

173. Sierra Silva, *Urban Slavery*, 30.

174. Dana Murillo, *Urban Indians in a Silver City: Zacatecas, Mexico, 1546–1810* (Stanford, CA: Stanford University Press, 2016), 55. According to Lane Fargher, Richard Blanton, and Verenice Heredia Espinoza, "an altepetl is defined by two basic features: a dynastic ruler (*tlatoani*) and corporate landholding groups (*calpulli*) that formed subdivisions of the altepetl" ("Egalitarian Ideology and Political Power in Prehispanic Central Mexico: The Case of Tlaxcallan," *Latin American Antiquity* 21, no. 3 [2010]: 232).

175. Murillo, *Urban Indians*, 55–110.

176. Miguel A. Valerio, "The Spanish Petition System, Hospital / ity, and the Formation of a Mulato Community in Sixteenth-Century Mexico," *Americas* 78, no. 3 (2021): 417–418.

177. According to Francisco de Solano in 1743, royal accounting records once covered the decades preceding 1590 as well, but "the land does not permit the survival of the papers that could illuminate [this period] . . . because in twenty years the moth or woodworm of the termite devours them." Francisco de Solano, *Relaciones geográficas del Arzobispado de México. 1743* (Madrid: Consejo Superior de Investigaciones Científicas, 1988), 1:24; "Caja de Acapulco," 1590–1592, AGI, Contaduría, 897. In 1590, the *Nuestra Señora de la Asunción* landed in Acapulco from Goa via Macau with a crew of forty lascars who were also described as "negros arabios" (Black Arabs). Those who converted to Christianity were permitted to stay in Acapulco after the ship left in 1591. Oropeza, *La migración asiática*, 115–116.

178. "Carta del virrey Diego Fernández de Córdoba, marqués de Guadalcázar," 1616, AGI, México, 28, N.33, fol. 4.

179. Seijas, *Asian Slaves*, 6; Schwaller, *Géneros de Gente*, 52–58.

180. Edward R. Slack Jr., "New Perspectives on Manila's Chinese Community at the Turn of the Eighteenth Century: The Forgotten Case of Pedro Barredo, Alcalde Mayor of the Parián 1701–1704," *Journal of Chinese Overseas* 17 (2021): 120–121. One of the few examples of "Sangley" appearing in the Americas is in Don Domingo de San Antón Muñón Chimalpahin Quauhtlehuanitzin, *Annals of His Time: Don Domingo de San Antón Muñón Chimalpahin Quauhtlehuanitzin*, ed. and trans. James Lockhart, Susan Schroeder, and Doris Namala (Stanford, CA: Stanford University Press, 2006). In 1605, news arrived in Mexico of the 1603 uprising. Chimalpahin Quauhtlehuanitzin reported that "not very many Spaniards died, but there were a great many more of the people there, the indigenous [macehualtzin] inhabitants called Sangleyes, who died and were killed" (89). In Nahuatl, he used "Sangreyes" for "Sangleyes," and this use demonstrates the journey of a loanword from Hokkien to Tagalog, Spanish, and finally Nahuatl.

181. "Nombre ussa abusibam.te y no con propiedad pues llaman así y expresan con este nombre a los yndios de las yslas filipinas que están muy distantes de la gran china cuyos moradores son los que propiam.te se deben llamar chinos y no los filipinenses que obserban distintos ritos y diferentes dogmas" (quoted in "Cartas de Audiencia," 1675, AGI, México, 82, R.2, N.51, fol. 2r). This exceptional description is all the more significant given that Miranda had arrived in Mexico only in 1671 and used this definition to question the broad applicability of emancipatory orders freeing "chinos" from bondage.

182. "Los indios nacidos en las islas filipinas como son japones, tartaros, malucos, sangleyes, mindanaos, vengalas, macasares, malayos, y de otras naciones . . . juntos y sercanos de la mayor ysla la gran china de que se enformaron el nombre en esta nueba españa y aun toda europa" (quoted in "Cartas de Audiencia," 1675, AGI, México, 82, R.2, N.51, fol. 3v).

183. "Los que por vía de las islas Filipinas vienen a estas partes desde el Oriente" (Ramos, *Los prodigios*, 1:88).

184. Pedro de Medina, *Libro de grandezas y cosas memorables de España* (Seville, Spain: En casa de Dominico de Robertis, 1549), JCBL, 21r.

185. Geraldine Heng, *The Invention of Race in the European Middle Ages* (New York: Cambridge University Press, 2018), 111.

186. Reséndez, *Conquering the Pacific*, 45.

187. Colín, *Labor evangélica*, 2.

188. Ricardo Padrón, *The Indies of the Setting Sun: How Early Modern Spain Mapped the Far East as the Transpacific West* (Chicago: University of Chicago Press, 2020), 32, 145, and 151–153; Reséndez, *Conquering the Pacific*, 129.

189. Navarrete, *Tratados*, 1–2.

190. "Chung Kue; esto es, Reyno de en medio" (Navarrete, *Tratados*, 2).

191. "Parecía mas negro que mulato" (quoted in "Proceso y causa criminal contra un chino esclavo de don Pedro, el abogado, por reniegos," 1665, AGN, Inquisición, vol. 600, exp. 23, fols. 422–428).

192. "Porque como paresse de mi cara . . . y facciones son de chino y no de mulato ni otro genero de esclavos" (quoted in "Autos sobre libertad promovidos por Domingo de la Cruz, chino y esclavo natural de Manila, contra Juan Sánchez Bañales vecino de Zapotlán," 1678, Archivo Real de la Audiencia de Nueva Galicia [ARANG], Caja 9, Exp. 9, Prog. 124, fol. 1r).

193. "En breve tiempo se fueron poco a poco secando y consumiendo sus carnes, y se mudaron las facciones de su rostro. Se enturbió el cabello y se achinó el color del rostro, de suerte que más parecía vieja, que niña; mas fea, que hermosa; mas retostada china, que blanca y rubia mogora; mas india avellanada de las muy tostadas del Occidente, que blanca y hermosa Oriental de los confines de la feliz Arabia" (Ramos, *Los prodigios*, 1:315). For more on miraculous changes in skin tones, see Erin Kathleen Rowe, "After Death, Her Face Turned White: Blackness, Whiteness, and Sanctity in the Early Modern Hispanic World," *American Historical Review* 121, no. 3 (2016): 727–754.

194. "Caja de Acapulco," 1615, AGI, Contaduría, 903, fols. 149–318.

195. "Caja de Acapulco," 1615, AGI, Contaduría, 903, fols. 28–107.

196. "Caja de Acapulco," 1600, AGI, Contaduría, 901, fols. 133v–277v.

197. Quoted in Oropeza, *La migración asiática*, 13.

198. "Caja de Acapulco," 1631, AGI, Contaduría, 905, fol. 35v.

199. "Caja de Acapulco," 1632, AGI, Contaduría, 905, fol. 80v.

200. "Marcos Garcia," AGN, 1608, Indiferente Virreinal, Caja 3724, exp. 022.

201. Oropeza, *La migración asiática*, 124.

202. "Caja de Acapulco," 1615, AGI, Contaduría, 903, fols. 217–218. Elen's salary of 171 pesos was also the standard rate paid to drummers from New Spain serving in the Philippines.

Several other "chinos" had similarly long records of service on the treasury payroll, including the logger Martín Pérez (1616–1636), the carpenter Francisco Encan (1599–1632), and the warehouse worker Pedro de la Cruz (1653–1679). Diego Javier Luis, "Galleon Anxiety: How Afro-Mexican Women Shaped Colonial Spirituality in Acapulco," *Americas* 78, no. 3 (2021): 408; Oropeza, *La migración asiática*, 130.

203. "Se tasso por ser chino" ("Caja de Acapulco," 1616, AGI, Contaduría, 904, fol. 378).

204. "Caja de Acapulco," 1616, AGI, Contaduría, 904, fol. 377.

205. Mayfield, "Galleons from the 'Mouth of Hell,'" 231 and 234; Luis, "Galleon Anxiety," 389–401.

206. Furlong, "Peasants, Servants, and Sojourners," 443.

207. "Grande ofensa" and "no los conocen se casan otra bez" ("Petición de Sebastián de Pineda de puesto en la armada que va a Filipinas," 1619, AGI, Filipinas, 38, N.12).

208. "Proceso y causa criminal contra Baltazar Mechor, chino, por casado dos veces," 1669, AGN, Inquisición, vol. 612, exp. 4. Although I use "citizen" to translate *vecino*, I share Dana Murillo's concern about the inadequacy of this word: "In many areas of New Spain *vecindad* was neither formal nor official and hence not legally restricted to Spaniards. Rather it was implicit, secured by the mere circumstance of birth for some and granted to others over time and through social consensus. Individuals earned vecindad by staying for long periods (officially around ten years, but often much less in practice), paying their taxes, and actively participating in community and civic life (for men that could entail attending town meetings and holding office). While the conditions of vecindad varied from one location to another, nothing prevented Indians (or Afro-descended peoples, for that matter) from meeting these residency and municipal requirements" (*Urban Indians*, 8).

209. Michelle A. McKinley, "The Unbearable Lightness of Being (Black): Legal and Cultural Constructions of Race and Nation in Colonial Latin America," in *Racial Formation in the Twenty-First Century*, ed. Daniel Martínez Hosang, Oneka LaBennett, and Laura Pulido (Berkeley: University of California Press, 2012), 135.

3. Merchants and Gunslingers

1. D. A. Brading, *Miners and Merchants in Bourbon Mexico 1763–1810* (New York: Cambridge University Press, 1971), 15.

2. "De los mas asperos, que he andado en mi vida, porque no ay otra cosa, que barrancos, montes, peñascos, y despeñaderos, de los mas profundos, que ay en el mundo: y puedo asegurar, que lo que es hasta llegar a Trisco, es vno de los mas asperos caminos de todos quantos he caminado" (Pedro Cubero Sebastián, *Peregrinacion del Mvndo* [Naples: Carlos Porfile, 1682], 391). "Trisco" must refer to Tixtla and not Atrixco (a town not on the route to Mexico City), in the present-day state of Guerrero.

3. Francisco Colín, *Labor evangélica, ministerios apostólicos de los obreros de la Compañía de Iesvs, fvndacion, y progresos de sv provincia en las islas Filipinas* (Madrid: por Ioseph Fernandez de Buendia, 1663), 640.

4. "Este camino si, que es malo, y trabajoso, montes hasta las nubes, asperos quanto se puede dezir; rios caudalosos . . . supongo que no ay puentes, mosquitos si, y muchos, y Caribes, quanto se puede dezir; algunas noches se duerme a las Estrellas" (Domingo Fernández Navarrete, *Tratados historicos, politicos, ethicos, y religiosos de la monarchia de china* [Madrid: Imprenta Real, 1676], 297).

5. Giovanni Francesco Gemelli Careri, *Viaje a Nueva España*, trans. Francisca Perujo (Mexico City: Universidad Nacional Autónoma de México, 1983), 16.

6. Careri, *Viaje a Nueva España*, 19.

7. "Es de los rios mas temidos de toda la nueua España, por auerse tragado tantos hombres" (Cubero Sebastián, *Peregrinacion del Mvndo*, 392).

8. "Causa grima, el ver aquella armazón tan ridícula" (Navarrete, *Tratados*, 297).

9. Francesco Carletti, *My Voyage around the World: The Chronicles of a 16th Century Florentine Merchant*, trans. Herbert Weinstock (New York: Pantheon Books, 1964), 57.

10. Careri, *Viaje a Nueva España*, 13–19; Carletti, *My Voyage Around the World*, 60. Tatiana Seijas notes that these inns (owned by Afro-Mexican or Indigenous people) tended to be costly because of the requirements of repartimiento labor, but they provided desperately needed supplies and even pulque ("Inns, Mules, and Hardtack for the Voyage: The Local Economy of the Manila Galleon in Mexico," *Colonial Latin American Review* 25, no. 1 (2016): 65–66). See also Sarah E. Owens, "Crossing Mexico (1620–1621): Franciscan Nuns and Their Journey to the Philippines," *Americas* 72, no. 4 (2015): 595.

11. Careri, *Viaje a Nueva España*, 9 and 13.

12. Navarrete, *Tratados*, 297–298.

13. Meha Priyadarshini, *Chinese Porcelain in Colonial Mexico: The Material Worlds of an Early Modern Trade* (Cham, Switzerland: Palgrave Macmillan, 2018), 8.

14. "Que el norte enfría ni que el sol calienta" (Bernardo de Balbuena, *Grandeza mexicana* [Mexico City: Diego Lopez Daualos, 1604], fol. 76r; see also fol. 73v).

15. "Y de Terrenate / Clauo fino, y canela de Tidoro. / De Cambray telas, de Quinsay rescate. . . . De la gran China sedas de colores" (Balbuena, *Grandeza mexicana*, 75–76). "Quinsay" is today's Hangzhou (杭州) in Zhejiang (浙江) province. Chinese silks predominantly came from Jiangnan (江南) and around Lake Tai (太湖). Most of the pottery came from Jingdezhen (景德镇) workshops. Ubaldo Iaccarino, "The 'Galleon System' and Chinese Trade in Manila at the Turn of the 16th Century," *Ming Qing Yanjiu* 16 (2011): 120.

16. Stephanie Merrim, *The Spectacular City, Mexico, and Colonial Hispanic Literary Culture* (Austin: University of Texas Press, 2010), 102.

17. Thomas Gage, *A New Survey of the West-Indies: Or, The English American His Travel by Sea and Land* (London: A. Clark, 1677), 123.

18. "Los hermanos de San Francisco, que se llama procesión de los chinos, por ser de indios de Filipinas. Cada una llevaba sus estatuas, con cantidad de luces, y una compañía de hombres armados, en el modo referido antes, además de algunos que iban a caballos, precedidos por trompetas lúgubres. Llegada la procesión al palacio real, entablaron contienda por la precedencia los chinos y los hermanos de la Santísima Trinidad, de modo que se dieron con las mazas y con las cruces en las espaldas de tal manera que muchos quedaron heridos" (Careri, *Viaje a Nueva España*, 73). The fact that the "chinos" were the brothers

of San Francisco is noteworthy because San Francisco's Saint Day in the Philippines was a public holiday, being the day that the Chinese pirate Limahong's attack on Manila was foiled. The San Francisco church in Mexico City was also a significant living and documentary archive of Indigenous knowledge production. Susan Schroeder, "Chimalpahin and Why Women Matter in History," in *Indigenous Intellectuals: Knowledge, Power, and Colonial Culture in Mexico and the Andes,* ed. Gabriela Ramos and Yanna Yannakakis (Durham, NC: Duke University Press, 2014), 108.

19. "Lunes 2, ahorcaron dos hombres, un chino y un mulato" (Antonio de Robles, *Diarios de sucesos notables [1665–1703]* [Mexico City: Editorial Porrúa, 1946], 1:298).

20. "Embustera" (Alonso Ramos, *Los prodigios de la Omnipotencia y milagros de la gracia en la vida de la venerable sierva de Dios Catarina de San Juan,* ed. Gisela von Wobeser [Mexico City: Universidad Nacional Autónoma de México-Instituto de Investigaciones Históricas, 2017], 2:13).

21. "Fidelidad" (Joseph del Castillo Graxeda, *Compendio de la vida, y virtudes de la venerable Catharina de San Juan* [Puebla, Mexico: Imprenta de Diego Fernandez de Leon, 1692], 20).

22. Edward R. Slack Jr., "Orientalizing New Spain: Perspectives on Asian Influence in Colonial Mexico," *México y la Cuenca del Pacífico* 15, no. 43 (2012): 125. Interestingly, in an earlier article, Slack had acknowledged that "chinos" experienced a wide range of racializing experiences in colonial Mexico ("The Chinos in New Spain: A Corrective Lens for a Distorted Image," *Journal of World History* 20, no. 1 [2009]: 25–67).

23. Melba Falck Reyes and Héctor Palacios, *El japonés que conquistó Guadalajara: La historia de Juan de Páez en la Guadalajara del siglo XVII* (Guadalajara, Mexico: Universidad de Guadalajara, 2009), 122.

24. Buschmann, Slack, and Tueller, *Navigating the Spanish Lake,* 95–96.

25. Lisa Sun-Hee Park, "Continuing Significance of the Model Minority Myth: The Second Generation," *Social Justice* 35, no. 2 (2008): 134–144.

26. Yoonmee Chang, "Asian Americans, Disability, and the Model Minority Myth," in *Flashpoints for Asian American Studies,* ed. Cathy Schlund-Vials (New York: Fordham University Press, 2018), 244.

27. For more on the model minority, see Erika Lee, *The Making of Asian America: A History* (New York: Simon and Schuster, 2016), 374–375.

28. Stanley J. Stein and Barbara H. Stein, *The Colonial Heritage of Latin America: Essays on Economic Dependence in Perspective* (New York: Oxford University Press, 1970), 118.

29. Edgar Llinás, "The Issue of Autonomy in the Royal and Pontifical University of Mexico," *Revista de Historia de América* 112 (1991): 111–119.

30. The famed bishop Juan de Palafox y Mendoza authored this statute in 1645, and the crown confirmed it in 1668. Déborah Oropeza, *La migración asiática en el virreinato de la Nueva España: Un proceso de globalización (1565–1700)* (Mexico City: El Colegio de México, 2020), 265.

31. Brian P. Owensby, *Empire of Law and Indian Justice in Colonial Mexico* (Stanford, CA: Stanford University Press, 2008), 1.

32. Camilla Townsend, *Fifth Sun: A New History of the Aztecs* (New York: Oxford University Press, 2019), 192–193.

33. Rubén Carrillo Martín, *Las gentes del mar Sangley* (Mexico City: Palabra de Clío, 2015), 112–116.

34. Tatiana Seijas, *Asian Slaves in Colonial Mexico: From Chinos to Indians* (New York: Cambridge University Press, 2014), 3–4.

35. Norah L. A. Gharala, *Taxing Blackness: Free Afromexican Tribute in Bourbon New Spain* (Tuscaloosa: University of Alabama Press, 2019), 5 and 33; Robert C. Schwaller, *Géneros de Gente in Early Colonial Mexico: Defining Racial Difference* (Norman: University of Oklahoma Press, 2016), 56–57. On the inaptness of the "Two Republics" model to describe the Spanish governance of Indigenous communities, see also Adrian Masters, "The Two, the One, the Many, the None: Rethinking the Republics of Spaniards and Indians in the Sixteenth-Century Spanish Indies," *The Americas* 78, no. 1 (2021): 3–36.

36. For more on the social politics of the "indio / a chino / a" label, see Oropeza, *La migración asiática*, 91–93; Seijas, *Asian Slaves*, 6.

37. Seijas, *Asian Slaves*, 4 and 147–148.

38. The *"cabecera-sujeto* system" of tribute emerged during the decades of the 1550s and 1560s (Charles Gibson, *The Aztecs under Spanish Rule: A History of the Indians of the Valley of Mexico, 1519–1810* [Stanford, CA: Stanford University Press, 1964], 33). See also Seijas, *Asian Slaves*, 147; Owensby, *Empire of Law,* 28.

39. Gharala, *Taxing Blackness*, 5 and 33; Seijas, *Asian Slaves*, 4–6.

40. "Caja de Acapulco," 1640, Archivo General de Indias (AGI), Contaduría, 905A, fols. 443r–v; Gibson, *The Aztecs under Spanish Rule*, 205.

41. Georgina Flores García et al., eds., *Catálogo y estudio introductorio de la presencia de las personas de origen africano y afrodescendientes durante los siglos XVI y XVII en la valle de Toluca* (Toluca, Mexico: Universidad Autónoma del Estado de México, 2017), 466.

42. However, these taxes were notoriously difficult to collect and "were not generally reciprocated [fiscally or in property] as they were for the much more common Indian pueblos" (Gharala, *Taxing Blackness*, 13; see also 31 and 37).

43. Matthew J. Furlong, "Peasants, Servants, and Sojourners: Itinerant Asians in Colonial New Spain, 1571–1720," PhD diss., University of Arizona, 516.

44. "Domingo de Villalobos," 1621, AGI, Contratación, 520, N.2, R.14.

45. See Danielle Terrazas Williams, *The Capital of Free Women: Race, Legitimacy, and Liberty in Colonial Mexico* (New Haven, CT: Yale University Press, 2022), 8.

46. R. Douglas Cope, *The Limits of Racial Domination: Plebeian Society in Colonial Mexico City, 1660–1720* (Madison: University of Wisconsin Press, 1994), 120.

47. Robert C. Schwaller, "'For Honor and Defence': Race and the Right to Bear Arms in Early Colonial Mexico," *Colonial Latin American Review* 21, no. 2 (2012): 261.

48. Owensby, *Empire of Law,* 59.

49. Owensby, *Empire of Law,* 163–164.

50. "Cariblancos" ("Ordenanza contra negros, mestizos, mulatos, chinos y zambaigos," 1647, Archivo General de la Nación México [AGN], Tierras, vol. 2984, exp. 111).

51. "T[iem]po nes[e]s[ari]o" ("Ordenanza contra negros, mestizos, mulatos, chinos y zambaigos").

52. Pablo Sierra Silva, *Urban Slavery in Colonial Mexico: Puebla de los Ángeles, 1531–1706* (Cambridge: Cambridge University Press, 2018), 36; Ben Vinson III, *Bearing Arms for His*

Majesty: The Free-Colored Militia in Colonial Mexico (Stanford, CA: Stanford University Press, 2001), 15, and *Before Mestizaje: The Frontiers of Race and Caste in Colonial Mexico* (New York: Cambridge University Press, 2017), 13.

53. Schwaller, *Géneros de Gente,* 65.

54. Homi Bhabha, "Of Mimicry and Man: The Ambivalence of Colonial Discourse," *October* 28 (1984): 125–133.

55. Manuel Valle Ortiz, "The *Destreza Verdadera:* A Global Phenomenon," in *Late Medieval and Early Modern Fight Books: Transmission and Tradition of Martial Arts in Europe (14th–17th Centuries),* ed. Daniel Jaquent, Karin Verelst, and Timothy Dawson (Boston: Brill, 2016), 325.

56. Kris Lane, ed., *Defending the Conquest: Bernardo de Vargas Machuca's Defense and Discourse of the Western Conquests* (University Park: Penn State University Press, 2010), 108.

57. Since 1592, "indios chinos" had been formally exempted from alcabalas unless they sold silks. Edward R. Slack Jr., "Sinifying New Spain: Cathay's Influence on Colonial Mexico via the *Nao de China," Journal of Chinese Overseas* 5, no. 1 (2009): 12, and "The Chinos in New Spain," 47–48; Ann Twinam, *Purchasing Whiteness: Pardos, Mulattos, and the Quest for Social Mobility in the Spanish Indies* (Stanford, CA: Stanford University Press, 2015), 103–104 and 114; Gharala, *Taxing Blackness,* 25; Seijas, *Asian Slaves,* 153; Oropeza, *La migración asiática,* 221.

58. Schwaller, "'For Honor and Defence,'" 252.

59. Miguel Valerio, "The Spanish Petition System, Hospital / ity, and the Formation of a Mulato Community in Sixteenth-Century Mexico," *Americas* 78, no. 3 (2021): 418–419 and 427–429. The alleged Gil Ávila-Martín Cortés conspiracy was an outgrowth of the tension of the New Laws of 1542, which outlawed perpetual encomienda inheritance. See also Matthew Restall, "Black Conquistadors: Armed Africans in Early Spanish America," *Americas* 57, no. 2 (2000): 171.

60. Twinam, *Purchasing Whiteness,* 104.

61. Twinam, *Purchasing Whiteness,* 104.

62. Joanne Rappaport, "'Asi lo paresçe por su aspecto': Physiognomy and the Construction of Difference in Colonial Bogotá," *Hispanic American Historical Review* 91, no. 4 (2011): 621.

63. Kathryn Burns, "Unfixing Race," in *Histories of Race and Racism: The Andes and Mesoamerica from Colonial Times to the Present,* ed. Laura Gotkowitz (Durham, NC: Duke University Press, 2012), 199–201.

64. Vinson, *Bearing Arms for His Majesty,* 15, and *Before Mestizaje,* 13.

65. "Juan Alonso," 1591, AGN, Indios, vol. 6a, exp. 1200.

66. "No se deue practicar con el d[ich]o orden," ("Juan Alonso," 1597, AGN, Indios, vol. 61, exp. 1202).

67. Schwaller, *Géneros de Gente,* 54. See also Owensby, *Empire of Law,* 46.

68. Oropeza, *La migración asiática,* 225–226.

69. Townsend, *Fifth Sun,* 183–184.

70. "Melchior de los Reyes portar espada y daga," 1610, AGN, Indiferente Virreinal, Caja 5713, exp. 057 (General de Parte Caja 5713).

71. Miguel A. Valerio, *Sovereign Joy: Afro-Mexican Kings and Queens, 1539–1640* (New York: Cambridge University Press, 2022), 82. See also María Elena Martínez, "The Black

Blood of New Spain: Limpieza de Sangre, Racial Violence, and Gendered Power in Early Colonial Mexico," *William and Mary Quarterly* 61, no. 3 (2004): 506.

72. Don Domingo de San Antón Muñón Chimalpahin Quauhtlehuanitzin, *Annals of His Time: Don Domingo de San Antón Muñón Chimalpahin Quauhtlehuanitzin*, ed. and trans. James Lockhart, Susan Schroeder, and Doris Namala (Stanford, CA: Stanford University Press, 2006), 218.

73. Valerio, *Sovereign Joy,* 115–119.

74. Townsend, *Fifth Sun,* 186–188.

75. "Don Balthazar de San Francisco indio chino traer espada y daga," 1612, AGN, Indiferente Virreinal, Caja 6422, exp. 086 (Indios Caja 6422).

76. "Chino libre de nación bengala" ("Francisco de Lima petición portar daga, espada y arcabuz," 1653, AGN, Indiferente Virreinal, Caja 6032, exp. 107). Tamar Herzog writes that despite variations in space and over time, "by the seventeenth and eighteenth centuries, the *vecindad* status . . . came to imply a wide range of fiscal, economic, political, social, and symbolic benefits in return for the fulfillment of certain duties" (*Defining Nations: Immigrants and Citizens in Early Modern Spain and Spanish America* [New Haven, CT: Yale University Press, 2003], 6).

77. Brading, *Miners and Merchants,* 98.

78. For more on the constructed nature of the term *Chichimeca,* see Charlotte M. Gradie, "Discovering the Chichimecas," *Americas* 51, no. 1 (1994): 68–69.

79. Schwaller, "'For Honor and Defence,'" 257.

80. Schwaller, *Géneros de Gente,* 204.

81. Dana Murillo, *Urban Indians in a Silver City: Zacatecas, Mexico, 1546–1810* (Stanford, CA: Stanford University Press, 2016), 31.

82. I have not been able to locate any documentation of that ordinance in the AGN.

83. François Chevalier, *Land and Society in Colonial Mexico: The Great Hacienda,* trans. Alvin Eustis (Berkeley: University of California Press, 1963), 290.

84. Chevalier, *Land and Society in Colonial Mexico,* 321–322.

85. "Despoblado" ("Juan de Lima," 1693, AGN, Procesos civiles, caja 92, exp. 3262).

86. "Ornato de su persona" ("Juan Tello de Guzman chino libre portar espada y daga," 1651, AGN, Indios, vol. 19, exp. 172).

87. "Hombre quieto y pacifico y que vive onrradam[en]te" ("Juan Tello de Guzman chino libre portar espada y daga," 1651, AGN, Indios, vol. 19, exp. 172).

88. "Marcos de Villanueva chino libre traer espada y daga," 1654, AGN, Indios, vol. 7, exp. 19 BIS.

89. Chimalpahin Quauhtlehuanitzin, *Annals of His Time,* 173.

90. "Real cédula a Martín Enríquez, virrey de Nueva España, ordenando que informe y envíe su parecer sobre el puerto que se utiliza en el Mar del Sur, para el carga y descarga de los navíos que van a las islas de Poniente, que calidad tiene y que distancia hay al puerto de Veracruz, y sobre los demás puertos de la Mar del Sur: Guatulco, Tehuantepeque y las Salinas, por si fuera conveniente mudarse," 1571, AGI, Mexico, 1090, L.6, fols. 358v–59r.

91. Reyes and Palacios, *El japonés que conquistó Guadalajara,* 16.

92. Nahui Ollin Vázquez Mendoza, "Huatulco, Oaxaca: Fragmentos de una historia colonial de abandonos y melancolías," *Relaciones* 134 (2013): 169; "Francisco de Cardenas usar arcabuz," 1644, AGN, Reales Cédulas Originales y Duplicados, vol. 48, exp. 327.

93. Lourdes de Ita, "Los viajes de circunnavegación de Francis Drake y Thomas Cavendish y su paso por el Pacífico novohispano, 1577–1588," in *Relaciones intercoloniales: Nueva España y Filipinas*, ed. Jaime Olveda (Zapopan, Mexico: El Colegio de Jalisco, 2017), 40.

94. See Terrazas Williams, *The Capital of Free Women*, 28.

95. "Fue persona de calidad" (quoted in "Hijos de Juan de la Barranca," 1666, AGN, Indios, vol. 24, exp. 21).

96. "Por sus particulares fines" ("Hijos de Juan de la Barranca").

97. The "chino" barbers are often thought to have been Chinese, given that "Sangleyes" filled the positions in most medicinal trades in the Philippines and harking back to Juan de Medina's assertion that Chinese doctors were more skilled than Spanish ones (Juan de Medina, *Historia de los sucesos de la Orden de N. Gran P. S. Agustín de estas islas Filipinas, desde que se descubrieron y se poblaron por los españoles, con las noticias memorables* [Manila: Tipo-Litografía de Chofré y Comp., 1893], 103). However, several barbers received the "indio chino" label or expressly identified themselves as being from the Philippines. These labels, though imprecise, suggest that the "chino" barbers of Mexico City may have been predominantly Philippine Natives, especially since few "Sangleyes" made the Pacific crossing as free migrants.

98. Oropeza, *La migración asiática*, 233–234.

99. Martín, *Las gentes del mar Sangley*, 135.

100. Gibson, *The Aztecs under Spanish Rule*, 399–400.

101. Nancy E. van Deusen, "Beatríz, India's, Lawsuit for Freedom from Slavery (Castile, Spain, 1558–1574)," in *Women in Colonial Latin America, 1526 to 1806: Texts and Contexts*, ed. Nora E. Jaffary and Jane E. Mangan (Indianapolis, IN: Hackett Publishing Company, 2018), 20.

102. "Siete del cuello arriba en la cabeza y diez en los brazos, y ocho en las piernas" (Alonso López de Hinojoso, *Summa y recopilacion de cirvgia, con vn arte para sangrar, y examen de barberos, compvesto por maestre Alonso Lopez de Hinojoso* [Mexico City: En casa de Pedro Balli, 1595], 88v).

103. Hinojoso, *Summa y recopilacion de cirvgia*, 91r.

104. "Francisco Antonio chino barbero," 1625, AGN, Indiferente Virreinal, Caja 3303, exp. 008 (Real Audiencia Caja 3303).

105. Martín, *Las gentes del mar Sangley*, 134–135.

106. "Gonzalo de la Mota chino barbero," 1639, AGN, Indiferente Virreinal, Caja 5795, exp. 055 (General de Parte Caja 5795); "Silvestre Vicente barbero," 1642, AGN, Indiferente Virreinal, Caja 6057, exp. 039 (General de Parte Caja 6057); "Antonio de la Cruz barbero," 1643, AGN, General de Parte, vol. 9, exp. 116.

107. This Juan Agustin may be the same "agustin chino barbero" living in the San Agustín neighborhood to whom Francisca Tereza fled in 1634. Tereza was married to Juan Peres, a "chino" and vecino of Mexico City, which further suggests shared social networks across the

"chino" communities of the viceregal capital. "Petición de Juan Peres," 1634, AGN, Indiferente Virreinal, exp. 029; "Francisco Velez indio chino libre tienda de barbero," 1649, AGN, Indios, vol. 15, cuaderno 2, exp. 86; "Pedro de Asquetta," 1648, AGN, Indios, vol. 15, exp. 29; "Juan Agustin," 1648, Indios, vol. 15, exp. 28; "Juan Agustin," 1648, AGN, Indios, vol. 15, exp. 62.

108. Guijo, *Gregorio M. de Guijo diario*, 2:108.

109. Guijo, *Gregorio M. de Guijo diario*, 1:4.

110. "Hernando Garcia contra Lucas de Aguilar," 1667, AGN, Causas criminales, caja 61, exp. 2109.

111. Linda A. Curcio-Nagy, "Native Icon to City Protectress: Ritual Political Symbolism and the Virgin of Remedies," *Americas* 52, no. 3 (1996): 383.

112. "Don Fernando Gaytan de Ayala," 1650, AGN, Arzobispos y Obispos Caja 2247, exp. 046.

113. Furlong, "Peasants, Servants, and Sojourners," 594.

114. "Pedro Ximenes contra Juan Salvador de Baeza barbeos chinos," 1634, AGN, Procesos Civiles, Caja 7, exp. 263.

115. "Francisco de la Cruz contra Lorenzo Lopez chinos barberos," 1634, AGN, Procesos Civiles, Caja 7, exp. 256.

116. José Luis Chong, "The 'Chinese Indians' of the Manila Galleon," in *Return Voyage: The China Galleon and the Baroque in Mexico 1565–1815*, ed. Marina Alfonso Mora and Luis Gerardo Morales Moreno (Mexico City: Gobierno del Estado de Puebla, 2016), 62.

117. Martín, *Las gentes del mar Sangley*, 137–138; Seijas, *Asian Slaves*, 159; Oropeza, *La migración asiática*, 232.

118. Furlong, "Peasants, Servants, and Sojourners," 377.

119. Antonio de Morga, *Svcesos de las islas Filipinas* (Mexico City: En Casa de Geronymo Balli, 1609), 127.

120. "Dixo que este declarante por ser chino y no saber de pleytos" ("Bienes de difuntos: Domingo de Villalobos," 1621–1622, AGI, Contratación, 520, N.2, R.14, fol. 17r).

121. "Por ser indio y en pueblo de indios bastaban" ("Bienes de difuntos," fol. 21v).

122. "Son de una tierra" ("Bienes de difuntos," fol. 156v).

123. Gibson, *The Aztecs under Spanish Rule*, 370.

124. Cope, *The Limits of Racial Domination*, 10; Gibson, *The Aztecs under Spanish Rule*, 371.

125. Oropeza, *La migración asiática*, 217–220.

126. Furlong, "Peasants, Servants, and Sojourners," 554.

127. Furlong, "Peasants, Servants, and Sojourners," 609.

128. Gregorio Martín de Guijo, *Gregorio M. de Guijo, diario, 1648–1664*, ed. Manuel Romero de Terreros (Mexico City: Editorial Porrúa, 1952), 2:42.

129. Guijo, *Gregorio M. de Guijo diario*, 2:114.

130. Gibson, *The Aztecs under Spanish Rule*, 395.

131. "Como natu[rale]s que son" ("Antonio de la Cruz indio chino," 1639, AGN, Indios, vol. 11, exp. 166).

132. Gharala, *Taxing Blackness*, 25. For more on chinos and alcabalas, see Slack, "The Chinos in New Spain," 47–48.

133. Martín, *Las gentes del mar Sangley,* 178.

134. Cope, *The Limits of Racial Domination,* 112 and 120.

135. "Antonio de la Cruz chino libre vender mercaderías," 1661, AGN, Indios, vol. 19, 336.

136. "Natural de la yndia de Portugal" ("Francisco Garcia indio chino vender ropa," 1651, AGN, Indios, vol. 16, exp. 28).

137. Perhaps the most detailed study of the vulnerability of traveling colonial documents is Sylvia Sellers-García, *Distance and Documents at the Spanish Empire's Periphery* (Stanford, CA: Stanford University Press, 2014).

138. "No solo se lo ympiden sino que le causan muchas molestias y amenasas" (quoted in "Antonio de Silva chino vender carne de ganado de cerdo," 1657, AGN, Indios, vol. 21, exp. 220).

139. "Gonzalo Marquez de la Cruz," 1658, AGN, Tierras, vol. 2956, exp. 52.

140. Seijas, *Asian Slaves,* 162.

141. Martín, *Las gentes del mar Sangley,* 119.

142. "Chino y no indio" (quoted in Martín, *Las gentes del mar Sangley,* 126).

143. "Sebastian de la Cruz," 1638, AGN, Fojas sueltas, Caja 331, exp. 10358.

144. "Peticion de Juan Peres," 1634, AGN, Matrimonios Caja 2430, exp. 029.

145. "Personas onrradas" (quoted in "Gonzalo de la Cruz," 1643, AGN, Criminal, vol. 187, exp. 19, fol. 5).

146. In the words of Brian Owensby, "Amparos were the Indians' first and chief recourse in disputes over land. But amparos did not aim to stop Spaniards from accumulating property; they sought only to make sure that Indians not lose land against their will" (*Empire of Law,* 104).

147. "Quieta y pacifica possession" ("Tomas Dominguez," 1677, AGN, Tierras, vol. 2862, exp. 4, fol. 3).

148. "Con fuersa y violencia" ("Tomas Dominguez").

149. Tamar Herzog, *Frontiers of Possession: Spain and Portugal in Europe and the Americas* (Cambridge, MA: Harvard University Press, 2015), 119.

150. Owensby, *Empire of Law,* 117 and 129.

151. Daniel Nemser, *Infrastructures of Race: Concentration and Biopolitics in Colonial Mexico* (Austin: University of Texas Press, 2017), 124.

152. Owensby, *Empire of Law,* 117.

153. "Soldado de batallon" and "e seruido y siruo al rey nro s.or a mi costa y mincion con armas y cauallo como los demas vecinos de aquella jurisdicion" (quoted in "Juan Geronimo," 1654, AGN, Indiferente Virreinal, Caja 4852, exp. 035 [Indios Caja 4852]; "Juan Jeronimo," 1654, AGN, Indios, vol. 17, exp. 40).

4. Contesting Enslavement in New Spain

1. "Ninguna manera" and "chinos ni esclabos" (quoted in "Manuel de la Cruz," 1642, Archivo General de la Nación México [AGN], Tribunal Superior de Justicia de la Ciudad de México, Procesos Civiles, exp. 461).

2. Alonso López de Hinojoso, *Summa y recopilacion de cirvgia, con vn arte para sangrar, y examen de barberos, compvesto por maestre Alonso Lopez de Hinojoso* (Mexico City: En casa de Pedro Balli, 1595), 126v–127v.

3. See Orlando Patterson, *Slavery and Social Death: A Comparative Study, with a New Preface* (Cambridge, MA: Harvard University Press, 2018); Vincent Brown, "Social Death and Political Life in the Study of Slavery," *American Historical Review* 114, no. 5 (2009): 1245; James H. Sweet, "Defying Social Death: The Multiple Configurations of African Slave Family in the Atlantic World," *William and Mary Quarterly* 70, no. 2 (2013): 272.

4. Laurent Dubois, "An Enslaved Enlightenment: Rethinking the Intellectual History of the French Atlantic," *Social History* 31, no. 1 (2006): 3.

5. See Gonzalo Aguirre Beltrán, *Medicina y magia: El proceso de aculturación en la estructura colonial,* 3rd ed. (Mexico City: Instituto Nacional Indigenista, 1987); Solange Alberro, *Inquisición y sociedad en México, 1571–1700* (Mexico City: Fondo de Cultura Económica, 1988), 492–493; Laura A. Lewis, *Hall of Mirrors: Power, Witchcraft, and Caste in Colonial Mexico* (Durham, NC: Duke University Press, 2003), 155.

6. For more on the emancipation of enslaved Africans and descendants of Africans in Mexico, see Dennis N. Valdés, "The Decline of Slavery in Mexico," *Americas* 44, no. 2 (1987): 167–194; Tatiana Seijas, *Asian Slaves in Colonial Mexico: From Chinos to Indians* (New York: Cambridge University Press, 2014), 139 and 223.

7. Homi K. Bhabha, "Introduction: On Disciplines and Destinations," in *Territories and Trajectories: Cultures in Circulation,* ed. Diana Sorensen (Durham, NC: Duke University Press, 2018), 9.

8. Giovanni Levi, "Frail Frontiers?," *Past & Present* 242, no. 14 (2019): 46–48.

9. Daniel Nemser, *Infrastructures of Race: Concentration and Biopolitics in Colonial Mexico* (Austin: University of Texas Press, 2017), 112.

10. Lewis, *Hall of Mirrors,* 152.

11. Ololiuhqui means "a thing that has become round like a ball" and is a species of morning glory (Hernando Ruiz de Alarcón, *Treatise on the Heathen Superstitions and Customs That Today Live among the Indians Native to This New Spain, 1629,* trans. and ed. J. Richard Andrews and Ross Hassig [Norman: University of Oklahoma Press, 1984], 250). See also Cecilia López Ridaura, "Notas sobre la variación en los conceptos de ciencia, superstición y minorías desde el primer Humanismo hasta el Tardobarroco," in *Las minorías: Ciencia y religión, magia y superstición en España y América (siglos XV al XVII),* ed. Rica Amrán (Santa Barbara, CA: eHumanista, 2015), 61; Amos Megged, *Rituals and Sisterhoods: Single Women's Households in Mexico, 1560–1750* (Louisville: University of Colorado Press, 2019), 200.

12. For more on convergence within enslaved communities in the Americas, see Stephanie E. Smallwood, *Saltwater Slavery: A Middle Passage from Africa to American Diaspora* (Cambridge, MA: Harvard University Press, 2008), 2; Matt Schaffer, "Bound to Africa: The Mandinka Legacy in the New World," *History in Africa* 32 (2005): 321–369.

13. For more on the two sides of the debate, see Evelyn Hu-DeHart, "Chinese Contract Labor in the Wake of the Abolition of Slavery in the Americas: A New Form of Slavery or Transition to Free Labor in the Case of Cuba?," *Amerasia Journal* 45, no. 1 (2019):

1–21; Lisa Yun, *The Coolie Speaks: Chinese Indentured Laborers and African Slaves in Cuba* (Philadelphia, PA: Temple University Press, 2008).

14. For a thorough rejection of the historiographical "replacement narrative," see Catherine R. Peters, "Imperatives, Impossibilities, and Intimacies in the Imperial Archive: Chinese Men and Women of Colour in Early Nineteenth-Century Trinidad," *Eighteenth-Century Fiction* 34, no. 2 (2022): 187–205.

15. For an example of the racial implications of this thinking, see James J. O'Kelly, *The Mambi-land, or Adventures of a Herald Correspondent in Cuba* (Philadelphia, PA: J. B. Lippincott, 1874), 53–73.

16. Quoted in Miguel Barnet, *Biography of a Runaway Slave: Fiftieth Anniversary Edition*, trans. W. Nick Hill (Evanston, IL: Northwestern University Press, 2016), 17–18 and 29.

17. See Silvana Testa, "La 'Lucumisation' des cultes d'origine africaine à Cuba: Le cas de Sagua la Grande," *Journal de la Société des américanistes* 91, no. 1 (2005): 120–121; Olga Portuondo Zúñiga, "Virgin of Charity of Cobre, Patron Saint," in *The Cuba Reader: History, Culture, Politics,* ed. Aviva Chomsky, Barry Carr, and Pamela Maria Smorkaloff (Durham, NC: Duke University Press, 2003), 495.

18. Kathleen López, *Chinese Cubans: A Transnational History* (Chapel Hill: University of North Carolina Press, 2013), 90 and 104.

19. Martin Tsang, "Yellow Blindness in a Black and White Ethnoscape: Chinese Influence and Heritage in Afro-Cuban Religiosity," in *Imagining Communities: Asians in the Americas,* ed. Zelideth María Rivas and Debbie Lee-DiStefano (New Brunswick, NJ: Rutgers University Press, 2016), 27, and "La Mulata Achinada: Bodies, Gender, and Authority in Afro-Chinese Religion in Cuba," in *Afro-Asian Connections in Latin America and the Caribbean,* ed. Luisa Marcela Ossa and Debbie Lee-DiStefano (Lanham, MD: Lexington Books, 2019), 218–219.

20. See Lisa Yun, "Introduction: Dethroning the Epics of Empire," in Ossa and Lee-DiStefano, eds., *Afro-Asian Connections,* xiii; Lok Siu, *Memories of a Future Home: Diasporic Citizenship of Chinese in Panama* (Stanford, CA: Stanford University Press, 2005), 201; Daryl J. Maeda, *Chains of Babylon: The Rise of Asian America* (Minneapolis: University of Minnesota Press, 2009), 5; Ossa and Lee-DiStefano, eds., *Afro-Asian Connections.*

21. The central texts in the study of enslaved "chinos" in colonial Mexico are Déborah Oropeza, *La migración asiática en el virreinato de la Nueva España: Un proceso de globalización (1565–1700)* (Mexico City: El Colegio de México, 2020); Seijas, *Asian Slaves;* Rubén Carrillo Martín, *Las gentes del mar Sangley* (Mexico City: Palabra de Clío, 2015); and Lucío de Sousa, *The Portuguese Slave Trade in Early Modern Japan: Merchants, Jesuits and Japanese, Chinese and Korean Slaves* (Boston: Brill, 2019).

22. Martín, *Las gentes del mar Sangley,* 112.

23. See Danielle Terrazas Williams, *The Capital of Free Women: Race, Legitimacy, and Liberty in Colonial Mexico* (New Haven, CT: Yale University Press, 2022), 30.

24. Dana Murillo, *Urban Indians in a Silver City: Zacatecas, Mexico, 1546–1810* (Stanford, CA: Stanford University Press, 2016), 136.

25. Pablo Sierra Silva, *Urban Slavery in Colonial Mexico: Puebla de los Ángeles, 1531–1706* (New York: Cambridge University Press, 2018), 173. Pablo Sierra Silva found that in 1648 a

"chino" confraternity housed in the Santa Veracruz Church of Puebla modeled the funding of its dedicated chapel and burials on a Black confraternity in the same church. Interestingly, the Santa Veracruz Church of Mexico City also housed numerous Afro-Mexican, Indigenous, and "chino" confraternities and administered sacraments to all of these populations (*Urban Slavery*, 173–174). See also Nicole von Germeten, "Black Brotherhoods in Mexico City," in *The Black Urban Atlantic in the Age of the Slave Trade*, ed. Jorge Cañizares-Esguerra, Matt D. Childs, and James Sidbury (Philadelphia: University of Pennsylvania Press, 2013), 254; Edgar F. Love, "Marriage Patterns of Persons of African Descent in a Colonial Mexico City Parish," *Hispanic American Historical Review* 51, no. 1 (1971): 79–91; Martín, *Las gentes del mar Sangley*, 128–129.

26. Seijas, *Asian Slaves*, 209.

27. Irene Silverblatt, *Modern Inquisitions: Peru and the Colonial Origins of the Civilized World* (Durham, NC: Duke University Press, 2004), 17–18.

28. Joan Bristol, *Christians, Blasphemers, and Witches: Afro-Mexican Ritual Practice in the Seventeenth Century* (Albuquerque: University of New Mexico Press, 2007), 7 and 16; Robert C. Schwaller, *Géneros de Gente in Early Colonial Mexico: Defining Racial Difference* (Norman: University of Oklahoma Press, 2016), 226; Joanne Rappaport, "'Asi lo paresçe por su aspecto': Physiognomy and the Construction of Difference in Colonial Bogotá," *Hispanic American Historical Review* 91, no. 4 (2011): 605.

29. Pablo Gómez, *The Experiential Caribbean: Creating Knowledge and Healing in the Early Modern Atlantic* (Chapel Hill: University of North Carolina Press, 2017), 3–8.

30. "Es evidente que una parte de las mercancías asiáticas que transportaba la nao de China se introdujo a tierra adentro por varios puntos del litoral noroccidental de manera legal y clandestina" (quoted in Jaime Olveda, "El Puerto de la Navidad," in *Relaciones intercoloniales: Nueva España y Filipinas*, ed. Jaime Olveda [Zapopan, Mexico: El Colegio de Jalisco, 2017], 115).

31. "Autos sobre libertad promovidos por Domingo de la Cruz, chino y esclavo natural de Maniola, contra Juan Sánchez Bañales vecino de Zapotlán," 1678, Archivo de la Real Audiencia de la Nueva Galicia (ARANG), Caja 9, Exp. 9, Prog. 124, fol. 1r.

32. Oropeza, *La migración asiática*, 149.

33. Flores García et al., eds., *Catálogo y estudio*, 210.

34. Oropeza, *La migración asiática*, 206 and 216.

35. Oropeza, *La migración asiática*, 235.

36. Frank T. Proctor, "African Diasporic Ethnicity in Mexico City to 1650," in *Africans to Spanish America: Expanding the Diaspora*, ed. Sherwin K. Bryant, Rachel Sarah O'Toole, and Ben Vinson III (Urbana: University of Illinois Press, 2012), 58; Pablo Miguel Sierra Silva, "The Slave Trade to Colonial Mexico: Revising from Puebla de los Ángeles, 1590–1640," in *From the Galleons to the Highlands: Slave Trade Routes in the Spanish Americas*, ed. Alex Borucki, David Eltis, and David Wheat (Albuquerque: University of New Mexico Press, 2020), 73–74.

By the end of the seventeenth century, many Afro-Mexicans residing in major urban centers were free. Some had been freed in wills or bought their own freedom, while others had been born to free women and were therefore declared free as well. Herman L. Bennett,

Colonial Blackness: A History of Afro-Mexico (Bloomington: Indiana University Press, 2009), 5; Gonzalo Aguirre Beltrán, *La población negra de México*, 2nd ed. (Mexico City: Fondo de Cultura Económica, 1972), 258–263; Ann Twinam, *Purchasing Whiteness: Pardos, Mulattos, and the Quest for Social Mobility in the Spanish Indies* (Stanford, CA: Stanford University Press, 2015), 87–88 and 91–92.

37. Sierra Silva, *Urban Slavery*, 66. For more on the history of creolization in the colonial Mexican context, see Miguel A. Valerio, *Sovereign Joy: Afro-Mexican Kings and Queens, 1539–1640* (New York: Cambridge University Press, 2022), 20–22.

38. For a broad overview of Mexican runaway communities in the context of North American and Caribbean maroons, see Patrick J. Carroll, "Mandinga: The Evolution of a Mexican Runaway Slave Community, 1735–1827," *Comparative Studies in Society and History* 19, no. 4 (1977): 488–505

39. Valdés, "The Decline of Slavery in Mexico," 189.

40. Frank T. Proctor, *Damned Notions of Liberty: Slavery, Culture, and Power in Colonial Mexico, 1640–1769* (Albuquerque: University of New Mexico Press, 2010), 130–131.

41. Seijas, *Asian Slaves*, 187.

42. Tamara J. Walker, "María Hipólita Lozano, Eighteenth-Century Lima (Peru)," in *As If She Were Free: A Collective Biography of Women and Emancipation in the Americas*, ed. Erica L. Ball, Tatiana Seijas, and Terri L. Snyder (New York: Cambridge University Press, 2020), 244–245.

43. "Luisa china trigueña," 1658, AGN, Indiferente Virreinal, Caja 6025, exp. 064 (Bienes Nacionales Caja 6025).

44. "Censuras ante Don Luis de Cifuentes," AGN, Indiferente Virreinal, Caja 2242, exp. 029.

45. Proctor, *Damned Notions of Liberty*, 132. See also Sierra Silva, *Urban Slavery*, 1.

46. Seijas, *Asian Slaves*, 164.

47. Proctor, *Damned Notions of Liberty*, 132.

48. Nancy E. van Deusen, *Global Indios: The Struggle for Justice in Sixteenth-Century Spain* (Durham, NC: Duke University Press, 2015), 138.

49. Sousa, *The Portuguese Slave Trade*, 27, 35, and 66, 111; Sierra Silva, *Urban Slavery*, 134; Javier Villa-Flores, "Talking through the Chest: Divination and Ventriloquism among African Slave Women in Seventeenth-Century Mexico," *Colonial Latin American Review* 14, no. 2 (2005): 303.

50. "Con poco temor de dios nuestro" (quoted in "Martín de Bisola pide cartas de censuras," 1626, AGN, Indiferente Virreinal, Clero Regular y Secular, Caja 3470, exp. 011).

51. Quoted in "Doña Margarita de Saavedra se le ausentó su esclavo chino," 1658, AGN, Indiferente Virreinal, Civil, Caja 2289, exp. 001.

52. "Casta sangley" and "delas que se husan y azen en las yslas philipinas" ("Simón casta sangley," 1631, AGN, Indiferente Virreinal, Caja 2173, exp. 010 (Civil Caja 2173).

53. "Carta monitoria para que se le restituya una china," 1660, AGN, Indiferente Virreinal, Caja 2306, exp. 009.

54. "Carta monitoria para que se le devuelve una china," 1663, AGN, Indiferente Virreinal, Caja 2306, exp. 022.

55. "Carta monitoria para descubrir una esclava china," 1661, AGN, Indiferente Virreinal, Caja 2306, exp. 008.

56. Seijas, *Asian Slaves,* 164n82.

57. "Maria de la Cruz negra," 1637, AGN, Indiferente Virreinal, Caja 0803, exp. 017 (Consolidación Caja 0803).

58. "Informe presentado por don Juan de Serecedo, Alcalde Mayor y de la Santa Hermandad del Real de Minas de Hostotipac, sobre la muerte intestada de Lucas García y el depósito de sus bienes en la persona de don Eugenio de la Gradilla. Por otra parte, el Escribano y Juez de la Diputación de Hostotipac notificó la existencia de una carta de obligación de pago otorgado por Juan García Bravo, Sebastián Ramos Jiménez y el Presbítero Nicolás Ramos Jiménez, mineros y vecinos de dicho real, en la que se comprometían a pagar 6,000 pesos en plata. Incluye inventario de sus bienes y el reclamo de un esclavo chino que estaba en poder de Antonio de León y Gálvez. Corresponde al índice de CJV: paquete 4 (49), año 1654, progresivo 210," 1654, ARANG, Caja 6, Exp. 4, Prog. 74, fols. 17r, 21r–v, 27r–28r.

59. "Encubrimiento de chino esclavo," 1635, AGN, Criminal, vol. 692, exp. 3, fol. 7r.

60. Oropeza Keresey, "La esclavitud asiática," 42; Oropeza, *La migración asiática,* 155.

61. Seijas, *Asian Slaves,* 189–193; "Testificación contra Andrés, esclavo, indio chino," 1621, AGN, Inquisición, vol. 486, exp. 39, fol. 201; Oropeza, *La migración asiática,* 111.

62. Javier Villa-Flores, "'To Lose One's Soul': Blasphemy and Slavery in New Spain, 1596–1669," *Hispanic American Historical Review* 82, no. 3 (2002): 468.

63. Quoted in Javier Villa-Flores, "Voices from a Living Hell: Slavery, Death, and Salvation in a Mexican Obraje," in *Local Religion in Colonial Mexico,* ed. Martin Austin Nesvig (Albuquerque: University of New Mexico Press, 2006), 235. Posadas's claim to be able to punish in the name of the Holy Office was no doubt a deception.

64. Villa-Flores, "'To Lose One's Soul,'" 458.

65. Walker, "María Hipólita Lozano," 245.

66. "Malsonante" and "de que se conocia el mal natural de este reo" (quoted in "Proceso y causa criminal contra Lucas de Araujo," 1661, AGN, Inquisición, vol. 583, exp. 5).

67. Beltrán, *Medicina y magia,* 112.

68. "No estaua borracho, sino en su entero juicio y depravada capacidad y voluntad" (quoted in "Proceso y causa criminal contra Lucas de Araujo," 1661).

69. "Proceso y causa criminal contra un chino esclavo de don Pedro," 1665, AGN, Inquisición, vol. 600, exp. 23.

70. Villa-Flores, "'To Lose One's Soul,'" 453.

71. "Anda hombre estas loco" (quoted in "Proceso y causa criminal contra un chino esclavo de don Pedro," 1665, AGN, Inquisición, vol. 600, exp. 23).

72. Henry Kamen, *The Spanish Inquisition: A Historical Revision* (New Haven, CT: Yale University Press, 1998), 145–146.

73. Proctor, *Damned Notions of Liberty,* 106.

74. "Porque tambien le dejaran a el de azotar" ("Testificación contra Luis chino," 1626, AGN, Inquisición, vol. 356, exp. 20, fol. 27).

75. Ivor Miller, "Aponte's Legacy in Cuban Popular Culture," *Afro-Hispanic Review* 37, no. 2 (2018): 130–131.

76. "Contra un esclavo llamado Tomás, de nación chino," 1663, AGN, Inquisición, vol. 598, exp. 15.

77. Alonso Ramos, *Los prodigios de la Omnipotencia y milagros de la gracia en la vida de la venerable sierva de Dios Catarina de San Juan,* ed. Gisela von Wobeser (Mexico City: Universidad Nacional Autónoma de México-Instituto de Investigaciones Históricas, 2017), 2:13.

78. "Mira padris, quando cautivaron para mi, hacieron esclava muchos ansias, muchos trabajos, solo sabe el divina Magestad, lo que yo pase" (quoted in Joseph del Castillo Graxeda, *Compendio de la vida, y virtudes de la venerable Catharina de San Juan* [Puebla, Mexico: Imprenta de Diego Fernandez de Leon, 1692], 17).

79. "Era suavissima para esta Virgen la memoria al gran Mogor" (Francisco de Aguilera, *Sermon que en las honras de la Venerable Madre Catharina de San Juan predicó* [Biblioteca de la Universidad de Sevilla, 1688], 2r).

80. See Jeanne Gillespie, "In the Right Place at the Right(?) Time: Catarina de San Juan's Visions and the Jesuit Missionary Efforts," in *Women's Voices and the Politics of the Spanish Empire,* ed. Jennifer L. Eich, Jeanne Gillespie, and Lucia G. Harrison (New Orleans, LA: University Press of the South, 2008), 304–315.

81. Aguilera, *Sermon,* 9r; Ramos, *Los prodigios,* 1:23 and 322–332; Castillo Graxeda, *Compendio de la vida,* 36.

82. "Lo que más frecuentemente he visto es a mis padres en el purgatorio . . . hasta que en un año de estos los vi venir acompañado a la nao de Filipinas al puerto de Acapulco, de donde, como de rodillas, vinieron a mi presencia" (quoted in Ramos, *Los prodigios,* 1:49).

83. Kathleen Ann Myers, *Neither Saints nor Sinners: Writing the Lives of Women in Spanish America* (New York: Oxford University Press, 2003), 46.

84. Proctor, *Damned Notions of Liberty,* 73; Villa-Flores, "Talking through the Chest," 304–305; Beltrán, *Medicina y magia,* 359; Ruth Behar, "Sex and Sin, Witchcraft and the Devil in Late-Colonial Mexico," *American Ethnologist* 14, no. 1 (1987): 34–54.

85. Bristol, *Christians, Blasphemers, and Witches,* 7.

86. Hinojoso, *Summa y recopilacion.*

87. Ruiz de Alarcón, *Treatise,* 64.

88. Ruiz de Alarcón, *Treatise,* 251. See also Domingo Lázaro de Arregui, *Descripcion de la Nueva Galicia,* ed. François Chevalier (Seville, Spain: Escuela de Estudios Hispano-Americanos de la Universidad de Sevilla, 1946), 51.

89. On the medicinal uses of peyote and ololiuhqui, see Angélica Morales-Sarabia, "Peyote and Ololiuhqui in the Medical Texts of New Spain and Their Circulation in Spain during the 16th and 17th Centuries," in *Transatlantic Trade and Global Cultural Transfers since 1492: More Than Commodities,* ed. Martina Kaller and Frank Jacob (New York: Routledge, 2020), 129–149.

90. Irving A. Leonard, "Peyote and the Mexican Inquisition, 1620," *American Anthropologist* 44, no. 2 (1942): 324–326; Melissa June Frost, "Herbs That Madden, Herbs That Cure: A History of Hallucinogenic Plant Use in Colonial Mexico," PhD diss., University of Virginia, 2017, 152–153.

91. Beltrán, *Medicina y magia*, 160–161.

92. Beltrán, *Medicina y magia*, 152–153.

93. "Denuncia de Antonio de Ibarra en contra de un chino esclavo de Martin de Aguilus," 1656, AGN, Inquisición, vol. (cajas) 1568 B, exp. 328.

94. Schwaller, *Géneros de Gente*, 212; Noemí Quezada, "The Inquisition's Repression of Curanderos," in *Cultural Encounters: The Impact of the Inquisition in Spain and the New World*, ed. Mary Elizabeth Perry and Anne J. Cruz (Berkeley: University of California Press, 1991), 41.

95. Ruiz de Alarcón, *Treatise*, 65.

96. Schwaller, *Géneros de Gente*, 212.

97. "China niña que le parece china" ("Contra Diego Palomino, chino, y su hija Teresa," 1675, AGN, Inquisición, vol. 626, exp. 4).

98. Ana María Silva Campo, "Fragile Fortunes: Afrodescendant Women, Witchcraft, and the Remaking of Urban Cartagena," *Colonial Latin American Review* 30, no. 2 (2021): 207–208.

99. Diego Javier Luis, "Galleon Anxiety: How Afro-Mexican Women Shaped Colonial Spirituality in Acapulco," *Americas* 78, no. 3 (2021): 408.

100. Ruiz de Alarcón, *Treatise*, 59.

101. Luis, "Galleon Anxiety," 408; Ruiz de Alarcón, *Treatise*, 59–67 and 200.

102. Ruiz de Alarcón, *Treatise*, 67–88.

103. Ruiz de Alarcón, *Treatise*, 68. For more on the use of protective pouches in the Afro-Atlantic world, see Cécile Fromont, "Paper, Ink, Vodun, and the Inquisition: Tracing Power, Slavery, and Witchcraft in the Early Modern Portuguese Atlantic," *Journal of the American Academy of Religion* 88, no. 2 (2020): 460–504; Matthew Francis Rarey, "Assemblage, Occlusion, and the Art of Survival in the Black Atlantic," *African Arts* 51, no. 4 (2018): 20–33.

104. Beltrán, *Medicina y magia*, 234–236.

105. "Vivir y morir en la ss[an]ta fee catolica de nuestra morir en jesu cpto" (quoted in "Comparecencia de Francisco López, natural del Reino de Bengola, en la India de Portugal," 1628, AGN, Indiferente Virreinal, caja-exp. 5633–073, fol. 1v).

106. "Proceso y causa criminal contra Leonor de Ontiveros, mulata de Toluca, por sospechosa de bruja y fama de serlo. Puebla de los Angeles. Mexico," 1652, AGN, Inquisición, vol. 454, exp. 40, fol. 563v.

107. Frank T. Proctor, "Afro-Mexican Slave Labor in the Obrajes de Paños of New Spain, Seventeenth and Eighteenth Centuries," *Americas* 60, no. 1 (2003): 40.

108. Proctor, "Afro-Mexican Slave Labor," 39.

109. Rhonda M. Gonzales, "No Friends in the Holy Office: Black and Mulatta Women Healing Communities and Answering to the Inquisition in Seventeenth-Century Mexico," *Journal of Pain African Studies* 6, no. 1 (2013): 11; Villa-Flores, "Talking through the Chest," 299.

110. Although he claimed to have learned how to divine in Kochi, it is important to point out that divination using hand measurements was present in Spain and among Indigenous people in central Mexico during this time as well. See Ruiz de Alarcón, *Treatise*, 143–145.

111. Ronald J. Quirk, "*Zajorí* in Puerto Rican Spanish," *Romance* 34, no. 3 (1994): 257.

112. For more on "natural" and "unnatural" magic, see Jonathan Seitz, *Witchcraft and Inquisition in Early Modern Venice* (New York: Cambridge University Press, 2011), 62. Pablo Gómez offers an interesting comparison between them and the accepted practices of the

saludadores, ensalmadores, and *santiguadores* of the Iberian Peninsula (*The Experiential Caribbean,* 152–154).

113. Sir William Barrett and Theodore Besterman, *The Divining Rod: An Experimental and Psychological Investigation* (New Hyde Park, NY: University Books, 1968), 277–282.

114. Beltrán, *Medicina y magia,* 27–28.

115. "Tierra de gentiles no de moros ni judíos" (quoted in "Proceso contra Antón, chino," 1659, AGN, Inquisición, vol. 456, exp. 2). See also Seijas, *Asian Slaves,* 201.

116. Ângela Barreto Xavier and Ines G. Županov, *Catholic Orientalism: Portuguese Empire, Indian Knowledge (16th–18th Centuries)* (New Delhi: Oxford University Press, 2015), 152–154.

117. Joan C. Bristol, "Ana de Vega: Seventeenth-Century Afro-Mexican Healer," in *The Human Tradition in Colonial Latin America,* 2nd ed., ed. Kenneth J. Andrien (Lanham, MD: Rowman and Littlefield, 2013), 210. See also James H. Sweet, *Domingos Álvares, African Healing, and the Intellectual History of the Atlantic World* (Chapel Hill: University of North Carolina Press, 2011); Gómez, *The Experiential Caribbean.*

118. Gregorio Martín de Guijo, *Gregorio M. de Guijo, diario, 1648–1664,* ed. Manuel Romero de Terreros (Mexico City: Editorial Porrúa, 1952), 2:77.

119. "De casta chino" (Alberro, *Inquisición y sociedad en México,* 480–481).

120. Seijas, *Asian Slaves,* 226.

121. Alberro, *Inquisición y sociedad en México,* 499–500.

122. María Juana is not the only person to have been labeled "achinado / a" in colonial Mexico. For example, "an achinado mulato slave" is listed in a will dictated in San José de Toluca in 1697 (Georgina Flores García et al., eds., *Catálogo y estudio introductorio de la presencia de las personas de origen africano y afrodescendientes durante los siglos XVI y XVII en la valle de Toluca* [Toluca, Mexico: Universidad Autónoma del Estado de México, 2017], 616).

123. Lyndal Roper, *Oedipus and the Devil: Witchcraft, Sexuality and Religion in Early Modern Europe* (New York: Routledge, 1994), 227.

124. "Yo echo todo lo que mis fuerzas an podido por reducir el mal natural de esa china" (quoted in "Contra Maria Juana de San Ignacio, mulata achinada," 1686, AGN, Inquisición, vol. 1551, exp. 37).

125. María Elisa Gutiérrez Velázquez, *Mujeres de origen africano en la capital novohispana, siglos XVII y XVIII* (Mexico City: Instituto Nacional de Antropología e Historia, 2006), 429.

126. Norah L. A. Gharala, "'From Mozambique in Indies of Portugal': Locating East Africans in New Spain," *Journal of Global History* 7, no. 3 (2022): 272. See also Oropeza, *La migración asiática,* 148.

127. For examples, see "Bartolome Diaz," AGN, 1605–1606, Civil, vol. 365, exp. 7, fol. 333v; "Francisco de Medina," AGN, 1604, Indiferente Virreinal, Caja 5571, exp. 043; "Phelipe de Silva," AGN, 1633, Indiferente Virreinal, Caja 0749, exp. 022.

5. Trajectories beyond Central Mexico

1. "Indio n[atura]l de la ciudad de lima residente" (quoted in "Información contra Alonso Coronel, de nación pampango," 1693, Archivo General de la Nación México [AGN], Inquisición, vol. 528, exp. 6, fols. 466r and 484r).

2. "Chino al parecer natural que dice ser de la ciudad de lima" (quoted in "Información contra Alonso Coronel," fol. 464r; emphasis added).

3. "Color i ojos que suelen tener lo que llaman chinos en la ciudad de mexico" ("Información contra Alonso Coronel, fol. 461r).

4. "Queda pendiente la exploración del caso peruano y de otros enclaves coloniales más allá del virreinato norteamericano" (Rubén Carrillo Martín, *Las gentes del mar Sangley* [Mexico City: Palabra de Clío, 2015], 239).

5. Quoted in "Decreto enviando petición del japonés Juan Antonio," 1624, Archivo General de Indias (AGI), Filipinas, 39, N.21.

6. "Yndios luzones" and "espías" ("Derrotero: Pedro de Unamuno, de Macao, Cantín a Acapulco," 1587, AGI, Patronato, 25, R.32, fol. 5).

7. Floro L. Mercene, *Manila Men in the New World: Filipino Migration to Mexico and the Americas from the Sixteenth Century* (Quezon City: University of the Philippines Press, 2007), 40.

8. "Derrotero," fol. 13.

9. "Derrotero," fol. 14.

10. The next instance was in 1595, when the *San Agustín* sailed from Manila and sank during a storm in Sir Francis Drake's Bay. During this period, it is possible that Asian sailors also traveled north from Acapulco on other voyages up the California coast, voyages for which only trace references remain. According to Warren Cook, "How many similar visits occurred but went unchronicled is beyond ascertaining" (*Flood Tide of Empire: Spain and the Pacific Northwest, 1543–1819* [New Haven, CT: Yale University Press, 1973], 7; see also 11). For more on the 1595 voyage of the *San Agustín* under Sebastián Rodríguez Cermeño, see "Carta del virrey Gaspar de Zúñiga Acevedo, conde de Monterrey," 1596, AGI, México, 23, N.50.

11. Déborah Oropeza, *La migración asiática en el virreinato de la Nueva España: Un proceso de globalización (1565–1700)* (Mexico City: El Colegio de México, 2020), 129. Buzos were expected to plug underwater leaks that a ship's carpenters and caulkers were unable to reach.

12. "Caja de Acapulco," 1602, AGI, Contaduría, 901, fols. 60v–65v.

13. "Caja de Acapulco," fols. 98r–99r.

14. "No ay tres marineros que pueden servir aferrar las velas de gavia" (quoted in "México 1602. Relación del viaje y derrotero de las naos que fueron al descubrimiento del puerto de Acapulco a cargo del general Sebastián Bizcaíno," AGI, MP-Libros_Manuscritos, 40, fol. 16v). See also Antonio de la Ascensión, "A Brief Report of the Discovery in the South Sea, by Fray Antonio de la Ascensión, 1602–1603," in *Spanish Exploration in the Southwest, 1542–1706,* ed. Herbert Eugene Bolton (New York: Charles Scribner's Sons, 1916), 104–134.

15. Cook, *Flood Tide of Empire,* 13.

16. Cook, *Flood Tide of Empire,* 13. The river was likely today's Rogue River.

17. "Caja de Acapulco," 1602, AGI, Contaduría, 901, fols. 112r–121r. For further evidence of early modern Asian presence in Oregon, see the scholarship on the "Beeswax wreck," now identified as the *Santo Cristo de Burgos* that ran aground in 1693 near the Ne-

halem Spit. Scott S. Williams, "The 'Beeswax Wreck': A Manila Galleon on the North Oregon Coast," *Alaska Journal of Anthropology* 15, nos. 1–2 (2017): 84; Scott S. Williams, Curt D. Peterson, Mitch Marken, and Richard Rogers, "The Beeswax Wreck of Nehalem: A Lost Manila Galleon," *Oregon Historical Quarterly* 119, no. 2 (2018): 204; Cook, *Flood Tide of Empire,* 31–32.

18. José Antonio Cervera, "Los planes españoles para conquistar China a través de Nueva España y Centroamérica en el siglo XVI," *Cuadernos de Intercambio sobre Centroamérica y el Caribe* 10, no. 12 (2013): 221–224.

19. Paul Lokken found records of two enslaved Africans from Mozambique in Guatemala during the early seventeenth century ("West Central Africans in the Province of Guatemala, 1605–1655," in *From the Galleons to the Highlands: Slave Trade Routes in the Spanish Americas,* ed. Alex Borucki, David Eltis, and David Wheat [Albuquerque: University of New Mexico Press, 2020], 114).

20. "Caja de Acapulco," 1602, AGI, Contaduría, 901, fols. 138r–139r. On the possibility of using Carlos de Sigüenza y Góngora's *Infortunios de Alonso Ramírez* (1690) as a source for tracking Asian mobility to the Yucatan, see Martín, *Las gentes del mar Sangley,* 229; Eugenio Chang-Rodríguez, "Chinese Labor Migration into Latin America in the Nineteenth Century," *Revista de Historia de América* 46 (1958): 377. For more about the *Infortunios,* see Aníbal González, "Los infortunios de Alonso Ramírez: Picaresca e historia," *Hispanic Review* 51, no. 2 (1983): 190; Mabel Moraña, "Máscara autobiográfica y conciencia criolla en *Infortunios de Alonso Ramírez,*" *Dispositio* 15, no. 40 (1990): 107; Patricio Boyer, "Criminality and Subjectivity in *Infortunios de Alonso Ramírez,*" *Hispanic Review* 78, no. 1 (2010): 28.

21. "Ahora es tiempo Lucifer aiudame" ("Informe de la comparecencia de Joseph Fernández de Isla," 1648, AGN, Indiferente Virreinal Caja 5388, exp. 071 [Inquisición Caja 5388], 1).

22. "Cierrale puta vieja" (quoted in "Informe de la comparecencia de Joseph Fernández de Isla," 1).

23. "Mateo de la Torre," 1648, AGN, Procesos Civiles, caja 79, exp. 2855.

24. "Bienes de difuntos: Diego Ruiz," 1671, AGI, Contratación, 455, N.2, R.3, fols. 4v–7v.

25. "Bienes de difuntos," fol. 4v.

26. Ignacio Muñoz, "Derroteros de los mares de Marruecos, Canarias, América y Filipinas, y otros documentos," Biblioteca Nacional de España, Mss / 7119, c. late 1600s, fol. 287v.

27. "Bienes de difuntos," fols. 17v–18r.

28. "Bienes de difuntos," fol. 18v.

29. The heavy emphasis in Sarmiento's history on Inca conquests paralleled Viceroy Francisco de Toledo's depiction of the Inca as tyrannical to justify continued violent action against them—a discursive tactic already well tested against the Mexica. Clements R. Markham, "Introduction," in Pedro Sarmiento de Gamboa, *Narratives of the Voyages of Pedro Sarmiento de Gamboa to the Straits of Magellan,* trans. Clements R. Markham (London: Printed for the Hakluyt Society, 1895), xix; Soledad Carmina González Díaz, "A Three-Century Journey: The Lost Manuscript of the *History of the Incas* by Pedro Sarmiento de Gamboa," *Americas* 78, no. 3 (2021): 467.

30. These and other conquests during the fifteenth century formed a vast territory known as the Tawantinsuyu empire. Tawantinsuyu (a Quechua word) referred to a realm that touched the four sides of the world. Józef Szykulsi, "Genesis and Expansion of the Tawantinsuyu Empire (Inca); Its Character, Course and Repercussions," *Tambo* 4 (2019): 220.

31. "Adonde había mucha gente y oro" (Pedro Sarmiento de Gamboa, *Historia de los Inca (Segunda parte de la Historia General Llamada Indica)* [Madrid: Ediciones Atlas, 1965], 251). See also Aleksín H. Ortega, "*Segunda parte de la historia general llamada índica (1572)* de Pedro Sarmiento de Gamboa. Estudio y edición anotada," PhD diss., City University of New York, 2018, 256n14.

32. "Con el mayor, mas solemne y mas rico triunfo que jamas inga habia entrado en la Casa del Sol" (Sarmiento de Gamboa, *Historia de los Inca*, 251–252).

33. This measurement is a gross underestimate.

34. Markham, "Introduction," xiii; Mercedes Maroto Camino, *Producing the Pacific: Maps and Narratives of Spanish Exploration (1567–1606)* (Amsterdam: Rodophi, 2005), 33. For modern reactions to the story of pre-Hispanic Andean contact, see Carmen Bernand, "Le Pacifique vu du Pérou (1567–1606)," *e-Spania* 14 (2012), https://doi.org/10.4000/e-spania.22060; Liliana Regalado de Hurtado, "Un contexto legendario para el origen de los Mitmaqkuna y el alcance del prestigio norteño," *Histórica* 7, no. 2 (1983): 255–286; Esteban Mayorga, *Gálapagos: Imaginarios y evolución textual en las islas encatadas* (West Lafayette, IN: Purdue University Press, 2019); Alec Hughes Pardo, *Atando cabos: Los contactos entre Perú y la Polinesia mediante la navegación a vela* (Toronto, CA: CreaLibros, 2020); Andrés Reséndez, *Conquering the Pacific: An Unknown Mariner and the Final Great Voyage of the Age of Discovery* (Boston: Houghton Mifflin Harcourt, 2021), 13–14; Alexander G. Ioannidis et al., "Native American Gene Flow into Polynesia Predating Easter Island Settlement," *Nature* 583 (2020): 576–577.

35. Jan Szemiński, "Horizonte geográfico inca," *Revista de Crítica Literaria Latinoamericana* 42, no. 84 (2016): 20–22.

36. For the representation of Potosí in China, see Kris Lane, "Potosí," in *New World Objects of Knowledge: A Cabinet of Curiosities*, ed. Mark Thurner and Juan Pimentel (London: University of London Press, 2021), 31–33.

37. Mariano Bonialian, "Asiáticos en Lima a principios del siglo XVII," *Bulletin de l'Institut Français d'Études Andines* 44, no. 2 (2015): 14.

38. Mariano Bonialian, "El Perú colonial en la temprana globalización: El caso del navío *Nuestra Señora del Rosario* (1591)," *Mediterranea* 18 (2021): 584 and 592.

39. William Lytle Shurtz, "Mexico, Peru, and the Manila Galleon," *Hispanic American Historical Review* 1, no. 4 (1918): 394–402.

40. Pablo E. Pérez-Mallaína, *Spain's Men of the Sea: Daily Life on the Indies Fleets in the Sixteenth Century* (Baltimore, MD: Johns Hopkins University Press, 1998), 14; Francesco Carletti, *My Voyage around the World: The Chronicles of a 16th Century Florentine Merchant*, trans. Herbert Weinstock (New York: Pantheon Books, 1964), 34.

41. Carletti, *My Voyage around the World*, 35.

42. Mariano A. Bonialian, *China en la América colonial: Bienes, mercados, comercio y cultura del consumo desde México hasta Buenos Aires* (Mexico City: Editorial Biblios, 2014), 37–54.

43. Bonialian, "Asiáticos en Lima," 6.

44. Rachel Sarah O'Toole, "Securing Subjecthood: Free and Enslaved Economies within the Pacific Slave Trade," in *From the Galleons to the Highlands: Slave Trade Routes in the Spanish Americas,* ed. Alex Borucki, David Eltis, and David Wheat (Albuquerque: University of New Mexico Press, 2020), 155.

45. "Caja de Acapulco," 1607, AGI, Contaduría, 902.

46. Norah L. A. Gharala, *Taxing Blackness: Free Afromexican Tribute in Bourbon New Spain* (Tuscaloosa: University of Alabama Press, 2019), 29; see also 34.

47. Michelle A. McKinley, "The Unbearable Lightness of Being (Black): Legal and Cultural Constructions of Race and Nation in Colonial Latin America," in *Racial Formation in the Twenty-First Century,* ed. Daniel Martínez Hosang, Oneka LaBennett, and Laura Pulido (Berkeley: University of California Press, 2012), 132.

48. Noble David Cook, "Introducción," in *Padrón de los indios de Lima en 1613,* ed. Mauro Escobar Gamboa (Lima: Universidad Nacional Mayor de San Marcos, 1968), iv; McKinley, "The Unbearable Lightness of Being (Black)," 133.

49. Gharala, *Taxing Blackness,* 35.

50. Cook, "Introducción," v.

51. "Indios e indias de La China, y el Xapón, e India de Portugal," in *Padrón de los indios de Lima en 1613,* 525.

52. Bonialian, "Asiáticos en Lima," 6–7 and 19.

53. McKinley, "The Unbearable Lightness of Being (Black)," 134.

54. Oropeza, *La migración asiática,* 246.

55. Lucío de Sousa guesses that "Xagua" and its derivatives could refer to Shanghai (上海), Sagwa, Luo Chaguo (羅剎國), or Java (*The Portuguese Slave Trade in Early Modern Japan: Merchants, Jesuits and Japanese, Chinese and Korean Slaves* [Boston: Brill, 2019], 80).

56. Confusingly, the padrón seems to document the same family twice but calls Isabel Mexia an "india china" from Manila in one entry and an Indigenous person from Tlaxcala in another. *Padrón de los indios de Lima en 1613,* 533.

57. *Padrón de los indios de Lima en 1613,* 528.

58. McKinley, "The Unbearable Lightness of Being (Black)," 134.

59. *Padrón de los indios de Lima en 1613,* 541 and 544; Sousa, *The Portuguese Slave Trade,* 453.

60. Rachel Sarah O'Toole, *Bound Lives: Africans, Indians, and the Making of Race in Colonial Peru* (Pittsburgh, PA: University of Pittsburgh Press, 2012), 162.

61. *Padrón de los indios de Lima en 1613,* 532.

62. *Padrón de los indios de Lima en 1613,* 267. For more on the occupation of abridor de cuellos, see Sousa, *The Portuguese Slave Trade,* 450n332; Bonialian, "Asiáticos en Lima," 16.

63. *Padrón de los indios de Lima en 1613,* 536.

64. "No hay cacique ni encomendero que todos los indios son libres" (*Padrón de los indios de Lima en 1613,* 535).

65. Sousa, *The Portuguese Slave Trade*, 230–231.

66. Sousa, *The Portuguese Slave Trade*, 456–457n360; José Vega Loyola, "Japoneses, chinos e indios en Lima cosmopolita de inicios del siglo XVII," *Cátedra Villareal* 3, no. 2 (2015): 162.

67. *Padrón de los indios de Lima en 1613*, 526.

68. "Va y viene" (*Padrón de los indios de Lima en 1613*, 537).

69. Sousa, *The Portuguese Slave Trade*, 230–231 and 242–243.

70. Leo J. Garofalo, "The Will of an Indian Oriental and Her *Chinos* in Peru," in *The Spanish Pacific, 1521–1815: A Reader of Primary Sources*, ed. Christina H. Lee and Ricardo Padrón (Amsterdam: Amsterdam University Press, 2020), 136.

71. Quoted in Sousa, *The Portuguese Slave Trade*, 254–255.

72. Quoted in Garofalo, "The Will of an Indian Oriental," 136.

73. Quoted in Garofalo, "The Will of an Indian Oriental," 136.

74. Danielle Terrazas Williams, "'My Conscience Is Free and Clear': African-Descended Women, Status, and Slave Owning in Mid-colonial Mexico," *Americas* 75, no. 3 (2018): 539 and 553, and *The Capital of Free Women: Race, Legitimacy, and Liberty in Colonial Mexico* (New Haven, CT: Yale University Press, 2022), 119–147; Tamara J. Walker, "María Hipólita Lozano, Eighteenth-Century Lima (Peru)," in *As If She Were Free: A Collective Biography of Women and Emancipation in the Americas*, ed. Erica L. Ball, Tatiana Seijas, and Terri L. Snyder (New York: Cambridge University Press, 2020), 242.

75. "Indias Occidentales" (Juan de Solórzano Pereira, *Política Indiana* [Madrid: Diego Díaz de la Carrera, 1648], 1:69). See also Oropeza, *La migración asiática*, 255.

76. See M. C. Mirow, "Juan Solórzano Pereira," in *Great Christian Jurists in Spanish History*, ed. Rafael Domingo and Javier Martínez-Torrón (New York: Cambridge University Press, 2018), 240–258.

77. "Que comercian los Portugueses por la via de Filipinas, i Mexico" (Solórzano Pereira, *Política Indiana*, 1:69).

78. James Muldoon, *The Americas in the Spanish World Order: The Justification for Conquest in the Seventeenth Century* (Philadelphia: University of Pennsylvania Press, 1994), 8.

79. "El d[ic]ho Alonso coronel is de mediana estatura, cara i gente ancha, de color i ojos que suelen tener lo que llaman chinos en la ciudad de mexico, cabello lapio todo negro y algunas canas de pocas barbas, su traxe es vestido de paño" ("Información contra Alonso Coronel, de nación pampango," 1693, AGN, Inquisición, vol. 528, exp. 6, fol. 461r).

80. The economy of Petatlán was intricately tied to that of the Pacific coast through the nearby port of Zihuantanejo.

81. "Información contra Alonso Coronel, de nación pampango," 1693, AGN, Inquisición, vol. 528, exp. 6, fol. 474r.

82. François Chevalier, *Land and Society in Colonial Mexico: The Great Hacienda*, trans. Alvin Eustis (Berkeley: University of California Press, 1963), 8; John Tutino, *Making a New World: Founding Capitalism in the Bajío and Spanish North America* (Durham, NC: Duke University Press, 2011), 128–130; Andrés Reséndez, *The Other Slavery: The Uncovered Story of Indian Enslavement in America* (Boston: Houghton Mifflin Harcourt, 2016), 327n16; Norah L. A.

Gharala, "'From Mozambique in Indies of Portugal': Locating East Africans in New Spain," *Journal of Global History* 7, no. 3 (2022): 267.

83. "Cara blanca" ("Información contra Alonso Coronel, de nación pampango," 1693, AGN, Inquisición, vol. 528, exp. 6, fol. 452r).

84. Garofalo, "The Will of an Indian Oriental," 132.

85. Woodrow Borah and Sherburne F. Cook, *Price Trends of Some Basic Commodities in Central Mexico, 1531–1570* (Berkeley: University of California Press, 1958); Tatiana Seijas, "Native Vassals: Chinos, Indigenous Identity, and Legal Protection in Early Modern Spain," in *Western Visions of the Far East in a Transpacific Age, 1522–1657*, ed. Christina Lee (Burlington, VT: Ashgate, 2012), 163–164. The ducado was worth approximately 1.25 pesos.

86. Nancy E. van Deusen, *Global Indios: The Struggle for Justice in Sixteenth-Century Spain* (Durham, NC: Duke University Press, 2015); Juan Gil, *La India y el Lejano Oriente en la Sevilla del Siglo de Oro* (Seville, Spain: Ayuntamiento de Sevilla—Instituto de la Cultura y las Artes de Sevilla, 2011).

87. Sanjay Subrahmanyam, *The Portuguese Empire in Asia, 1500–1700: A Political and Economic History*, 2nd ed. (Chichester, UK: Wiley-Blackwell, 2012), 240; Stephanie Hassell, "Inquisition Records from Goa as Sources for the Study of Slavery in the Eastern Domains of the Portuguese Empire," *History in Africa* 42 (2015): 410.

88. Sousa, *The Portuguese Slave Trade*, 461.

89. Sousa, *The Portuguese Slave Trade*, 34.

90. Gil, *La India y el Lejano Oriente*, 148–168.

91. Martín, *Las gentes del mar Sangley*, 37.

92. Van Deusen, *Global Indios*, 1.

93. Van Deusen, *Global Indios*, 10 and 36.

94. Van Deusen, *Global Indios*, 49.

95. At least one petition for manumission by an enslaved Bengali man in Spain referred to an attempted escape in Havana. The man eventually received his freedom in 1657 because he claimed to be an "indio" of the Philippines and therefore legally protected. Seijas, "Native Vassals," 161.

96. See Ángel Núñez Ortega, *Noticia histórica de las relaciones políticas y comerciales entre México y el Japón, durante el siglo XVII* (Mexico City: Imprenta del Gobierno, 1879), 21–26.

97. Christina Lee, "The Perception of the Japanese in Early Modern Spain: Not Quite 'the Best People Yet Discovered,'" *eHumanista* 11 (2008): 348.

98. Marco Musillo, "Travelers from Afar through Civic Spaces: The Tenshō Embassy in Renaissance Italy," in *Western Visions of the Far East in a Transpacific Age*, 167, 170, 173, 176, and 179.

99. Melba Falck Reyes and Héctor Palacios, *El japonés que conquistó Guadalajara: La historia de Juan de Páez en la Guadalajara del siglo XVII* (Guadalajara, Mexico: Universidad de Guadalajara, 2009), 36–37.

100. "Por ser gentil su nación" (C. Lee, "The Perception of the Japanese," 360).

101. C. Lee, "The Perception of the Japanese," 357 and 362; Mayu Fujikawa, "The Borghese Papacy's Reception of a Samurai Delegation and Its Fresco-Image at the Palazzo del Quirinale, Rome," in *Western Visions of the Far East in a Transpacific Age*, 194.

102. C. Lee, "The Perception of the Japanese," 367; "Tomas Felipe Japon," 1623, AGI, Contratación, 5387, N.53.

103. Martín, *Las gentes del mar Sangley,* 102.

104. Oropeza, *La migración asiática,* 220.

105. Oropeza, *La migración asiática,* 278.

106. "Petición de Antonio Pérez de oficio de intérprete de chino," 1608, AGI, Filipinas, 5, N.57, fol. 1.

107. "Estoi informado que es muy buen polvorista y que saue de fuegos artificiales si no es de ympedimento el ser chino por la suficiencia era proposito" ("Petición de Ríos Coronel de que se prorroge el diezmo de oro," 1609, AGI, Filipinas, 36, N.50, fol. 546r).

108. "Indio natural de la ciudad de Manila" and "vecino de Manila" (quoted in "Antonio Perez," 1610, AGI, Contratación, 5317, N.2, R.49, fol. 1r).

109. "Indio natural de la ciudad de Manila" (quoted in "Antonio Perez," fol. 2v).

110. "De poca barba lanpiño color parda al sumas puntas de viruelas en el rrostro" (quoted in "Antonio Perez," fol. 1v).

111. "Honrrado," "virtuoso," and "valiente" (quoted in "Petición de Diego de Maracot de encomienda de Guagua," 1623, AGI, Filipians, 39, N.20, fols. 78–83).

112. "[Como] si fueran esclauos" (quoted in "Petición de Diego de Maracot," fol. 10).

113. An escudo was worth sixteen silver reales.

114. Luciano Santiago, "The Filipino Indios Encomenderos (ca. 1620–1711)," *Philippine Quarterly of Culture and Society* 18, no. 3 (1990): 168.

115. Santiago, "The Filipino Indios Encomenderos," 166–167.

116. Santiago, "The Filipino Indios Encomenderos," 170–173.

117. "Su natural" (quoted in "Lucas Luis," 1612, AGI, Contratación, 5324, N.26, fol. 2r).

118. "Su natural" (quoted in "Lucas Luis," fol. 2r).

119. "Anda desmanparado padesiendo necesidad y falto de su dotrina" (quoted in "Diego Farfán," 1612, AGI, Contratación, 5324, N.25, fol. 1v).

120. Van Deusen, *Global Indios,* 119.

121. "En defensa de la fee catholica" (quoted in "Petición del japonés Juan Antonio de licencia para ir a Nueva España," 1624, AGI, Filipinas, 39, N.24).

122. "Tanbien saue este chino aderezar biobos y toda cosa de su tierra que este maltratada" and "es pobre y mui humilde" ("Decreto enviando petición del japonés Juan Antonio," 1624, AGI, Filipinas, 39, N.21).

123. "Gastado quanto tenia por ser el camino tan largo, pasa estrema necesidad por estar donde no tiene conozimiento con nadie para poderse valer" (quoted in "Decreto enviando petición del japonés Juan Antonio," 1624, AGI, Filipinas, 39, N.21).

124. "Porque el es hombre platico en las lenguas de aquellas partes y las sabe muy bien"and "que se suele dar a los que tienen semejantes oficios" (quoted in "Petición del japonés Juan Antonio de que se le nombre intérprete," 1624, AGI, Filipinas, 39, N.23).

125. "Porque de otra manera no tiene con que por su mucha necesidad" ("Petición del japonés Juan Antonio de licencia para ir a Nueva España").

126. "Que se le da licencia pa[ra] que buelba" ("Petición del japonés Juan Antonio de licencia para ir a Nueva España).

127. "Tratados con el amor y enseñanza que si fueran hijos," "ingratos," and "injustos" (quoted in "Real decreto para que se vea el memorial de Pedro de Mendoza," 1655, AGI, Filipinas, 4, N.40).

128. "Si el conss[ej]o juzgare . . . que deuen ser dados por libres . . . los entregara y embiara . . . con mui buena volunt[a]d porque le son de mayor gasto que servicio" (quoted in "Real decreto para que se vea el memorial de Pedro de Mendoza").

129. "Donde tiene sus padres" (quoted in "Petición de Juan Castelín Dala de licencia para volver a Filipinas," 1632, AGI, Filipinas, 5, N.413).

6. The Elusive Eighteenth Century

1. "Autos seguidos sobre el fallecimiento intestado de Alejandro Mauricio de Arabo, vecino de Guadalajara y originario de China. Nota: se realizó un inventario de sus bienes," 1746, Archivo de la Real Audiencia de la Nueva Galicia (ARANG), Caja 74, Exp. 6, Prog. 975, fols. 1r, 18r.

2. "3 pares de medias de china," "un par de calsetas nuebas de China," "quatro platos finos de China," "dos posuelos chocolateros de china," and "setenta y dos cartillas de china" ("Autos seguidos sobre el fallecimiento intestado de Alejandro Mauricio de Arabo, vecino de Guadalajara y originario de China. Nota: se realizó un inventario de sus bienes," 1746, ARANG, Caja 74, Exp. 6, Prog. 975, fols. 2r–10r).

3. Tatiana Seijas, "Asian Migrations to Latin America in the Pacific World, 16th–19th Centuries," *History Compass* 14 (2016): 577. See also Déborah Oropeza, *La migración asiática en el virreinato de la Nueva España: Un proceso de globalización (1565–1700)* (Mexico City: El Colegio de México, 2020), 29. Scholarship on Asians in Mexico in the late colonial period is largely restricted to selected passages from Rubén Carrillo Martín, *Las gentes del mar Sangley* (Mexico City: Palabra de Clío, 2015); Jaime Olveda, "El Puerto de la Navidad," in *Relaciones intercoloniales: Nueva España y Filipinas,* ed. Jaime Olveda (Zapopan, Mexico: El Colegio de Jalisco, 2017), 115; and Ben Vinson III, *Before Mestizaje: The Frontiers of Race and Caste in Colonial Mexico* (New York: Cambridge University Press, 2017). The only writing dedicated to the subject is Tatiana Seijas, "*Indios Chinos* in Eighteenth-Century Mexico," in *To Be Indio in Colonial Spanish America,* ed. Mónica Díaz (Albuquerque: University of New Mexico Press, 2017), 123–141.

4. Carrillo Martín, *Las gentes del mar Sangley,* 188–201; Edward R. Slack Jr., "Orientalizing New Spain: Perspectives on Asian Influence in Colonial Mexico," *México y la Cuenca del Pacífico* 15, no. 43 (2012): 126, "The Chinos in New Spain: A Corrective Lens for a Distorted Image," *Journal of World History* 20, no. 1 (2009): 57–67, and "Sinifying New Spain: Cathay's Influence on Colonial Mexico via the *Nao de China*," *Journal of Chinese Overseas* 5, no. 1 (2009): 20–24.

5. Ilona Katzew, "Casta Painting: Identity and Social Stratification in Colonial Mexico," *Laberinto* 1 (1997): 7; Magali M. Carrera, *Imagining Identity in New Spain: Race, Lineage, and the Colonial Body in Portraiture and Casta Paintings* (Austin: University of Texas Press, 2003), 94; Beatriz de Alba-Koch, "*Celestina* and Agustín Arrieta's *China Poblana*: Mexico's Female Icon Revisited," in *A Companion to Celestina,* ed. Enrique Fernandez (Leiden,

the Netherlands: Brill, 2017), 347; Ilona Katzew, *Casta Painting: Images of Race in Eighteenth-Century Mexico* (New Haven, CT: Yale University Press, 2004), 44.

6. Katzew, *Casta Painting*, 49.

7. Katzew, *Casta Painting*, 44.

8. Andrés Reséndez, *The Other Slavery: The Uncovered Story of Indian Enslavement in America* (Boston: Houghton Mifflin Harcourt, 2016), 172–195.

9. Ignacio María Barreda, *Castas de Nueba España*, 1777. Albrazado means "white-spotted." See Katzew, *Casta Painting*, 44.

10. Alexander von Humboldt, *Political Essay on the Kingdom of New Spain*, trans. John Black (New York: I. Riley, 1811), 184. See also Luis Andrade Ciudad and Fred Rohner, "Usos y acepciones de chino, china en el norte del Perú, siglos XVIII–XIX," *Lexis* 38, no. 1 (2014): 40.

11. Humboldt, *Political Essay*, 98.

12. Quoted in Eliette Soulier, "'China' y 'Chino' en los diccionarios castellanos (1611–1791)," in *"Ars longa": Actas del VIII Congreso Internacional Jóvenes Investigadores Siglo de Oro (JISO 2018)*, ed. Carlos Mata Induráin and Sara Santa Aguilar (Pamplona, Spain: Servicio de Publicaciones de la Universidad de Navarra, 2019), 389.

13. Soulier, "'China' y 'Chino,'" 389–390.

14. Martín, *Las gentes del mar Sangley*, 188–201; Slack, "The Chinos in New Spain," 57–67.

15. Carrera, *Imagining Identity*, 25; Marco Polo Hernández Cuevas, "The Mexican Colonial Term 'Chino' Is a Referent of Afrodescendant," *Journal of Pan African Studies* 5, no. 5 (2012): 124–143; Alba-Koch, *Celestina*, 347.

16. Melba Falck Reyes and Héctor Palacios, *El japonés que conquistó Guadalajara: La historia de Juan de Páez en la Guadalajara del siglo XVII* (Guadalajara, Mexico: Universidad de Guadalajara, 2009), 51.

17. Reyes and Palacios, *El japonés*, 67 and 90–91.

18. Reyes and Palacios, *El japonés*, 60.

19. As an example of his prosperity, Páez owned twenty-eight enslaved men, women, and children. For decades, he managed the accounts of the cathedral of Guadalajara as its steward, and he was an astute financier. His daughter Juana inherited his estate, including its enslaved people, after her mother died in 1680. Juana died in 1704 at the age of fifty-nine. Reyes and Palacios, *El japonés*, 84–85.

20. As Ann Twinam reminds us, many "historians rightfully reject the detailed hierarchies and rigidities epitomized by the casta paintings or inherent in descriptions of an inflexible casta system" (*Purchasing Whiteness: Pardos, Mulattos, and the Quest for Social Mobility in the Spanish Indies* [Stanford, CA: Stanford University Press, 2015], 48).

21. For example, see Haydée Quiroz Malca, "Acapulco y la Costa Chica, construcciones coloniales de la diversidad cultural: Reflexiones a partir del padrón de 1777," *Investigaciones sociales* 20, no. 37 (2017): 73–74.

22. Vinson, *Before Mestizaje*, 63–65.

23. See "Sumaria contra Antonio de Arano y otros: motín de México," 1692, Archivo General de Indias (AGI), Patronato, 226, N.1, R.6; "Contra Agustin Miguel de Estrada,

Lobo o Chino, por casado dos veces," 1736, Archivo General de la Nación México (AGN), Inquisición, vol. 872, exp. 2; "Ygnacio Vásquez, mulato o chino," 1782, AGN, Matrimonios, Caja 315, exp. 41.

24. According to Twinam, "Early expressions of naturaleza trace back to the *Siete Partidas,* the law code of medieval Spain (1252–1284). . . . 'Nature' was the God-given essence that set what 'was.' In contrast, 'naturaleza' was the 'was' that governed the flow of that positive or negative essence from father and mother to offspring" (*Purchasing Whiteness,* 50).

25. Seijas, "Asian Migrations to Latin America," 577.

26. Mariano A. Bonialian, *China en la América colonial: Bienes, mercados, comercio y cultura del consumo desde México hasta Buenos Aires* (Mexico City: Editorial Biblios, 2014), 56–60, and *El pacífico hispanoamericano: Política y comercio asiático en el imperio español (1680–1784)* (Mexico City: El Colegio de México, 2012), 225.

27. John Tutino, *Making a New World: Founding Capitalism in the Bajío and Spanish North America* (Durham, NC: Duke University Press, 2011), 162–164.

28. Antonio de Robles, *Diarios de sucesos notables (1665–1703)* (Mexico City: Editorial Porrúa, 1946), 3:75 and 91.

29. Tutino, *Making a New World,* 160.

30. Robles, *Diarios,* 3:114 and 129.

31. Robles, *Diarios,* 3:310.

32. "Petición del capitán Pedro Alonso Davalos y Bracamonte alcalde ordinario de la ciudad de Mexico," 1703, AGN, Indiferente Virreinal, 2463, exp. 007.

33. Oropeza, *La migración asiática,* 249–252. Compare to the antislavery rhetoric of Alonso de Montúfar. Alonso de Montúfar, "Carta de Alonso de Montúfar o.p., arzobispo de México, considerando la esclavitud de los negros tan injusta como la de los indios," in *La conquista espiritual de la América Española: 200 documentos-siglos XVI,* ed. Paulo Suess (Quito, Ecuador: Abya-Yala, 2002), 432; Emily Berquist Soule, "Early Spanish Antislavery and the Abolition of the Slave Trade to Spanish America," in *From the Galleons to the Highlands: Slave Trade Routes in the Spanish Americas,* ed. Alex Borucki, David Eltis, and David Wheat (Albuquerque: University of New Mexico Press, 2020), 278–279.

34. "Voluminoso" and "total[ent]e independiente" (quoted in "Mateo de la Torre," 1648, AGN, Procesos Civiles, Caja 79, exp. 2855, fol. 20).

35. "Le toca reconocer a quien pertensca el conocim[ien]to desta causa" (quoted in "Mateo de la Torre," fol. 20).

36. "Justam[en]te temeroso de litigar" and "tan valida y poderosa" (quoted in "Mateo de la Torre," fol. 20).

37. "Fernando Haro y Monterroso," 1670, AGI, Contratación, 5437, N.1, R.68.

38. "Servicios personales" ("Cartas de Audiencia," 1671, AGI, Guadalajara, 11, R.10, N.84).

39. "Cartas de Audiencia," 1671, AGI, Guadalajara, 11, R.10, N.84.

40. Oropeza, *La migración asiática,* 253–254.

41. There is some tantalizing evidence that Haro y Monterroso appreciated the Asian presence in Mexico. On March 23, 1671, he argued that the coconut wine called *colima* should

not be banned but merely regulated. "Chinos" had originally brought this drink to the Pacific coast a century earlier and were prominent in its production as both plantation laborers and owners. Haro y Monterroso wrote that "used with moderation, it is very healthy" and that it was often consumed in "religious communities" (quoted in "Cartas de Audiencia," 1671, AGI, Guadalajara, 11, R.10, N.61; "Méritos: Fernando Haro y Monterroso," 1689, AGI, Indiferente, 132, N.22, 3). For more on coconut wine, see Chapter 3.

42. See Juan de Solórzano Pereira, *Política Indiana* (Madrid: Diego Díaz de la Carrera, 1648), 1:69.

43. "Ay grandissimo numero destos chinos . . . rreputados comúnmente por esclavos y las mujeres chinas tambien y sus hijos sin diferencia alguna" (quoted in "Cartas de Audiencia," 1672, AGI, Guadalajara, 12, R.1, N.9).

44. "Todas las mugeres de qualquiera hedad, y todos los barones, que tenían menos de catorce años al tiempo que los tomaron en justa guerra sean declarados por libres" (quoted in "Cartas de Audiencia").

45. Virginia González Claverán, "Un documento colonial sobre esclavos asiáticos," *Hmex* 38, no. 3 (1989): 528. It seems doubtful that Spanish officials took the care to deport these newly liberated "chinos."

46. "Cartas de Audiencia."

47. "Cartas de Audiencia," fol. 31v.

48. "Celo" and "es tan justo y conveniente dejar a Libert[di]os en su liuertad"(quoted in "Libertad de los indios," 1672, AGI, Guadalajara, 231, L.4, fols. 68v–69rv).

49. "Cartas de Audiencia," 1675, AGI, México, 82, R.2, N.51; Reséndez, *The Other Slavery,* 132; Tatiana Seijas, *Asian Slaves in Colonial Mexico: From Chinos to Indians* (New York: Cambridge University Press, 2014), 140.

50. "Cartas de Audiencia," 1675, AGI, México, 82, R.2, N.51.

51. "Los retiren a obrajes y reales de minas con animo de ocultarlos pa[ra] que no puedan alcansar justicia" ("Cartas de Audiencia," 1675, AGI, México, 82, R.2, N.51).

52. "Muy distinta de la mansedumbre y sinseridad delos indios naturales de este reyno, por ser aquellos mas hábiles, y no de tan buenas inclinaciones, y costumbres" (quoted in "Cartas de Audiencia," 1675, AGI, México, 82, R.2, N.51). The strange decision to use the term *Biblical Philippians* to refer to Philippine natives may have served to characterize them as in need of spiritual guidance.

53. For an excellent discussion of Miranda's anti-Muslim rhetoric, see Seijas, *Asian Slaves,* 236–238.

54. "Aunque esta materia fue facil de practicar en la real audiencia de Guadalaxara por no llegar a veinte el numero de estos esclabos en todo aquel districto, aquí se ha reconocido muy perjudicial, y peligrosa" (quoted in "Cartas de Audiencia," 1675, AGI, México, 82, R.2, N.51).

55. "El fin de su magestad, no es de ganar vasallos sino es aumentar el gremio de la iglesia y la esclavitud es medio contrario" (quoted in "Cartas de Audiencia," 1675, AGI, México, 82, R.2, N.51, fol. 3v).

56. Miranda's hostility to emancipation led to many disputes between him and Haro y Monterroso over the next several years. Little came of these disputes because Miranda had

the support of the viceroy, Payo Enríquez de Ribera. See "Represión a Martín de Solís, fiscal de la Audiencia de México," 1676, AGI, Guadalajara, 231, L.4, fols. 157r–158v; "Proceder del fiscal de la Audiencia de México," 1678, AGI, México, 50, N.49; "Cartas del virrey Payo Enríquez de Ribera," 1678, AGI, México, 50, N.21.

57. Robles, *Diarios*, 3:170–171.

58. Oropeza, *La migración asiática*, 255.

59. Oropeza, *La migración asiática*, 256.

60. See "Liberación de indios esclavos," 1674, AGI, Guadalajara, 231, L.4, fol. 95v; "Cartas de Audiencia," 1673, AGI, Guadalajara, 12, R.2, N.24.

61. Alberto Carrillo Cázares, *Partidos y padrones del obispado de Michoacán: 1680–1685* (Zamora, Spain: El Colegio de Michoacán, 1996), 334.

62. "Autos sobre Libertad promovidos por Domingo de la Cruz, chino y esclavo natural de Manila, contra Juan Sánchez Bañales vecino de Zapotlán," 1678, ARANG, Caja 9, Exp. 9, Prog. 124, fol. 5v.

63. Jorge Delgadillo Núñez, "Becoming Citizens: Afro-Mexicans, Identity, and Historical Memory in Guadalajara, 17th to 19th Centuries," PhD diss., Vanderbilt University, 2021, 77.

64. Olveda, "El Puerto de la Navidad," 120–121.

65. "No se puede dudar que entre los gravísimos desconsuelos que padeció en tan arrastrado cautiverio esta inocente virgen, especialmente en los repetidos y casi continuados peligros de muerte, sería el mayor no estar bautizada" (Alonso Ramos, *Los prodigios de la Omnipotencia y milagros de la gracia en la vida de la venerable sierva de Dios Catarina de San Juan*, ed. Gisela von Wobeser [Mexico City: Universidad Nacional Autónoma de México-Instituto de Investigaciones Históricas, 2017], 1:55).

66. James Muldoon, *The Americas in the Spanish World Order: The Justification for Conquest in the Seventeenth Century* (Philadelphia: University of Pennsylvania Press, 1994), 47.

67. "No la tratasen como a señora, ni como a hija, sino como a esclava" (Ramos, *Los prodigios*, 1:81).

68. "Esclava de sus esclavos" (quoted in Ramos, *Los prodigios*, 2:53–92).

69. Kate Risse, "Catarina de San Juan and the China Poblana: From Spiritual Humility to Civil Obedience," *Confluencia* 18, no. 1 (2002): 73; Gauvin Alexander Bailey, "A Mughal Princess in Baroque New Spain: Catarina de San Juan (1606–1688), the China Poblana," *Anales del instituto de investigaciones estéticas* 71 (1997): 41.

70. "Orden sobre esclavos que llegan a Acapulco desde Filipinas," 1700, AGI, 332, L.10, fol. 142v.

71. "Profesar muchos la seta de Maometana" ("Orden sobre esclavos que llegan a Acapulco desde Filipinas," fol. 142v).

72. Sabrina Smith, "Slave Trading in Antequera and Interregional Slave Traffic in New Spain, 1680–1710," in *From the Galleons to the Highlands: Slave Trade Routes in the Spanish Americas*, ed. Alex Borucki, David Eltis, and David Wheat (Albuquerque: University of New Mexico Press, 2020), 135–136.

73. "Autos del Liberta Nuestra Señora del Rosario del cargo de Miguel de Elorriaga," 1712, AGI, Contaduría, 908, N.1, fols. 917–923.

74. "Expediente sobre el comercio entre Filipinas y Nueva España," 1712–22, AGI, Filipinas, 206, N.1, fols. 221v–225v.

75. "El Capitán de Fragata, Don Pedro de la Guardia, solicitó al Cura Párroco Don Benito Vélez que bautizara e instruyera en la fe a su esclavo negro, natural de las costa [*sic*] de Mozambique," 1800, ARANG, Caja 376, exp. 12, prog. 5719; Norah L. A. Gharala, "'From Mozambique in Indies of Portugal': Locating East Africans in New Spain," *Journal of Global History* 7, no. 3 (2022): 264.

76. "Aspecto ser natural de aquellas islas, o panpango" (quoted in "Instancia presentada por Juan de Valenzuela," 1718, AGN, Indiferente Virreinal, 3044, exp. 008).

77. "Porque todos los chinos de d[ich]as islas gozan de libertad" (quoted in "Instancia presentada por Juan de Valenzuela").

78. Significantly, people described as "achinado / a" were not necessarily guaranteed freedom during the eighteenth century. In 1743, a twenty-year-old woman named María Unsuelo ("achinada") was enslaved on a hacienda called Santa Clara in the town of San Lucas near Tampico. Francisco de Solano, *Relaciones geográficas del Arzobispado de México. 1743*, ed. Catalina Romero (Madrid: Consejo Superior de Investigaciones Científicas, 1988), 1:216.

79. Danielle Terrazas Williams, *The Capital of Free Women: Race, Legitimacy, and Liberty in Colonial Mexico* (New Haven, CT: Yale University Press, 2022), 29–30.

80. "Los cuales por la próxima o remota, tenían procedencia de esclavos" ("Bando en que se prohíbe el casamiento de blancos con negros, mulatos, chinos y cualquier casta," AGN, Indiferente Virreinal, Caja 0469, exp. 005).

81. For more on the haphazard process of emancipation in the Philippines, see Oropeza, *La migración asiática*, 258.

82. "No habitan Indios en esta Ciudad, sino en los Pueblos de su Jurisdiccion, y en ella solo, se hallan avecindados cerca de quatrocientas familias de Chinos, Mulatos, y Negros" (Joseph Antonio de Villa-Señor y Sánchez, *Theatro americano: Descripcion general de los Reynos y provincias de la Nueva-España y sus jurisdicciones* [Mexico City: Viuda de D. Joseph Bernardo de Hogal, 1746], 186–187). The figure of four hundred families had also been recorded three years earlier by Francisco de Solano (Solano, *Relaciones geográficas*, 1:22).

83. "La una de Chinos, la otra de Negros, y la tercera de Mulatos, las que hacen sus Guardias en continua atalaya, assi en las Vigias del Puerto, como en las de ambas Costas" (Villa-Señor y Sánchez, *Theatro americano*, 187).

84. Solano, *Relaciones geográficas*, 1:22.

85. Solano, *Relaciones geográficas*, 1:23.

86. According to Solano, "chinos" could still be found in 1743 in the jurisdiction of Tixtla between Acapulco and Mexico City as well, particularly the towns of Chilpanzingo and Zumpango that were entirely dependent on the arrival of the Manila galleons to Acapulco (Solano, *Relaciones geográficas* 2:468). See also D. A. Brading, *Miners and Merchants in Bourbon Mexico 1763–1810* (New York: Cambridge University Press, 1971), 27–28.

87. Villa-Señor y Sánchez, *Theatro americano*, 189; Solano, *Relaciones geográficas*, 1:25.

88. Villa-Señor y Sánchez, *Theatro americano*, 189.

89. Slack, "The *Chinos* in New Spain," 41.

90. "Indios luzones filipinos que vulgarmente llaman chinos" (Solano, *Relaciones geográficas*, 1:25).

91. Solano, *Relaciones geográficas*, 1:25. Oropeza's research shows that not all "chinos" in Coyuca married Indigenous women: some married "mulatas," "chinas," "mestizas," or "negras" (*La migración asiática*, 196).

92. Matthew J. Furlong, "Peasants, Servants, and Sojourners: Itinerant Asians in Colonial New Spain, 1571–1720," PhD diss., University of Arizona, 2014, 522; Solano, *Relaciones geográficas*, 1:23.

93. Solano, *Relaciones geográficas*, 1:25.

94. "Nuestro barrio de San Nicolás se fundó desde el tiempo antiguo por los indios philipinos que venían anualmente de Manila . . . formando la población hasta el aumento que hoy tiene" (quoted in Oropeza, *La migración asiática*, 194; see also 162). See also Carrillo Martín, *Las gentes del mar Sangley*, 183.

95. José Antonio Calderón Quijano, *Historia de las fortificaciones en Nueva España* (Seville, Spain: Escuela de Estudios Hispano-Americanos de Sevilla, 1953), 238.

96. Vinson, *Before Mestizaje*, 94.

97. However, it should be noted that some of the 1,292 "mulatos" in Acapulco had a "chino" or "china" parent. Quiroz Malca, "Acapulco y la Costa Chica," 73–74; Vinson, *Before Mestizaje*, 94.

98. Stanley J. Stein and Barbara H. Stein, *The Colonial Heritage of Latin America: Essays on Economic Dependence in Perspective* (New York: Oxford University Press, 1970), 86–88; Katzew, *Casta Painting*, 111.

99. According to Jackie R. Booker, "The Bourbon reforms . . . threatened to erode the advantages enjoyed by Cádiz and Mexico City entrepreneurs who united through status, family, and ideology" ("The Veracruz Merchant Community in Late Bourbon Mexico: A Preliminary Portrait, 1770–1810," *Americas* 45, no. 2 [1998]: 188).

100. D. A. Brading, *Church and State in Bourbon Mexico: The Diocese of Michoacán 1749–1810* (New York: Cambridge University Press, 1994), 7.

101. Brading, *Miners and Merchants*, 30.

102. Brading, *Miners and Merchants*, 29.

103. Stein and Stein, *The Colonial Heritage of Latin America*, 100–101.

104. Ruth Hill, *Hierarchy, Commerce, and Fraud in Bourbon Spanish America: A Postal Inspector's Exposé* (Nashville, TN: Vanderbilt University Press, 2005), 109, 111, and 115.

105. Bonialian, *China en la América colonial*, 75.

106. Eric Van Young, *Hacienda and Market in Eighteenth-Century Mexico: The Rural Economy of the Guadalajara Region, 1675–1820* (Berkeley: University of California Press, 1981), 26.

107. Young, *Hacienda and Market*, 29–31.

108. Brading, *Miners and Merchants*, 14–15.

109. Olveda, "El Puerto de la Navidad," 121–122.

110. Jorge Alberto Ruiz and María Concepción Gavira, "Mezclas y desorden en la población de una provincia fronteriza: Zacatula—México en el siglo XVIII," *Cuadernos interculturales* 11, no. 21 (2013): 152.

111. Cázares, *Partidos y padrones*, 344–346.

112. Roberto Junco Sanchez, Guadalupe Pinzón, and Etsuko Miyata, "The Chinese Porcelain from the Port of San Blas, Mexico," in *Archeology of Manila Galleon Seaports and Early Maritime Globalization*, ed. Chunming Wu, Roberto Junco Sanchez, and Miao Liu (Singapore: Springer, 2019), 2:241.

113. Salvador Bernabéu and José María García Redondo, "Mapas trastornados: Análisis histórico-visual de los derroteros del galeón de Manila en el siglo XVIII," in *Nueva España, puerta americana al Pacífico asiático*, ed. Carmen Yuste López (Mexico City: Universidad Nacional Autónoma de México, 2019), 185.

114. Young, *Hacienda and Market*, 146.

115. "Natural del Reyno de Manila" ("Ante la Junta de Requisición de Guadalajara de Bienes Europeos; compuesta por el Licenciado Don Miguel Marin, Alcalde Ordinario de Guadalajara; Don Vicente Garro, Administrador de Correos; Don Manuel Porres Baranda de Estrada, vocales de dicha junta y su Fiscal, Don Francisco González de Velasco, se presentaron Don Manuel Ruiz, natural de los reinos de Castilla, del comercio de Sayula y residente en Guadalajara y Miguel Sales, natural del reino de Manila, para acusar a Agustín Madrigal, vecino de Tequila, de haberles quitado sus pertenencias; por lo que, debido a que el acusado ya estaba preso, piden se les devuelvan sus propiedades o se le embarguen sus bienes," 1811, ARANG, Caja 445, exp. 3, Prog. 7335, fols. 2r–12r).

116. These merchants were likely part of the new wave of European-born Spaniards (many from the Basque region) who arrived in the Americas to do business during the latter half of the eighteenth century. Booker, "The Veracruz Merchant Community," 188 and 197; Brading, *Miners and Merchants*, 35–37.

117. Other records attest to Asian "chinos'" distant trajectories, going as far as Spain in at least one case and to Buenos Aires in another. Interestingly, the first known Asian in what would later become Argentina was Francisco Xapón, an enslaved Japanese man brought to the Córdoba region via Buenos Aires. He had been sold for the princely sum of eight hundred pesos and litigated successfully for his freedom in 1597–1598. Lucío de Sousa, *The Portuguese Slave Trade in Early Modern Japan: Merchants, Jesuits and Japanese, Chinese and Korean Slaves* (Boston: Brill, 2019), 459–461; "Felix Lince," 1729, AGI, Contratación, 5477, N.12; Rubén Carrillo Martín, "Asians to New Spain: Asian Cultural and Migratory Flows in Mexico in the Early Stages of 'Globalization' (1565–1816)," PhD diss., Universitat Oberta de Catalunya, 2015, 136.

118. Carrillo Martín, *Las gentes del mar Sangley*, 182–183.

119. Carrillo Martín, *Las gentes del mar Sangley*, 182.

120. Ernest Sánchez Santiró, "La población de la ciudad de México en 1777," *Secuencia* 60 (2004): 35.

121. Susan Migden Socolow, "Introduction to the Rural Past," in *The Countryside in Colonial Latin America*, ed. Louisa Schell Hoberman and Susan Migden Socolow (Albuquerque: University of New Mexico Press, 1996), 7.

122. Brading, *Church and State in Bourbon Mexico*, 8. See also D. A. Brading, "Tridentine Catholicism and Enlightened Despotism in Bourbon Mexico," *Journal of Latin American Studies* 15, no. 1 (1983): 1–22, and *Miners and Merchants*, 26–27; Frank T. Proctor III, "'Amores

perritos': Puppies, Laughter and Popular Catholicism in Bourbon Mexico City," *Journal of Latin American Studies* 46, no. 1 (2014): 1–28.

123. Ruth Behar, "Sex and Sin, Witchcraft and the Devil in Late-Colonial Mexico," *American Ethnologist* 14, no. 1 (1987): 49–51.

124. Brading, *Church and State in Bourbon Mexico,* 150–170, and "'Tridentine Catholicism and Enlightened Despotism,'" 22.

125. "Jose de la Asencion, mulato libre y natural de la villa de Colima, denuncia a un indio o chino de Filipinas," 1719, AGN, Inquisición, vol. 1169, exp. SN, fol. 263r.

126. Gonzalo Aguirre Beltrán, *Medicina y magia: El proceso de aculturación en la estructura colonial,* 3rd ed. (Mexico City: Instituto Nacional Indigenista, 1987), 128, 152, 175, and 179.

127. "Jose de la Asencion, mulato libre y natural de la villa de Colima, denuncia a un indio o chino de Filipinas," 1719, AGN, Inquisición, vol. 1169, exp. SN, fol. 263r. See also Carrillo Martín, *Las gentes del mar Sangley,* 60.

128. Seijas, *"Indios Chinos,"* 130; "Autos seguidos en Orizaba contra Pascuala de los Reyes, casada según dice con Jose Feliciano, chino," 1701, AGN, Inquisición, vol. 718, exp. SN, fols. 341r–v.

129. "Es alto Delgado, ojos chicos, como de sangley, narizes chattas, color de chino, y pelo corto negro, y que usa birrete a su parecer" ("Para que se aprehendiera a un hombre llamado Nicolas, de calidad chino," 1772, AGN, Inquisición, vol. 1103, exp. 11, fol. 136r).

130. "Ni otra casta" ("Para que se aprehendiera a un hombre llamado Nicolas," fol. 139r; emphasis added).

131. "Chino puro" ("Para que se aprehendiera a un hombre llamado Nicolas," fol. 135v).

132. Seijas, *"Indios Chinos,"* 134.

133. "Vulgarmente llaman Chinos" and "los de las islas philipinas, que residen en su distrito" (quoted in "Consulta que hizo a este tribunal," 1766, AGN, Inquisición, vol. 1037, exp. 6, fol. 291r).

134. "Consulta que hizo a este tribunal," fols. 291r–v.

135. Bonialian, *China en la América colonial,* 59, and *El pacífico hispanoamericano,* 380.

136. Pedro Manuel de Arandia y Santestevan, *Ordenanzas de marina, para los navios del rey, de las islas Philipinas, que en Guerra, y con reales permissos hacen viages al Reyno de la Nueva España, ù otro destino del Real servicio* (Manila: Imprenta de la Compañía de Jesús, 1757), 121.

137. Although casta descriptors are missing from the list, we should assume that, like other groupings of transpacific sailors during this period, the majority of the crew members were Asian. One sick convict named Jose Mariano was specifically designated as *sianes* (Thai). "Acapulco, Pedro de Ossorio da lista de individuos de la tripulación y guarnición de la nao San Andrés," 1790, AGN, Indiferente Virreinal, Caja 2834, exp. 021.

138. Bonialian, *El pacífico hispanoamericano,* 375.

139. "Por lo general, todos los barcos que se requieren para el comercio con Acapulco están ahí. Aquí se pueden ver de manera constante entre doscientos y trescientos indígenas, a veces hasta seiscientos, que trabajan cargando los barcos de guerra y los galeones españoles" (quoted in Laura Ibarra García, "El comercio entre Nueva España y Filipinas según un alemán del siglo XVIII," in *Relaciones intercoloniales: Nueva España y Filipinas,* ed. Jaime Olveda [Zapopan, Mexico: El Colegio de Jalisco, 2017], 14). For more on wealthy

foreign traders who conducted trade in Manila, see Kristie Patricia Flannery and Guillermo Ruiz-Stovel, "The Loyal Foreign Merchant Captain: Thomé Gaspar de León and the Making of Manila's Intra-Asian Connections," *Vegueta. Anuario de la Facultad de Geografía e Historia* 20 (2020): 189–215.

140. "Expediente sobre tripulaciones y caja de ahorros," 1753–1755, AGI, Filipinas, 157, N.1, fols. 97–145.

141. For example, Edward Slack found that in 1760, the *Santísima Trinidad* "was manned by 370 sailors, consisting of 30 officers (Europeans or Mexican *criollos*), 40 artillerymen (27 *chinos*), 120 sailors (109 *chinos*), 100 'Spanish' cabin boys (96 *chinos*), and 80 'plain' cabin boys (78 *chinos*). In sum, 84 percent (310) of the crew were born and raised in Spain's Asian colony, with 68 percent (250) hailing from the port of Cavite alone" ("The Chinos in New Spain," 39).

142. Spanish grumetes were paid a hundred pesos per year and could bring a chest of belongings with them, while simple grumetes received only thirty-five pesos per year and could not bring a chest. Arandia y Santestevan, *Ordenanzas de marina*, 8 and 41.

143. Seijas, "Indios Chinos," 135.

144. This observation coincides with Eva Maria Mehl's finding that convict deportations from Mexico to the Philippines increased during the late colonial period (*Forced Migration in the Spanish Pacific World: From Mexico to the Philippines, 1765–1811* [Cambridge: Cambridge University Press, 2016], 17).

145. *Trigueño* is also sometimes translated as "olive-skinned" or "swarthy."

146. Alex Kerner, "Beard and Conquest: The Role of Hair in the Construction of Gendered Spanish Attitudes towards the American Indians in the Sixteenth Century," *Revista de historia iberoamericana* 6, no. 1 (2013): 105–112; Michael Schreffler, "'Their Cortés and Our Cortés': Spanish Colonialism and Aztec Representation," *Art Bulletin* 91, no. 4 (2009): 408–412.

147. Jorge Cañizares-Esguerra, "New World, New Stars: Patriotic Astrology and the Invention of Indian and Creole Bodies in Colonial Spanish America, 1600–1650," *American Historical Review* 104, no. 1 (1999): 57.

148. See Slack, "The Chinos in New Spain," 39; Arturo Giráldez, *The Age of Trade: The Manila Galleons and the Dawn of the Global Economy* (Lanham, MD: Rowman and Littlefield, 2015), 140.

149. Bonialian, *El pacífico hispanoamericano*, 375 and 398.

150. See "Categoría: Galeón de Manila," Historia Naval de España, February 27, 2021, https://todoavante.es/index.php?title=Categor%C3%ADa%3AGale%C3%B3n_de _Manila&fbclid=IwAR37f4PMmuSevf3ZsInSzEUCosh3xWoTenE1pKqTLe8UKVIxDnlvI KeQlNE.

151. Bonialian, *El pacífico hispanoamericano*, 404 and 407. See also Joshua Eng Sin Kueh, "The Manila Chinese: Community, Trade and Empire, c. 1570–c. 1770," PhD diss., Georgetown University, 2014, 163.

152. For a thorough examination of the Company and its operations, see María Lourdes Díaz-Trechuelo Spinola, *La Real Compañía de Filipinas* (Seville, Spain: Escuela de Estudios Hispano-Americanos de Sevilla, 1965).

153. William Lytle Schurz, *The Manila Galleon: Illustrated with Maps* (New York: E. P. Dutton, 1939), 314–318.

154. Alberto Baena Zapatero, "El comercio asiático en los barcos de la armada: Generales y equipajes entre Manila y Cádiz," in *Nueva España: Puerta americana al Pacífico asiático siglos XVI–XVIII*, ed. Carmen Yuste López (Mexico City: Universidad Nacional Autónoma de México, 2019), 283.

155. Curiously, sixty-eight Jesuits who had been expulsed from the colonies, along with the others of their religious order, were also aboard the *Santa Rosa de Lima* and disembarked in Cádiz. "Registro de venida de la fragata: Santa Rosa de Lima," 1770, AGI, Contratación, 2436, N.2, R.1; Zapatero, "El comercio asiático," 287.

156. Zapatero, "El comercio asiático," 316–319.

157. Salvador P. Escoto, "Governor Anda and the Liquidation of the Jesuit Temporalities in the Philippines, 1770–1776," *Philippine Studies* 23, no. 3 (1975): 303; "Cartas del Gobernador de Filipinas," 1772, AGN, Indiferente Virreinal, 4427, exp. 042, fols. 64r–5v.

158. "Restituirse a Manila su patria" ("Cartas del Gobernador de Filipinas," 1772, AGN, Indiferente Virreinal, 4427, exp. 042, fol. 63r).

159. "Marcha" ("Cartas del Gobernador de Filipinas," fol. 67v).

160. "Cartas del Gobernador de Filipinas," 1772, AGN, Indiferente Virreinal, 4427, exp. 042.

161. Refer to the "Caja de Acapulco" records at the AGI.

162. For example, see Filomeno V. Aguilar Jr., "'Filibustero,' Rizal, and the Manilamen of the Nineteenth Century," *Philippine Studies* 59, no. 4 (2011): 442–452.

163. Francis Drake, Thomas Cavendish, Joris van Speilbergen, Woodes Rogers, William Dampier, and George Anson were among the captains of privateers on this route. Schurz, *The Manila Galleon*, 303–360.

164. Warren Cook, *Flood Tide of Empire: Spain and the Pacific Northwest, 1543–1819* (New Haven, CT: Yale University Press, 1973); Buschmann, Slack, and Tueller, *Navigating the Spanish Lake*, 37–62; Rainer Buschmann, *Iberian Visions of the Pacific Ocean, 1507–1899* (New York: Palgrave Macmillan, 2014).

165. Giráldez, *The Age of Trade*, 178–179.

166. Giráldez, *The Age of Trade*, 175.

167. Mehl, *Forced Migration*, 74.

168. Dutch officials in Batavia had attempted to trade directly with colonial Mexico in 1747 via two ships, the *Hervating* and the *Herstheller*, but both were captured off the Mexican Pacific coast. Guadalupe Pinzón Ríos, "La expedición neerlandesa de 1747: Un intento inglés y holandés por comerciar con Nueva España," in *Nueva España: Puerta americana al Pacífico asiático siglos XVI–XVIII*, 211; Giráldez, *The Age of Trade*, 187–189. For more on the meanings of comercio libre during this period, see Stanley J. Stein and Barbara H. Stein, *Apogee of Empire: Spain and New Spain in the Age of Charles III, 1759–1789* (Baltimore, MD: Johns Hopkins University Press, 2003), 69–80, 143–185, 223–265.

169. Bonialian, *China en la América colonial*, 75–76.

170. See Malcolm Churchill, "Louisiana History and Early Filipino Settlement: Searching for the Story," *Bulletin of the American Historical Collection Foundation* 27, no. 2 (1999): 25–48;

Lafcadio Hearn, "Saint Malo: A Lacustrine Village in Louisiana," *Harper's Weekly,* March 31, 1883, 196–199.

171. Lucas Alamán, "The Siege of Guanajuato," in *The Mexico Reader: History, Culture, Politics,* ed. Gilbert M. Joseph and Timothy J. Henderson (Durham, NC: Duke University Press, 2002), 173.

172. John Tutino, "Breaking New Spain, 1808–21: Remaking Power, Production, and Patriarchy before Iguala," *Mexican Studies / Estudios Mexicanos* 37, no. 3 (2021): 369. Although the soldier rosters for this period rarely give soldiers' castas, I strongly suspect that Asians and / or Asian descendants participated in the siege of Acapulco. Significantly, the militias of Guadalajara and Michoacán defected and joined the rebels. Brading, *Miners and Merchants,* 345.

173. Shirley Fish, *The Manila-Acapulco Galleons: The Treasure Ships of the Pacific* (Milton Keynes, UK: AuthorHouse UK, 2011), 466–491; Schurz, *The Manila Galleon,* 60.

174. Tutino, "Breaking New Spain," 373–374.

175. Giráldez, *The Age of Trade,* 190.

176. Fish, *The Manila-Acapulco Galleons,* 466–491.

177. For an overview of the meanings of "americano," see John Charles Chasteen, *Americanos: Latin America's Struggle for Independence* (New York: Oxford University Press, 2008), 1–4.

178. "No sólo a los nacidos en América, sino a los europeos, africanos y asiáticos que en ella residen" (quoted in "Plan de Independencia de la América Septentrional: Iguala," in *Derechos del pueblo mexicano: México a través de sus constituciones,* ed. Eduardo Ferrer Mac-Gregor and Luis René Guerrero Galván, 9th ed. [Mexico City: Miguel Ángel Porrúa, 2016], 1:235; emphasis added). While it is very rare to see "asiático" in reference to Asian populations during the early modern period, the word had become more common by the early nineteenth century.

179. Chasteen, *Americanos,* 93–94.

180. Lisa Yun, *The Coolie Speaks: Chinese Indentured Laborers and African Slaves in Cuba* (Philadelphia, PA: Temple University Press, 2008), 5; Richard B. Allen, "Slaves, Convicts, Abolitionism and the Global Origins of the Post-Emancipation Indentured Labor System," *Slavery & Abolition* 35, no. 2 (2014): 333–335.

181. Leonard Blussé, "Batavia, 1619–1740: The Rise and Fall of a Chinese Colonial Town," *Journal of Southeast Asian Studies* 12, no. 1 (1981): 166; Manel Ollé, "Del barrio al océano: Los chinos de Manila entre el comercio del Galeón, la convivencia municipal y las redes diásporas regionales," in *Los chinos de utramar: Diásporas, sociabilidad e identidades,* ed. Ricardo Martínez Esquivel (Mexico City: Palabra de Clío, 2007), 28; Markus Vink, "'The World's Oldest Trade': Dutch Slavery and Slave Trade in the Indian Ocean in the Seventeenth Century," *Journal of World History* 14, no. 2 (2003): 140 and 142–144; Kerry Ward, "'Tavern of the Seas'? The Cape of Good Hope as an Oceanic Crossroads during the Seventeenth and Eighteenth Centuries," in *Seascapes: Maritime Histories, Littoral Cultures, and Transoceanic Exchanges,* ed. Jerry H. Bentley, Renate Bridenthal, and Karen Wigen (Honolulu: University of Hawai'i Press, 2007), 143; Robert C.-H. Shell, "The March of the Mardijckers: The Toleration of Islam at the Cape, 1633–1861," *Kronos* 22 (1995): 6–7; Martha W. McCartney, *A Study of the Africans and African Americans on Jamestown Island and at Green Spring, 1619–1803* (Wil-

liamsburg, VA: Colonial Williamsburg Foundation, 2003), 52; Iris H. Wilson Engstrand, "Introduction," in José Mariano Mozino, *Noticias de Nutka: An Account of Nootka Sound in 1792,* trans. and ed. Iris H. Wilson Engstrand (Seattle: University of Washington Press, 1991), xxxi.

182. Erika Lee, *The Making of Asian America: A History* (New York: Simon and Schuster, 2016), 34.

183. Allen, "Slaves, Convicts," 332–333.

184. See Lisa Lowe, *The Intimacies of Four Continents* (Durham, NC: Duke University Press, 2015); Yun, *The Coolie Speaks;* Evelyn Hu-DeHart, "Chinese Coolie Labor in Cuba and Peru in the Nineteenth Century: Free Labor or Neoslavery?," *Journal of Overseas Chinese Studies* 2, no. 2 (1992): 38–54, and "On Coolies and Shopkeepers: The Chinese as Huagong (Laborers) and Huashang (Merchants) in Latin America / Caribbean," in *Displacements and Diasporas: Asians in the Americas,* ed. Wanni W. Anderson and Robert G. Lee (New Brunswick, NJ: Rutgers University Press, 2005), 78–111; Matthew Pratt Guterl, "After Slavery: Asian Labor, the American South, and the Age of Emancipation," *Journal of World History* 14, no. 2 (2011): 209–241; Moon-Ho Jung, "Outlawing 'Coolies': Race, Nation, and Empire in the Age of Emancipation," *American Quarterly* 57, no. 3 (2005): 677–701; Edlie L. Wong, *Racial Reconstruction: Black Inclusion, Chinese Exclusion, and the Fictions of Citizenship* (New York: New York University Press, 2015).

185. Olveda, "El Puerto de la Navidad," 125; Kathleen López, *Chinese Cubans: A Transnational History* (Chapel Hill: University of North Carolina Press, 2013), 16–21; Ana Paulina Lee, *Mandarin Brazil: Race, Representation, and Memory* (Stanford, CA: Stanford University Press, 2018), 5–6.

186. López, *Chinese Cubans,* 22.

187. Quoted in Yun, *The Coolie Speaks,* 243.

188. Quoted in Yun, *The Coolie Speaks,* 249.

189. Isabelle Lausent-Herrera, "Tusans (Tusheng) and the Changing Chinese Community in Peru," *Journal of Chinese Overseas* 7, no. 1 (2009): 116.

190. Beth Lew-Williams, *The Chinese Must Go: Violence, Exclusion and the Making of the Alien in America* (Cambridge, MA: Harvard University Press, 2018), 21.

191. James L. Huesmann, "The Chinese in Costa Rica, 1855–1897," *Historian* 53, no. 4 (1991): 715.

192. Robert Chao Romero, *The Chinese in Mexico, 1882–1940* (Tucson: University of Arizona Press, 2010), 26.

193. Jason Oliver Chang, *Chino: Anti-Chinese Racism in Mexico, 1880–1940* (Urbana: University of Illinois Press, 2017), 10.

194. Steve J. Stern, "The Tricks of Time: Colonial Legacies and Historical Sensibilities in Latin America," *Princeton University Library Chronicle* 57, no. 3 (1996): 378.

Conclusion

1. "Tal vez en el traje de Catarina de San Juan tenga origen el zangalejo ó castor de la *China de Puebla,* como le decían" (Antonio Carrión, *Historia de la ciudad de Puebla de los Angeles [Puebla de Zaragoza]* [Puebla, Mexico: Tipografía de las Escuelas Salesianas de Artes y Oficios, 1897], 1:184). Also see Rubén Carrillo Martín, "Asians to New Spain: Asian Cultural

and Migratory Flows in Mexico in the Early Stages of 'Globalization' (1565–1816)," PhD diss., Universitat Oberta de Catalunya, 2015, 153.

2. Ricardo Pérez Montfort, "La china poblana como emblema nacional," *Artes de México* 66 (2003): 40–51.

3. "Vivió en distintas partes, y en ellas siempre vivió en unos aposentillos lóbregos, llenos de animalexos immundos, despoblandos los suelos de la compostura que los pule, y calzados de unas lajas frías que los acompanaba" (Joseph del Castillo Graxeda, *Compendio de la vida, y virtudes de la venerable Catharina de San Juan* [Puebla, Mexico: Imprenta de Diego Fernandez de Leon, 1692], 82).

4. "Huyendo de la delicadez de la seda" (Castillo Graxeda, *Compendio*, 81).

5. "Siempre el mas grosero, el mas tosco" (Castillo Graxeda, *Compendio*, 81). See also Rubén Carrillo Martín, *Las gentes del mar Sangley* (Mexico City: Palabra de Clío, 2015), 71.

6. "Coma yo el panis que dan para el perros: porque yo, que soy sino perra china bautizada en pe" (quoted in Castillo Graxeda, *Compendio*, 83).

7. "Que china es esta, ni que santa. . . . Toma vuesasted tu pesso, que santa ni q[ue] china? Yo no ha menester pesso: ay esta mi Redemptor mio, que cuida de mi" (quoted in Castillo Graxeda, *Compendio*, 106). This episode also appears in Alonso Ramos's account, with a little more polish. The confessor had apparently decided to test Catarina's holiness with the peso, suspecting that she was a trickster. Ramos attributes an additional line to Catarina, "And know that I have very good blood in these veins, even though I seem and am taken for a china" (*Los prodigios de la Omnipotencia y milagros de la gracia en la vida de la venerable sierva de Dios Catarina de San Juan*, ed. Gisela von Wobeser [Mexico City: Universidad Nacional Autónoma de México-Instituto de Investigaciones Históricas, 2017], 2:155).

8. Lok Siu terms this feeling of connection to other diasporic journeys "diasporic affect" ("Diasporic Affect: Circulating Art, Producing Relationality," in *Circles and Circuits: Chinese Caribbean Art*, ed. Alexandra Chang [Durham, NC: Duke University Press, 2018], 215).

9. Quoted in Camila Osorio, "La disculpa diplomática de López Obrador por la masacre de chinos en 1911," *El País*, May 17, 2021, https://elpais.com/mexico/2021-05-17/la -disculpa-diplomatica-de-lopez-obrador-a-china.html. The apology was López Obrador's third in a long series of planned apologies to minority communities in Mexico that have endured historical atrocities.

10. Juan Esteban Rodríguez-Rodríguez et al., "Admixture Dynamics in Colonial Mexico and the Genetic Legacy of the Manila Galleon," *bioRxiv* (2021): 9, https://doi.org /10.1101/2021.10.09.463780; Juan Esteban Rodríguez-Rodríguez, "The Genetic Legacy of the Manila Galleon Trade in Mexico," *Philosophical Transactions Royal Society B* 377 (2022): 1–10.

11. See Evelyn Hu-DeHart and Kathleen López, "Asian Diasporas in Latin America and the Caribbean: An Historical Overview," *Afro-Hispanic Review* 27, no. 1 (2008): 9–21; Erika Lee, *The Making of Asian America: A History* (New York: Simon and Schuster, 2016); Lok Siu, *Memories of a Future Home: Diasporic Citizenship of Chinese in Panama* (Stanford, CA: Stanford University Press, 2005); Ana Paulina Lee, *Mandarin Brazil: Race, Representation, and Memory* (Stanford, CA: Stanford University Press, 2018); Jeffrey Lesser, ed., *Searching for Home*

Abroad: Japanese Brazilians and Transnationalism (Durham, NC: Duke University Press, 2003); Junyoung Verónica Kim, "Asia-Latin America as Method: The Global South Project and the Dislocation of the West, *Verge* 3, no. 2 (2017): 97–117; Robert G. Lee and Wanni W. Anderson, eds., *Displacements and Diasporas: Asians in the Americas* (New Brunswick, NJ: Rutgers University Press, 2005).

12. See Daryl J. Maeda, *Chains of Babylon: The Rise of Asian America* (Minneapolis: University of Minnesota Press, 2009); Min Zhou, Anthony C. Ocampo, and J. V. Gatewood, "Introduction: Revisiting Contemporary Asian America," in *Contemporary Asian America: A Multidisciplinary Reader*, ed. Min Zhou and Anthony C. Ocampo (New York: New York University Press, 2016), 1–22.

13. Maeda, *Chains of Babylon*, 155.

14. E. Lee, *The Making of Asian America*, 2; Malcolm Churchill, "Louisiana History and Early Filipino Settlement: Searching for the Story," *Bulletin of the American Historical Collection Foundation* 27, no. 2 (1999): 25–48; Peggy Nagae, "Immigration and Citizenship in Oregon," *Oregon Historical Quarterly* 113, no. 3 (2012): 340; Barbara Yasui, "The Nikkei in Oregon, 1834–1940," *Oregon Historical Quarterly* 76, no. 3 (1975): 228.

15. Thi Bui, *The Best We Could Do: An Illustrated Memoir* (New York: Abrams ComicArts, 2018), 39–41.

16. Alejo Carpentier, *Viaje a la semilla / Concierto barroco* (Girona, Spain: Ediciones Atalanta, 2008).

17. "La eternidad a que voló compite: / que en la pira que yace Catarina, / águila viva, fénix resucite" (quoted in Ramos, *Los prodigios*, 3:172).

Selected Bibliography

The following compilation of primary and secondary sources does not list every source cited in the notes. Rather, it is designed specifically to aid the study of Asians in the early modern Americas, as well as to provide a point of entry for readers interested in Spanish colonialism in the Philippines and the Manila galleons.

Primary Sources

Aduarte, Diego. *Historia de la provincia del Sancto Rosario de la Orden de Predicadores en Philippinas, Iapon y China.* 2 vols. Manila: Luis Beltrán, 1640.

Aguilera, Francisco de. *Sermon que en las honras de la Venerable Madre Catharina de San Juan predicó.* N.p., 1688. Biblioteca de la Universidad de Sevilla.

Argensola, Bartolomé Leonardo de. *Conqvista delas islas Malvcas.* Madrid: Alonso Martín, 1609.

Balbuena, Bernardo de. *Grandeza mexicana.* Mexico City: Diego Lopez Daualos, 1604.

Bañuelos y Carrillo, Guillermo de. *Tratado del estado de las islas Philipinas, y de sus conueniencias.* Mexico City: Imprenta de Bernardo Calderon, 1638.

Blair, Emma Helen, and James Alexander Robertson, eds. *The Philippine Islands, 1493–1898.* 55 vols. Cleveland, OH: Arthur H. Clark, 1903–1909.

Careri, Giovanni Francisco Gemelli. *Viaje a Nueva España.* Translated by Francisca Perujo. Mexico City: Universidad Nacional Autónoma de México, 1983.

Carletti, Francesco. *My Voyage around the World: The Chronicles of a 16th Century Florentine Merchant.* Translated by Herbert Weinstock. New York: Pantheon Books, 1964.

Castillo Graxeda, Joseph del. *Compendio de la vida, y virtudes de la venerable Catharina de San Juan.* Puebla, Mexico: Imprenta de Diego Fernandez de Leon, 1692.

Cázares, Alberto Carrillo. *Partidos y padrones del obispado de Michoacán: 1680–1685.* Zamora, Mexico: El Colegio de Michoacán, 1996.

Chimalpahin Quauhtlehuanitzin, Don Domingo de San Antón Muñón. *Annals of His Time: Don Domingo de San Antón Muñón Chimalpahin Quauhtlehuanitzin.* Edited and translated by James Lockhart, Susan Schroeder, and Doris Namala. Stanford, CA: Stanford University Press, 2006.

Chirino, Pedro. *Relacion de las islas Filipinas i de lo que en ellas an trabaiado los padres de la Compañia de Iesvs.* Rome: Esteban Paulino, 1604.

Colín, Francisco. *Labor evangélica, ministerios apostólicos de los obreros de la Compañia de Iesvs, fvndacion, y progresos de sv provincia en las islas Filipinas.* Madrid: por Ioseph Fernandez de Buendia, 1663.

Cubero Sebastián, Pedro. *Peregrinacion del Mvndo.* Naples: Carlos Porfile, 1682.

Fernández Navarrete, Domingo. *Tratados historicos, politicos, ethicos, y religiosos de la monarchia de china.* Madrid: Imprenta Real, 1676.

Flores García, Georgina, María Elena Bribiesca Sumano, María Guadalupe Zárate Barrios, and Brenda Jacqueline Vázquez Monte de Oca, eds. *Catálogo y estudio introductorio de la presencia de las personas de origen africano y afrodescendientes durante los siglos XVI y XVII en la valle de Toluca.* Toluca, Mexico: Universidad Autónoma del Estado de México, 2017.

Gage, Thomas. *A New Survey of the West-Indies: Or, The English American His Travel by Sea and Land.* London: A. Clark, 1677.

Gamboa, Mauro Escobar, ed. *Padrón de los indios de Lima en 1613.* Lima: Universidad Nacional Mayor de San Marcos, 1968.

Guijo, Gregorio Martín de. *Gregorio M. de Guijo diario, 1648–1664.* 2 vols. Edited by Manuel Romero de Terreros. Mexico City: Editorial Porrúa, 1952.

Herrera y Tordesillas, Antonio de. *Historia general de los hechos de los castellanos en las islas i Tierra Firme del Mar Oceano.* Vol. 4. Madrid: En la Emprenta Real, 1601.

Lee, Christina, and Ricardo Padrón, eds. *The Spanish Pacific, 1521–1815: A Reader of Primary Sources.* Amsterdam: Amsterdam University Press, 2020.

Maldonado, Miguel Rodríguez. *Relacion verdadera del levantamiento de los sangleyes en las Filipinas, y el milagroso castigo de su rebelion: Con otros sucessos de aquellas Islas.* Seville, Spain: Clemente Hidalgo, 1606.

Medina, Juan de. *Historia de los sucesos de la Orden de N. Gran P. S. Agustín de estas islas Filipinas, desde que se descubrieron y se poblaron por los españoles, con las noticias memorables.* Manila: Tipo-Litografía de Chofré y Comp., 1893.

Mendoza, Juan González de. *Historia de las cosas mas notables, ritos y costumbres, del gran reyno dela china.* Rome: Vincentio Accolti, 1585.

Morga, Antonio de. *Svcesos de las islas Filipinas.* Mexico City: En Casa de Geronymo Balli, 1609.

Navarrete, Domingo Fernández. *Tratados historicos, politicos, ethnicos, y religiosos de la monarchia de china.* Madrid: Imprenta Real, 1676.

Ramos, Alonso. *Los prodigios de la Omnipotencia y milagros de la gracia en la vida de la venerable sierva de Dios Catarina de San Juan.* 3 vols. Edited by Gisela von Wobeser. Mexico City: Universidad Autónoma de México, Instituto de Investigaciones Históricas, 2017.

Robles, Antonio de. *Diarios de sucesos notables (1665–1703).* 3 vols. Mexico City: Editorial Porrúa, 1946.

"Sino-Spanish Codex (a.k.a. Boxer Codex)." Manila, ca. 1590, Lilly Library.

Solano, Francisco de. *Relaciones geográficas del Arzobispado de México. 1743.* Edited by Catalina Romero. Vol. 1. Madrid: Consejo Superior de Investigaciones Científicas, 1988.

Solórzano Pereira, Juan de. *Política Indiana.* 2 vols. Madrid: Diego Díaz de la Carrera, 1648.
Villa-Señor y Sánchez, Joseph Antonio de. *Theatro americano: Descripcion general de los Reynos y provincias de la Nueva-España y sus jurisdicciones.* Mexico City: Viuda de D. Joseph Bernardo de Hogal, 1746.

Secondary Sources

Bailey, Gauvin Alexander. "A Mughal Princess in Baroque New Spain: Catarina de San Juan (1606–1688), the China Poblana." *Anales del instituto de investigaciones estéticas* 71 (1997): 37–73.
Barreto Xavier, Ângela, and Ines G. Županov. *Catholic Orientalism: Portuguese Empire, Indian Knowledge (16th–18th Centuries).* New Delhi: Oxford University Press, 2015.
Barrón Soto, Cristina E. "La migración filipina en México." In *Destino México: Un estudio de las migraciones asiáticas a México, siglos XIX y XX,* edited by María Elena Ota Mishima, 365–412. Mexico City: El Colegio de México, 1997.
Bjork, Katherine. "The Link That Kept the Philippines Spanish: Mexican Merchant Interests and the Manila Trade, 1571–1815." *Journal of World History* 9, no. 1 (1998): 25–50.
Bonialian, Mariano A. "Asiáticos en Lima a principios del siglo XVII." *Bulletin de l'Institut Français d'Études Andines* 44, no. 2 (2015): 1–32.
———. *China en la América colonial: Bienes, mercados, comercio y cultura del consumo desde México hasta Buenos Aires.* Mexico City: Editorial Biblios, 2014.
———. *El pacífico hispanoamericano: Política y comercio asiático en el imperio español (1680–1784).* Mexico City: El Colegio de México, 2012.
Borao Mateo, José Eugenio. "Contextualizing the Pampangos (and Gagayano) Soldiers in the Spanish Fortress in Taiwan (1626–1642)." *Anuario de Estudios Americanos* 70, no. 2 (2013): 581–605.
Buschmann, Rainer F., Edward R. Slack Jr., and James B. Tueller. *Navigating the Spanish Lake: The Pacific in the Iberian World, 1521–1898.* Honolulu: University of Hawai'i Press, 2014.
Cervera, José Antonio. "Los planes españoles para conquistar China a través de Nueva España y Centroamérica en el siglo XVI." *Cuadernos de Intercambio sobre Centroamérica y el Caribe* 10, no. 12 (2013): 207–234.
Chaunu, Pierre. *Las Filipinas y el Pacífico de los Ibéricos siglos XVI-XVII-XVIII.* Mexico City: Instituto Mexicano de Comercio Exterior, 1974.
Cope, R. Douglas. *The Limits of Racial Domination: Plebeian Society in Colonial Mexico City, 1660–1720.* Madison: University of Wisconsin Press, 1994.
Crewe, Ryan Dominic. "Connecting the Indies: The Hispano-Asian Pacific World in Early Modern Global History." *Jornal de Estudos Historicos* 30, no. 60 (2017): 17–34.
———. "Pacific Purgatory: Spanish Dominicans, Chinese Sangleys, and the Entanglement of Mission and Commerce in Manila, 1580–1640." *Journal of Early Modern History* 19 (2015): 337–365.
———. "Transpacific Mestizo: Religion and Caste in the Worlds of a Moluccan Prisoner of the Mexican Inquisition." *Itinerario* 39, no. 3 (2015): 463–485.

Deusen, Nancy E. van. "Indios on the Move in the Sixteenth-Century Iberian World." *Journal of Global History* 10, no. 3 (2015): 387–409.

Dubs, Homer H., and Robert S. Smith. "Chinese in Mexico City in 1635." *Far Eastern Quarterly* 1, no. 4 (1942): 387–389.

Fish, Shirley. *The Manila-Acapulco Galleons: The Treasure Ships of the Pacific.* Milton Keynes, UK: AuthorHouse UK, 2011.

Flannery, Kristie Patricia. "Can the Devil Cross the Deep Blue Sea? Imagining the Spanish Pacific and Vast Early America from Below." *William and Mary Quarterly* 79, no. 1 (2022): 31–69.

Flynn, Dennis O., Arturo Giráldez, and James Sobredo, eds. *European Entry into the Pacific: Spain and the Acapulco-Manila Galleons.* New York: Routledge, 2001.

Furlong, Matthew J. "Peasants, Servants, and Sojourners: Itinerant Asians in Colonial New Spain, 1571–1720." PhD diss., University of Arizona, 2014.

García-Abásolo, Antonio. "La audiencia de Manila y los chinos de Filipinas: Casos de integración en el delito." In *Homenaje a Alberto de la Hera,* edited by José Luis Soberanes Fernández and Rosa María Martínez de Codes, 339–368. Mexico City: UNAM, Instituto de Investigaciones Jurídicas, 2008.

———. "La difícil convivencia entre españoles y chinos en Filipinas." In *Élites urbanas en Hispanoamérica,* edited by Luis Navarro García, 487–494. Seville, Spain: Secretariado de Publicaciones de la Universidad de Sevilla, 2005.

———. "Los chinos y el modelo colonial español en Filipinas." *Cuadernos de Historia Moderna* 10 (2011): 223–242.

Gebhardt, Jonathan. "Global Cities, Incoherent Communities: Communication, Coexistence, and Conflict in Macau and Manila, 1550–1700." PhD diss., Yale University, 2015.

Gharala, Norah L. A. "'From Mozambique in Indies of Portugal': Locating East Africans in New Spain." *Journal of Global Slavery* 7, no. 3 (2022): 243–281.

Gil, Juan. *La India y el Lejano Oriente en la Sevilla del Siglo de Oro.* Seville, Spain: Ayuntamiento de Sevilla—Instituto de la Cultura y las Artes de Sevilla, 2011.

———. *Los chinos en Manila: Siglos XVI y XVII.* Lisbon: Centro Científico e Cultural de Macau, 2011.

Giráldez, Arturo. *The Age of Trade: The Manila Galleons and the Dawn of the Global Economy.* Lanham, MD: Rowman and Littlefield, 2015.

Gommans, Jos, and Ariel Lopez, eds. *Philippine Confluence: Iberian, Chinese and Islamic Currents, c. 1500–1800.* Leiden, the Netherlands: Leiden University Press, 2020.

González Cleverán, Virginia. "Un documento colonial sobre esclavos asiáticos." *Historia Mexicana* 38, no. 3 (1989): 523–532.

Hawkley, Ethan P. "The Birth of Globalization: The World and the Beginnings of Philippines Sovereignty, 1565–1610." PhD diss., Northeastern University, 2014.

Hespanha, António Manuel. *Filhos da terra: Identidades mestiças nos confins da expansão portuguesa.* Lisbon: Tinta-da-china, 2019.

Hu-DeHart, Evelyn. "Spanish Manila: A Transpacific Maritime Enterprise and America's First Chinatown." In *Oceanic Archives, Indigenous Epistemologies, and Transpacific Amer-*

ican Studies, edited by Yuan Shu, Otto Heim, and Kendall Johnson, 49–61. Hong Kong: Hong Kong University Press, 2019.

Hu-DeHart, Evelyn, and Kathleen López. "Asian Diasporas in Latin America and the Caribbean: An Historical Overview." *Afro-Hispanic Review* 27, no. 1 (2008): 9–21.

Iaccarino, Ubaldo. "The 'Galleon System' and Chinese Trade in Manila at the Turn of the 16th Century." *Ming Qing Yanjiu* 16 (2011): 95–128.

Lach, Donald F. *Asia in the Making of Europe.* 3 vols. Chicago: University of Chicago Press, 1965–1977.

Laufer, Berthold. "The Relations of the Chinese to the Philippine Islands." *Smithsonian Miscellaneous Collections* 50, no. 1789 (1908): 248–283.

Lee, Christina. "The Perception of the Japanese in Early Modern Spain: Not Quite 'The Best People Yet Discovered.'" *eHumanista* 11 (2008): 345–380.

———. *Saints of Resistance: Devotions in the Philippines under Early Spanish Rule.* New York: Oxford University Press, 2021.

———, ed. *Western Visions of the Far East in a Transpacific Age, 1522–1657.* Burlington, VT: Ashgate, 2012.

Lee, Erika. *The Making of Asian America: A History.* New York: Simon and Schuster, 2015.

Leibsohn, Dana, and Meha Priyadarshini. "Transpacific: Beyond Silk and Silver." *Colonial Latin American Review* 25, no. 1 (2016): 1–15.

Loyola, José Vega. "Japoneses, chinos e indios en Lima cosmopolita de inicios del siglo XVII." *Cátedra Villareal* 3, no. 2 (2015): 155–172.

Luis, Diego Javier. "The Armed Chino: Licensing Fear in New Spain." *Journal of Colonialism and Colonial History* 20, no. 1 (2019): 1–23.

———. "Diasporic Convergences: Tracing Knowledge Production and Transmission among Enslaved Chinos in New Spain." *Ethnohistory* 68, no. 2 (2021): 291–310.

———. "Galleon Anxiety: How Afro-Mexican Women Shaped Colonial Spirituality in Acapulco." *Americas* 78, no. 3 (2021): 389–413.

Machuca Chávez, Claudia Paulina. "Cabildo, negociación y vino de cocos: El caso de la villa de Colima en el siglo XVII." *Anuario de Estudios Americanos* 66, no. 1 (2009): 173–192.

Martín, Rubén Carrillo. "Asians to New Spain: Asian Cultural and Migratory Flows in Mexico in the Early Stages of 'Globalization' (1565–1816)." PhD diss., Universitat Oberta de Catalunya, 2015.

———. *Las gentes del mar Sangley.* Mexico City: Palabra de Clío, 2015.

Matsuda, Matt. *Pacific Worlds: A History of Seas, Peoples, and Cultures.* New York: Cambridge University Press, 2012.

Mawson, Stephanie. "Rebellion and Mutiny in the Mariana Islands, 1680–1690." *Journal of Pacific History* 50, no. 2 (2015): 128–148.

Mayfield, Alex R. "Galleons from the 'Mouth of Hell': Empire and Religion in Seventeenth Century Acapulco." *Journal of Early Modern Christianity* 5, no. 2 (2018): 221–245.

McKinley, Michelle A. "The Unbearable Lightness of Being (Black): Legal and Cultural Constructions of Race and Nation in Colonial Latin America." In *Racial Formation in the Twenty-First Century*, edited by Daniel Martínez HoSang, Oneka LaBennett, and Laura Pulido, 116–142. Berkeley: University of California Press, 2012.

Mehl, Eva Maria. *Forced Migration in the Spanish Pacific World: From Mexico to the Philippines, 1765–1811.* Cambridge: Cambridge University Press, 2016.

Myers, Kathleen Ann. *Neither Saints nor Sinners: Writing the Lives of Women in Spanish America.* New York: Oxford University Press, 2003.

Newson, Linda A. *Conquest and Pestilence in the Early Spanish Philippines.* Honolulu: University of Hawai'i Press, 2009.

Núñez Ortega, Ángel. *Noticia histórica de las relaciones políticas y comerciales entre México y el Japón, durante el siglo XVII.* Mexico City: Imprenta del gobierno, 1879.

Ollé, Manel. "Del barrio al océano: Los chinos de Manila entre el comercio del Galeón, la convivencia municipal y las redes diásporas regionales." In *Los chinos de ultramar: Diásporas, sociabilidad e identidades,* edited by Ricardo Martínez Esquivel, 21–56. Mexico City: Palabra de Clío, 2007.

Ollé, Manel, and Joan-Pau Rubiés, eds. *El Códice Boxer: Etnografía colonial e hibridismo cultural en las islas Filipinas.* Barcelona: Edicions de la Universitat de Barcelona, 2019.

Olveda, Jaime, ed. *Relaciones intercoloniales: Nueva España y Filipinas.* Zapopan, Mexico: El Colegio de Jalisco, 2017.

Oropeza, Déborah. *La migración asiática en el virreinato de la Nueva España: Un proceso de globalización (1565–1700).* Mexico City: El Colegio de México, 2020.

Oropeza Keresey, Déborah. "La esclavitud asiática en el virreinato de la Nueva España, 1565–1673." *Historia Mexicana* 61, no. 1 (2011): 5–57.

Owens, Sarah E. "Crossing Mexico (1620–1621): Franciscan Nuns and Their Journey to the Philippines." *Americas* 72, no. 4 (2015): 583–606.

Padrón, Ricardo. *The Indies of the Setting Sun: How Early Modern Spain Mapped the Far East as the Transpacific West.* Chicago: University of Chicago Press, 2020.

———. "A Sea of Denial: The Early Modern Spanish Invention of the Pacific Rim." *Hispanic Review* 77, no. 1 (2009): 1–27.

Phelan, John Leddy. *The Hispanization of the Philippines: Spanish Aims and Filipino Responses, 1565–1700.* Madison: University of Wisconsin Press, 1959.

Priyadarshini, Meha. *Chinese Porcelain in Colonial Mexico: The Material Worlds of an Early Modern Trade.* Cham, Switzerland: Palgrave Macmillan, 2018.

Quiroz Malca, Haydée. "Acapulco y la Costa Chica, construcciones coloniales de la diversidad cultural: Reflexiones a partir del padrón de 1777." *Investigaciones sociales* 20, no. 37 (2017): 69–78.

Rafael, Vicente. *Contracting Colonialism: Translation and Christian Conversion in Tagalog Society under Early Spanish Rule.* Quezon City: Ateneo de Manila University Press, 2017.

Reséndez, Andrés. *Conquering the Pacific: An Unknown Mariner and the Final Great Voyage of the Age of Discovery.* Boston: Houghton Mifflin Harcourt, 2021.

———. *The Other Slavery: The Uncovered Story of Indian Enslavement in America.* Boston: Houghton Mifflin Harcourt, 2016.

Reyes, Melba Falck, and Hectór Palacios. *El japonés que conquistó Guadalajara: La historia de Juan de Páez en la Guadalajara del siglo XVII.* Guadalajara, Mexico: Universidad de Guadalajara, 2009.

Risse, Kate. "Catarina de San Juan and the China Poblana: From Spiritual Humility to Civil Obedience." *Confluencia* 18, no. 1 (2002): 70–80.

Ruiz, Jorge Alberto, and María Concepción Gavira. "Mezclas y desorden en la población de una provincia fronteriza: Zacatula—México en el siglo XVIII." *Cuadernos interculturales* 11, no. 21 (2013): 141–160.

Ruiz-Stovel, Guillermo. "Chinese Merchants, Silver Galleons, and Ethnic Violence in Spanish Manila, 1603–1686." *México y la Cuenca del Pacífico* 12, no. 36 (2009): 47–63.

Santiago, Luciano. "The Filipino Indios Encomenderos (ca. 1620–1711)." *Philippine Quarterly of Culture and Society* 18, no. 3 (1990): 162–184.

Schurz, William Lytle. *The Manila Galleon: Illustrated with Maps.* New York: E. P. Dutton, 1939.

———. "Mexico, Peru, and the Manila Galleon." *Hispanic American Historical Review* 1, no. 4 (1918): 389–402.

Scott, William Henry. *Barangay: Sixteenth-Century Philippine Culture and Society.* Quezon City: Ateneo de Manila University Press, 1994.

Seijas, Tatiana. "Asian Migrations to Latin America in the Pacific World, 16th–19th Centuries." *History Compass* 14 (2016): 573–581.

———. *Asian Slaves in Colonial Mexico: From Chinos to Indians.* New York: Cambridge University Press, 2014.

———. "*Indios Chinos* in Eighteenth-Century Mexico." In *To Be Indio in Colonial Spanish America*, edited by Mónica Díaz, 123–142. Albuquerque: University of New Mexico Press, 2017.

———. "Inns, Mules, and Hardtack for the Voyage: The Local Economy of the Manila Galleon in Mexico." *Colonial Latin American Review* 25, no. 1 (2016): 56–76.

———. "Native Vassals: Chinos, Indigenous Identity, and Legal Protection in Early Modern Spain." In *Western Visions of the Far East in a Transpacific Age, 1522–1657*, edited by Christina Lee, 153–164. Burlington, VT: Ashgate, 2012.

———. "Portuguese Slave Trade to Spanish Manila: 1580–1640." *Itinerario* 32, no. 1, 2008: 19–38.

Sierra Silva, Pablo Miguel. *Urban Slavery in Colonial Mexico: Puebla de los Ángeles, 1531–1706.* Cambridge: Cambridge University Press, 2018.

Slack, Edward R., Jr. "The Chinos in New Spain: A Corrective Lens for a Distorted Image." *Journal of World History* 20, no. 1 (2009): 35–67.

———. "New Perspectives on Manila's Chinese Community at the Turn of the Eighteenth Century: The Forgotten Case of Pedro Barredo, Alcalde Mayor of the Parián 1701–1704." *Journal of Chinese Overseas* 17 (2021): 117–146.

———. "Orientalizing New Spain: Perspectives on Asian Influence in Colonial Mexico." *México y la Cuenca del Pacífico* 15, no. 43 (2012): 97–128.

———. "Sinifying New Spain: Cathay's Influence on Colonial Mexico via the *Nao de China*." *Journal of Chinese Overseas* 5, no. 1 (2009): 5–27.

Sousa, Lucío de. *The Portuguese Slave Trade in Early Modern Japan: Merchants, Jesuits and Japanese, Chinese and Korean Slaves.* Boston: Brill, 2019.

Terrazas Williams, Danielle. *The Capital of Free Women: Race, Legitimacy, and Liberty in Colonial Mexico.* New Haven, CT: Yale University Press, 2022.

Tremml-Werner, Birgit. *Spain, China, and Japan in Manila, 1571–1644: Local Comparisons and Global Connections*. Amsterdam: Amsterdam University Press, 2015.

Vinson, Ben, III. *Before Mestizaje: The Frontiers of Race and Caste in Colonial Mexico*. New York: Cambridge University Press, 2017.

Williams, Scott S., Curt D. Peterson, Mitch Marken, and Richard Rogers. "The Beeswax Wreck of Nehalem: A Lost Manila Galleon." *Oregon Historical Quarterly* 119, no. 2 (2018): 192–209.

Woods, Damon L. *The Myth of the Barangay and Other Silenced Histories*. Quezon City: University of the Philippines Press, 2017.

Yuste López, Carmen, ed. *Nueva España: Puerta americana al Pacífico asiático*. Mexico City: Universidad Nacional Autónoma de México, 2019.

Acknowledgments

Fully expressing my gratitude to the people and institutions that have made this work possible would require a volume unto itself. My first thank you goes to Evelyn Hu-DeHart at Brown University, who first introduced me to the wonders of the Spanish Pacific. At the end of my second year in graduate school, she empowered me to pursue a topic of immediate relevance to both my historical interests and identity—a novelty to me at the time. Shortly thereafter, she sent me to the John Carter Brown Library (JCBL) to read Juan González de Mendoza's monumental *Historia de las cosas mas notables, ritos y costumbres, del gran reyno dela china* (1585), which ignited in me an undying curiosity about and fascination with early modern connections between Asia and Latin America. Even when my semesters became hectic, she always made time to cook an elaborate array of dishes (crowned with homemade chili pepper sauce [辣椒]) that she would invariably call a simple dinner.

Jeremy Mumford and Neil Safier played similarly formative roles in my career. Jeremy introduced me to the world of Spanish paleography and helped transform works in arcane scripts into legible texts. He was also among the first of my professors to read my writing as carefully and critically as he would that of any other scholar. Meanwhile, in his former role as director of the JCBL, Neil welcomed me to the institution that would become my first and last stop for any question I had about Latin American, Atlantic World, and even Pacific histories. With his and the JCBL's support, the only limits on my research were those of my imagination. When one of my committee members, the late and much missed R. Douglas Cope, tragically passed away in the fall of 2019, Neil did not hesitate to step in as his replacement.

Cope's passing stunned his students. His vast knowledge, subtle wit, and unparalleled generosity opened the field of Latin American history to generations of students at Brown, and I was no exception. I will never forget an exchange I witnessed after one of his undergraduate lectures, when a student approached him, clearly awed, and said, "I've never seen a professor lecture like that before. How can you remember everything?" Cope replied with something characteristically humble along the lines of, "Well, it's my job, and I've been doing it for many years." He was a model scholar and human being. I had the great pleasure of conversing with him about my manuscript after he had read an early version of it. I shall always cherish my memory of his enthusiasm for the topic and the work.

I have deep gratitude for the other professors at Brown who played important roles in my intellectual development, like Jonathan Conant, Linford Fisher, and Jennifer Lambe. Of course, there is a special place in my heart for the hallowed halls of the JCBL and the tremendous staff members who run it—in particular, Bertie Mandelblatt, Kim Nusco, and Val Andrews. I am grateful that I had the opportunity to spend a year at that wonderful institution as a J. M. Stuart Fellow. During that time, I met Kristen Block, Norah Gharala, Guillaume Candela, and many others, whose stimulating company greatly enriched my thinking. I also thank the staff members of the other main archives I used in this book: the Archivo General de Indias, the Archivo General de la Nación México, the Archives of the University of Santo Tomas, and the Archivo de la Real Audiencia de la Nueva Galicia.

I probably had no single greater intellectual influence than the unforgettable community of PhD students, candidates, and postdoctoral students, who were with me in the trenches the whole way. They included James Wang, Julian Saporiti, Juan Betancourt, René Cordero, Sherri Cummings, Grazia Deng, Morris Karp, Darcy Hackley, Mallory Matsumoto, Stacey Murrell, Brooke Grasberger, Alessandro Moghrabi, Julia Gettle, Mahmoud Nowara, Leland Grigoli, and many others. Their support, ideas, contentions, ramblings, and creativity have provided nourishment for my soul that will last all my life.

Further afield, I was and continue to be fortunate to dialogue with scholars all over the world whose work I deeply admire and who have shown selfless generosity toward my research and professional development in ways both big and small. Some of their names appear repeatedly in the notes of this book: Christina Lee, Rubén Carrillo Martín, Pablo Sierra Silva, Dana Murillo, Luis Castellví Laukamp, and Matteo Lazzari.

During the difficult early years of the COVID pandemic, Davidson, North Carolina, became my home, and the steadfast faculty members there (both temporary and permanent) consistently went out of their way to create a community and support me and my work. I would like to recognize particularly the ever supportive Scott Denham, Jane Mangan, Caroline Fache, Sharon Green, Anne Wills, David Robb, Rachel Pang, Jae Kim, Heather Offerman, Tony Pasero O'Malley, Fuji Losada, Jeremy Whitson, and Anastasia Whitson (little Flora, too).

On a practical level, this book could not have been written without the institutions that funded its research and writing. In addition to the abovementioned Brown University and JCBL, I extend a sincere thanks to the Conference on Latin American History, Davidson College, the American Historical Association, and the Huntington Library for their support. On a similar note, I am grateful to the journals that published early versions of this research. Several passages of Chapter 3 reprint text first published in "The Armed *Chino:* Licensing Fear in New Spain," *Journal of Colonialism and Colonial History* 20, no. 1 (2019). Portions of Chapter 4 were first published as "Diasporic Convergences: Tracing Knowledge Production and Transmission among Enslaved Chinos in New Spain," *Ethnohistory* 68, no. 2 (2021).

Perhaps the institution that was most critical to this project has been Harvard University Press. My editor, Emily Silk, has set a gold standard with her support of this book. She has consistently exceeded every expectation by large margins and has made innumerable invaluable suggestions that repeatedly improved the writing. To her, the rest of the press's team, and my anonymous reviewers, *mil gracias.*

My academic trajectory began at Emory University, where I wrote an honors thesis for the history department under the tutelage of three amazing professors whose kindness, patience, and passion I remember with great fondness: Cynthia Patterson, Laura Otis, and Yanna Yannakakis. It is a testament to the strength of Emory's undergraduate history program that I decided to devote my professional life to academia.

Along the way, I have had heroic mentors, perhaps none more so than my peerless martial arts instructors at the Francis Fong Martial Arts Academy. There, I spent many hours discussing the power of creativity in all things—including writing and intellectual thought—with Sifu Fong (known affectionately by his students as "Sifu"). Under his instruction, I explored the panorama of Southeast Asian martial arts (including Wing Chun, Kali, Silat, and Muay Thai), which undoubtedly planted the seed of my fascination with the region in my earliest college days.

In May 2021, I suffered a terrible neck injury that made the process of writing and revising this book a great test of fortitude and willpower. In desperate moments, I thought of my coach Annie Malaythong, who taught me to persevere against terrific odds. I also remembered the late David García, a close family friend, who finished his dissertation at Vanderbilt University while paralyzed from the neck down. His story of triumph—and the positivity and faith he expressed through it all—was an unparalleled motivation to keep going.

However, I have had no greater inspiration to persist against all adversity than my family—especially my parents, William Luis and Linda Tracey, to whom I have lovingly dedicated this book. Their example and their everlasting love and support have made every success I can claim possible. I owe them a great debt that I can never repay. Thank you.

One family history is immediately relevant to that told in this book and is worth recounting in brief. In the first decades of the twentieth century, my grandfather traveled to Cuba from a small village near Taishan (台山), China. His family had already been coming and going from Cuba for a couple of generations. After his arrival there, he was given the name Domingo Luis, a Hispanicization of his family name (pronounced Lui in Taishanese [雷]). In Havana, he met my grandmother, Petra Liduvina Santos del Río. She was the daughter of Ventura Santos Santos, who was the son of an enslaved woman named Rita. Ventura fought in the Cuban Independence army and became a master mason of the Logia San Juan in Caibarién. Together, Petra and Domingo moved to New York City in the 1940s, where they married and had two children. Much of my father's adult life and my own have been spent recovering our Afro-Asian roots. Although the histories in this book occurred hundreds of years before the births of my *abuela* and *abuelo,* writing the book has nonetheless been a centerpiece of my personal journey.

Finally, I have saved the best for last. My dear wife, Hillary Li, has been a godlike pillar of support. She has meant so much to me during these writing years that trying to express my gratitude in mere words would be foolhardy. I shall say only that she has been a beacon of light through the darkest trials of this process. For now, there is nothing more to do than to give her this book.

INDEX

Page numbers in italics refer to figures and tables.